The Discovery of Being
& Thomas Aquinas

The Discovery of Being
& Thomas Aquinas

Philosophical and Theological Perspectives

EDITED BY CHRISTOPHER M. CULLEN, SJ
& FRANKLIN T. HARKINS

The Catholic University of America Press
Washington, D.C.

The paper used in this publication meets the minimum requirements of American
National Standards for Information Science—Permanence of Paper for Printed
Library Materials, ANSI Z39.48-1984.
∞

Design and composition by Kachergis Book Design

Cataloging-in-Publication Data available
from the Library of Congress
ISBN 978-0-8132-3187-7

CONTENTS

ACKNOWLEDGMENTS

The essays that constitute this collection were first presented at the 31st Annual Conference of the Center for Medieval Studies at Fordham University in 2011, entitled "The Metaphysics of Aquinas and Its Modern Interpreters: Theological and Philosophical Perspectives." We wish to acknowledge Fordham's Center for Medieval Studies, particularly its former director, Professor Maryanne Kowaleski, for sponsoring and hosting the conference on this important theme. We are most grateful to the world-class scholars of Thomistic philosophy and theology who participated in the conference and revised their papers for inclusion in the present volume. A special thanks is due to John Martino, acquisitions editor in philosophy and theology at the Catholic University of America Press, for his enthusiastic support of this project from the outset and his helpful suggestions along the way. We owe a debt of gratitude to Austin Holmes, Franklin's research assistant at Boston College School of Theology and Ministry, for reading and making corrections to the entire manuscript. Finally, we are most grateful for the support of the Jesuit community at Fordham, of which Chris is a member, and of Franklin's family—his wife, Angela, and their son, Joseph.

CHRISTOPHER M. CULLEN, SJ
New York, N.Y.

FRANKLIN T. HARKINS
Boston, Mass.

Feast of the Visitation of the Blessed Virgin Mary, 2018

Individual Works of Thomas Aquinas

Comp. Theol.	*Compendium theologiae seu brevis compilatio theologiae ad fratrem Raynaldum*
De Ente	*Sermo sive tractatus De ente et essentia*
De Malo	*Quaestiones disputatae De malo*
De Pot.	*Quaestiones disputatae De potentia Dei*
De Spir.	*Quaestio disputata De spiritualibus creaturis*
De Ver.	*Quaestiones disputatae De veritate*
Expos. de Trin.	*Expositio super librum Boethii de Trinitate*
In de Heb.	*Expositio libri Boetii De Hebdomadibus*
In Ioh.	*Lectura super Ioannem*
In Meta.	*Sententia super Metaphysicam*
In Peri Her.	*Expositio libri Peryermenias*
In Phys.	*Sententia super Physicam*
In Sent.	*Scriptum super libros Sententiarum*
Quodl.	*Quaestiones de quodlibet I–XII*
SCG	*Summa Contra Gentiles*
ST	*Summa Theologiae*

Other Works

DS	*Enchiridion Symbolorum* (ed. Denzinger)
Leon.	Editio Leonina (Aquinas)
PG	Patrologia Graeca (ed. Migne)

Introduction

CHRISTOPHER M. CULLEN, SJ
& FRANKLIN T. HARKINS

Metaphysics is among the more disputed subjects of human inquiry, especially since the eighteenth-century Enlightenment in which various thinkers dismissed the very possibility of the endeavor, at least as a "science" of being. One might think of Immanuel Kant's critique of metaphysics as a science in name only, incapable of yielding any knowledge about the world independent of the mind—*a posteriori* knowledge. Or one might think, for example, of David Hume's famous skeptical critique of the mind's ability to make judgments concerning the relation of effect and cause, which undermines any science of reality. The twentieth century has not been any kinder, especially in light of the twin attacks launched against such a science by the great Protestant theologian Karl Barth and the influential German philosopher Martin Heidegger. The latter, however, pays tribute to its questions: "Is Being a mere word and its meaning a vapor, or does what is named with the word 'Being' hold within the spiritual fate of the West?"[1]

There is no doubt, however, that Aristotle and Thomas Aquinas regarded metaphysics as the highest branch of philosophy, the one that goes further than any other science in fulfilling reason's quest for knowledge in its contemplation of the highest things. Aristotle had expressed the view at the beginning of his *Metaphysics* that every man naturally

1. Martin Heidegger, *Introduction to Metaphysics*, trans. Gregory Fried and Richard Polt (New Haven, Conn.: Yale University Press, 2000), 45.

desires to know, and that some ultimately desire to know reality, the things that are. Aristotle speaks in *Metaphysics* VI of first philosophy as the science of being *qua* being:

There is a science which studies Being *qua* Being, and the properties inherent in it in virtue of its own nature. This science is not the same as any of the so-called particular sciences, for none of the others contemplates Being generally *qua* Being; they divide off some portion of it and study the attribute of this portion, as do for example the mathematical sciences. But since it is for the first principles and the most ultimate causes that we are searching, clearly they must belong to something in virtue of its own nature. Hence if these principles were investigated by those also who investigated the elements of existing things, the elements must be elements of Being not incidentally, but *qua* Being. Therefore it is of Being *qua* Being that we too must grasp the first causes.[2]

Aquinas follows Aristotle in holding that the subject of metaphysics is being, not a particular domain of beings, as in more restricted sciences, but the whole domain and under the aspect of the mere fact that they are rather than are not.[3] Aquinas summarizes the subject matter and various names for metaphysics in the prologue to his commentary on Aristotle's *Metaphysics*:

Therefore in accordance with the three things mentioned above from which this science [metaphysics] derives its perfection, three names arise. It is called divine science or theology inasmuch as it considers the aforementioned substances. It is called metaphysics inasmuch as it considers being and the attributes which naturally accompany being (for things which transcend the physical order are discovered by the process of analysis, as the more common are discovered after the less common). And it is called first philosophy inasmuch as it considers the first causes of things. Therefore it is evident what the subject of this science is, and how it is related to the other sciences, and by what names it is designated.[4]

While there has been agreement among followers of Aquinas that being insofar as it is being (being *qua* being) is the subject of metaphysics, there is not agreement on how this being *qua* being is to be under-

2. Aristotle, *Metaphysics*, trans. Hugh Tredennick (Cambridge, Mass.: Harvard University Press, 1989), IV.1, 1003a21–25. See also VI.1, 1026a31.

3. Aristotle, *Metaphysics* IV.1, 1003a22–23: "There is a science that investigates being qua being and what belongs essentially to it."

4. Thomas Aquinas, *Commentary on the Metaphysics of Aristotle*, trans. John P. Rowan (Chicago: H. Regnery, 1961), prologue.

stood, nor on how we come to know the being that is the object of meta-physical investigation. To say much more on the being of metaphysics is to determine the nexus of questions involved in the dispute. To go one step further is to enter into a whole set of distinctio and qualifica-tions that are made in any Thomistically inspired account. Indeed, the questions of what being is, as the object of the science of metaphysics, and how to account for the "discovery" of the being of metaphysics have emerged as central problems for the contemporary retrieval of Aquinas and for post-Leonine Thomism in general. This lack of agreement has hampered the retrieval of Aquinas's metaphysics. One of the challenges for a Thomistic account of the mind's knowledge of being is its founda-tional epistemological empiricism, namely the view that the proper ob-ject of the intellect is the essence abstracted from the sensible singular.

To begin to understand the debate about the foundations of Thom-istic metaphysics, we do well to consider a recent textbook on Thomistic metaphysics by the Dominican scholar Benedict Ashley.[5] The discov-ery of being emerges as a crucial criterion for trying to account for the diversity of approaches among contemporary Thomists. The question of the discovery comes first, as it is usually determinative of what con-stitutes the object of discovery and investigation, that is, what is the being, as in the subject matter, of metaphysics. The solutions to this foundational question of discovery have differed widely among Thom-ists: some, for example, have insisted that the being investigated by metaphysics is known through a concept derived from the third degree of abstraction (Thomas de Vio Cajetan); some others have held that it is known through an intuition (Jacques Maritain);[6] still others have main-tained that it is known through a negative judgment of *separatio*; and

5. Benedict Ashley, OP, *The Way toward Wisdom: An Interdisciplinary and Intercultural Intro-duction to Metaphysics* (Notre Dame, Ind.: University of Notre Dame Press, 2006), 44–54. There are other accounts of the branches of the Thomist tradition: see Helen James John, *The Thomist Spectrum* (New York: Fordham University Press, 1966); and Brian J. Shanley, OP, *The Thomist Tradition* (Dordrecht: Kluwer Academic, 2002).

6. Jacques Maritain, *A Preface to Metaphysics: Seven Lectures on Being* (New York: New American Library, 1962 [1934]). Maritain shifted his position toward Existential Thomism in *Ex-istence and the Existent*, trans. Lewis Galantiere and Gerald B. Phelan (Garden City, N.Y.: Image Books, 1948 [1947]), 35–44. He tries to reconcile his intuition of being with a negative judgment of *separatio* in light of the scholarly work done on Aquinas's *Expositio super librum Boethii De Trinitate*. See Armand Maurer's translation, *The Division and Method of the Sciences*, 4th ed., Mediaeval Sources in Translation 3 (Toronto: Pontifical Institute of Mediaeval Studies, 1986).

finally, some have argued that being is known *a priori* (Transcendental Thomism). Ashley speaks of eight different varieties of Thomism, and although he uses various criteria to distinguish these (e.g., the nature of metaphysics, the "concerns" of the practitioners about various applications for metaphysics), the single most determinative of these is that of how the mind comes to a knowledge of "being qua being, understood analogically."[7] A closely allied criterion for his genealogy of Thomisms, as Ashley also makes clear, is the question of exactly what must be established before one can enter into a science of being *qua* being. Does this science involve first proving the existence of a positively immaterial being? Or is the bar lower, such that it is merely necessary to establish what has been called "negatively immaterial being," that is, that being is not necessarily material?

One of the first ways of categorizing approaches to the question of discovery is to focus on which operation of the mind provides us with access to knowledge of metaphysical being. The first division is between those Thomists, on the one hand, who have maintained that being is known by the intellect through abstraction, and those, on the other, who have held that being is known by the judgment, and indeed a specific kind of judgment, namely *separatio*. *Separatio* is a negative judgment, in short, that being is not necessarily material. Those Thomists who hold that the being of metaphysics is known through the first act of the mind, or abstraction, take it to be known through abstraction to the third and highest degree. This position is commonly thought to rely on the work of the Renaissance Dominican Thomas de Vio Cajetan (1468–1534) and was famously defended in the twentieth century by Reginald Garrigou-Lagrange, OP (1877–1964).[8] Those Thomists who hold that the being of metaphysics is known by a judgment tend to give precedence to Aquinas's commentary on Boethius's *De Trinitate*, specifically the fifth question, where Aquinas discusses the operations of the intellect and says that the operation of "joining and dividing, which is properly called separation," belongs to "divine science or metaphysics."[9] No small part

7. Ashley, *The Way toward Wisdom*, 46. Ashley's eight varieties of Thomistic metaphysics are (a) Essentialist (or Conceptualist), (b) Platonizing, (c) Transcendental, (d) Existential, (e) Phenomenological, (f) Analytic, (g) Semiotic, and (h) Aristotelian (ibid., 44–54).

8. Reginald Garrigou-Lagrange, OP, *Reality: A Synthesis of Thomistic Thought*, trans. Patrick Cummins (St. Louis, Mo.: Herder, 1950).

9. Aquinas, *The Division and Method of the Sciences*, 41.

of the debate is the weight to be given to this somewhat earlier text of Aquinas.[10]

The present volume is divided into three major parts: the essays in part 1 treat the foundation of metaphysics within Thomism; those in part 2 exemplify the use of metaphysics with respect to fundamental philosophical issues within Thomism; and those in part 3 concern the role of metaphysics *vis-à-vis* central theological topics. Taken together, the essays gathered here aim at two major goals. The first is to contribute to the clarification of the issues concerning the foundation of a Thomistic metaphysics; the second is to examine how, from a Thomistic perspective, metaphysics is used in various branches or areas of philosophy and theology.

Concerning the first of these goals, the five essays in part 1 offer decisive interpretations of Aquinas on the issue of the foundation of metaphysics. Indeed, the first part of the volume—with essays by John F. Wippel, Rudi te Velde, John F. X. Knasas, Stephen Fields, and Jason A. Mitchell—attempts a sort of "genealogy" of Thomists on this issue. It is hoped that these essays will introduce students to a central debate in Thomistic metaphysics while also being of help to scholars who are looking for a consideration of the issues for their own reflection and writing. Of course, in the face of the manifest pluralism among Thomists, their substantial agreement on many points of metaphysics must be borne in mind. Nevertheless, this volume embraces the pluralism of positions within the Thomistic school, not to defend pluralism for its own sake, but rather in order to pursue the truth of the matter through dialectical discussion of the questions. The essays that constitute this volume were gathered with the conviction that the pluralism found within contemporary Thomism is a rich resource, insufficiently tapped to date, for achieving greater clarity on the foundation of metaphysics.

With regard to the second goal, it is hoped that the essays in parts 2 and 3 will demonstrate the essential value and vital necessity of a sound foundation in metaphysics for the practice of both philosophy and theology. The four essays in part 2—Gregory Doolan's on the categories, James M. Jacobs's on the ontology of artifacts, Alice Ramos's on the tran-

---

10. For a discussion of editions, translations, and the biographical context of Aquinas's *Expositio*, see Jean-Pierre Torrell, OP, *Saint Thomas Aquinas*, vol. 1, *The Person and His Work*, trans. Robert Royal (Washington, D.C.: The Catholic University of America Press, 1993), 345.

scendentals, and Steven Long's on the analogy of being—exemplify the important role of metaphysics with respect to fundamental philosophical issues. Similarly, the four essays in part 3 demonstrate the significance of metaphysics for understanding central theological themes, such as human nature and Christology (Paul Gondreau), divine accommodation and angelology (Franklin T. Harkins), grace and salvation (Shawn M. Colberg), and God as the ultimate object of human fulfillment (Aaron Canty). In short, these last four essays demonstrate that, whereas theology without metaphysics is problematic, Thomistic theology without metaphysics is surely impossible.

This volume does not address the whole range of objections and attacks against Thomistic metaphysics, including those that have come from certain analytic philosophers. The most famous of these is Anthony Kenny's *Aquinas on Being*.[11] The challenge posed to the very foundation of Aquinas's metaphysics is one of many such objections that could be brought against the very possibility of metaphysics as Aquinas conceives it. This volume's first section presents a range of positions within Thomism on a particular dispute about the starting point of metaphysics. It does not attempt to defend Thomistic metaphysics against its major objectors, whether from the Middle Ages, the Renaissance, modernity, or contemporary analytic philosophy. Such a defense is a worthwhile endeavor, but it is not our task here. Furthermore, the inclusion of this sort of analytic critique would require a different organizing principle for the volume as a whole. This volume attempts to present a thorough, scholarly investigation of what is admittedly an intramural dispute within the Thomistic tradition.

---

11. Anthony Kenny, *Aquinas on Being* (Oxford: Oxford University Press, 2002). Kenny first raises concerns about Aquinas's doctrine of being in *Aquinas* (Oxford: Oxford University Press, 1980). He expanded this critique in *Aquinas on Mind* (London: Routledge, 1993). See Edward Feser's *Aquinas: A Beginner's Guide* (Oxford: Oneworld Publications, 2009) for a summary of this dispute and a discussion of the various philosophers within the analytic tradition who have come to the defense of Aquinas's metaphysics: e.g., Brian Davies, "Kenny on Aquinas on Being," *The Modern Schoolman* 82, no. 2 (2005): 111–29, and "Aquinas, God, Being," *Monist* 80, no. 4 (1997): 500–521; and Gyula Klima, "On Kenny on Aquinas on Being: A Critical Review of *Aquinas on Being* by Anthony Kenny," *International Philosophical Quarterly* 44, no. 4 (2004): 567–80. See also Alfred J. Freddoso's overview and discussion of the revival of interest in Aquinas among analytic philosophers, "The Vindication of St. Thomas: Thomism and Contemporary Anglo-American Philosophy," *Nova et Vetera* 14, no. 2 (2016): 565–84; and the famous issue of the *Monist* on "Analytical Thomism" edited by John Haldane, *Monist* 80, no. 4 (October 1997).

Finally, in an age that has turned away from metaphysically grounded theology, the essays gathered here remind us of why "the remembrance of being" is essential to the understanding of the Christian faith. This volume attempts to show the importance of metaphysics, from its foundation, through its employment in various areas of philosophy, to its fruition in theology. To take but one example, we can see the theological importance of understanding being aright very clearly in Aquinas's discussion of the most proper name of God as "He Who Is" (*Qui est*) in *Summa Theologiae* I, q. 13, a. 11. Any other name would signify some mode of substance. "Hence, Damascene says that 'He Who Is' [*Qui est*] is the principal of all names applied to God; for comprehending all in itself, it contains existence itself [*ipsum esse*] as an infinite and indeterminate sea of substance."[12]

12. *The Summa Theologica of St. Thomas Aquinas*, trans. the English Dominicans (New York: Benziger, 1947–48), I, q. 13, a. 11, co.

PART ONE

The Foundation of Metaphysics

I

Aquinas on *separatio* and Our Discovery of Being as Being

JOHN F. WIPPEL

My purpose here, as in my earlier discussions of this issue, is to offer an account that is historically accurate insofar as this can be derived from Aquinas's texts, and one that is in accord with his general theory of knowledge and his understanding of being as being as the subject of metaphysics.[1] This is easier said than done because nowhere in his writings does Thomas offer us a complete account of all that is involved in this. One is required to draw on texts scattered throughout his corpus and then to try to bring them together in a coherent whole that will be historically accurate and philosophically sound. In certain cases one may have to supply material not explicitly addressed by Thomas as best as one can to complete the account.

As is well known, according to Aquinas's theory of knowledge, all of our knowledge derives in some way from sense experience.[2] Presumably

---

1. See my *Metaphysical Themes in Thomas Aquinas* (Washington, D.C.: The Catholic University of America Press, 1984), chap. 4, and *The Metaphysical Thought of Thomas Aquinas: From Finite Being to Uncreated Being* (Washington, D.C.: The Catholic University of America Press, 2000), chap. 2.

2. See, for instance, *Expos. de Trin.*, q. 6, a. 2, editio Leonina (hereafter, Leon.) 50 (Rome: Leonine Commission, 1992), 164.71–76: "Principium igitur cuiuslibet nostre cognitionis est in sensu, quia ex apprehensione sensus oritur appreensio phantasiae, que est 'motus a sensu factus' ... a qua iterum oritur appreensio intellectiva in nobis, cum phantasmata sint intellective

this must also apply to his explanation of how we come to know being as being. This would seem to rule out as historically unreliable any account that appeals to an *a priori* knowledge of being on our part.

At the same time, it is well known that Thomas often refers to being as that which the intellect first discovers. At times he indicates that this priority of being means that whatever other concept or notion we may examine, if we analyze it or, as he puts it, use the process of *resolutio*, we are ultimately going to be driven back to recognizing it as in some way involving being. Here I have in mind especially his language in *De Ver.*, q. 1, a. 1, and the discussion of *resolutio* and *compositio* that he works out in his *Expos. de Trin.*, q. 6, a. 1. Thus he writes in the first text: "That which the intellect first conceives, and into which it resolves all of its other conceptions, is being [*ens*]."[3] And in the text from the *Expos. de Trin.* he points out that when we are following the path of resolution and reason from more particular to more general concepts, the last we discover by using this process is being. While this is for him to say that a knowledge of being is implied in our knowledge of less extended conceptions, it is not for him to assert that an explicit knowledge of being is present in our minds before we can form any other concept or notion.[4]

More important for my immediate purpose is the contrast between those texts which imply that a knowledge of being is available to everyone, and other texts where Thomas stresses how difficult it was for

---

anime ut obiecta," and *De Ver.*, q. 12, a. 3, ad 2, Leon. 22.2 (Rome: Leonine Commission, 1972), 378.379–82: "Sed quia primum principium nostrae cognitionis est sensus, oportet ad sensum quodam modo resolvere omnia de quibus iudicamus."

3. *De Ver.*, q. 1, a. 1, Leon. 22.1:4.100–102: "illud autem quod primo intellectus concipit quasi notissimum et in quod conceptiones omnes resolvit est ens."

4. *Expos. de Trin.*, q. 6, a. 1, Leon. 50:162.372–82: "Quandoque vero procedit de uno in aliud secundum rationem, ut quando est processus secundum causas intrinsecas ... resolvendo autem quando e converso, eo quod universalius est simplicius; maxime autem universalia sunt que sunt communia omnibus entibus, et ideo terminus resolutionis in hac via ultimus est consideratio entis et eorum que sunt entis in quantum huiusmodi." For further discussion see my *Metaphysical Thought of Thomas Aquinas*, 42–43 and n62. Also see Jan Aertsen, "Method and Metaphysics: The *via resolutionis* in Thomas Aquinas," *New Scholasticism* 63 (1989): 405–18, and *Medieval Philosophy and the Transcendentals: The Case of Thomas Aquinas* (Leiden: Brill, 1996), 130–36. While my account will differ from that offered by Jacques Maritain in various ways, I find him making a similar point when he describes being as the "first of all concepts." See his *Existence and the Existent* (New York: Pantheon Books, 1948), 25n12. After referring to the idea of being as implicitly present in the minds of the primitive men who use languages that do not possess the word "being" he remarks: "The first idea formed by a child is not the idea of being; but the idea of being is implicit in the first idea the child forms."

the first philosophers to arrive at a knowledge of being as such. Indeed, in one text whose interpretation continues to be disputed, he seems to say that along with all the other earlier philosophers, even Plato and Aristotle failed to reach this level of understanding (*ST* I, q. 44, a. 2), even though in a slightly earlier text from his *De Pot.*, q. 3, a. 5, he does attribute such knowledge to them.

Thus in *De Pot.* he writes: "Still later philosophers such as Plato, Aristotle, and their followers came to a consideration of universal *esse* itself."[5] But in *ST* I, q. 44, a. 2, as part of his effort to show that prime matter is created, he finds earlier philosophical thought passing through three stages: (1) the earliest philosophers, being "grossiores" in their thinking, posited only sensible bodies as beings, and thought only of accidental motion and causes of the same; (2) others reached a higher level and distinguished between form and matter (which they viewed as uncreated) and posited more universal causes such as Plato's ideas or Aristotle's ecliptic circle of the sun. But both groups still regarded being in some particular way, either as "this being" (*hoc ens*) or "such being" (*tale ens*); (3) finally some arrived at a knowledge of being insofar as it is being and hence investigated the causes of beings not only insofar as they are "these" or "such," but insofar as they are beings.[6]

The surprising thing here is that Thomas does not include Plato and Aristotle within this highest level, where being as being was discovered. While some have tried to show that this text does not exclude them from belonging there, that is not what the text says.[7] But for my purposes, however this particular text may be interpreted, it, along with many others, proves the point that in Aquinas's eyes philosophical thinking only gradually succeeded in discovering being as being.

Moreover, in *SCG* I.4, while arguing that it was fitting for God to

5. See *De Pot.*, ed. Paul Pession (Turin: Marietti, 1965), 49: "Posteriores vero philosophi, ut Plato, Aristoteles et eorum sequaces, pervenerunt ad considerationem ipsius esse universalis; et ideo ipsi soli posuerunt aliquam universalem causam rerum, a qua omnia alia in esse prodirent."

6. *ST* I, q. 44, a. 2, Leon. (Rome: Leonine Commission, 1988), 4.457–58.

7. On this see Étienne Gilson, *The Spirit of Mediaeval Philosophy* (New York: Sheed and Ward, 1940), 439–40; Mark Johnson, "Did St. Thomas Attribute a Doctrine of Creation to Aristotle?," *New Scholasticism* 63 (1989): 129–55; Lawrence Dewan, OP, "Thomas Aquinas, Creation and Two Historians," *Laval théologique et philosophique* 50 (1994): 363–87; Jan Aertsen, "La scoperta dell'ente in quanto ente," in *Studi di filosofia 29: Tommaso d'Aquino e l'oggetto della metafisica*, ed. S. Brock, 35–48 (Rome: Armando Editore, 2004); John F. Wippel, "Aquinas on Creation and Preambles of Faith," *The Thomist* 78 (2014): 1–36.

reveal truths such as his existence and his unity (which in other contexts he refers to as *praeambula fidei*) even though they can and have been discovered by human reason, Thomas emphasizes the difficulty of such reasoning and of metaphysical thinking in general. So true is this that he makes it clear that the majority of human beings would never arrive at metaphysical knowledge by relying on reason alone.[8]

In order to reconcile these two seemingly divergent lines in Thomas's texts—(1) that being is that which the intellect first conceives, and (2) that relatively few humans arrive at philosophical knowledge of being as being—and along with a number of other interpreters of Thomas's thought, I maintain that we must credit him with making a distinction between the knowledge of being that is available to everyman, on the one hand, and the knowledge of being as being that is the subject of metaphysics, on the other hand.[9] Given this conviction, I propose to make some remarks here about how, in light of what Thomas does explicitly state, one can offer a coherent account of how one discovers both of these notions of being, what I will call a primitive or prephilosophical understanding, on the one hand, and a metaphysical notion of being as being, on the others.

The Primitive or Prephilosophical Notion of Being

First, then, I turn to an account of a prephilosophical notion of being in light of Thomas's theory of knowledge. I have already recalled that according to Aquinas all of our knowledge must in some way be derived from sense experience. I would also like to recall that, for Thomas, being (or *ens* in Latin) is not a simple but a complex notion. He refers to it as

8. See SCG I.4, Editio Leonina Manualis (Rome: Leonine Commission, 1934), 4. Note especially: "Ad cognitionem enim eorum quae de Deo ratio investigare potest, multa praecognoscere oportet: cum fere totius philosophiae consideratio ad Dei cognitionem ordinatur, propter quod metaphysica, quae circa divina versatur, inter philsophiae partes ultima remanet addiscenda. Sic ergo non nisi cum magno labore studii ad praedictae veritatis inquisitionem perveniri potest. Quem quidem laborem pauci subire volunt pro amore scientiae."

9. For others who distinguish in various ways between a primitive notion of being and a philosophical notion see Henri Renard, "What Is St. Thomas' Approach to Metaphysics?," *New Scholasticism* 30 (1956): 63–84, at 73; A. M. Krapiec, "Analysis formationis conceptus entis existentialiter considerati," *Divus Thomas (Piac.)* 59 (1956): 320–50, at 341–44; George Klubertanz, *Introduction to the Philosophy of Being*, 2nd ed. (New York: Appleton-Century-Crofts, 1963), 45–52; Robert W. Schmidt, "L'emploi de la séparation en métaphysique," *Revue philosophique de Louvain* 58 (1960): 373–93, at 377–80.

id quod est (that which is) or as *quod est,* and at times as "that which has *esse*" (*habens esse*).[10] I take it that these descriptions should apply both to his prephilosophical notion of being, and to his notion of being as being.

As regards the prephilosophical notion of being, when it is described as "that which is," a question may be raised about the meaning of "is" or *est* as it appears in this description. Does it simply refer to our recognition of being as "that which exists," or does it include something more— the intrinsic *actus essendi* that Thomas posits in every existing entity to account for the fact that it exists? This is an extremely important distinction within Thomas's metaphysics, and one that is often blurred or confused, and I would give credit to Cornelio Fabro for having emphasized its meaning and importance, even though my subsequent account will differ from his in various ways.[11] If we follow the order of discovery and concentrate on the awareness of being that is available to everyman, then I suggest that we understand "that which is" as simply referring to a notion that recognizes both the quidditative aspect and the existential aspect of the notion of being. If at some further point within one's development of Thomas's metaphysics one shows that there must be a real composition of essence and a distinct *actus essendi* within all finite beings, then one may also understand "that which is" in a fuller sense, as including the act of existing in its meaning. But this should not be assumed at the beginning.

Accordingly, in discussing a prephilosophical notion of being, one must account for the content found in that notion. Here Thomas provides some helpful and well known texts, especially in his *In Sent.* I and

---

10. See, for instance, *In de Heb.* 2, Leon. 50:271.57–59: "ens, sive id quod est"; *ST* I-II, q. 26, a. 4, Leon. 6 (Rome: Leonine Commission, 1891), 190: "ens simpliciter est quod habet esse"; *In Meta.* IV, n. 535, ed. M.-R. Cathala and R. M. Spiazzi (Turin: Marietti, 1950), 151: "dicit quod ens sive quod est dicitur multipliciter"; *De Pot.*, q. 7, a. 7, ed. Paul Pession (Turin: Marietti, 1965), 204: "substantia est ens tamquam per se habens esse"; *SCG* I.22: "Amplius, omnis res est per hoc quod habet esse" (12). Also see *In Meta.* XII, n. 2419: "Nam ens dicitur quasi esse habens, hoc solum est substantia quae subsistit" (567).

11. See, for instance, his "Elementi per una dottrina tomistica della partecipazione," in his *Esegesi tomistica* (Rome: Libreria, 1969), 435: "Perciò l'autentica nozione tomistica di partecipazione esige di distinguere l'*esse* come atto non solo dall'essenza ch'è la sua potenza, ma anche dall'esistenza ch'è il *fatto* di essere e quindi un 'resultato' e non un principio metafisico: di qui nasce l'errore di quei tomisti i quali, seguendo la spinta dell'apriori di Kant, fondano l'esperienza o l'apprensione dell'*esse* nell'atto del giudizio (Maréchal, Lotz, Rahner …) e parlano perciò, con espressione assai equivoca, di un 'esistenzialismo tomistico.'"

in his *Expos. de Trin.*, q. 5, a. 3. In these texts he distinguishes between two operations of the intellect, one called the understanding of indivisibles, and the other referred to as composition and division. The first operation, often referred to as simple apprehension, is directed toward the nature or quiddity of a thing, while the second, often referred to as judgment, is directed toward a thing's *esse*. It follows from this that in order to account for the quidditative aspect of our notion of being—"that which"—Thomas would have us appeal to the intellect's first operation, and in order to account for our inclusion of the fact of existence within the same notion, he would have us appeal to judgment. This, of course, is the judgment of existence that has been discussed and utilized to good effect by Gilson, by Maritain in a somewhat different way, by Joseph Owens, and by many of Gilson's other followers. And I myself acknowledge my debt to Gilson for the valuable work he has done concerning this in various writings, especially in his *Being and Some Philosophers*.[12]

In brief, therefore, I would agree with Gilson that it is only through judgment that we first come to a knowledge of anything as existing and that as a result of one or perhaps a series of such judgments we are then in position to formulate a general notion or conception of being as "that which is." Among Thomas's texts, one may begin with one taken from his *In Sent.* I, d. 38, q. 1, a. 3, sol.:

> Since in a thing there are two [factors], the quiddity of a thing and its *esse*, to these two there correspond two operations on the part of the intellect. One which is called by the philosophers *formatio* whereby it apprehends the quiddities of things, which is also called by the Philosopher in *De anima* III the "understanding of indivisibles." The other grasps [*comprehendit*] the *esse* of a thing by composing an affirmation because also the *esse* of a thing composed of matter and form, from which it takes its knowledge, consists in a certain composition of form with matter or of an accident with a subject.[13]

12. See Étienne Gilson, *Being and Some Philosophers*, 2nd ed. (Toronto: Pontifical Institute of Mediaeval Studies, 1952), chap. 6.

13. "Cum in re duo sint, quidditas rei, et esse eius, his duobus respondet duplex operatio intellectus. Una quae dicitur a philosophis formatio, qua apprehendit quidditates rerum, quae etiam a Philosopho, in III *De anima*, dicitur indivisibilium intelligentia. Alia autem comprehendit esse rei, componendo affirmationem, quia etiam esse rei ex materia et forma compositae, a qua cognitionem accipit, consistit in quadam compositione formae ad materiam, vel accidentis ad subjectum." *In Sent.*, ed. Pierre Mandonnet (Paris: Lethielleux, 1929), I, d. 38, q. 1, a. 3, sol. (1:903). For Aristotle see *De anima* III.5, 430a26–28.

In this text Thomas assigns to judgment an apprehending (or to transliterate, a comprehending) grasp of *esse*, although a certain ambiguity remains about how *esse* itself is to be taken here. I would think that at the very least it refers to the actual existence of a thing and would acknowledge that it may also refer to the intrinsic *actus essendi* from which its actual existence results (to use Fabro's description of this). For earlier on in this same work Thomas had already introduced his view of composition (and hence distinction) of essence and *esse* in creatures.[14]

A second well-known description is found at the beginning of q. 5, a. 3, of the corpus of Aquinas's *Expos. de Trin.* Here he is addressing the question whether mathematics treats without matter and motion what exists in matter. The question is occasioned by the Boethian text on which he is commenting and in order to answer it Thomas finds it necessary to explain how the intellect is able to abstract, that is to say, how it can distinguish intellectually. Here, too, he recalls from Aristotle's *De anima* III.6 that the intellect's operation is twofold—one whereby it knows what something is, called the "understanding of indivisibles" and another whereby it composes and divides, that is, judges by forming affirmative and negative propositions. Then he writes:

And these two operations correspond to two [factors] that are present in things. The first operation looks to [*respicit*] the very nature of a thing, according to which the thing understood holds some grade among beings, whether it be a complete thing, such as some whole, or an incomplete thing, such as a part or accident. The second operation looks to [*respicit*] the very *esse* of the thing, which results from the union of the principles of a thing in composites, or accompanies the simple nature of the thing, as in simple substances.[15]

---

14. For example, in d. 8, q. 1, a. 1; q. 5, a. 1, sol.; and a. 2. For the first of these texts see Mandonnet (ed.), 1:195: "Cum autem ita sit quod in qualibet re creata essentia sua differat a suo esse, res illa proprie denominatur a quidditate sua, et non ab actu essendi"; for the second (q. 5, a. 1 and the *sed contra*) see 226–27; and for q. 5, a. 2 see 229–30. For texts where Thomas uses *esse* in judgments of existence see *In Peri Her.*, revised Leonine ed., 1*.1.II.2: "hoc verbum 'est' quandoque in enuntiatione praedicatur secundum se, ut cum dicitur 'Sortes est,' per quod nichil aliud intendimus significare quam quod Sortes est in rerum natura" (88.36–40); also see *ST* II-II, q. 83, a. 1, arg. 3: "secunda vero est compositio et divisio, per quam scilicet apprehenditur aliquid esse vel non esse" (Leon. 9 [Rome: Leonine Commission, 1889], 192). See ad 3 for confirmation that Thomas accepts this as his own view.

15. "Et hee quidem due operationes duobus quae sunt in rebus respondent. Prima quidem operatio respicit ipsam naturam rei, secundum quam res intellecta aliquem gradum in entibus obtinet, sive sit res completa, ut totum aliquod, sive res incompleta, ut pars vel accidens. Secunda vero operatio respicit ipsum esse rei; quod quidem resultat ex congregatione principiorum rei in

Here Thomas uses the verb *respicit* ("look to") to refer to judgment's grasp of *esse* (which I will take here as referring to actual existence, in the sense of facticity). This might seem not to be as strong as the term "comprehend" which he applies in the text from d. 38 of his *In Sent.* I. Nonetheless, in the present passage he also uses the same verb (*respicit*) to refer to the intellect's first operation whereby it understands the nature of a thing and apprehends this. Moreover, he writes: "the first operation looks to [*respicit*] the quiddity of a thing; the second looks to [*respicit*] its *esse.*"[16] Hence it seems clear that he is assigning an apprehensive role to judgment in the case of judgments of existence.

But this is not enough to explain how one reaches a prephilosophical notion of being because, as has already been mentioned, according to Aquinas all our knowledge begins with sense experience. It follows that collaboration between the senses and the intellect is required for judgments of existence. While I cannot treat of Aquinas's entire theory of knowledge here, I would like to single out the following steps. First of all, according to his theory, sense perception requires that a sensible object must act on one or more external sense power. This is important for our purposes because it assigns an active role to the object perceived and implies that in order for an act of perception to occur, a sense power must be acted on by a sensible object. The sense power itself then reacts to this and, by means of what Thomas calls a sensible species, enables the form of the object perceived to take on a new mode of existence within the sense power, an *esse immateriale* or an *esse intentionale*, while retaining its physical or material *esse* within the sensible object.[17]

---

compositis, vel ipsam simplicem naturam rei concomitatur, ut in substantiis simplicibus." *Expos. de Trin.*, q. 5, a. 3, Leon. 50:147.96–105.

16. *In Sent.* I, d. 19, q. 5, a. 1, ad 7: "Ad septimum dicendum, quod cum sit duplex operatio intellectus: una quarum dicitur a quibusdam imaginatio intellectus, quam Philosophus, III *De anima*, nominat intelligentiam indivisibilium, quae consistit in apprehensione quidditatis simplicis, quae alio etiam nomine formatio dicitur; alia est quam dicunt fidem, quae consistit in compositione vel divisione propositionis: prima operatio respicit quidditatem rei; secunda respicit esse ipsius" (ed. Mandonnet, 1:489).

17. See *Sententia libri De anima* II.24, Leon. 45.1 (Rome: Leonine Commission, 1984), 169.45–56: "Quandoque vero forma recipitur in paciente secundum alium modum essendi quam sit in agente, quia dispositio materialis pacientis ad recipiendum non est similis dispositioni materiali quae erat in agente, et ideo forma recipitur in paciente sine materia in quantum paciens assimilatur agenti secundum formam et non secundum materiam; et per hunc modum sensus recipit formam sine materia, quia alterius modi esse habet forma in sensu et in re sensibili: nam in re sensibili habet esse naturale, in sensu autem habet esse intentionale sive spirituale." It is

Aquinas, of course, posits four internal senses, and the first of these—the common sense (*sensus communis*) is important for our purposes. He assigns two functions to it. The first is a function whereby individual sense perceptions as reported by different external senses are distinguished appropriately, such as this sound from this color or odor, etc. The second function is that it is by means of the common sense that a higher animal or a human being is made aware that a given external sense is perceiving a certain sensible object. While no organic power can immediately know itself, the common sense is aware when the external senses are actually perceiving.[18]

Also at the level of the internal senses is the imagination which, of course, produces phantasms or sense images of appropriately organized perceptions delivered to it by the common sense. The imagination submits these to the abstractive power of the intellect—the agent intellect. The agent intellect then renders actually intelligible the potentially intelligible content conveyed by phantasms, and, impressing this upon the possible intellect by means of an intelligible species, moves the possible intellect to understand this abstracted and universalized content.[19] But

---

interesting to note that the Latin translation of Aristotle's *De anima* used here by Thomas refers to a sense power as *susceptivum specierum sine materia* (169), but Thomas takes this as meaning that the sense power receives the *form* of the thing known without its matter. Unlike some contemporary interpreters of Aquinas, M. F. Burnyeat gets this point right in his interesting "Aquinas on 'Spiritual Change' in Perception," in *Ancient and Medieval Theories of Intentionality*, ed. Dominik Perler (Leiden: Brill, 2001), 129–53, at 149.

18. *Sentensia libri De Anima*, c. 13: "circa ipsas inmutationes sensuum propriorum a suis obiectis habet sensus communis aliquas operationes proprias quas sensus proprii habere non possunt, sicut quod percipit ipsas inmutationes sensuum et discernit inter sensibilia diversorum sensuum: sensu enim communi percipimus nos videre et discernimus inter album et dulce" (120.99–105), and c. 26: "huiusmodi autem actiones sunt duae: una est secundum quod nos percipimus actiones sensuum propriorum, puta quod sentimus nos videre et audire; alia est secundum quod discernimus inter sensibilia diversorum sensuum, puta quod aliud sit dulce, et aliud album" (178.8–14). Also see c. 27 for more on the common sense. See also *ST* I, q. 78, a. 4, ad 2 (Leon. 5:256).

19. On this see *Quodl.* VIII.2.1, Leon. 25.1 (Rome: Leonine Commission, 1996), 55–57.74–104. In terms of context, here Thomas is responding to a question about the need for the soul to depend on species (here he is not speaking of forms) derived from objects of cognition outside the soul. In answering he discusses both sensible and intelligible species. These species should not be viewed as the forms or objects of cognition but are rather likenesses of such forms or objects which are required for the forms or objects themselves to be present to a cognitive power. Also see, for instance, *De Spir.* IX, ad 6, Leon. 24.2 (Rome: Leonine Commission, 2000), 97.427–35. Note in particular: "unde species visibilis non se habet ut quod videtur set ut quo videtur. Et similiter est de intellectu possibili, nisi quod intellectus possibilis reflectitur supra se ipsum et supra speciem suam, non autem visus."

insofar as judgments of existence are directed to individual things, in order for the original object to be understood as this individual, the intellect turns back to a knowledge of its own act of cognition, then to the species that serves as the principle for that act, and then to the phantasm preserved in the imagination, and reunites the abstracted universal content with the individual differences preserved in the phantasm, thereby recognizing the abstracted universal content, of dog, for instance, as realized in this individual dog.[20]

At this point Thomas does not explicitly tell us how the intellect then moves on to judge that this originally perceived object actually exists. Here, or so it seems to me, the common sense plays a critical role because it is by means of this internal sense power that one is aware that the external sense power is actually perceiving something. At this point, I suggest, the possible intellect is also aware that the common sense reports that one or more external senses are perceiving the individual sensible object and are acted upon by it. Being aware of this, the possible intellect judges that this particular thing is or exists, or that "this x exists," or makes an existential judgment to the effect that this particular thing exists.[21] As the knowing being encounters other external objects and perceives each of them through one or more external sense power,

---

20. Note how Aquinas describes this in *De Ver.*, q. 10, a. 5: "Et sic mens singulare cognoscit per quandam reflexionem, prout scilicet mens cognoscendo obiectum suum, quod est aliqua natura universalis, redit in cognitionem sui actus, et ulterius in speciem quae est sui actus principium, et ulterius in phantasma a quo species est extracta; et sic aliquam cognitionem de singulari accipit" (Leon. 22.2:309.73–81). For a very similar presentation see his slightly earlier *In Sent.* IV, d. 50, q. 1, a. 3, ed. Roberto Busa, *S. Thomae Aquinatis Opera Omnia* (Stuttgart-Bad Constatt: Frommann-Holzboog, 1980), 1:704. On this see George P. Klubertanz, "St. Thomas and the Knowledge of the Singular," *New Scholasticism* 26 (1952): 135–66, esp. 149–51; François-Xavier Putallaz, *Le sens de la réflexion chez Thomas d'Aquin* (Paris: J. Vrin, 1991), 118–23; Camille Bérubé, *La Connaissance de l'individuel au Moyen Âge* (Montréal/Paris: Presses de l'Université de Montréal/Presses Universitaires de France, 1964), 42–64. See also *Quaestiones disputatae de anima*, a. 20, ad 1 in contrarium, ed. Bernardo C. Bazán, Leon. 24.1:174–75.465–76. There after again repeating the solution he had presented in the previously mentioned texts, Thomas adds this remark: "Set hec reflexio compleri non potest nisi per adiunctionem virtutis cogitative et ymaginative, quae non sunt in anima separata." Bérubé notes this and, after considering Thomas's fuller discussions in *ST* I, q. 85, a. 1 and q. 84, a. 7, remarks (at 60–64) that a number of modern scholars have rediscovered the role of the "forgotten sense"—the cogitative power, in Thomas's account of knowledge of the individual but see below.

21. For a good albeit brief description of this general process see *De Ver.*, q. 10, a. 5, as cited above in note 20. Also see *ST* II-II, q. 173, a. 2 (Leon. 10:386), within the context of a comparison between natural knowledge and prophetic revelations.

this process is repeated with the consequence that a series of existential judgments will be made. Perhaps as a result of the first judgment of existence, or perhaps as the result of a series of such judgments, the human being in question will formulate a vague general idea or notion of the real or "that which is," in other words, of being, probably without having ever heard of the term "being" itself. This notion of the real or of "that which is" is what I mean by a primitive or prephilosophical notion of being.

Various questions may be raised about this procedure as I have presented it. For instance, some interpreters, such as Jacques Maritain and especially A. M. Krapiec, emphasize the role of the internal sense known as the cogitative power in humans as playing an indispensable role in the formation of individual judgments of existence. Krapiec goes so far in stressing the role of this internal sense power that he at times refers to it almost as though such judgments should be attributed to it. Yet he does not deny that existence as such, and hence the notion of being as "that which is," can be grasped explicitly only by the intellect.[22] In my view he overstates the role of the cogitative power in his very interesting account, and neglects the part played in it by the *sensus communis*. This, I think, is because he has misinterpreted an important text from Thomas's commentary on *De anima* II.13, where Thomas is not really discussing how we discover existence as such, or being as existing, as Krapiec thinks, but rather how the human knower goes about applying an abstract and universal notion or concept or principle to an individual in the case of practical action. It should be noted that Thomas also brings out very clearly the difference between these two procedures in *De Ver.*, q. 10, a. 5, that is, between the way in which the motion of the sensitive part of the soul terminates in the mind as happens in a motion running from things to the soul whereby the mind knows an individual by a certain *reflexio* or turning back, as outlined above,[23] and the way in which the motion runs from the soul to the sensitive part of the soul and thus the soul uses particular reason (the cogitative power) which, while it is a certain power of the sensitive part with a determined organ in the body, composes and

22. See Krapiec, "Analysis formationis conceptus entis existentialiter considerati," 331–36. For Maritain, see *Existence and the Existent*, 26–29 and n13, as well as 27 in the note for his reference to "'judgment' (improperly so-called) of the external senses and the aestimative."

23. See the text partially quoted above in note 20.

divides individual "intentions" and thus plays an important mediating role in enabling the soul to apply the universal knowledge possessed by the mind to individual actions.[24]

But this second procedure or motion is very different from that involved in individual judgments of existing. In discussing these we are concerned about one's discovery of an individual as existing and hence with the first kind of motion that runs from things to the soul. In accounting for this, therefore, I prefer to emphasize the role of the common sense. Because the intellect at the terminus of its turning back upon a phantasm must also be aware by means of the common sense that an object is being perceived by an external sense, it appears to me to be best suited to assist the possible intellect in judging that a given object exists.

Another question may be raised concerning whether this prephilosophical notion of being is gained by some form of abstraction. Because its content is complex—that which is—abstraction or the intellect's first operation is not sufficient for the intellect to recognize that something is or exists. As we have already seen, Thomas at times states explicitly that judgment is required for this. Nonetheless, after one has recognized that a given thing exists, or that "x exists," one then is in position to formulate a complex notion of being as "that which is." In order to form a general notion that may be applied to anything about which one can judge "it is," one may still ask whether abstraction of some kind occurs here. On the one hand, as Klubertanz maintains, it may suffice for the intellect to recall that it has made such judgments about a number of other objects perceived by the external senses and simply on the strength of these judgments to recognize that the "is" is common to all of these judgments, whereas the subjects of the judgments vary. Then one will realize that the subject of "is" in such judgments is not restricted to any particular subject and recognize that "something is," thereby reaching the prephilosophical notion of being as that which is.[25]

24. For Thomas's text see Sentencia libri de anima II.13, Leon. 45.1 (Rome: Leonine Commission, 1984), 120–22. Note 122.206: "nam cogitativa apprehendit individuum ut existentem sub natura communi, quod contingit ei in quantum unitur intellective in eodem subiecto, unde cognoscit hunc hominem prout est hic homo, et hoc lignum prout est hoc lignum."

25. Introduction to the Philosophy of Being, 2nd ed. (New York: Wipf and Stock, 2005), 45–47. Klubertanz insists that this is not a process of abstraction. He argues that abstraction "leaves some part of our initial reality out of consideration." If being is reached by abstraction, there is something in the real thing that is left out, and this will be not-being, or nothing (45–46). We

On the other hand, if such a notion is formed by abstraction, it is not an abstraction of essence or quiddity from existence, as existence must be retained in the resulting notion of being, even of a prephilosophical notion of being, as "that which is." And the grave concern would then remain about how the differences from which one would abstract this notion of being could still enjoy being or be real. For Thomas has denied that being can be divided by adding differences to it from without. Hence we should not conclude that a prephilosophical notion of being is reached by abstraction.[26]

Next, there is a question about which comes first in a judgment of existence—one's discovery of the subject of the judgment through the intellect's first operation, for instance, "this x," or of the verb "is" through the intellect's second operation. While I have outlined a series of steps involved in one's discovery of a prephilosophical notion of being, these steps apply to the order of nature, but perhaps not necessarily to the order of time. Accordingly, because I do not find an explicit answer to this in Thomas's texts, I am sympathetic with Maritain's (and Owens's) suggestion that the intellect's apprehension of the quidditative content expressed by the subject through its first operation—the understanding of indivisibles—and the resulting judgment of existence are in fact simultaneous, with the understanding of indivisibles being first in the order of nature in terms of material causality, and the judgment of existence being first in the order of formal causality.[27]

---

have not abstracted "something" from anything, but, as he puts it, we have a "negative judgment of generalization." Thus we move from (1) "this is," "that is," etc., to (2) "is" is not necessarily identical with this or that to (3) "something is" and hence we form the notion of "that which is" (47–48).

26. *De Ver.*, q. 1, a. 1, Leon. 22.1: "Sed enti non possunt addi aliqua quasi extranea per modum quo differentia additur generi vel accidens subiecto, quia quaelibet natura est essentialiter ens, unde probat etiam Philosophus in III Metaphysicae quod ens non potest esse genus; sed secundum hoc aliqua dicuntur addere super ens inquantum exprimunt modum ipsius entis qui nomine entis non exprimitur, quod dupliciter contingit" (5.105–14). *In Meta.* V, l. 9, n. 889: "Sciendum est enim quod ens non potest hoc modo contrahi ad aliquid determinatum, sicut genus contrahitur ad species per differentias. Nam differentia, cum non participet genus, est extra essentiam generis. Nihil autem posset esse extra essentiam entis, quod per additionem ad ens aliquam speciem entis constituat: nam quod est extra ens, nihil est, et differentia esse non potest. Unde in tertio huius probavit Philosophus, quod ens, genus esse non potest." On this see my *Metaphysical Themes*, 80–81, and references concerning this point in nn33–34 to Robert and Geiger.

27. See Maritain, *Existence and the Existent*, 26. See also Owens, "Judgment and Truth in Aquinas," in *St. Thomas Aquinas on the Existence of God: The Collected Papers of Joseph Owens*, ed. John R. Catan (Albany: State University of New York Press, 1980), 43–44.

Finally, how can this account be reconciled with Thomas's frequent references to being as that which is first discovered by the intellect? As I have briefly indicated above, in some texts Thomas refers to being as that which the intellect first conceives in the sense that it is that into which it "resolves" all its other conceptions. On the other hand, there is the need of sense perception of some existing thing and, as a result of abstraction, grasp of its essence in universal fashion followed by reflection back on the phantasms if the notion of being is to have both existential and quidditative content. In light of this, and in agreement with some other scholars, I conclude that an explicit notion of being need not be that which is first conceived in the temporal sense. It is first in this sense that, no matter what conception may be explicitly formed by the human knower, the process of resolution (analysis) will ultimately lead one to recognize whatever it is as real, that is, as being.[28]

Formation of the Metaphysical Notion of Being

So much, then, for my account of Thomas's views on formulating a prephilosophical notion of being. Such a notion, I have contended, is not identical with the notion of being as being, which is the subject of metaphysics for Thomas. Because the subjects of the existential judgments one may formulate based on sense perception are all material and changing, one has not yet arrived at an understanding of the kind of object of theoretical science he assigns to metaphysics in his *Expos. de Trin.*, q. 5, a. 1. There he indicates that a theoretical science must have a distinctive object of speculation, and that depending on their degree of freedom from matter and motion, there are three distinctive kinds of such objects: (1) those that depend on matter and motion in order to exist and in order to be understood, that is, those whose definitions include sensible matter, and which are studied in physics; (2) those that depend on matter to exist, but do not depend on sensible matter in order to be understood such as lines and numbers, which are studied by mathematics; (3) those that do not depend on matter to exist (or to be

28. See J. Aertsen, "Method and Metaphysics: The *via resolutionis* in Thomas Aquinas," *New Scholasticism* 63 (1989): 405–18, at 416: "Being is the 'first known.' But is 'first' becomes explicit, as the beginning of *De Ver.* 1, 1 makes clear, only on the basis of a resolution." See notes 3 and 4 above as well as my *Metaphysical Thought of Thomas Aquinas*, 41–44.

understood), in one of two ways, either in the sense that they are never found in matter (such as God and angels), which I call the " positively immaterial" because they positively exclude matter, and those that may or may not be found in matter such as substance, quality, being (*ens*), act, the one and the many, etc., which are studied in philosophical divine science, that is, in metaphysics and which I call the "negatively or neutrally immaterial" in that they need not be found in matter.[29]

Thomas's reply to the sixth objection should be noted. The objection argues that a whole should not be divided against its parts. But divine science (metaphysics) seems to be a whole with respect to physics and mathematics, as their subjects are parts of its subject; for the subject of divine science or first philosophy is being, and mobile substance, which the natural philosopher studies, is a part of this and quantity, which is studied by the mathematician, is another part.[30]

In responding Aquinas agrees that the subjects of the other sciences are parts of being, which is the subject of metaphysics. Thus *ens mobile* and *ens quantum* are parts of being. But it does not follow from this that the other sciences are parts of metaphysics. This is because each particular science considers one part of being according to its particular mode of consideration, which is different from the mode whereby being is studied in metaphysics. Hence, speaking properly, the subject of such a particular science is not a part of the subject of metaphysics. "For it is not a part of being under that aspect [*ratio*] whereby being is the subject of metaphysics."[31]

This reply is important for at least two reasons. First, it makes it clear that in discussing the different degrees to which the things studied by the theoretical sciences depend on matter and motion, Thomas has in mind especially the subjects of each of them. Second, it brings out Aris-

---

29. Leon. 50:138.135–62. Note especially the third type, because the distinction he introduces there is crucial to his position: "Quaedam vero speculabilia sunt que non dependent a materia secundum esse, quia sine materia possunt esse, sive numquam sint in materia, sicut Deus et angelus, sive in quibusdam sint in materia et in quibusdam non, ut substantia, qualitas, ens, potentia, actus, unum et multa et huiusmodi" (ll. 154–60). On the terminology of "positively" immaterial and "negatively" or "neutrally immaterial" see my *Metaphysical Thought of Thomas Aquinas*, 8 and 17.

30. Leon. 50:136–37.42–51.

31. Leon. 50:141.322–33. Note especially: "non enim est pars entis secundum illam rationem qua ens est subiectum metaphysice."

totle's point in *Metaphysics* IV.1 about two aspects of the science of being as being: (1) unlike physics and mathematics it does not cut off a part of being and study the properties of that part, but it studies being taken universally; and (2) it studies being from its unique perspective, that is, as being. Hence, as Thomas will say explicitly elsewhere, in metaphysics one may indeed study material being and quantified being, but in that case one studies them *as* being rather than as material or quantified.[32] Both of these aspects are reinforced by Thomas's response to the seventh objection according to which philosophy should rather be divided by reason of the division of being by potency and act, by the one and the many, and by substance and accident. To this Thomas simply replies that those parts of being require the same mode of consideration as does *ens commune* because they too do not depend on matter and hence fall under the same mode of consideration as does *ens commune*. Therefore the science that studies them is the same as the science of *ens commune*.[33] Note also that this reference to *ens commune* reinforces the point that Thomas is here dealing with the subject of metaphysics.

In q. 5, a. 4 of this same treatise, Thomas explicitly asks whether divine science studies the kinds of things that are without matter and motion.[34] He begins his response by noting that if a science has a given subject genus, "it must consider the principles of that genus; for science is not perfected except through a knowledge of principles."[35] Here he also refers to metaphysics as the science which studies those things that are common to all beings and states explicitly that its subject is being as being (*ens inquantum est ens*).[36] He then indicates that the subject of

---

32. Cf. *In Meta.* VI, l. 1, n. 1165: "Advertendum est autem, quod licet ad considerationem primae philosophiae pertineant ea quae sunt separata secundum esse et rationem a materia et motu, non tamen solum ea; sed etiam de sensibilibus, inquantum sunt entia, Philosophus perscrutatur."

33. For the objection see Leon. 50:137.55–59. For Thomas's reply see 141.338–42: "Ad septimum dicendum, quod illae partes entis exigunt eundem modum tractandi cum ente communi, quia etiam ipsa non dependent ad materiam; et ideo scientia de ipsis non distinguitur a scientia que est de ente communi."

34. For Thomas's formulation of the question see Leon. 50:136.8–9: "quarto utrum divina scientia sit de his que sunt sine materia et motu."

35. Leon. 50:153.82–86: "Sciendum siquidem est quod quecumque scientia considerat aliquod genus subiectum, oportet quod consideret principia illius generis, cum scientia non perficiatur nisi per cognitionem principiorum."

36. Ibid., 154.157–62: "unde et huiusmodi res divine non tractantur a philosophis nisi prout sunt rerum omnium principia, et ideo pertractantur in illa doctrina in qua ponuntur ea que sunt communia omnibus entibus, que habet subiectum ens in quantum est ens."

metaphysics does not depend on matter and motion in order to exist only in the weaker of the two senses he had already distinguished in q. 5, a. 1, that is, as the negatively immaterial. Being insofar as it is being does not depend on matter in order to exist only in this sense that it may or may not be present in matter. As he puts it, "it is not of its nature or essence to be in matter and motion, but it can exist without matter and motion even though it is sometimes present in them." It is in this way that being and substance and potency and act are separate from matter and motion.[37]

Or as he describes this in the Prooemium to his *In Meta.*, it belongs to one and the same science (metaphysics) to study separate substances, which he identifies here as the first causes of things, and being in general (*ens commune*), which is the subject of that science. Again he explains that this is because it belongs to one and the same science to study the proper causes of its subject-genus, and that genus itself. Hence, he continues, while the subject of this science is being in general (and not separate substances), it is entirely concerned with what is separate from matter both in the order of existence (*esse*) and in the order of understanding. This is because "not only are those things that can never exist in matter such as God and intellectual substances said to be separate according to existence and according to understanding, but also those that can exist without matter, such as *ens commune*."[38] It is therefore obviously very important for him to explain how one can discover being in general or being as being—the subject of metaphysics, which is only negatively or neutrally immaterial.

---

37. Ibid., ll. 182–95: "Utraque [philosophical divine science or metaphysics, and the divine science based on revelation] autem est de his quae sunt separata a materia et motu secundum esse, sed diversimode, secundum quod dupliciter potest esse aliquid a materia et motu separatum secundum esse: uno modo sic quod de ratione ipsius rei que separata dicitur sit quod nullo modo in materia et motu esse possit, sicut Deus et angeli dicuntur a materia et motu separati; alio modo sic quod non sit de ratione eius quod sit in materia et motu, set possit esse sine materia et motu quamvis quandoque inveniatur in materia et motu, et sic ens et substantia et potentia et actus sunt separata a materia et motu, quia secundum esse a materia et motu non dependent sicut mathematica dependebant." See also his reply to obj. 5 (156.305–13).

38. *In Meta.*, Prooemium (1–2). Note: "Quamvis autem subiectum huius scientiae sit ens commune, dicitur tamen tota de his quae sunt separata a materia secundum esse et rationem. Quia secundum esse et rationem separari dicuntur, non solum illa quae nunquam in materia esse possunt, sicut Deus et intellectuales substantiae, sed etiam illla quae possunt sine materia esse, sicut ens commune."

Fortunately, he has devoted q. 5, a. 3 to explaining how one discovers the subjects of each of the three theoretical sciences and, in doing so, explicitly introduces an intellectual operation which he refers to there as *separatio*. In terms of context he is addressing another question occasioned by the Boethian text: "Whether mathematics studies without motion and matter things that exist in matter and motion."[39]

In order to clarify this issue Thomas writes that he must indicate how the intellect in its operation can abstract. As he makes clear a little later, here he is using this verb "to abstract" in a broad sense, so as to apply to any way in which the intellect can distinguish. After recalling Aristotle's distinction between the intellect's first operation (understanding of indivisibles) and its second operation (judgment) and, as we have seen, correlating them respectively with a knowledge of the nature of a thing and its *esse*,[40] he notes that in the case of judgment the intellect can truly abstract, that is, distinguish, only things that are separate in reality.[41] In its first operation, however, it can abstract things that are not separate in reality in some cases, but not in others. Simply put, if one of the things that is united with another depends on the latter for its intelligibility, the intellect cannot understand the former without understanding the latter; if one of the things does not depend on the other for its intelligibility, the intellect through its first operation can understand the former without the latter. He applies this principle both to various part-whole relationships and matter-form relationships.[42]

Thomas then introduces a new precision into his terminology. In its judging operation, the intellect distinguishes one thing from another by understanding that one does not exist in the other. But in its first operation (simple apprehension) it understands what something is without understanding anything about another, neither that the one is united with the other nor that it is separate from it. Hence, he writes, the latter operation is not properly referred to as *separatio* as is the for-

---

39. For his statement of this question see *Expos. de Trin.*, Leon. 50:136.6–7: "utrum mathematica consideratio sit sine motu et materia de his quae sunt in materia."

40. See above in my text, 16–18.

41. *Expos. de Trin.*, q. 5, a. 3, Leon. 50:147.105–18. Note especially: "Et quia veritas intellectus est ex hoc quod conformature <rei>, patet quod secundum hanc secundam operationem intellectus non potest vere astraere quod secundum rem coniunctum est; quia in abstraendo significaretur esse separatio secundum ipsum esse rei."

42. Ibid., 147.132–58.

mer; it is rightly called abstraction, but only when the two things, one of which is understood without the other, are united in reality.[43] Here then, as the autograph of this text reveals, it was only after some false starts that Aquinas hit upon this terminology.[44] To repeat, now instead of using the term "abstraction" broadly so as to apply to distinguishing intellectually through the intellect's first operation and through its second, he restricts this so that it applies only to the first, that is, simple apprehension. When one distinguishes intellectually through a negative judgment, this process should be called *separatio*. Because Thomas goes on to associate *separatio* with metaphysics and with the discovery of that which does not depend on matter to exist in the sense of the neutrally immaterial, it is of special interest to us. But before making this application, he introduces important divisions into abstraction when it is taken strictly.

First he considers things that are united as form and matter, and concentrates on the relation between accidental forms and substance. While no accident can be abstracted from its underlying substance because it depends on the latter for its existence, accidents do befall substance according to a certain order. The accident of quantity first informs a substantial subject, followed by quality, *passiones*, and motions. Therefore one can think of a substance as subject to quantity without thinking of it as subject to sensible qualities, and the others that follow. And, Thomas notes, it is by reason of sensible qualities that matter is referred to as sensible matter. Hence he refers to this as the abstraction of a form from sensible matter. And thus it is with this form, the accidental form of quantity, that mathematics is concerned, along with those things that follow upon quantity such as configuration. In other words, it is by

43. Ibid., 148.159–71. "Sic ergo intellectus distinguit unum ab altero aliter et aliter secundum diversas operationes: quia secundum operationem qua componit et dividit distinguit unum ab alio per hoc quod intelligit unum alii non inesse, in operatione vero qua intelligit quid est unumquodque, distinguit unum ab alio dum intelligit quid est hoc, nichil intelligendo de alio, neque quod sit cum eo, neque quod sit ab eo separatum; unde ista distinctio non proprie habet nomen separationis, sed prima tantum. Hec autem distinctio recte dicitur abstractio, set tantum quando ea quorum unum sine altero intelligitur sunt simul secundum rem."

44. For the autograph's presentation of several different attempts by Thomas to get the first part of his response right see 146A, with reference to the text beginning on l. 86 and following; for two attempts to express the different ways in which the intellect can distinguish see 148A, with reference to l. 159 and following. The technical distinction between abstraction and separation appears only in the final version.

means of abstraction of the form (quantity) that one reaches the subject of mathematics—quantity or being as quantified but not as subject to sensible qualities.[45]

As for things that are united as part and whole, the intellect cannot abstract a whole from the kind of part or parts upon which that whole depends for its intelligibility, for instance, a mixed body cannot be abstracted from its elements, or a syllable from its letters. These are called parts of the form or parts of the species. But the intellect can abstract a whole from the kind of part upon which the whole does not depend for its intelligibility, and such parts are called parts of matter. And so, Thomas writes, this is the relationship that obtains between a human being and his or her designated parts such as this soul and this body and this fingernail and this bone, etc. These are indeed parts of the essence of this individual human being, but not of human being insofar as it is human being. This is the abstraction of the universal from the individual whereby a nature is considered absolutely according to its essential intelligibility (*rationem*) without its designated or individuated parts.[46]

In summing up, Thomas notes that two kinds of abstraction taken in the strict sense are found in the intellect. One corresponds to the

45. Ibid., 148.184–202. Note how Thomas sums this up: "Et de huiusmodi abstractis est mathematica, que considerat quantitates et ea que quantitates consequuntur, ut figuras et huiusmodi." For an interesting discussion of the ontological status of mathematical objects according to Thomas see Armand Maurer, "A Neglected Thomistic Text on the Foundation of Mathematics," reprinted in his *Being and Knowing: Studies in Thomas Aquinas and Later Medieval Philosophers* (Toronto: Pontifical Institute of Mediaeval Studies, 1990), 33–41. Also see his later "Thomists and Thomas Aquinas on the Foundation of Mathematics," *Review of Metaphysics* 47 (1993): 43–61. On *ens mobile* as the subject of natural philosophy and *ens quantum* as the subject of mathematics see *In Meta.* I, l. 2, n. 47 (Turin: Marietti, 1950), 14: "Sed scientiae particulares sunt posteriores secundum naturam universalibus scientiis, quia subiecta earum addunt ad subiecta scientiarum universalium: sicut patet, quod ens mobile de quo est naturalis philosophia, addit supra ens simpliciter, de quo est metaphysica, et supra ens quantum de quo est mathematica." The same is implied by Thomas's presentation of and response to obj. 6 in his *Expos. de Trin.*, q. 5, a. 1 (for which see above notes 30 and 31).

46. *Expos. de Trin.*, q. 5, a. 3, Leon. 50:148–49.204–38. There is a textual problem concerning l. 233: "et hoc modo se habent ad hominem omnes partes signate, sicut hec anima, et hoc corpus, et *hic unguis*, et hoc os, et huiusmodi: hee enim partes sunt quidem partes essentie Sortis et Platonis, non autem hominis in quantum homo" (emphasis added). But one wonders how "this nail" can be included within the essence of this individual human being. As the edition points out (see also Preface, 27n1), the autograph reads *hic ignis* ("this fire"), which one branch of the manuscript tradition followed. It seems to me likely that the autograph reading is correct, because to be composed of an element such as this individual instance of the element fire would be part of the essence of this individual human being, whereas "this nail" would not be.

union of form and matter or of an accidental form with its substantial subject and is the abstraction of a form (quantity) from sensible qualities and hence from sensible matter. The other corresponds to the union of a whole and a part and is the abstraction of a universal from an individual. In considering and rejecting the possibility that there might be abstractions opposed to these whereby a part would be abstracted from a whole or matter from form, he makes two important remarks about *separatio*. As regards a part being abstracted from a whole, this is impossible if it is simply a part of matter, as such a part includes the whole in its definition. And if it is a part of the species, then it can exist without the whole, such as a line without a triangle, or a letter without a syllable, or an element without a mixture. But, he writes: "In those things that can be divided in the order of existence, *separation* obtains rather than abstraction."[47]

As for possibly abstracting matter from form, Thomas immediately rules out substantial form and prime matter, as they are correlative to one another and depend on one another. It is only abstraction of the accidental form of quantity and configuration that is at issue here, and sensible matter cannot be abstracted from these because sensible qualities presuppose quantity. "Substance, however, which is the intelligible matter for quantity, can exist without quantity. Therefore, to consider substance without quantity pertains to the genus of separation rather than of abstraction."[48] This is most important because, as we have seen, substance, like being, is one of the items he has listed to illustrate those things that do not depend on matter and motion to exist in the negative or neutral sense in that they need not be found in matter, but can be. Because substance is the primary instance of being within the predicaments, we can read this as also meaning that being can exist without quantity, and that to consider this pertains to *separatio*.

Thomas concludes by correlating these three different ways in which the intellect can distinguish with the three theoretical sciences. One way the intellect can distinguish is according to its second or judging op-

---

47. See Leon. 50:149.239–58. Note in particular: "In his autem que secundum esse possunt esse divisa magis habet locum separatio quam abstractio."

48. Ibid., 149.258–74. Note especially: "Substantia autem, quae est materia intelligibilis quantitatis, potest esse sine quantitate; unde considerare substantiam sine quantitate magis pertinet ad genus separationis quam abstractionis."

eration and is properly called *separatio,* and pertains to divine science or metaphysics.[49] If one asks why, this is because *separatio* enables one to consider substance (or being) without quantity and hence without matter and as not restricted to any particular kind of being, and thus by negating any such restriction to one's understanding of being, enables one to grasp it universally and *as* being. The second way of distinguishing pertains to the intellect's first operation and is the abstraction of a form—quantity—and this pertains to mathematics. The third also pertains to the intellect's first operation and is the abstraction of the universal from the particular, and this pertains to physics, although Thomas adds that it is common to all the sciences, because in science one sets aside that which is *per accidens* and retains that which is *per se.*[50]

This does not mean that Aquinas is here saying that one attains the subject of metaphysics by abstracting a universal from individuals, as he has just assigned that task to *separatio.* And if someone should claim that Thomas has not explicitly said that it is through separation that one discovers the subject of metaphysics, it seems clear to me that he has. For he has said that it is through separation that one discovers the kind of freedom from matter that is required by the subject of metaphysics—being as being. He has listed both substance and being as enjoying that kind of freedom from matter, that is to say, negative or neutral immateriality. Moreover, he has indicated that it is through abstraction of the form of quantity that one arrives at an understanding of being as quantified, and as he has indicated in replying to the sixth objection in q. 5, a. 3 of this same treatise, this would be the subject of a particular science, that is, mathematics, whereas being is the subject of metaphysics. Finally, he has associated abstraction of the universal from the particular especially with physics, although he has added that this kind of abstraction is also practiced in the other sciences. But, to repeat my point, he does not say that abstraction is used to discover the subject of metaphysics.

49. Ibid., ll. 279–86.
50. Ibid., 149.275–86.

Some Disputed Issues

To conclude by touching on some disputed points, I would first note that in these texts Thomas has not in any way implied that one must have first discovered the existence of positively immaterial being, whether this be the soul or the first mover or God, in order to discover the subject of metaphysics and hence to begin this science. As we have already seen, he has indicated the opposite by noting in q. 5, a. 4 of his *Expos. de Trin.* that if a science has a subject, it belongs to that science to consider the principles of that subject. Only then will the task of that science be completed.[51]

And as we have also already seen, he brings this out even more explicitly in the Prooemium to his *In Meta.* There again he offers his personal solution to the dilemma left by Aristotle concerning whether the science of being as being can be identified with the science of separate or divine being. Central to his solution is his identification of separate substances with the universal and first causes of being and his observation that it belongs to one and the same science to consider the proper causes of a given genus and that genus itself. Therefore it belongs to the same science to consider separate substances and *ens commune*, which is the genus of which such substances are the general and universal causes. Only *ens commune*, he continues, is the subject of this science. For the subject of a science is that whose causes and properties one seeks, not the causes themselves. For knowledge of causes of a given genus is the end (*finis*) at which the consideration of the science arrives.[52]

And yet he also writes that the entire science deals with that which is separate from matter in the order of existence as well as the order of understanding. Not only are those things said to be separate that can never exist in matter, such as God and intellectual substances, but also those that can exist without matter, such as *ens commune*. He adds: "It [this science] is called metaphysics insofar as it considers being [*ens*] and those things that follow upon it. For these transphysicals are found on the way of *resolution* just as the more universal things are found after the less universal."[53] In these texts there can be no doubt that Aquinas is ex-

---

51. See above, notes 35–37.

52. See his *In Meta.*, Prooemium (1–2).

53. Ibid. (2). Note: "Dicitur ... metaphysica, in quantum considerat ens et ea quae consequuntur ipsum. Haec enim transphysica inveniuntur in via resolutionis, sicut magis communia post minus communia."

pressing his own view about the nature and subject of metaphysics.[54] It begins only with the discovery of its subject—being as being or *ens commune*—as attained by means of *separatio* and then pursues knowledge of the cause (or causes) of its subject—separate substances—as its goal.

But as we turn to the body of Thomas's commentary on Aristotle's *Metaphysics* VI.1 the issue becomes more difficult. To provide some context we should first turn briefly to his commentary on IV.1. There Thomas follows Aristotle and explains, as does Aristotle, that there is a science that investigates being as being and the properties that pertain to it *per se*. The science of being as being is distinguished from particular sciences because unlike them, it does not cut off a particular part of being, and simply study the attributes of that part. None of them studies universal being insofar as it is being. Hence in this science we are studying being taken universally and seeking the principles of being insofar as it is being. Therefore, Thomas states explicitly, "being is the subject of this science because every science seeks after the proper causes of its own subject."[55] Here his interpretation of Aristotle is in perfect conformity with his own views as expressed in the texts we have examined above.

When one turns to Thomas's commentary on *Metaphysics* VI.1, however, things become more complicated, just as they do in Aristotle's own text. The opening lines of Aristotle's text in this chapter, and hence of Thomas's exposition of it as well, about the need to seek for the principles and causes of beings as beings, are consistent with what we have just seen from Aristotle's discussion in IV.1 and in Thomas's commentary on this. And so, too, is the contrast that is drawn by both writers between the effort in this science to seek for the causes of being as such and that carried out in particular sciences to arrive at a knowledge of the causes and principles of their own restricted subject genera.[56] Both

---

54. Indeed, the final sentence from his Prooemium merits quotation: "Sic igitur patet quid sit subiectum huius scientiae, et qualiter se habeat ad alias scientias, et quo nomine nominetur" (ibid.)

55. For Thomas see his *In Meta.* IV, l. 1, nn. 532–33 (151). Note especially: "ergo in hac scientia quaerimus principia entis inquantum est ens: ergo ens est subiectum huius scientiae, quia quaelibet scientia est quaerens causas proprias sui subiecti." For Aristotle see his *Metaphysica*, ed. W. Jaeger (Oxford: Oxford University Press, 1978), I.1, 1003a21–32.

56. For Aristotle see *Metaphysics* VI.1, 1025b3–10. For Thomas see *In Meta.* VI, l. 1, nn. 1145–47 (295).

thinkers note that the things studied in physics include a reference to sensible matter and to motion in their definition (Thomas recalls that the subject of physics is *ens mobile*) and that mathematics studies things *as* immobile and *as* separate from sensible matter even though presumably they are not separate from matter in the order of existence (*secundum esse*).[57] Both Aristotle and Thomas in commenting on Aristotle's text write that if there is something that is sempiternal and separate from matter in the order of existence, some kind of theoretical philosophy must study this. Both Aristotle and Thomas consider and reject physics as well as mathematics as unqualified for study of this kind of entity and conclude that this must belong to a prior kind of philosophy, first philosophy or, as Aristotle also refers to it, "theology."[58]

Finally Thomas raises the question that Aristotle himself saw and tried to resolve: can the science that studies separate entity and hence seems to study only one particular kind of being be identified with the universal science of being as being? Thomas responds by almost literally citing Aristotle's less than satisfying answer:

If there is not some other substance apart from those that exist according to nature, with which physics deals, physics will be the first science. But if there is some immobile substance, it will be prior [to natural substance: added by Thomas] and consequently the philosophy that studies substance of this kind will be first philosophy. And because it is first it will be universal, and it will belong to it to investigate being insofar as it is being, both what it is, and those things that pertain to it as being.

And, as Thomas has obviously picked out the weak step in Aristotle's argument, that is, the transition from "first philosophy" to the universal science, he adds the key to his own solution: "For the science of the first being and the science of *ens commune* are one and the same, as was said at the beginning of Bk IV."[59] But, it should be noted, Thomas

---

57. For Aristotle see 1025b30–1026a6. For Thomas see nn. 1155 and 1157 ("Ens enim mobile est subiectum naturalis philosophiae"), 1159–61 (296–97).

58. For Aristotle see 1026a10–23. For Thomas see nn. 1162–66.

59. See *In Meta.*, l. 1, n. 1170: "si non est aliqua alia substantia praeter eas quae consistunt secundum naturam, de quibus est physica, physica erit prima scientia. Sed, si est aliqua substantia immobilis, ista erit prior substantia naturali; et per consequens philosophia considerans huiusmodi substantiam, erit philosophia prima. Et quia est prima, ideo erit universalis, et erit eius speculari de ente inquantum est ens, et de eo quod quid est, et de his quae sunt entis

does not say that the first being is the *subject* of metaphysics; for such a claim would contradict his personal view that a theoretical science must have a subject, and that it is the task of one who practices that science to arrive at knowledge of the principles of that subject. Moreover, I should note, if only in passing, for Thomas not only is God not the subject of metaphysics; he is not included within *ens commune*, which is its subject. Hence he can be studied by the metaphysician only indirectly, as cause or principle of its subject.[60]

This passage, along with the parallel to it from Thomas's commentary on *Metaphysics* XI, is often cited to support the claim that Thomas would require a prior knowledge of the existence of some separate entity in order for one to discover the subject of metaphysics and hence in order to begin metaphysics.[61] It is difficult to reconcile such an inter-

---

inquantum est ens: eadem enim est scientia primi entis et entis communis, ut in principio quarti habitum est."

60. On this see Albert Zimmermann, *Ontologie oder Metaphysik? Die Diskussion über den Gegenstand der Metaphysik im 13. und 14. Jahrhundert*, 2nd ed. (Leuven: Peeters, 1998), 216–23.

61. For the parallel in Thomas's commentary on Book XI see *In Meta.* VII, n. 2267 (536). Thomas's explanation here is essentially the same as that in the text just quoted from his commentary on Book VI.1, which is not surprising insofar as Aristotle's text presents the same position in XI.7 and VI.1. To explain the transition from the science of the first beings to the universal science this time Thomas adds two sentences: "Eadem enim est scientia quae est de primis entibus, et quae est universalis. Nam prima entia sunt principia aliorum." For some who attribute this to Thomas as his personal view see A. Moreno, "The Nature of Metaphysics," *The Thomist* 30 (1966): 109–35, at 113–15; Thomas C. O'Brien, *Metaphysics and the Existence of God* (Washington, D.C.: Thomist Press, 1960), 160; James Doig, *Aquinas on Metaphysics: A Historico-Doctrinal Study of the Commentary on the Metaphysics* (The Hague: Martinus Nijhoff, 1972), 243n1 and 303n1; James A. Weisheipl, "The Relationship of Medieval Natural Philosophy to Modern Science: The Contribution of Thomas Aquinas to its Understanding," *Manuscripta* 20 (1976): 181–96, at 194–96; Leo Elders, *Faith and Science: An Introduction to St. Thomas's* Expositio in Boethii De Trinitate (Rome: Herder, 1974), 107–8; Mark Jordan, *Ordering Wisdom: The Hierarchy of Philosophical Discourses in Aquinas* (Notre Dame, Ind.: University of Notre Dame Press, 1986), 158–60; Louis-B. Geiger "Abstraction et séparation d'après s. Thomas *In De Trinitate* q. 5, a. 3," *Revue des sciences philosophiques et théologiques* 31 (1947): 3–40, at 24–25 (an otherwise very sound article); Benedict Ashley, *The Way toward Wisdom: An Interdisciplinary and Intercultural Introduction to Metaphysics* (Notre Dame, Ind.: University of Notre Dame University Press, 2006), 153–58; and Ralph McInerny, *Praeambula Fidei: Thomism and the God of the Philosophers* (Washington, D.C.: The Catholic University of America Press, 2006), 194–96. Few of these discussions, in my opinion, pay sufficient attention to the problem in Aristotle's own text of reconciling his presentation in IV.1–2 with that in VI.1, and the major attempts made in the subsequent history of Aristotelianism, especially in Avicenna and Averroes and in various recent efforts, to work this out. For my own discussions of these texts and this issue see my *Metaphysical Themes in Thomas Aquinas*, 82–95; *Metaphysical Thought of Thomas Aquinas*, 51–59; and *Metaphysical Themes in Thomas Aquinas II* (Washington, D.C.: The Catholic University of America Press, 2007),

pretation with all that Thomas has said in the texts we have already considered where he is clearly writing in his own name, and where the opposite procedure is indicated. One should move from knowledge of the subject of a science to knowledge of its cause or principle, in this case from a knowledge of being as being as gained by means of *separatio* to a knowledge of God as the cause of *ens commune*. In such a case I have previously suggested that Thomas is writing here as the expositor of Aristotle and that while respecting Aristotle's text, he is especially concerned to show how Aristotle's identification of the science of separate entity with the universal science of being as being can be justified.[62] This need not imply that he is also necessarily endorsing the chronological sequence implied by Aristotle's own text if this runs counter to what he has already indicated elsewhere where he is writing in his own name; for this is not his primary concern here as the expositor of Aristotle. In such a case we should give priority to those texts where Thomas writes in his own name.

A second difficulty might be raised, based on the interesting fact that in his later texts Thomas does not seem to refer to *separatio* as such, which might lead one to think that he has abandoned this doctrine. Moreover, in *ST* I, q. 85, a. 1, in replying to obj. 2, Thomas again reviews the kind of abstraction associated with physics (abstraction from individual sensible matter) and with mathematics (abstraction of quantity from common sensible matter). Certain things, he adds, can be abstracted from common intelligible matter, such as being, *unum*, potency and act, and other things of this kind, which can also exist without any matter, as is evident in immaterial substances. Here, it might be argued, Thomas speaks of abstraction rather than of separation in referring to our knowledge of being and other negatively or neutrally immaterial things.[63]

In responding to this one should recall the broader usage of "abstraction" that Thomas had used at the beginning of q. 5, a. 3 of his

---

chap. 10, especially 246–55 (also 34n8 for references to some of the recent literature on this) as well as the whole of chap. 10 for my claim that we cannot assume that in his *In Meta.* Thomas himself always accepts as his own view the position he finds in Aristotle's text.

62. See the references given in the previous note.

63. Leon. 5:331. Note: "Quaedam vero sunt quae possunt abstrahi etiam a materia intelligibili communi, sicut ens, unum, potentia et actus, et alia huiusmodi, quae etiam esse possunt absque omni materia, ut patet in substantiis immaterialibus."

Expos. de Trin., where he took it as being equivalent to distinguishing intellectually in any way, whether through the intellect's first operation or its second operation. Later in that context he noted that when this term is used strictly or properly, it applies only to distinguishing through the intellect's first operation, and proposed the term *separatio* to describe distinguishing intellectually through a negative judgment. Hence in the text from *ST* I, q. 85, a. 1, he is using the term *abstract* broadly rather than strictly. That this is so is indicated by his reply to the first objection in that same article where he writes that abstraction may occur through the operation whereby the intellect composes and divides (i.e., judgment) as when we understand that one thing is not in another or is separated from it. Or it may occur through the operation whereby the intellect simply understands one thing without understanding another. Hence while there may be a move away from the precise terminology he had introduced in q. 5, a. 3 of the *Expos. de Trin.* in the passage from the *Summa*, there is no change in doctrine.

A third objection to my general interpretation has been proposed by John Knasas. He maintains that, according to Thomas, one can begin the science of metaphysics without having discovered its subject, *ens commune* (or being as being) in its full sense, that is, as studying that which is neutrally immaterial. Then in the course of one's metaphysical investigations, one can demonstrate the existence of God, positively immaterial being. Then, by appealing to this, one can extend one's understanding of *ens commune* to cover being that does not depend on matter and motion in order to exist and thereby discover the subject of metaphysics in the full sense.[64]

---

64. See Knasas, *The Preface to Thomistic Metaphysics: A Contribution to the Neo-Thomist Debate on the Start of Metaphysics* (New York: Peter Lang, 1990), 4 and 18 (Aquinas never says that the metaphysician attains his subject in a *separation*); 21 (two arguments against Wippel); chap. 5, especially at the end (113); and *Being and Some Twentieth-Century Thomists* (New York: Fordham University Press, 2003), 66–69 (where he seems more confident that his position was also held by Joseph Owens), esp. 67: "The metaphysician need not understand separateness from matter as true of the subject at the initiation of the science." Note that on 68 Knasas cites *In VI Meta.*, l. 1, n. 1163, where he "calls metaphysics immaterial simply because it treats God and the angels." In this text Thomas simply repeats Aristotle's text. But Knasas does not there cite the very relevant n. 1165: "Advertendum est autem, quod licet ad considerationem primae philosophiae pertineant ea quae sunt separata secundum esse et rationem a materia et motu, non tamen solum ea; sed etiam de sensibilibus, inquantum sunt entia, Philosophus perscrutatur. Nisi forte dicamus, ut Avicenna dicit, quod huiusmodi communia de quibus haec scientia perscrutatur, dicuntur separata

This is very difficult to reconcile with Aquinas's understanding of the subject of a science. He regards science as a habit that informs the possible intellect viewed as a potency or power. And he writes that "the habit of a power is distinguished specifically by reason of the difference of that which is the per se object of that power."[65] Hence in *ST* I, q. 1, a. 7, he writes: "Thus the subject of a science is related to that science just as an object is related to a power or habit." In light of this, in his magisterial review of the thirteenth- and fourteenth-century controversies concerning the subject of metaphysics, Albert Zimmermann writes about Aquinas's view: "Therefore the subject of a science is the object through which the habit of this science differs from those of the other sciences."[66] As Zimmermann points out, Thomas also maintains that every science has its unity from its subject, and cites Thomas's commentary on the *Posterior Analytics* I.41: "The unity of any science is to be determined in accord with the unity of its subject."[67]

---

secundum esse, non quia semper sint sine materia, sed quia non de necessitate habent esse in materia, sicut mathematica." This distinction, which Thomas here attributes to Avicenna, is the one that Thomas himself defends in his *Expos. de Trin.*, q. 5, aa. 1 and 4, and in the Prooemium to his *In Meta*. On Avicenna as a likely source for Aquinas's notion of *separation* as distinguished from abstraction see Pasquale Porro, "Tommaso d'Aquino, Avicenna, e la struttura della metafisica," in *Tommaso d'Aquino e l'oggetto della metafisica (Studi di filosofia 29)*, ed. Stephen Brock (Rome: Armando, 2004), 65–87. Porro notes that the distinction between abstraction and *separatio* has been found in the works of Arts Masters at Paris in 1230–50, and that Alfarabi via Avicenna could have been the remote source for this in those Masters as shown by Claude Lafleur and Joanne Carrier in pursuing a suggestion made by Alain de Libera. See their "Abstraction, séparation et tripartition de la philosophie theorétique: quelques élements de l'arrière-fond farabien et artien de Thomas d'Aquin," *Recherches de Théologie et Philosophie médiévales* 67 (2000): 248–71. On Avicenna as the proximate source for Aquinas's distinction between *separatio* and abstraction at least at the conceptual level if not the terminological see esp. 81–83. For my own suggestion that Thomas was inspired by Avicenna in developing this distinction, although based on different texts from those offered by Porro, see my "The Latin Avicenna as a Source for Thomas Aquinas's Metaphysics," in *Metaphysical Themes in Thomas Aquinas II*, 39–43.

65. See his *Sentencia Libri De sensu et sensato*, Prooemium, Leon. 45.2:3.9–19: "Et quia habitus alicuius potenciae distinguntur specie secundum differenciam eius quod est per se obiectum potenciae, necesse est quod habitus scienciarum, quibus intellectus perficitur, distinguantur secundum differenciam separabilis a materia et ideo Philosophus in VI Metaphysicae distinguit genera scienciarum secundum diversum modum separationis a materia: nam ea quae sunt separata a materia secundum esse et rationem pertinent ad methaphysicum."

66. Leon. 4:19: "Sic enim se habet subiectum ad scentiam, sicut obiectum ad potentiam vel habitum." Zimmermann writes: "Subjekt einer Wissenschaft ist also das Object, durch welches sich der Habitus dieser Wissenschaft von denen anderer Wisssenschaften unterscheidet." *Ontologie oder Metaphysik?*, 204.

67. "Unde relinquitur quod cuiuslibet scienciae unitas secundum unitatem subiecti est

And in that same context Thomas goes on to explain that just as
the unity of the subject genus of one science is more general than that
of another, for instance, the unity of being or substance is more general than the unity of mobile being, so also one science is more general
than another. Thus metaphysics, which treats of being or of substance,
is more general than physics, which deals with mobile being. Thomas
also quotes with approval Aristotle's statement to the effect that every
demonstrative science deals with three things, one of which is the subject genus whose *per se* properties (*passiones*) it investigates; second are
the common principles (*dignitates*) from which it demonstrates as from
that which is first; and third are the properties about which each science
accepts what they signify. Thomas also follows Aristotle's statement to
the effect that the sciences "suppose" (accept without proving) the principles in the sense "that they are" (*quia sunt*), the properties in terms
of "what they are," and their subjects both with regard to "that they are"
and "what they are."[68] In other words, which is of paramount importance regarding Knasas's proposal, Thomas follows Aristotle in denying
that any science can demonstrate the "if it is" and the "what it is" of its
own subject. He states this in another way, for instance, in his commentary on Aristotle's *Physics*: "Nulla scientia probat suum subiectum."[69]

Second, Knasas's proposal contradicts Thomas's statement in the
Prooemium to his *In Meta.* to this effect:

Although the subject of this science is *ens commune*, the whole science [*tota*] is
said to deal with that which is separate from matter according to *secundum esse
et rationem*. For not only are those things that can never exist in matter such as
God and intellectual substances said to be separate *secundum esse et rationem*,
but also those that can exist without matter and motion, such as *ens commune*.[70]

---

attendenda." Thomas goes on to remark: "Set, sicut unius generis subiecti unitas est communior
quam alterius, ut puta entis sive substanciae quam corporis mobilis, ita etiam una sciencia communior est quam alia, sicut metaphysica, quae est de ente sive de substantia, communior est quam
phisica, quae est de corpore mobile." See *Expositio Libri Posteriorum* I.42, Leon. 1*2:153.145–53.

68. See *Expositio Libri Post.*, I.18: "*Omnis enim demonstrativa scientia circa tria est*, quorum
unum est *genus* subiectum *cuius per se passiones* scrutatur; et aliud est *communes dignitates, ex
quibus sicut primis demonstrant*; tercium est *passiones*, de quibus *unaquaque scientia accipit quid
significet*" (68.128–33). See also ll. 136–38: "Quia enim dixerat quod sciencie supponunt de principiis quia sunt, de passionibus quid sunt, de subiectis autem utrumque ..."

69. *In Phys.* I, l. 1, n. 4: After noting that the subject of physics is *ens mobile* he writes: "Non
dico autem *corpus mobile*, quia omne mobile esse corpus probatur in isto libro: nulla autem scientia probat suum subiectum." On all of this see Zimmermann, *Ontologie oder Metaphysik?*, 202–7.

70. *In Meta.*, Prooemium (2), cited above in note 38.

According to Knasas, the science would originally study only material being, but not being in the sense of that which is negatively immaterial. Yet this is not how Aquinas describes the subject of metaphysics. He holds that the *entire science* deals with that which is separate from matter *secundum esse et secundum rationem*. Hence Knasas's proposal should not be regarded as a defensible interpretation of Aquinas's understanding of our discovery of the subject of metaphysics.

Concluding Remarks

Underlying the opposition to my proposal on the part of many who maintain that according to Aquinas one must have demonstrated the existence of positively immaterial being before beginning metaphysics is a philosophical position on their part, namely, that it is impossible for one to speak meaningfully of negatively immaterial being or to propose it as the subject of metaphysics without prior knowledge of positively immaterial being. On philosophical grounds I also defend the opposite position, as I have already indicated elsewhere.[71]

To summarize my thinking on this, just as it is possible for us to investigate a material and changing being from different perspectives, for instance, as mobile, as quantified, as living or dead, it is also possible for us to investigate such a being simply insofar as it is real or insofar as it enjoys being. This does not require that we investigate it insofar as it is material or quantified even though such a being may exist only in that way. Once we have formulated a prephilosophical notion of being as "that which is," we can always ask ourselves how widely we can apply it: must we restrict it to the particular kinds of beings we have experienced, or can we extend this notion so that it may be applied to anything of which we can say "it is"? To accept the latter alternative is to acknowledge that if we should encounter or demonstrate the reality of some positively immaterial being, we could then recognize it as enjoying being and hence as "that which is." To acknowledge this does not require us to assume in advance that such a being exists, or even to defend its possibility in the absolute sense, that is, intrinsically (as lacking contradiction) and extrinsically in that causes might exist that could

71. For more on this see my *Metaphysical Themes in Thomas Aquinas*, 102–4, and *Metaphysical Thought of Thomas Aquinas*, 59–62.

bring such an entity into existence. All we need to do is not to exclude any such entity from being recognized as a being if we should encounter or demonstrate its existence. And to do this we need only distinguish between that by which a being is the kind of thing it is (including being material or perhaps immaterial), from that by reason of which it is real or enjoys being. (Note that this is not to distinguish its essence from its *actus essendi*, but to distinguish its whatness from its being, i.e., "that which is.") This is what we do through the negative judgment called separation. We consider being simply as being without necessarily restricting it to any particular kind, whether material or immaterial.

2

The Knowledge of Being

Thomistic Metaphysics in the Contemporary Debate

RUDI TE VELDE

To speak of "Thomistic metaphysics" in a more than formal or program-matic sense is quite problematic, except perhaps in a Wittgensteinian sense of family resemblance. Even after seven centuries of Thomistic tra-dition—of schools, common reading-practices, manuals, commentators, debates, and so forth—there still exists a fundamental lack of consensus with regard to the status and nature of the science of metaphysics in Thomas's thought. This is not to say that there are no candidates for the title of "Thomistic metaphysics"; on the contrary, in a certain sense there are too many candidates, none of which succeeds, it would appear, to establish itself as the final and official version of "Thomistic meta-physics." Whole libraries can be filled with books of all kinds, about the metaphysics of Aquinas: textbooks to be used in Catholic educational institutions (e.g., Norris Clarke's *The One and the Many: A Contempo-rary Thomistic Metaphysics*), systematic expositions of metaphysics *ad mentem Sancti Thomae* (e.g., the impressive study by Benedict Ashley, *The Way toward Wisdom*), or scholarly studies on metaphysical themes as present in the works of Thomas Aquinas (e.g., John Wippel, *The*

Metaphysical Thought of Thomas Aquinas).[1] But behind the common label of Thomism as used in titles of numerous books containing serious philosophy, one finds a great variety of schools, each with their own distinctive approach. Nowadays, these schools, such as Transcendental Thomism (Marechal, Rahner, Lotz, Lonergan), Existential Thomism (Gilson, Maritain, Owens), or Aristotelian Thomism (Ashley[2]), may not be as vital as they were half a century ago, but they are still alive and recognizable in their contributions to the ongoing debate on how metaphysics in the Thomistic sense must be understood. Thus there are different schools, allowing for different approaches to what metaphysics is and should be, and different views on the foundation of metaphysical thought as proposed and practiced by Aquinas himself.

Of course, one might speak here of a "valuable multiplicity of Thomistic orientations," a diversity which should be seen as a sign of the richness of the philosophical possibilities hidden in Aquinas's writings, which offer each generation of readers something new to think about, something which is neglected or misunderstood in the traditional interpretations. One should always return to the texts of Thomas, not so much in order to find there the ultimate truth of his thought behind the proliferation of Thomistic schools, but rather to seek a sort of new and philosophically inspiring understanding of Thomas, with regard to the contemporary philosophical situation.

In the history of philosophy Thomas stands as an exceptional figure: although not primarily a philosopher himself, he displays in his thought a profound and genuine philosophical quality. Part of this qual-

---

1. Wippel, *The Metaphysical Thought of Thomas Aquinas: From Finite Being to Uncreated Being* (Washington, D.C.: The Catholic University of America Press, 2000); Clarke, *The One and the Many* (Notre Dame, Ind.: University of Notre Dame Press, 2001). In the introduction, Clarke writes that his "aim is to provide an advanced textbook of systematic metaphysics in the Thomistic tradition, one which is alert not only to developments within Thomism but also to contemporary problems and other movements in philosophy." His book is not intended as a work of historical scholarship, but it is rather a "creative retrieval" of the metaphysical thought of Aquinas. Benedict M. Ashley, OP, *The Way toward Wisdom: An Interdisciplinary and Intercultural Introduction to Metaphysics* (Notre Dame, Ind.: University of Notre Dame Press, 2006).

2. Ashley provides a nice overview of all the varieties of Thomistic metaphysics (*The Way toward Wisdom*, 44–55); see also Fergus Kerr, OP, *After Aquinas: Versions of Thomism* (Oxford: Blackwell, 2002), as well as his "The Varieties of Interpreting Aquinas," in *Contemplating Aquinas: On the Varieties of Interpretation*, ed. Kerr (London: SCM Press, 2003), 27–40. Kerr quotes Alaisdair MacIntyre who wonders whether there are not "too many Thomisms."

ity is the combination of an extreme clarity of expression with a certain elusiveness. If one can speak of his metaphysical "system," it is a system that is never formally exposed as such in a logical, coherent, and explicit manner. The metaphysical system of Thomism is necessarily the product of our interpretation, and thus something which is always in the making and object of an ongoing dispute. And this dispute will never be completely silenced by textual evidence and its correct interpretation, as what matters most in philosophy is something of which there cannot be textual evidence. Reading Thomas in order to find out some aspects of his thought is often but a first step in rethinking the argument, in order to find out for oneself the truth of the matter. And this is what the text invites you to do. The most interesting books about Thomas are not always the scholarly studies which try to remain faithful to the evidence of the text, but books in which the author proposes to offer a sort of creative retrieval. This will necessarily result in a "valuable multiplicity of Thomistic orientations."

Variety and multiplicity are acceptable to a certain extent, but there has to exist a common spirit, some sort of identity tag, if the name "Thomism" is to mean anything at all. Instead of putting forward disputable doctrinal criteria, I want to suggest that the great variety of Thomistic orientations has its unity in the spirit of metaphysical realism. There exists a widespread consensus as to the fact that Thomistic philosophy has a definite realistic self-understanding in the sense that it claims that human thinking attains to the very being of things. Realism in its Thomistic sense has to do with the characteristic focus on being (*ens, esse*) and on the cognitive openness of the human mind to the being of things. In order to stress the realistic orientation of Thomistic philosophy one often uses the seemingly pleonastic expression "real being," instead of just "being," as signifying reality in itself, which human thought is directed to beyond its immanent conceptual form. It appears to me that this bears a slightly antimodern tone: according to the realistic philosophy of Saint Thomas, the human mind is able to reach beyond the subjective appearances, toward that which exists objectively, outside and independent from our mind: *real* being.

It is not easy to characterize in a more precise way the metaphysical realism which underlies the philosophical orientation of Thomas's thought. In the premodern period of philosophy, "realism" (as opposed to all kinds of modern idealism, phenomenologism, and subjectivism) was not really an issue which had to be defended against alternatives. However, this changed during the modern period with its "turn to the subject." Modern philosophy is born from the scattering experience of skepticism according to which the human subject becomes aware of itself, as distinguished from the world outside itself, to which it no longer enjoys immediate and unproblematic access. In such a situation, realism becomes something one has to argue for, something to be defended against forms of subjectivism or skepticism ("our mind is really able to know how things are in themselves"). However, in the thought of Thomas there is no explicit awareness of realism as something one has to fight for, no awareness of a problematic gap between mind and world. Contrary to the implicit and unproblematic realism of Thomas himself, the realism which is the hallmark of Thomism (in all its varieties) has the character of a thesis to be exposed, and defended against the subjectivism of modern thought.

To clarify in what sense the metaphysical thought of Aquinas can be called "realistic," and how deep this realism is, remains an important desideratum. The recent discussions among Thomists, with respect to the nature and possibility of metaphysics as understood by Thomas and the related question of our knowledge of being, often circle around the issue of realism.

A Pretheoretical Notion of Being?

The knowledge of being, or more specifically, the question of how our mind has access to being as the subject of metaphysics, serves as the theme of the following reflections. Let us begin, as a point of departure, with the opening sentence of Wippel's book *The Metaphysical Thought of Thomas Aquinas*: "One of the more notable developments in recent decades in our understanding of Aquinas's metaphysical thought has been a growing appreciation of the distinctive way in which he accounts for our discovery of being as real and, consequent upon this, for our knowledge of being as being."[3] Wippel refers to two different "discov-

3. Wippel, *Metaphysical Thought*, 3.

eries" with respect to being, the first one by which the human mind becomes acquainted with being (real being, being as existing) in a still pretheoretical sense, and another by which being as object of the science of metaphysics is established (being as being). Both forms of knowledge of being dominate the discussion in the Thomistic literature about the nature and possibility of metaphysics. The discussion about the first discovery—how do we come to know being as real?—has its origin in a passage in *Expos. de Trin.* (q. 5, a. 3), where Thomas distinguishes between the intellect's first operation, by means of which we grasp or conceive the "whatness" of a thing, and the second operation, which is related to the thing's existence.[4] This second operation is commonly known as judgment, as distinct from the first operation of concept formation. Now, Thomas seems to appeal to judgment to account for our discovery of the existence of things, as distinct from their conceivable content (essence or whatness). It is through an act of judgment that we affirm that something *is* as we conceive it. Gilson in particular has emphasized the role of the judgment in our knowledge of the existence of things: being precisely as existing (*actus essendi*) is not known through the conceptual mode of knowledge, but only through the act of judgment.[5]

The second discovery, the one concerning being in its metaphysical sense, stands at the center of a long and continuing debate in the literature about the so-called separation, the special kind of abstraction to which Thomas refers in the same commentary on the *De trinitate* and which he presumably regards as constitutive of the science of metaphysics.[6] Wippel connects the judgment of *separatio* with the way in which we attain knowledge of being as being, the subject of metaphysics. Many scholars have emphasized the importance of this *separatio* for our un-

---

4. *Expositio super librum Boethii De trinitate*, q. 5, a. 3, ed. B. Decker (Leiden: E. J. Brill, 1965), 182: "Prima quidem operatio respicit ipsam naturam rei, secundum quam res intellecta aliquem gradum in entibus obtinet, ut pars vel accidens. Secunda vero operatio respicit ipsum esse rei ..." Cf. Thomas Aquinas, *The Division and Methods of the Sciences*, trans. Armand Maurer (Toronto: Pontifical Institute of Mediaeval Studies, 1984), 35.

5. See in particular Etienne Gilson's *Being and Some Philosophers*, 2nd ed. (Toronto: Pontifical Institute of Mediaeval Studies, 1952).

6. Aquinas, *Expos. de Trin.*, q. 5, a. 3: "Sic ergo in operatione intellectus triplex distinctio invenitur. Una secundum operationem intellectus componentis et dividentis, quae separatio dicitur proprie; et haec competit scientiae divinae sive metaphysicae" (ed. Decker, 186). See *Division and Methods*, 41.

derstanding of Thomas's conception of metaphysics, but at the same time it remains a source of confusion and conflicting interpretations.

But before addressing the problems concerning the founding operation of *separatio* and the possibility of metaphysics, we will first look at how Wippel describes our discovery of being in the pretheoretical sense. What he has in mind is a common notion of being, which is formed on the basis of our initial intellectual awareness that the objects of our daily experience actually exist. Essential for the process by which we arrive at such an understanding of being as actual existence is the role of judgment, the second operation of the intellect. Following Gilson, he assigns to the act of judgment the special role of grasping the *esse* of things in the sense of their actual existence. The epistemic process whereby we arrive at such a notion of being is described by Wippel as follows.[7] Our knowledge begins with sense experience. A concrete sensible object of whatever kind is presented to us, and our intelligence grasps that object in a confused way as "something that exists." This initial knowledge of existence will become more explicit by making a judgment of existence regarding the particular thing one is perceiving: "this thing is." As one experiences other extramental objects, one will make more particular judgments of existence; and reflection upon this procedure will bring one to form, in a vague and general fashion, an idea of reality, of being, of "that which is." This primitive notion of being is based on our original experience of material and changing beings. This notion, according to Wippel, has not yet been freed from restriction to matter. Hence, it cannot be identified with the notion of being as being, the subject of metaphysics. The meaning of "being" in its primitive and pretheoretical sense can be explained as "an indeterminate existing object of experience," something that is, not absolutely, but relative to the context of human experience.

Although such an empirical notion of being may have its value, I seriously doubt whether this notion can be found in the thought of Thomas. Aquinas often refers to being as that which is first grasped or conceived by the intellect, being as the *primum notum*, for instance in the first article of *De Ver.*: "That which the intellect first conceives as most known and into which it resolves all of its conceptions is being, as Avi-

---

7. Wippel, *Metaphysical Thought*, 35.

cenna says in the beginning of his *Metaphysics*."[8] Now, Wippel suggests in his book that the notion of being, which is formed by the intellect on the basis of its discovery of being as existing through several judgments of existence, may be identified with what Thomas has in mind when he refers to being as that which is first known.[9]

I strongly disagree with this suggestion. Whatever the value of the primitive notion of being in the sense of the "indeterminate object of experience," being in the sense of the proper object of the intellect (*ens ut primum notum*) is something completely different. It seems to me that Wippel's epistemological sketch, of how we get acquainted with the notion of being in the sense of real existence, already presupposes a prior awareness of reality ("that which is"). We do not acquire such a prior knowledge of being by way of several judgments of existence with respect to concrete existing objects within our experience. Prior to any concrete specimen of knowledge we acquire of things on the basis of sense perception, is the intellect's universal openness to being. It seems to me that Wippel's view, of how we arrive at the knowledge of being as existing, begs the question.

In the thought of Thomas, the notion of being expresses the *a priori* horizon of the intellect, and as such it is immediately and naturally known when the intellect comes into contact with any singular object which is given by sense experience. Being is said to be the proper object of the intellect. This means that things can only be known by the intellect insofar as they *are*. Being relates to the intellect like sound relates to the ear, Thomas says.[10] It is the inner reason of the intelligibility (*ratio intelligibilitatis*) of any given object, and as such it grounds the relationship of the intellect to its object. My difference of opinion with Wippel follows from a different interpretation of what it means that "being"

8. *De Ver.*, q. 1, a. 1: "... illud autem quod primo intellectus concipit quasi notissimum et in quod conceptiones omnes resolvit est ens, ut Avicenna dicit in principio suae Metaphysicae" (Leon. 22.1:5.100–104).

9. Wippel, *Metaphysical Thought*, 44: "What one first discovers through original judgments of existence can be summed up, as it were, under the heading of being, or reality, or something similar. Once the intellect makes this discovery, it expresses it in a complex concept or notion, as 'that which is.' This, I am suggesting, is what Thomas has in mind when he refers to being (*ens*) as that which is first known."

10. Cf. *ST* I, q. 5, a. 2: "Unde ens est proprium obiectum intellectus: et sic est primum intelligibile, sicut sonus est primum audibile."

is the *first* thing the intellect conceives. In my view, it does not mean that "being" is the first thing I intellectually grasp from some existing object I encounter when I come into contact with reality; rather, "being" expresses precisely this "standing-in-contact-with-reality-as-such." What Wippel is looking for is a kind of immediate contact with a singular existing object, as expressed in a judgment of existence; and through this contact we come in touch with a singular instance of "is." But in this way of looking at the relationship between mind and reality, the perspective remains epistemological, that is, presupposing the distinction between reality on the one hand and our representational knowledge on the other. From this perspective the question arises of how we get in touch with reality, or how we discover being as real. But for Thomas, I think, this is not the most fundamental question, as we are already, from the outset, in touch with reality, just like the ear is already, naturally, in touch with the world of sound. Only as already open to the world of sound can the ear hear a concrete specimen of sound.

The Metaphysical Notion of Being
and the Act of Separation

I turn now to the metaphysical notion of being, and to the question of how we discover being in this sense. According to Wippel, we discover being in its metaphysical sense by means of a special negative judgment, the judgment of *separatio*. The notion of separation is one of the most debated issues in the interpretation of the metaphysics of Thomas, ever since the publication of the famous article by Geiger, who was the first to point out the significance of the notion of *separatio* in Thomas's *Expos. de Trin.*[11] Considering the ongoing debate on the subject of *separatio*, and the difficult questions it raises, it is clear that this metaphysical type of abstraction is complicated and not easy to understand.

Let us begin with noting that *separatio* is introduced by Thomas as a special kind of abstraction, which differs from the regular form of abstraction in that it has the formal structure of a negative judgment. Abstraction as such is a kind of distinction, made by the intellect, by

---

11. L.-B. Geiger, "Abstraction et séparation d'après s. Thomas," *Revue des sciences philosophiques et théologiques* 31 (1947): 3–40.

which it considers one thing without the other, while in reality they are connected. *Separatio*, in contrast, is a distinction, expressed in the form of a negative judgment, whereby the intellect distinguishes one thing from another by stating that the one *exists* without the other. Abstraction, as pertaining to the intellect's first operation, goes hand in hand with the suspension of the truth-relation between thought and reality; separation, however, entails the affirmation of the conformity between thought and reality. By way of separation we judge that both things exist in separation from one another, for instance, the negative judgment by which it is stated that "a man is not a donkey."

Now, Thomas discusses the different kinds of abstraction in view of the question of the division of the three speculative sciences: physics, mathematics, and metaphysics. These sciences are distinguished from each other according to their object. In order to be the object of a science, something must be free from matter and motion, two features which are contrary to the required intelligibility of the object. Thomas wants to show that there are three different ways in which reality can be made the object of a science, corresponding to the degrees in which something is free (or can be made free by way of abstraction) from matter and motion. Thus, it is by way of abstraction that a science is established in relationship to its defining object, that is, some intelligible aspect of reality as formally disclosed to the intellect. Now, the two particular sciences of physics and mathematics are based on abstraction in the strict and proper sense; they investigate intelligible aspects of sensible and material reality, aspects which can be understood without matter, but do not exist according to this mode of intelligibility. The objects of physics (universals such as "man" or "tree") and of mathematics ("circle," "line") possess a mode of intelligibility which does not coincide with their mode of existence. The intelligible content of the object must be abstracted from the material conditions of its existence. Metaphysics, on the contrary, considers intelligible aspects of reality as such, whether material or not. Metaphysical objects are not *abstracta* in the proper sense, but *separata*; they are separated from matter in themselves, either because their mode of existence excludes all matter (transcendent objects such as God and the angels), or because they are neutrally immaterial, or common to material and immaterial things (objects such as being, substance, unity, act, and so forth). So the metaphysical science is constituted in its defining object-relationship to reality by means of a special mode of abstraction, the act of *separatio*, by which the intrinsic intelligibility of things, insofar as they are beings, is disclosed to the intellect. Thus, metaphysical objects are not abstract; they have their mode of intelligibility in identity with their mode of existence.

Aquinas's fascinating thoughts about metaphysical abstraction have led to a serious and still unresolved controversy among his interpreters. Metaphysics, the science of being as being, is grounded in a specific judgment of separation, in which it is expressed that being does not depend on matter. This view has occasioned the question of how such a judgment about the neutrally immaterial character of being can be justified. A considerable number of interpreters hold that one must have already demonstrated the existence of something positively immaterial in order to justify the judgment of separation, and consequently, to establish thereby the science of metaphysics. For instance, Ashley, in his *The Way toward Wisdom*, argues with great conviction that the possibility of metaphysics depends on the prior knowledge of the existence of a first mover in natural philosophy. He contends that metaphysics, or first philosophy, should be validated by the prior science of physics[12] because only in this way, by transcending the domain of being in the restricted sense of physical reality, and proving the existence of an immaterial being, does it become clear that being does not depend on matter, and that it exhibits an intelligibility that is proper to metaphysics. As long as one remains within the physical domain of human experience, one cannot find any justification of the judgment of *separatio*, by which metaphysics is established.

What should we think of this view? The judgment of separation, in this view, requires a prior knowledge of at least one immaterial being. As long as we restrict ourselves to the physical realm, we will not discover the metaphysical and profounder sense of being as transcending the merely empirical and material. There are certainly some texts in Thomas's writings which might be read as supporting such an interpretation. But it is not primarily a matter of textual evidence; the controversy goes deeper still.

12. See esp. chap. 4, part D ("Natural Science Validates First Philosophy").

Before looking at such a piece of textual evidence, I want to formulate two objections to Ashley's position. My first point would be that it does not seem very plausible that a prior proof of the existence of some immaterial being should be required in order to demonstrate, within the newly founded science of metaphysics, another immaterial being, namely God, who is the first principle of all things. For Ashley, the demonstration of the first mover in Aristotle's *Physics* serves as a means to arrive at the metaphysical standpoint of consideration, which is required for dealing with the issue of the existence and nature of God. But Aristotle's argument from his *Physics* is to Aquinas one of the recognized proofs for the existence of God. The consequence would be that the final and metaphysical demonstration of God is preceded by a physical demonstration of God (or of some other immaterial being). This strange two-step procedure is very close to a vicious circle: one needs to prove the existence of an immaterial being in order to be able, within metaphysics, to prove the existence of an immaterial being.

The second problem with Ashley's interpretation has to do with the *a priori*-character of the notion of being. What I mean is this: in order to conceive the possibility of an immaterial being, and to affirm its existence, one must have a notion of being as something which admits realization without matter. The human mind can only rise above the physical horizon of sense experience when its conceptual openness to being allows it. Being, as *primum cognitum*, defines the formal openness of the intellect, which from the outset is not restricted to that part of being which falls under our experience. In other words: it seems reasonable to assume that the (indirect) affirmation of the existence of an immaterial being presupposes, on the part of our intellect, an intelligible perspective on reality in which the dependence on matter is transcended. Now, "being" expresses the formal intelligibility of reality which does not depend on that external aspect of matter. Therefore, in order to conceive and affirm some immaterial being, the intellect must consider reality under the aspect of being, that is, according to its intrinsic intelligibility as being. Thomas is quite clear about his view that immaterial beings ("God and the angels") can only be known and affirmed as (extrinsic) principles of the subject of metaphysics, that is, of reality considered as being.

The most important piece of textual evidence for Ashley's position with regard to metaphysics' dependence on a prior demonstration of the existence of some immaterial being, is drawn from some passages in Thomas's *In Meta.* I want to discuss one text in particular, taken from *In Meta.* IV. Here, Aristotle is criticizing the ancient philosophers of nature for having dealt with the first principles of demonstration. To Aristotle, considering the first principles of demonstration does not pertain to the particular science of physics, but to first philosophy, because they are common to all scientific knowledge. In his commentary Thomas explains that the ancient philosophers thought that only corporeal and mobile substance exists. In their view, there exists nothing besides nature, and therefore to them, the philosophy of nature was identical with first philosophy. But this is not the case, Thomas says, as there is another science which is superior to natural science; for nature is only one class within the totality of being. Not all being is of this kind, as it had been proven in the *Physics* that there is an immobile being. "And because the consideration of *ens commune* pertains to that science to which it belongs to consider the First Being, therefore the consideration of *ens commune* also belongs to a science different from natural philosophy."[13]

Can one use this text as evidence for the position that Thomas justifies separation by appealing to the existence of an immaterial first mover? The reference to the final conclusion of the *Physics*, concerning the existence of an immobile being, seems to serve as a necessary step toward the metaphysical consideration, beyond physics, of "common being," *common* in the sense of not restricted to the material objects of physics. Read in this way, the possibility of the metaphysical consideration depends on the prior demonstration of the existence of an immobile being in the *Physics*.

In my view, one should read this, and similar texts from *In Meta.*, in a different way. Thomas is commenting on the text in which Aristotle is criticizing the ancient philosophers for having identified first philosophy with the study of nature. To them, nature, the whole of material reality, is all there is. But if the study of nature would coincide with first philosophy, that is, the study of being as common to all there is (*ens commune*),

---

13. *In Meta.* IV, l. 5, n. 593: "Non enim omne ens est huiusmodi: cum probatum sit in octavo *Physicorum*, esse aliquod ens immobile .... Et quia ad illam scientiam pertinent consideratio entis communis, ad quam pertinent consideratio entis primi, ideo ad aliam scientiam quam ad naturalem pertinent consideratio entis communis" (ed. Cathala-Spiazzi, 164).

then nature must have a self-sufficient intelligibility, in the sense that it must be understandable completely through itself, as nature would then coincide with being as being. That this is not the case, says Thomas, is evident from the argument of the first mover in the *Physics*. In this argument, Aristotle has shown that nature is not self-sufficient and absolute, but that the physical domain of mobile being (being-in-motion) ultimately depends on a principle and source of motion, which is not itself part of nature. The intellect, with being as its formal object, cannot come to rest within the science of nature. Pushed forward by the unrestricted intellectual dynamism toward being, the physicist in us must transform himself into a metaphysician.

The Proof of the First Mover in the *Physics*

Closely related to the question of how one arrives at the subject of metaphysics, is the discussion on the allegedly physical character of the demonstration of the existence of the first mover. In Ashley's view this argument, which grounds metaphysics, clearly belongs to physics or natural science.[14] It is the task of natural science to prove the existence of at least one immaterial being, by which the foundational judgment of metaphysics—that being as such does not depend on matter—is justified. In support of this view, one can point to the evident fact that Aristotle's argument for the first mover is included in his *Physics*. By demonstrating the existence of an immaterial being, it is in fact shown that being is not restricted to physical being (*ens mobile*), and hence does not depend on matter. Only then, according to Ashley and other students of Thomas, one can validly assume a higher science, prior to physics, which considers being as being.

Hence, the crucial question is whether Aristotle's proof for the existence of the first mover should be taken as a physical, or rather as a metaphysical, argument. This is an old discussion. The proof of the unmoved mover, the first of the five ways in the *Summa Theologiae*, has always been controversial.[15] Many commentators considered the argument as merely

14. Ashley, *The Way toward Wisdom*, 96: "Since this work [*Physics*] pertains to *physica*, that is, natural science, this demonstration cannot be metaphysical, but is presupposed to metaphysics, that is, First Philosophy."

15. See my *Aquinas on God* (Aldershot: Ashgate, 2006), 48.

a physical argument, concluding to a first principle of physical change and motion, not to a first metaphysical principle of being. Others, such as Suarez, have rejected this argument, maintaining that it cannot even conclude to an immaterial first mover, let alone an uncreated one. It is, therefore, not immediately evident in which sense it might be considered as a genuinely metaphysical argument. On the other hand, the Aristotelian argument on the basis of motion is clearly Thomas's favorite proof for the existence of God. In *ST* I, q. 2, a. 3, he calls it the "first and most manifest" way, and the reason for this seems to be the fact that the argument takes as its starting point the manifest fact of motion.

Now, the common assumption among the interpreters of Aquinas seems to be that the five ways belong formally to the science of metaphysics. Because it is the acknowledged task of metaphysics—Thomas is quite clear about this—to prove the existence of God, who is the first principle of all being. In his *Expos. de Trin.*, Thomas points out that "divine things" are knowable by the light of natural (philosophical) reason, insofar as they are the *principles of all things*. Consequently, the natural knowledge of God belongs to that science which investigates that which is common to all beings, and which takes as its subject *being as being*. This is the science of metaphysics, also called "divine science."[16]

The subject (*subiectum*) of metaphysics is being as being or as common to all things (*ens commune*). Metaphysics considers reality in light of the intelligibility things possess, insofar as they are beings. God is approached in metaphysics as "the principle of its subject," that is to say: things are ultimately not intelligible in their being unless they are reduced to a first cause of their being which is called "God." It is by way of this reduction that God's existence is indirectly known, *per effectum*.

But is this formal perspective of being *as being* not absent in the argument on the basis of motion? The argument starts from the phenomenon of motion, which is the defining concept of the subject of physics. For the subject of physics is determined as *ens mobile*, that being which is susceptible of movement and change. Thus, the question is where in the argument the formal perspective of metaphysics can be recognized.

It is not possible to present here an exhaustive analysis of Thomas's version of Aristotle's argument on the basis of motion. I will present a

---

16. *Expos. de Trin.*, q. 5, a. 4, ed. Bruno Decker (Leiden: E. J. Brill, 1965), 194.

reading of the argument, in which the formal perspective of being as being is made explicit. The argument, as I read it, wants to prove that motion—the defining concept of the domain of physics—is not something absolute (nonrelative), intelligible through itself; the argument shows that motion does not coincide with being as such, because its intelligibility requires something else which is itself not in motion, thus something outside the domain of physics. Therefore, being-in-motion (*ens mobile*) is but a *part* of being, thus something *particular*, as it exhibits only a restricted intelligibility. In other terms: what the argument proves is that being in motion—the whole of nature—is not intelligible *as being* unless it is reduced to something which is itself not in motion, something beyond nature, which is nevertheless the principle and the source of the being-in-motion of natural things. Here we see the formal perspective of metaphysics at work: being in motion as such, or being in motion considered as being, is not intelligible unless it is reduced to something which is itself not in motion. But it must be intelligible, for otherwise the whole domain of material and changeable reality could not be affirmed as being. This last point is not always sufficiently appreciated in the literature. The underlying assumption of the argument is that the changeable reality of nature is asserted as *being* in and through itself (instead of just empirical existence) and, therefore, it must be intelligible by reason of its being. But the whole of nature is not intelligible if it is taken absolutely in itself, as Aristotle argues against the ancient philosophers of nature.

One could say that Aristotle's argument, in the strict sense, is neither physical nor metaphysical in character, but that it proves the necessity of the *transition* from physics to metaphysics. Contrary to Ashley (and many others), I do not think that the founding judgment of separation, by which the intrinsic intelligibility of metaphysical objects is disclosed to the intellect, is only justified as the result of the "physical" proof of the existence of the first mover. The science of metaphysics comes after physics, Thomas says, in the sense that the more universal is known after the particular.[17] The objects of physics are still particular in char-

---

17. *In Meta.*, Prooemium (ed. Cathala-Spiazzi, 2): "[*Dicitur*] *metaphysica*, in quantum considerat ens et ea quae consequuntur ipsum. Haec enim transphysica inveniuntur in via resolutionis, sicut magis communia post minus communia." These "trans-physica" are the common objects of metaphysics, such as being, substance, one, act, and potency.

acter, meaning that physics studies reality in its categorial aspects of being-*this* and being-*such*. Now, because of this particular character of physical objects, the intellectual search for knowledge, realizing itself within the unlimited horizon of universal being, cannot find its complete satisfaction within the science of physics. The intellect, in its search for understanding reality under the aspect of being, must go beyond physics, because the domain of physics appears to have a restricted degree of intelligibility, in which the intellect cannot come to rest. The typical mode of explanation in physics is such that a particular instance of motion is explained by reference to another particular instance of motion, which is the former's active mover. However, being-in-motion-as-such, which is common to all particular instances of motion, cannot be explained in this way. Consequently, the whole domain of physical motion must be related to a principle or source of motion external to this domain. Through this reduction, the intellect becomes reflectively aware of the particular character of nature, insofar as its particularity is understood as the particular way of having something universal ("this" is understood and expressed as "this-*being*"). But this reflective movement (this "as such") does not take place prior to the establishment of metaphysics, as a preparing step toward it; it is in fact the movement toward metaphysics, by which the intellect transcends its particular, and thus restricted, physical perspective of knowledge and becomes metaphysical. The movement, by which the transition of physics to metaphysics takes place, is called "resolution": metaphysics comes after physics insofar as its objects are discovered by way of resolution, as the more universal after the less universal. In my interpretation, the emphasis lies on the reflective movement of *resolution*, by which the intellect transcends the physical perspective on reality as relative to our sense experience, toward a way of understanding reality insofar as it is being, whether it is material or not.

Metaphysical Realism

I want to conclude with some provisional remarks about metaphysical realism. Realism is a difficult topic in philosophy, not only because there are so many different "realisms," but also because the metaphysical realism of being *qua* being cannot exist without a certain form of idealism of the first notion of being, as that concept which allows our intellect to conceive and to assert such a thing as a mind-independent world. One cannot think or speak of the world without the conceptual means to think such a world. Now, the mind-independent world of realism is often identified, in a quite naive and unproblematic way, with the physical universe, that is, the universe which consists of the physical objects we all are familiar with, the trees in the park, the stars in the heavens, water in the oceans, animals, our planet; in short, everything which belongs to what we call nature, the visible reality which surrounds us. And we usually take this physical reality in a direct, realistic sense, as something which exists independently from how we take it to be, independently from the conceptual perspective, in relation to which something can appear as "a physical universe." And then we go on to attribute this realistic or better empiricist attitude of thought, with respect to physical reality, to the philosophy of Thomas.

However, we can learn from Thomas that "all that exists" does not coincide simply with the collection of physical objects. To account for reality in its concrete sense as being, the differentiated whole of all that is, the intellect must transcend its physical (and still abstract) perspective on the many particular objects of nature, and relate this particular field of nature to the being that all things have in common. Thus, "physical objects" are not simply reality itself, but they correspond to the way in which intelligible aspects of sensible reality are considered by the intellect. When we look at reality from the point of view of physics, we see particular things, things which exist in matter and motion. But what exists in the full and concrete sense is more than *physical* being, or form in matter. Let us phrase it this way: there is more in things than meets the eye from the perspective of physics. And that more is not something supernatural, not something which is added from the outside to the physical part of reality. It is that same reality, but considered concretely as *being*, that is to say, each physical thing, as a particular nature, is now understood as related in a particular way to the act of being. The difference is that physics considers intelligible aspects of sensible reality, and thus intelligible aspects of reality relative to our experience, while metaphysics considers intelligible aspects of reality as such, absolutely. Metaphysics may have the appearance of being the most abstract science, but it is in fact the science of the most concrete, of being in its intrinsic intelligibility.

To speak of the world as consisting merely of physical objects is already a reduction, a flattening of the full sense of being. That which exists should not be understood according to the defining relationship of physics, that is, the composition of form and matter, but according to the relationship of essence and the act of being: the concrete thing which exists. And this essence may include the aspect of matter or not, as this is not relevant for the intelligibility of a thing as being. So from a different angle, we encounter here the same "separation"; being as (in itself) constituted by the relationship of essence and the act of being does not depend on matter. Separation has to do with what we can call "concrete intelligibility." Realism? Yes! But only insofar as the intelligibility is grounded in being, and not in a naive empirical or physical realism.

3

The Role of Sense Realism in the Initiation of Thomistic Metaphysics

JOHN F. X. KNASAS

By "sense realism" I mean the reflexively discernible fact that my sense cognition, for example, what I am doing right now as I look this way and listen, directly and immediately presents me with something real. By "real" I mean to say that the object presents itself as an existent ontologically independent of the sensor. Accordingly, I understand that if my sensing stopped because I was rendered blind or deaf, the sensed item would be still existing. By "something" I do not mean full-bodied substances like people, cats and dogs, rocks and trees. Such are not given as perceptually basic. I mean simply colored and shaped extension perhaps in motion and noisy. By "directly and immediately" I mean, first, as the focus of my cognitive attention, or not on the periphery, and, second, without the use of "ideas" as seems to be the case in remembering and imagining. By "reflexively" I mean a bending back of my attention upon a presently exercised act of sensation. This reflective capacity is crucial to verifying sense realism. In contrast to my reflecting upon current remembering and imagining, my reflecting upon what I am doing right now as I look this way reveals my vision to be an idea-free zone. Though I can bend back upon remembering and imagining and locate "ideas" in and through which I am remembering or imagining this or that, I cannot produce similar results when I reflect upon my current sensation.

Usually the role of sense realism is to serve as an anchor for our concepts. We need to know that our concepts are connected to reality and sense realism provides that contact. But once the anchor catches, we busy ourselves with other things. I want to argue that the fact that the anchor catches is a most important thing with which to busy ourselves. In other words, the direct presence of something real in sense cognition is the *sine qua non* both for the development of a meaning of being different from *ens mobile* and for grasping the essence/existence distinction that fundamentally characterizes that unique meaning.[1]

The basic content of Aquinas's metaphysics is twofold: its subject matter and the causes thereof, *viz.*, God and the separate substances. The metaphysician unfolds this basic content by beginning with the subject matter. Formulae for the subject matter include: *ens commune, ens qua ens*, and *ens inquantum ens*. Aquinas compares the subject to the *ratio animalis* which abstracts from reason, though some animals are rational.[2] The subject, then, is an intelligibility, an object of abstraction. Aquinas further describes it as possessing two characteristics. The first is what I will call "immateriality." Though every object of intellection is immaterial, what I mean is involved in Aquinas's just-mentioned comparison to animal. The *ratio entis* abstracts from matter, though sometimes it is within matter, just as the meaning of animal abstracts from reason though some animals are rational. The *ratio entis* is an intelligibility that need not be realized in matter, just as animal is an intelligibility that need not be realized in rational substances, though the *abstractum* of animal must be realized materially. While unspecified, the other things in which *ens* is found are presumably the angels, also called

1. Thus I am not defending sense realism itself but its use for Thomistic metaphysical purposes. For remarks in defense of realism, see my *Being and Some Twentieth-Century Thomists* (New York: Fordham University Press, 2003), 289–92, and Joseph Owens, *Cognition: An Epistemological Inquiry* (Houston, Tex.: Center for Thomistic Studies, 1992), chap. 2. For the cognitional development of real substances from knowing real accidents, see Richard J. Connell, *Substance and Modern Science* (Houston, Tex.: Center for Thomistic Studies, 1988), esp. chaps. 2–3.

2. "We say that being [*ens*] and substance are separate from matter and motion not because it is of their nature to be without them, as it is of the nature of ass to be without reason, but because it is not of their nature to be in matter and motion, although sometimes they are in matter and motion as animal abstracts from reason, although some animals are rational." Aquinas, *Expos. de Trin.*, q. 5, a. 4, ad 5, *The Division and Methods of the Sciences*, trans. Armand Maurer (Toronto: Pontifical Institute of Mediaeval Studies, 1963), 48–49.

the intelligences.[3] Though a characteristic of the *ratio entis*, immateriality in my sense does not seem to be especially characteristic of *ens*. In his *Expos. de Trin.*, q. 5, a. 4, co., Aquinas notes that immateriality also characterizes other notions, for example, substance, act, potency, one, and many.[4]

Besides immateriality, the subject of metaphysics is marked by composition. It is a composite commonality. Compositeness is its second earmark. At SCG II.54, Aquinas describes this compositeness.[5] The potency/act composition has a greater extension than the matter/form composition. The matter/form composition ranges only through material substances. The potency/act composition extends to immaterial created substances as well. Furthermore, the potency/act composition divides common being. Hence, the *ens commune* mentioned here is the same *ens commune* elsewhere characterized as the subject of metaphysics. Only now a further wrinkle is mentioned. The notion is composite. It harbors a potential and an actual element.

Earlier in II.54, Aquinas identifies these elements.[6] The potency/act composition common both to material and immaterial things is the substance/being (*esse*) composition. Elsewhere Aquinas uses for the

3. "In the divine science taught by the philosophers, however, the angels, which they call Intelligences." Aquinas, *Expos. de Trin.*, q. 5, a. 4, ad 3 (89).

4. "For something can exist separate from matter and motion ... because by its nature it does not exist in matter and motion; but it can exist without them, though we sometimes find it with them. In this way being [*ens*], substance, potency, and act are separate from matter and motion, because they do not depend on them for their existence, unlike the objects of mathematics, which can only exist in matter. Thus philosophical theology [also called metaphysics] investigates beings separate in [this] second sense as its subjects." Aquinas, *Expos. de Trin.*, q. 5, a. 4, co. (45).

5. "It is therefore clear that composition of act and potentiality has greater extension than that of form and matter. Thus, matter and form divide natural substance, while potentiality and act divide common being [*ens commune*]. Accordingly, whatever follows upon potentiality and act, as such, is common to both material and immaterial created substances, as *to receive* and *to be received*, *to perfect* and *to be perfected*. Yet all that is proper to matter and form, as such, as *to be generated* and *to be corrupted*, and the like, are proper to material substances, and in no way belong to immaterial created substances." *Summa Contra Gentiles*, trans. James F. Anderson (Notre Dame, Ind.: University of Notre Dame Press, 1975), 2:158.

6. "There is in [intellectual and immaterial] substances but one composition of act and potentiality, namely, the composition of substance and being [*substantia et esse*], which by some is said to be of that which is [*quod est*] and being [*esse*], or of *that which is* and *that by which a thing is*. On the other hand, in substances composed of matter and form there is a twofold composition of act and potentiality: the first, of the substance itself which is composed of matter and form; the second, of the substance thus composed, and being; and this composition also can be said to be of *that which is* and being or of *that which is* and that by which a thing is" (ibid., 157–58).

term *esse* the expression *actus essendi*.[7] Substance and act of being are intelligibilities that in turn comprise another intelligibility—that of *ens commune* itself.

Of these two earmarks of *ratio entis*, the second seems to be the defining one. As mentioned, immateriality is not particularly distinctive of the *ratio entis*. It is shared by the notions of substance, act, potency, etc. Also, throughout his writings Aquinas repeats that something is called a being in virtue of possessing its *esse* or *actus essendi*.[8] Consequently, a being is a "quasi habens esse."[9] A being is "as if a haver, or possessor, of *esse*."

7. Thomists translate *esse rei* as the existence or being of a thing. Unfortunately, contemporary readers can take that to mean the fact of the thing. That would make *esse* to mean what Aquinas calls *ens*. Aquinas distinguishes the two with these analogies: Just as a man is called a runner (*currens*) by his running (*currere*), so too the man is a being (*ens*) by his *esse* (*In de Heb.*, chap. II). Also, just as motion is the act of the mobile, so too *esse* is the act of the existent insofar as it is existent: "Sicut autem motus est actus ipsius mobilis inquantum mobile est, ita esse est actus existentis, inquantum ens est" (*In Sent.* I, d. 19, q. 2, a. 2, co.). *Esse* means something like these accidental acts of running and motion. For further discussion and texts, see Knasas, *Being and Some Twentieth-Century Thomists*, 175–77.

8. "Cum autem in re sit quidditas ejus et suum esse, veritas fundatur in esse rei magis quam in quidditate, sicut et nomen entis ab esse imponitur" (*In Sent.* I, d. 19, q. 5, a. 1, co.); "Sicut autem motus est actus ipsius mobilis inquantum mobile est; ita esse est actus existentis, inquantum ens est" (*In Sent.* I, d. 19, q. 2, a. 2, co.); "quod cum dicitur: *Diversum est esse*, et quod est, distinguitur actus essendi ab eo cui actus ille convenit. Ratio autem entis ab actu essendi sumitur, non ab eo cui convenit actus essendi" (*De Ver.*, q. 1, a. 1, ad 3, second set); "esse dicitur actus entis inquantum est ens, idest quo denominatur aliquid ens actu in rerum natura" (*Quodl.* IX, q. 2, a. 3, co.); "et ipsum esse est quo substantia denominatur ens" (SCG II.54); "Et ulterius aliqui erexerunt se ad considerandum ens inquantum est ens, et consideraverunt causam rerum, non solum secundum quod sunt haec vel talia, sed secundum quod sunt entia. Hoc igitur quod est causa rerum inquantum sunt entia, oportet esse causam rerum, non solum secundum quod sunt talia per formas accidentales, nec secundum quod sunt haec per formas substantiales, sed etiam secundum omne illud quod pertinet ad esse illorum quocumque modo" (*ST* I, q. 44, a. 2, co.).

9. "Nam ens dicitur quasi esse habens, hoc autem solum est substantia, quae subsistit" (*In Meta.* XII, l, 1). Aquinas elucidates the qualification. In respect to the substance rendered a being by composition with *esse*, *esse* is *prius* (SCG I.22), *primus* (*De Pot.*, q. 3, a. 4, co.), *profundius*, and *magis intimum* (*ST* I, q. 8, a. 1, co.). Hence, "esse est accidens, non quasi per accidens se habens, sed quasi actualitas cuiuslibet substantiae (*Quodl.* II, q. 2, a. 1, ad 2). One Neo-Thomist metaphysician explains the relation of *esse* to the thing this way: "The notion that there is an accident prior to substance in sensible things is repellent to the ingrained human way of thinking. Yet the effort has to be made for the metaphysical understanding of existence. Not substance, but an accident, being is absolutely basic in sensible things. This has to be understood, however, in a way that does not make being function as the substance. Strictly, it is not the being that is there, but the substance that has the being. The nature cannot take on an adverbial relation to its being. Man cannot be regarded as basically a certain portion of being that exists humanly, or a horse as another portion of being that exists equinely. The man and the horse are not portions of being, but substances that have being. They, and not their being, have to be expressed substantively, even

With these two characteristics of the subject of metaphysics in mind, how does the Thomist metaphysician present them? Does one begin by establishing immateriality and then compositeness or vice versa? Or are the two somehow given simultaneously? Almost unanimously the twentieth-century Thomist attempts to answer this first question have presumed that the philosopher begins metaphysics with the immateriality earmark. Without the immateriality earmark one does not have Aquinas's metaphysical science. But the attempts in that regard have come to naught.

In a long footnote in his *Existence and the Existent*, Jacques Maritain presents one striking expression of his thesis.[10] Commenting on *Expos. de Trin.*, q. 5, a. 3, co., Maritain explains that the *ratio entis* is separated from matter thanks to a confrontation with the act of existing of sensible things—an act that "over-passes the line of material essences." The

---

though their being is prior to their natures." Joseph Owens, *An Elementary Christian* Metaphysics (Houston, Tex.: Center for Thomistic Studies, 1985), 75. For further Thomistic texts on *ens* as *habens esse*, see Knasas, *Being and Some Twentieth-Century Thomists*, 174n4.

10. "This doctrine [of Aquinas at *Expos. de Trin.*, q. 5, a. 3, co.] shows indeed that what properly pertains to the metaphysical concept of being is that it results from an abstraction (or a separation from matter) which takes place *secundum hanc secundam operationem intellectus*.... If it can be separated from matter by the operation of the (negative) judgment, the reason is that it is related in its content to the act of existing which is signified by the (positive) judgment and which over-passes the line of material essences, - the connatural object of simple apprehension." Jacques Maritain, *Existence and the Existent*, trans. Lewis Galantiere and Gerald B. Phelan [New York: Vantage Books, 1966), 28n14. Likewise, "When, moving on to the queen-science, metaphysics, ... the intellect disengages being from the knowledge of the sensible in which it is immersed, in order to make it the object or rather the subject of metaphysics; when, in a word, it conceptualizes the metaphysical intuition of being ... what the intellect releases into that same light is, here again, first and foremost, the act of existing" (ibid., 26; similarly on 20 and 21). Also in an earlier publication, "the metaphysical trans-sensible, since it is transcendental and polyvalent (analogous), is not only free from matter in its notion and definition but can also exist without it. That is why the order to existence is emboweled in the objects of metaphysics.... If moreover, as we remarked above, metaphysics descends to the actual existence of things in time, and rises to the actual existence of things outside time, it is not only because actual existence is the sign par excellence of the intrinsic possibility of existence." Jacques Maritain, *The Degrees of Knowledge*, trans. Gerald B. Phelan (New York: Charles Scribner's Sons, 1959), 218. At the end of his life in "Réflexions sur la nature blessée et sur l'intuition de l'être," *Revue Thomiste* 68 (1968): 5–41 (later republished in *Approches sans entrave* [Paris: Fayard, 1973]), Maritain plied the same thesis. For a collection and translation of Maritain's remarks along with Gilson's critique from his "Propos sur l'être et sa notion," *San Tommaso et it pensiero moderno*, ed. Antonio Piolanti (Citta Nuova: Pontificia Academia Romana de S. Tommaso d'Aquino, 1974), see my *The Preface to Thomistic Metaphysics: A Contribution to the Neo-Thomist Debate on the Start of Metaphysics* (New York: Peter Lang, 1990), appendix.

immateriality of the *ratio entis* squarely rests upon the immateriality of *esse*. Maritain notes that Aquinas prefaced his discussion of metaphysical separation, or negative judgment, with a discussion of the grasp of *esse* in the composing mode of the mind's second act—positive judgment. Maritain is confident, then, that for Aquinas also an appreciation of *esse* is the key for an appreciation of the subject of metaphysics. The judgment negating matter from *ens* has its reason in a positive judgment whose content includes the act of existing.

The philosophical difficulty with Maritain's approach to *ens commune* is that it claims more from experience than experience can give. From a number of judgments I can see that *esse* is an act that need not actuate this body or that body. But in every case, *esse* is still presented as the act of some body. From the data there is no indication that *esse* possesses an ability to actuate more than bodies. Maritain's approach is also at odds with the Thomistic texts on abstraction. Aquinas understands abstraction to be determined by the data. The comparison of the *ratio entis* with the *ratio animalis* suggests that *ens* is abstracted as immaterial from data that includes some immaterial instances. Just as one would never abstract animal from rational if one knew it only in humans, so too one would never abstract being from matter if one grasped being only in bodies.

But where abstraction fails, perhaps the application of reasoning will succeed. According to the natural philosophy approach to Thomistic metaphysics, the entry into metaphysics is consequent upon natural philosophy's demonstration of the immaterial. From the study of motion in the *Physics*, the natural philosopher proves separate substance as a required immaterial and immovable mover. From the study of intellection in the *De anima*, the natural philosopher proves the human soul to be immaterial. Such conclusions enable us to stretch our original notion of being so that it is seen to apply analogically both to the material and immaterial orders.[11]

11. Natural philosophy Thomists were quite a significant group. "In physics we prove that there is an Unmoved Mover and that the intellective soul is a principle of immaterial operations, and so we know that there are beings which are not material things. The metaphysical object is not attained by abstraction, and presupposes a preliminary separation or distinction of immaterial beings from material beings. After this we can grasp both in the unity of a single concept of being." William H. Kane, "Abstraction and the Distinction of the Sciences," *The Thomist* 17 (1954): 43–68, at 62. "But for St. Thomas there are two ways to establish the existence of such a sub-

The natural philosophy approach is also at odds with the Thomistic texts. At *ST* I, q. 44, a. 2, co., Aquinas expressly says that reasoning based on matter/form principles takes the philosopher to a first body only: "These transmutations (of essential forms) they attributed to certain more universal causes, such as the oblique circle, according to Aristotle." The oblique circle is a reference to the celestial sphere that moves the sun. If the philosopher reasons further, the text continues, it is on the basis of *ens inquantum ens*. Aquinas says that this third viewpoint involves a reference to the *esse* of sensible things.[12] (In passing I wish to

_____

stance separate from matter and motion. The first is through a consideration of physical motion, such as Aristotle undertakes in Books VII and VIII of the *Physics*, where he demonstrates that the cause of all physical motions in the world must itself be immaterial and immovable. The second is through a consideration of human intellection and volition, such as Aristotle gives in Book III of *De anima*, where he demonstrates that the human intellective soul must be immaterial and immortal .... Thus for St. Thomas natural philosophy is prior *quoad nos* to metaphysics. Natural philosophy establishes by demonstration that there is some being which is not material. This negative judgement, or more properly, the judgement of separation is the point of departure for a higher study, which can be called 'First Philosophy' or metaphysics." James A. Weisheipl, "The Relationship of Medieval Natural Philosophy to Modern Science: The Contribution of Thomas Aquinas to Its Understanding," *Manuscripta* 20 (1976): 181–96, at 194–95. "This subject [of metaphysics] is set up by a double negative judgment, 'Not all being is material.' This is the result of the discovery in physics and psychology of immaterial beings. 'Therefore, being itself is neither material nor immaterial.'" Melvin A. Glutz, "Being and Metaphysics," *The Modern Schoolman* 35 (1958): 271–85, at 282–83. "In natural science we discover that the First Cause of the existence and action of ens mobile is not itself a physical object which can be studied by the principles of natural science, and that this is also true of the human intellectual soul." Benedict M. Ashley, OP, "The River Forest School and the Philosophy of Nature Today," in *Philosophy and the God of Abraham: Essays in Memory of James A. Weisheipl, OP*, ed. R. James Long (Toronto: Pontifical Institute of Mediaeval Studies, 1991), 1–15, at 4. "The subject of metaphysics is best clarified after one has established in natural philosophy and in psychology the existence of non-material reality such as the unmoved mover and the human soul." William Wallace, *The Elements of Philosophy* (New York: Alba House, 1977), 85. Others holding the general thesis that natural science's proof of the immaterial is a doctrinal prerequisite to Thomistic metaphysics include Vincent Smith, "The Prime Mover: Physical and Metaphysical Considerations," *Proceedings of the American Catholic Philosophical Association* 28 (1954): 78–94, at 91; Thomas C. O'Brien, *Metaphysics and the Existence of God* (Washington, D.C.: Thomist Press, 1960), 158–64; James Doig, *Aquinas on Metaphysics* (The Hague: Martinus Nijhoff, 1972), 241–47; Ralph McInerny, *Being and Predication* (Washington, D.C.: The Catholic University of America Press, 1986), 51–52; Antonio Moreno, "The Subject, Abstraction, and Methodology of Aquinas' Metaphysics," *Angelicum* 61 (1984): 580–601; and Mark Jordan, *Ordering Wisdom: The Hierarchy of Philosophical Discourses in Aquinas* (Notre Dame, Ind.: University of Notre Dame Press, 1986), 172–73.

12. "Then others advanced further and raised themselves to the consideration of being as being [*ens inquantum est ens*], and who assigned a cause to things ... according to all that belongs to their being [*esse*] in any way whatever." Aquinas, *ST* I, q. 44, a. 2, co., in *Basic Writings of Saint Thomas Aquinas*, ed. Anton C. Pegis (New York: Random House, 1945), 1:429.

note that my comment should not be confused with Gilson's comment, which claims that in q. 44, a. 2 Aquinas says that Aristotle does not get to *ens inquantum ens*. Neither here nor in my other discussions of a. 2 am I speaking of Aristotle, but rather about natural philosophy reasoning based upon the defining notes of *ens mobile*—matter/form.)[13] Also, Aquinas restricts philosophical knowledge of God and angels together to metaphysics. In *Expos. de Trin.*, q. 5, a. 4, co., and in a context of coming to know their existence, Aquinas says: "Philosophers, then, study these divine beings only insofar as [*nisi prout*] they are the principles of all things."[14] Finally, at *In Phys.* II, l. 4, n. 175, Aquinas explicitly assigns to metaphysics even the consideration of the rational soul as separable from matter. Natural science deals with the soul only as a part of a generable and corruptible thing. As I will note, this natural consideration of the rational soul is very indirect, *viz.*, from bodily changes underlying phantasms.

I find no Thomistic texts that unequivocally give natural philosophy a demonstration of the immaterial. Often cited remarks that if there were nothing beyond sensible things then physics would be first philosophy do not say that physics proves the immaterial.[15] Nor do they imply it. In line with q. 44, a. 2, their meaning may simply be that without further causes sensible things would not contain an effect that could specify another science than physics. Second, *Expos. de Trin.*, q. 5,

13. In his *The Way toward Wisdom: An Interdisciplinary and Intercultural Introduction to Metaphysics* (Notre Dame, Ind.: University of Notre Dame Press, 2006), 159, Ashley confuses me with Gilson's point and so misses my point.

14. Also, "[Aristotle] puts a question about things that exist immaterially: whether, that is, our intellect, though conjoined with spatial magnitude (i.e., the body), can understand 'anything separated,' i.e., any substance separated from matter. He undertakes to pursue this enquiry later, —not at present, because it is not yet evident that any such substances exist nor, if they do, what sort of thing they are. It is a problem for metaphysics [*haec quaestio pertinent ad Metaphysicum*]." Aquinas, *In De An.* III, l. 12, n. 785, in *Commentary on Aristotle's De Anima*, trans. Kenelm Foster and Silvester Humphries (Notre Dame, Ind.: Dumb Ox Books, 1994), 233.

15. "If there is no substance other than those which exist in the way that natural substances do, with which the philosophy of nature deals, the philosophy of nature will be the first science. But if there is some immobile substance, this will be prior to natural substance; and therefore the philosophy which considers this kind of substance will be first philosophy [*per consequens philosophia considerans huiusmodi substantiam erit philosophia prima*]." *In Meta.* VI, l. 1, n. 1170, in *Commentary on the Metaphysics of Aristotle*, trans. John P. Rowan (Chicago: Henry Regnery, 1961), 462. In his Dumb Ox republishing of the Rowan translation, Ralph McInerny changes the last line to "therefore the philosophy of nature, which considers this kind of substance, will be first philosophy." See also *In Meta.* III, l. 4, n. 398, and XI, l. 7, n. 2267.

a. 2, ad 3 speaks of natural philosophy treating the first mover, *primus motor*, as the end to which natural science leads.[16] The text does not identify the first mover as God. Moreover, at SCG I.13 *Quia vero*, Aquinas employs a similar phrase (*primum movens*) to refer to the outermost celestial sphere. Nor in the *Expos. de Trin.* text does Aquinas characterize the first mover as immaterial. Rather, it is "of a different nature from natural things." This could well apply to the ungenerable and incorruptible heavenly spheres and their matter not being subject to loss of form. In sum, nothing in this text necessarily goes beyond q. 44, a. 2.[17] Third, the closing lines of the commentary on the *Physics* state that Aristotle ends his general discussion of natural things with the first principle of the whole of nature, *primum principium totius naturae*, who is God.[18] But the only preceding discussion of the *primum principium* is early in the commentary on the eighth book. There the first principle is the *principium totius esse*, not of *forma substantiale*. In short the discussion is metaphysical. Moreover, earlier at *In Phys.* II, l. 11, n. 245, Aquinas insists that physics does not deal with every mover. For instance, it does not deal with a moving principle that is altogether immobile and the first of all movers and such is the topic of Book VIII.[19] This indicates that Book VIII is metaphysical. It also fits in with the restriction in q. 44, a. 2 of matter/form reasoning to the material cosmos and the noted introduction of a *primum principium* into Book VIII. Finally, neither is

16. "Natural science does not treat of the First Mover as its subject or as part of its subject, but as the end to which natural science leads.... So also the First Mover is of a different nature from natural things, but it is related to them because it moves them. So it falls under the consideration of natural science, not in itself, but insofar as it is a mover" (Maurer, *Division and Methods*, 23).

17. At *Expos. de Trin.*, q. 6, a. 3, co., Aquinas insists that for the natural philosopher heavenly and terrestrial bodies do not belong in the same genus. For further discussion see my "Materiality and Aquinas' Natural Philosophy: A Reply to Johnson," *The Modern Schoolman* 68 (1991): 245–57, at 249–51.

18. *In Phys.* VIII, l. 2, n. 974.

19. "Natural philosophy does not consider every mover. For there are two kinds of moving principles, namely, the moved and the non-moved. Now a mover that is not moved is not natural because it does not have in itself a principle of motion. And such is the moving principle which is altogether immobile and the first of all movers, as will be shown in Book VIII." *In Phys.* II, l. 11, n. 245, in *Commentary on Aristotle's Physics*, trans. Richard J. Blackwell et al. (Notre Dame, Ind.: Dumb Ox Books, 1999), 122–23. A few paragraphs earlier at n. 243, Aquinas describes the consideration of an immobile mover as a third philosophical study. Aquinas assigns the study to metaphysics. Book VIII would, then, be metaphysics.

the *prima via* decisive, for the terminology is open to a metaphysical interpretation.[20]

Struck by the *a posteriori* inabilities to reveal the immaterial, Transcendental Thomists take an *a priori* route to the subject of metaphysics. *Esse* remains grasped in judgment. Yet *esse* now is divine *esse* and judgment is an *a priori* dynamism to that term. In the wake of this dynamism, material being is seen to be the limited and finite thing that it is. Material being is not expressive of being as such. In this way the subject of metaphysics is reached. Hence, Karl Rahner, echoing Joseph Maréchal, says in *Spirit in the World*:

So it follows from the problematic of the modus significandi in the simple apprehension that abstraction as the apprehension of what is metaphysically universal must be an act that preapprehends metaphysical being without representing it objectively. Then, on the other hand, the represented content can correctly be liberated from its relation to matter by a negation ... without itself being eliminated as really possible, or at least becoming unknowable: ... the decisive abstraction of metaphysical determinations takes place in judgment.[21]

The preapprehension of metaphysical being belongs *a priori* to the agent intellect and is "the condition of every objective knowledge."[22]

The philosophical difficulty with the Transcendental Thomist approach is that it seems locked in Kantianism. Is the dynamism of judgment expressive of anything more than a peculiarity of thought? Even the claim that the dynamism cannot be denied without contradiction would fail to move a Kantian. "Just what you would expect, if it is a condition for thought alone," he would say. This lingering doubt would mean that the objectivity of the subject of metaphysics is still problematic.[23]

Thomistically speaking, the Transcendental Thomist approach is

20. See Knasas, *Preface to Thomistic Metaphysics*, 155–58, and "Thomistic Existentialism and the Proofs *Ex Motu* at C. G. I, 13," *The Thomist* 59 (1995): 591–616. Also see many of Joseph Owens's groundbreaking articles on the motion proof in *St. Thomas Aquinas on the Existence of God: The Collected Papers of Joseph Owens*, ed. John R. Catan (Albany: State University of New York Press, 1980).

21. Karl Rahner, *Spirit in the World*, trans. William Dych (New York: Herder and Herder, 1968), 200.

22. Ibid., 221. "Insofar as [the agent intellect] apprehends this material of sensibility within its anticipatory dynamism to *esse*, it illumines this material" (ibid., 225). See also Karl Rahner, "Aquinas: the Nature of Truth," trans. Andrew Tallon, *Continuum* 2 (1964): 60–71, at 67.

23. Aquinas's use of "the indirect proof" of first principles at *In Meta*. IV, l. 7, is directed

at odds with Aquinas's texts on the *secunda operatio*. The *esse* that the second operation grasps is the *esse rei*, not the divine *esse*. Also, cited texts for an apriorism in Aquinas do not prove to be so. When Aquinas claims at *De Ver.*, q. 1, a. 4, ad 5 that the "truth by which we judge things proceeds exemplarily from the divine intellect," he is not speaking of some direct divine infusion of truth into our intellect. Rather, "exemplarily" means from things made in the likeness of divine truth. Likewise, when he asserts at *De Ver.*, q. 22, a. 2, ad 1 that "all cognitive beings also know God implicitly in any known object," the context and parallel passages show that Aquinas does not mean that God is an *a priori* condition for our consciousness of objects. Rather Aquinas means that cognitive beings implicitly know God in any known object because any thing is made in God's likeness. To know the copy is *ipso facto* to know in some way the original. Finally, texts mentioning the natural and inborn knowledge of the first principles, e.g., *De Ver.*, q. 10, a. 6 and *In Meta.* IV, l. 6, are simply referring to the agent intellect's natural capacity to abstract with ease the notion of being from which the first principles follow. Similarly someone is a natural-born baseball player not because he is born with the capacity to throw a curve ball but because he is born with the talent to easily acquire that capacity.

So in light of this gloomy tale, very few others—I am thinking of Etienne Gilson and Joseph Owens[24]—have dared to buck the assumption that initiating metaphysics requires establishing the immateriality earmark. Sufficient unto the day is starting metaphysics with the discov-

---

against philosophical realists. It is anachronistic to claim that Aquinas is refuting Kantians. See my *Being and Some Twentieth-Century Thomists*, 126–28.

24. "The chronic disease of metaphysical being is not existence, but its tendency to lose existence. To restore existence to being is therefore the first prerequisite to the restoring of being itself to its legitimate position as the first principle of metaphysics." Etienne Gilson, *Being and Some Philosophers* (Toronto: Pontifical Institute of Mediaeval Studies, 1952), 214. "The being that places a thing under the subject of metaphysics is the being that is immediately known in sensible things through each ordinary, everyday judgment, and that is everywhere universalized by the ordinary man in a subsequent concept.... Rather, [being] is what is first grasped through the concretion of the sensible thing, as the thing is immediately known in sensible experience. It is not something esoteric or farfetched, but is familiar to everyone in every cognitive act." Owens, *An Elementary Christian Metaphysics*, 370–71. See also ibid., 97n21: "As originally grasped by the human intellect, being, though a transcendent aspect, does not at once manifest itself as transcendent. When its primary sense is reached in subsistent being, its literal meaning is seen to extend beyond the sensible and beyond the finite orders."

ery of the compositeness of thing and *esse*. An understanding of the *ratio entis* as *habens esse* is a distinctive enough consideration for launching metaphysics even if the *habens* is still understood as material and sensible. Indeed at *Expos. de Trin.*, q. 5, a. 1, co., Aquinas presents any number of possibilities for a third speculative science whose object includes independence from matter. First, the science could deal with something that never exists in matter, for instance, God and the angels. Second, it could deal with objects able to be in matter and apart from it, such as substance, quality, being, potency, and act. Third, the science could deal with both of the previous. These manifold possibilities should cause one to hesitate to say just how metaphysics is separate from matter. Interestingly, at *In Meta.* VI, l. 1, n. 1163, Aquinas calls metaphysics immaterial simply because it treats God and the angels.

Yet recently attempts of Gilson, Owens, and others have also met with criticism. In his *The Way toward Wisdom: An Interdisciplinary and Intercultural Introduction to Metaphysics*, Benedict Ashley mentions two criticisms. First, echoing a comment by John Deely, Ashley insists that if we still lack the immaterial sense of the *ratio entis*, then any results of analyzing sensible things remain under the umbrella of *ens mobile*, the subject of natural philosophy. Hence, even the discovery of the most profound and intimate *actus* of *esse* does not mean that we have left the neighborhood of physics.[25] Second, quoting a remark of John Wippel, Ashley then notes that by leaving for later the establishing of the immateriality characteristic of the *ratio entis*, this minority approach would, on the one hand, inappropriately have a science without a subject matter and, on the other hand, have the metaphysician proving, rather than discovering, his subject matter.[26] My project here is to argue that an ap-

25. "*Esse* and essence are *correlative* causes, related as form to matter, and act to potency. Hence, though they are really distinct, one cannot be separated or known apart from the other. To say that 'something has *esse*' means nothing unless we understand it in relation to the essence of that which has this '*esse*.' It is untenable to suppose ... that what material beings of different kinds have in common is simply a neutral *esse*. It has to be at least some generic essence that is correlative to and limits that *esse*. The broadest genus that we can judge from direct experience to have *esse* is *ens mobile* that is restricted to matter and motion.... The *esse* that material things have is the ultimate act and perfection of material things, and as such its study falls within the scope of natural science and leaves nothing over as the object of an independent Metascience." Ashley, *Way toward Wisdom*, 160–61.

26. Wippel's remark is: "This approach fails to do justice to Thomas's understanding of the subject of a science, knowledge of which is required for one to begin the science. It also

preciation of the role of sense realism replies to these recent objections.

First, that Aristotle's and Aquinas's understanding of sensation is realist in the sense described above is evinced by how their understanding of the mechanics of sensation scrupulously guards and preserves realism. Those mechanics are summed up in the thesis that the senses "susceptivus specierum sine materia." The senses are receptive of the species without the matter.[27] What does this mean? Aquinas admits that the formula is odd. It is so because reception of form without matter is true of any change whatsoever, even changes that do not result in cognition. In any change the patient receives only form from the agent, not the agent's matter.

To convey the aptness of the formula, Aquinas distinguishes different ways of receiving a form from an agent. In the first way, the received form has the same material mode of existence as in the agent. This first kind of reception of form occurs when any passive thing in nature receives the action that alters its natural quality. For example, consider the way air receives the influence of fire. The air loses one of its temperatures and acquires another. Apparently, in sensation form is received without involving the matter of the sensor in the way that alteration in nature involves the matter of the thing altered.

But a second way to receive form exists. In this case, the received form appears to remain the very form of the agent. But now the form has an *esse intentionale et spirituale* in the sensor.[28] How is the form picked up? Because the sensor is a hylemorphic substance and the matter of the sensor has been excluded as a recipient of the form, a fair answer is that the sensor's form is the recipient of the formal determina-

---

contradicts a principle Thomas accepts from Aristotle to the effect that no science can establish the existence of its own subject." John Wippel, *The Metaphysical Thought of St. Thomas Aquinas: From Finite Being to Uncreated Being* (Washington, D.C.: The Catholic University of America Press, 2000), 58n110.

27. *In De An.* I, n. 418, and II, l. 24.

28. "Sometimes, however, the recipient receives the form into a mode of existence other than that which the form has in the agent; when, that is, the recipient's material disposition to receive form does not resemble the material disposition in the agent. In these cases the form is taken into the recipient 'without matter,' the recipient being assimilated to the agent in respect of form and not in respect to matter. And it is thus that a sense receives form without matter, the form having in the sense, a different mode of being from that which it has in the object sensed. In the latter it has a material mode of being [*esse naturale*], but in the sense, a cognitional and spiritual mode [*esse intentionale et spirituale*]." *In De An.* II, l. 24, n. 553 (340).

tion of the agent: as Aquinas remarks, "the recipient being assimilated to the agent in respect of form and not in respect to matter." "Matter" here is the matter of the sensor; hence, the mentioned "form" should also be that of the sensor.

This understanding of the mechanics of sensation is tailor-made to underwrite the previous phenomenology of sense realism and shows that the phenomenology is being respected all along. According to that phenomenology, reflection discerns that a current act of sensation is an idea-free zone. As Aquinas himself notes at *ST* I, q. 84, a. 8, ad 2, if one ingests a sleep-inducing volume of food or drink and if the vapors' movements are slight, "not only does the imagination retain its freedom, but even the common sense is partly freed; so that sometimes while asleep a man may judge that what he sees is a dream, discerning, as it were, between things and their images [*similitudines discernat a rebus*]." Notice that as the more external senses are freed, one's attention is taken away from the similitudes to the things. Now according to the mechanics, the formally received form stays the very form of some real item, for example the color, the motion, or the shape. The received form should make the sensor the reality directly and immediately. It should not be a sign, not even a formal sign of the real. In this regard, maximum caution should be exercised regarding the vocabulary of "species" when talking about sensation. In the case of sensation an understanding of its mechanics makes us understand the species not as a likeness but as the very form of the agent present in the sensor. Speaking both of sense and intellect at *De Ver.*, q. 2, a. 2, co., Aquinas does describe knowing as when "the existing perfection of one thing is brought to be in another" (*existens perfectio unius, est nata esse in altero*). And, as mentioned, that is just what is found by the phenomenology. Reflection upon a current act of sensation finds no *tertium quid* between knower and known.[29]

29. "The sense-objects which actuate sensitive activities—the visible, the audible, etc.—exist outside the soul; the reason being that actual sensation attains to the individual things which exist externally." *In De An.* I, l. 12, n. 375 (249). "For what is seen is color which exists in an exterior body." *In De An.* III, l. 8, n. 718 (419). Richard Sorabji thinks that Aristotle's interpretation of cognition has been made less material than it is by commentators influenced by the "contraries problem" and the logical problem of accidents existing apart from substances as seems apparent in long-range detection of odor. "From Aristotle to Brentano: The Development of the Concept of Intentionality," in *Festschrift for A. C. Lloyd: On the Aristotelian Tradition*, ed. H. Blumenthal and H. Robinson, *Oxford Studies in Ancient Philosophy*, supp. vol. (Oxford: Oxford University Press, 1991), 227. Though these problems are concerns for Aquinas, it is clear that Thomas also

Second, what has this to do with my project? Simply this: despite the heavy use of form/matter vocabulary, Aquinas regards sense's reception of form without the matter to be a type of change off the radar screen of natural philosophy. It should then be a datum that allows us to frame a sense of being wider than *ens mobile* but without having to employ a knowledge of immaterial realities. In his *In De Anima* III, l. 12, Aquinas provides a summary comparison of sense and intellect. He first speaks of the kind of movement that sensation involves and then extends it to intellect.

The sense-object appears to play an active part in sensation insofar as sensitivity as a whole is, to start with, in potency. For the sense-object and the sense-faculty are not mutually exclusive things, as though, when one acted on the other it had to transform and alter the latter by destroying something within it. In fact, all that the object does to the faculty is to actualize it; so he adds that sensitivity is not passive [*neque patitur neque alteratur*] to the change producing activity of the sense-object in the ordinary sense [*proprie accepta*] of the terms "passivity" [*passione*] and "change" [*alteratione*], which generally connote the substitution of one of two mutually exclusive qualities for the other.[30]

Sense involves a *sui generis* passivity. Ordinarily, what is passive involves a contrary to what is in the agent. The agent proceeds by destroy-

---

wants to accommodate the direct realism of sense perception. In his "Aristotle on Sense Perception," in *Aristotle: De Anima in Focus*, ed. Michael Durrant (New York: Routledge, 1993), 75–89, at 84, Thomas J. Slakey emphasizes that for Aristotle "the problem (with sensation) is to explain how we get knowledge of other things *as other* things." Slakey says (85) that the unity of form and matter is the paradigmatic case of unity and so one cannot construe the *De anima* as saying that the effect of the external object on a part of the body, the sense organ, is distinct from perception itself, which is an effect in the soul. Slakey is incognizant of Aquinas's nuancing of hylemorphism at *ST* I, q. 14, a. 1, co., to include amplitude (*amplitudo et extensio*) of form in order to accommodate sensing changeable substances. Yet other authors who emphasize the "materiality" of sensation are Terrell Ward Bynum, "A New Look at Aristotle's Theory of Perception," in *Aristotle: De Anima in Focus*, 90–109, and John E. Sisko, "Material Alteration and Cognitive Activity in Aristotle's *De Anima*," *Phronesis* 41 (1996): 138–57. Taking advantage of Searle's interpretation of intentionality, Bynum says, "If I seem to perceive an object in my environment, the would-be perception could not be genuine unless there really is such an external object there causing the perception" (106–7). The problem here is to understand how a "purely physiological" (107) understanding of sensation would know there are external objects. Sisko remarks that "Once the right sort of external cause is provided, material alteration within the organ is sufficient for episodes of perception" (154). The talk of sufficiency seems to indicate that for Sisko perception is simply physiology. Aquinas would insist that over and above the physiology, sensation involves formal reception of form.

30. *In De An.* III, l. 12, n. 765 (445).

ing that contrary and substituting another. The sense faculty involves
no such contrary, and so it is not passive in this proper sense. In the
immediately following lines, Aquinas locates where the study of motion from one contrary to another occurs. In the Foster and Humphries
translation, Aquinas says: "Since, as he shows in the *Physics* [V.5] changes of bodies are of this latter kind, it is clear that if we call sensation a
change we mean a different sort of change."[31] Yet the translation fails
to do justice to the Latin according to which the change of sensation
is another species of motion than the species considered in the entire
book itself of the *Physics*: "Et quia motus, qui est in rebus corporalibus, de quo determinatum est in libro Physicorum, est de contrario
in contrarium, manifestum est, quod sentire, si dicatur motus, est alia
species motus ab ea de qua determinatum est in libro Physicorum."[32]
Now, the "book" may contain more than the general science of nature.
As I noted, indications exist that Aquinas considered Book VIII to be
metaphysical.[33] But no one thinks that the "book" of the *Physics* fails to
contain the general science of nature. Hence, Aquinas's placing of sensation outside the "book" of the *Physics* because it is a different kind of
motion than that studied in the book is one and the same with placing
sensation outside of the general science of physics and any subdivision
thereof. Aquinas does remark: "et ideo iste motus [sentire] simpliciter
est alter a motu physico."[34]

Furthermore, the *De anima* commentary affirms that the *sui generis*
movement and passivity found in the sense is also found in understanding (*intelligere*) and willing (*velle*) and is properly called *operatio*.[35] Yet
earlier in his *De trinitate* commentary (1258–59), while explaining how
metaphysics does not deal with things in motion despite treating the angels, in which there is choice and movement in regard to place, Aquinas
says, "motion with respect to choice [*secundum electionem*] is reducible

31. Ibid., n. 766.

32. "And because motion, which is in corporeal things, about which it is determined in the
book of the *Physics*, is from contrary to contrary, it is clear that to sense, if it is called a motion,
is another species of motion from that about which it is determined in the book of the *Physics*"
(ed. Pirotta, author's translation).

33. See note 00 above.

34. At *ST* I, q. 78, a. 3, co., Aquinas distinguishes "duplex immutatio: una naturalis et alia
spiritualis." The operation of sense requires the latter.

35. *In De An.* III, l. 12, n. 766 (ed. Pirotta, 251–52).

to the sense in which the act of the intellect or will [*actus intellectus uel uoluntatis*] is called motion; which is an improper sense of the term [*improprie dictum*], motion being understood as operation [*pro operatione sumpto*]."[36] Is not Aquinas telling us that metaphysics considers choice along with the act of intellect and will because they all fall in the category of motion improperly speaking? One could hardly blame a reader for thinking so. As another instance of motion improperly speaking, sensation also would be reserved for metaphysical treatment. Sensation is not mentioned here because angels do not sense.

But if any doubt remains about the metaphysical assignment here, the *De trinitate* commentary also affirms: "Spiritual creatures, moreover, are mutable only with regard to choice [*secundum electionem*]; and this sort of motion [*talis mutatio*] is not the concern of the natural philosopher [*ad naturalem*] but rather of the metaphysician [*diuinum*]."[37] Now we know the "sort of motion" being talked about. The sort is motion improperly speaking. The sort includes sensation, intellection, and will. Aquinas unequivocally assigns the sort to metaphysics, for in a philosophical context, which is that of the above quotation, metaphysics is divine science.[38]

Natural philosophy Thomists might insist upon other texts assigning to natural philosophy a study of the passions and likenesses of the intellectual soul. But surely if natural philosophy can do that, then natural philosophy can study sensation. And so my fellow Thomists could cite Aquinas's *Peri hermeneias* comment that "ad naturale" pertains to how the conceptions of the soul are passions of the soul and likenesses of things.[39]

---

36. *Expos. de Trin.*, q. 5, a. 4, ad 3 (47).

37. *Expos. de Trin.*, q. 5, a. 2, ad 7 (25).

38. "The science that treats of all these is theology or divine science [*scientia diuina*], which is so called because its principal object is God. By another name it is called metaphysics [*metaphisica*]." *Expos. de Trin.*, q. 5, a. 1, co. (8). "Accordingly there are two kinds of science concerning the divine. One follows our way of knowing, which uses the principles of sensible things in order to make the Godhead known. This is the way the philosophers handed down a science of the divine, calling the primary science 'divine science' [*philosophiam primam scientiam diuinam*]." *Expos. de Trin.*, q. 2, a. 2, co., in *Faith, Reason and Theology*, trans. Armand Maurer (Toronto: Pontifical Institute of Mediaeval Studies, 1987), 41.

39. "[Aristotle] excuses himself from a further consideration of these things, for the nature of the passions of the soul and the way in which they are likenesses of things does not pertain to logic but to philosophy of nature [*non enim hoc pertinent ad logicum negocium, sed ad naturale*]

But elsewhere the assignment is given both to natural science and metaphysics.[40] Also, as the first *lectio* to the commentary on the *Nicomachean Ethics* displays, Aquinas can use "natural philosophy" to designate the two sciences of the real: physics and metaphysics.[41] Finally, just previous to the *Peri hermeneias* comment, Aquinas allows the conceptions of the intellect to be passions insofar as corporeal passion is required for the phantasm from which the possible intellect suffers the *sui generis* passion of the conception.[42] It seems that Aquinas restricts natural philosophy to a physiological, and so indirect, account of the soul's passions.

So my point is this: as falling outside the data encompassed by *ens mobile*—that is, generation and corruption, alteration, increase and decrease, and locomotion—sensation prompts the intellect to conceive a wider sense of being than *ens mobile*. As wider, this notion of being will distinguish itself from the subject of physics and so permit the development of another science of the real. Moreover, this notion of being will not be proved or demonstrated but discovered in its own data just as *ens mobile* is discovered in its data.

Does Aquinas ever speak about this protometaphysical sense of being that spans the real and the cognitional? I believe that he does when he speaks of the *ratio entis* as the *primum cognitum* at the start of *De*

---

and has already been treated in the book *De Anima*." *Aristotle: On Interpretation, Commentary by St. Thomas and Cajetan*, trans. Jean T. Oesterle (Milwaukee, Wis.: Marquette University Press, 1962), I, l. 2, n. 12 (28–29).

40. "... because no science, except natural philosophy and metaphysics [*nisi naturalis et metaphysica*] is concerned with [species existing in the possible intellect]" (Aquinas, SCG II.75). "For universals, about which are the sciences, are what are known through the intelligible species, not the intelligible species themselves about which clearly are not all the sciences but only physics and metaphysics [*sola physica et metaphysica*]." Aquinas, *In De An.* II, ad 5, ed. James Robb (Toronto: Pontifical Institute of Mediaeval Studies, 1968), 73 (author's translation).

41. "... ad philosophiam naturalem pertinent considerare ordinem rerum quem ratio humana considerat sed non facit; ita quod sub naturali philosophia comprehendamus et metaphysicam." Aquinas, *Ethica* I, l. I, no. 2, ed. Spiazzi (Turin: Marietti, 1964), 3.

42. "Since Aristotle did not customarily speak of the conceptions of the intellect as passions, Andronicus took the position that this book was not Aristotle's. In I *De Anima*, however, it is obvious that he calls all of the operations of the soul 'passions' of the soul. Whence even the conception of the intellect can be called a passion and this either because we do not understand without a phantasm, which requires corporeal passion (for which reason the Philosopher calls the imaginative power the passive intellect); or because by extending the name 'passion' to every reception, the understanding of the possible intellect is also a kind of undergoing, as is said in III *De Anima*." Aquinas, *In Peri Her.*, l. 2, n. 6 (trans. Oesterle, 26).

Ente and *De Ver.*, q. 1, a. 1, co. Being also includes the true. Aquinas understands the true in terms of the *ens rationis* that is the proposition. For at *De Ver.*, q. 1, a. 3, co., he says that the intellect begins to have truth when the intellect has something proper to itself that nevertheless has a conformity to things. This moment is when the intellect judges and says that something is or is not. Also at *SCG* I.58, Aquinas describes the proposition as existing in the intellect, not in the thing that is outside the soul (*in ipso intellectu existit, non in re quae est extra animam*). But besides being found in the intellectual composing of the proposition, Aquinas insists that truth is also found in sense. What is the truth of the senses? At *ST* I, q. 16, a. 2, co., Aquinas says that "sight has the likeness of a visible thing [*similitudinem visibilis*]."[43] But from the *De anima* commentary, we know how to take the sensible likeness. The likeness is the very determination of something real existing in the amplitude of form that is the sense power. Aquinas says that sense is unable to know this likeness because it is insufficiently reflective. But the intellect can. As noted, the reflective phenomenology shows sense to be so suffused with the real that sense can be described as an idea-free zone. That fact is what leads to a mechanics of sensation in which the similitude or likeness is delineated as the very form of the reality that is sensed. So if being as the *primum cognitum* includes the true, then being also includes the cognitional presence of the real in sensation.

One could object that my immediate realism so rivets the *primum cognitum* to real natures that the *primum cognitum* cannot be my *ratio entis* that spans both the real and the cognitional. In fact, Aquinas repeatedly describes the *primum cognitum* as divided by the ten genera. But Aquinas also follows Aristotle's observation that with us science and perception are of things but indirectly of themselves.[44] The admitted realist focus of cognition does not preclude an immediate but indirect awareness of one's very awareness. The idea of formal reception of form achieves a unity so that both knower and known appear in cognition. Hence, the data

43. Also, "Now truth is not in [the senses] in such a way that the senses know truth, but in so far as they have a true apprehension of sensible things, as was said above. This takes place through the sense apprehending things as they are ... now the knowledge of things by the senses is in proportion to the existence of their likeness in the senses [*inquantum similitudo rerum est in sensu*]." Aquinas, *ST* I, q. 17, a. 2, co., in *Basic Writings*, ed. Pegis, 1:182.

44. Aquinas, *In Meta.* XII, l. 11, n. 2617. For commentary, see Owens, *Elementary Christian Metaphysics*, 223.

for the abstraction of the *primum cognitum* are never just real natures. The data include the cognition that makes those natures available. The something real is not the total object of awareness but its focus. I believe that Aquinas's remarks about the ten genera simply bear upon that focus. Immediate realism does not understand human awareness to be so sunk into things that it loses all awareness of itself.

Another indication that this wider sense of being is of metaphysical relevance is its fruitfulness for metaphysical analysis. An analysis of the data of the real thing juxtaposed to itself cognitionally existing leads one to the *habens esse* sense of being. Just as the analysis of the data in which *ens mobile* is discovered leads to the distinction of substrate and determination as defining notes of *ens mobile*, so too the analysis of the real thing juxtaposed to itself cognitionally existing leads to the distinction between a thing and its real existence. For something real to genuinely take on another way of existing as is implied by sense realism, the thing cannot be real of itself. An assumed intrinsic reality for the thing would render it bulletproof to take on another way of existing. That we confront real things in sensation implies that these things are real not in virtue of themselves but rather in virtue of their existence understood as an act distinct from them.[45]

If one prefers, one can state the above reflection in terms of the mechanics of sensation. It is not just the form that enters the sensor; it is the form as real. Otherwise, the sensor would not sense something real. What does this imply? Is not the implication that the form is not real of itself? Only as not real of itself could the form genuinely exist in the different way that it does in sensation. Likewise for cognitional existence: the form is not cognitional of itself under pain of not genuinely really existing. In these ways, one grasps the form as existence-neutral. This conclusion alerts one to further nonformal acts that render the form real or cognitional.

---

45. As a voice in the minority expressed it: "In fact, one may claim that it is exactly this double existence of the same thing, say the Parthenon or a man or a horse, that enables metaphysics after Avicenna to get off the ground. The one thing is found to exist in two different ways. This shows that the thing itself is not the same as either existence thereby setting up the basic problem of metaphysics, namely being *qua* being in contradistinction to the things that have being." Joseph Owens, "The Range of Existence," *Proceedings of the Seventh Inter-American Congress of Philosophy* (Québec: Les Presses de L'Universite Laval, 1967), 44–59, at 57. On whether at this point the distinction is real or not, see my comments on Wippel in *Preface to Thomistic Metaphysics*, 151n41.

In this metaphysical analysis it is some individual, not the individual's essence, that one grasps as common to the two existences. But there should be no mystery that the individual is in some sense common. We note this fact with individuals and their other accidents. I grasp *this* coffee as both hot and cold and so conclude that *this* coffee is temperature-neutral while its temperatures are acts distinct from itself. Also, individuals neutral in certain respects are as much objects of intellection as universal essences like human and animal. I certainly cannot imagine the coffee as temperature-neutral nor myself as complexion-neutral.

Aquinas regularly juxtaposes the individual substance to its *esse*. For example, at SCG I.15 and II.15, Aquinas uses the phrase "possibile esse et non esse" for the individual generable and corruptible thing in relation to its *esse*. Later, in II.54, Aquinas considers the individual substance made up of matter and form to be composed with *esse* as a potency with its act. These texts suggest that Aquinas can carry out what the *De Ente* calls an *absolute consideratio* not just on a universal essence but also on an individual. The strongest confirmation of an absolute consideration of the individual is SCG I.65. In one argument for God's knowledge of singulars, Aquinas speaks both of the universal essence (*essentia universalis*) and the singular essence (*essentia singularis*).[46] For example, the universal essence of man as composed of soul and body and the essence of Socrates as composed of this body and this soul. Aquinas goes on to explain that because *esse* is had by individuals and because God is the universal principle of being, then God in knowing his essence knows

46. "Again by knowing the principles of which the essence of a thing is composed, we necessarily know that thing itself. Thus, by knowing a rational soul and a certain sort of body, we know man. Now, the singular essence [*singularis essentia*] is composed of designated matter and individuated form. Thus, the essence of Socrates is composed of this body and this soul, just as the universal essence [*essentia hominis universalis*] of man is composed of soul and body, as may be seen in *Metaphysics* VII. Hence, just as the latter principles fall within the definition of universal man, so the former principles would fall in the definition of Socrates if he could be defined. Hence, whoever has a knowledge of matter and of what designates matter, and also of form individuated in matter, must have a knowledge of the singular. But the knowledge of God extends to matter and to individuating accidents and forms. For, since His understanding is His essence, He must understand all things that in any way are in His essence. Now within His essence, as within the first source, there are virtually present all things that in any way have being [*esse*]. Matter and accidents are not absent from among these things, since matter is a being [*ens*] in potency and an accident is a being [*ens*] in another. Therefore, the knowledge of singulars is not lacking to God." SCG I.65, taken from *Summa Contra Gentiles*, trans. Anton C. Pegis (Notre Dame, Ind.: University of Notre Dame Press, 1975), 1:211–12. See also *De Pot.* VII, a. 2, ad 9.

singulars. So Aquinas does not understand the potency to *esse* that is essence simply as the universal. Potential essence is also the singular and individual. Without that admission the previous argument for God's knowledge of singulars would be impossible to understand. The data consisting of the individual's real existence and cognitional existence in sensation are what lead the mind to form an understanding of the individual as essence, or potency to *esse*. Among Thomists essence is regularly discussed in terms of the universal. The unfortunate result is that *esse* becomes just the fact of some instance of that universal. To arrive at the understanding of *esse* as a distinctive act of its own, the ability of essence to stand for a singular must be appropriated.

In conclusion, I wish to repeat my replies to Ashley's two objections. His first objection is that without knowledge of a real immaterial as at least possible the existential Thomist is still laboring under *ens mobile*. Hence, any results of his analysis of sensible things, even *actus essendi*, belong to natural philosophy. The objection does not realize that the analysis is being conducted in light of the real thing juxtaposed to itself cognitionally existing in sense. As a *sui generis* case of alteration, sensation is an instance outside the umbrella of *ens mobile*. As employing that instance, the analysis and its results are outside of the science of *ens mobile*. The second objection is that starting metaphysics without a knowledge of real immaterials would have the metaphysician beginning without a subject matter and then later proving its own subject matter. The objection fails to realize that an appropriation of sense cognition precisely as cognition enables one to intellect a wider sense of being than *ens mobile*. In the instances of the real thing juxtaposed to itself cognitionally existing, the intellect discovers a wider sense of being than *ens mobile*, which is discovered in cases of change that involve the destruction of a previous form. Both the physicist and the metaphysician discover the intelligibility that is their subject matter. Each then proceeds by an analysis of their respective data and folds the results of that analysis into the commonality that each had discovered. Hence, the physicist comes to grasp *ens mobile* as a composite of substrate and determination, while the metaphysician comes to grasp his intelligibility as a composite of essence and existence. It is correct that in this approach to metaphysics the metaphysician does not yet understand that the *ratio entis* could be instantiated in a *habens esse* that is a real immaterial. That knowledge can be left to the unfolding of the science. No philosopher knows everything about his subject matter at the beginning of his science. Even the physicist knows *ens mobile* before he understands its composite nature. Why cannot the immateriality characteristic of what is an intelligibility already distinct from *ens mobile* be left to the unfolding of metaphysical science?

4

Contraries in One

Contingency, Analogy, and God in
Transcendental Thomism

STEPHEN M. FIELDS, SJ

"Oh to vex me," said the seventeenth-century poet and divine John Donne, "contraries meet in one."[1] The history of thought has long venerated the doctrine of analogy as overcoming the paradoxes that mesmerized the Jacobean sensibility. Heraclitus and the Stoics adumbrated it, for instance, in their principle of "the sympathy of the whole," which claimed that the tensions immanent in the visible world are ultimately reconciled in an underlying invisible harmony.[2] Plato located analogy's ground in his anamnetic epistemology, which links sensible realities to the infinite world of spiritual forms.[3] Aristotle found it in the *eros* of the mind. Knowledge obtains only because the intellect is impelled by something divine toward which it aims, but never satisfactorily reaches.[4] In Christianity, analogy has been closely linked with the sacramental vision of reality. Finding inspiration in Bishop Butler's magnum opus,

1. John Donne, "Holy Sonnet 19," line 1.
2. Ernst Cassirer, *An Essay on Man* (New Haven, Conn.: Yale University Press, 1944), 94–95 and 222–23.
3. See especially *Phaedo*.
4. Cited in Maurice Blondel, *Action (1893)*, trans. Oliva Blanchette (South Bend, Ind.: University of Notre Dame Press, 1984), 388 (original pagination).

John Henry Newman, for instance, spoke of the church as the earthly society that unfolds the hidden economy of grace.[5] Developing this point more recently, Avery Dulles included analogy in his list of the fifteen indispensable criteria of authentic Catholic theology.[6]

The school of Thomism known as "transcendental" has made its own creative contribution to analogy's development. Philosophical at root, it has been harnessed by theology as a dogmatic hermeneutic. The Jesuit Joseph Maréchal (1878–1944), a francophone Belgian or Walloon, produced between 1922 and 1926 one of the movement's groundbreaking works, *The Point of Departure of Metaphysics*.[7] Most significant is the last of the series' five volumes, *Le Thomisme devant la philosophie critique*, loosely rendered as *Thomism in Dialogue with Kant*.[8] Several contemporary philosophers owe their inspiration to Maréchal, including the Canadian Bernard Lonergan (1904–84), the Austrian Emerich Coreth (1919–2006), and the German Johannes Baptist Lotz (1903–92). This study will deal with another German, Karl Rahner (1904–84), Maréchal's most renowned disciple. It will first explain the logic according to which the Belgian develops his distinctive understanding of analogy. Subsequently, it will explain how Rahner expands his mentor's insights in order to rethink the traditional Thomist doctrine of God. Two sections constitute this essay; each considers how our thinkers seek to resolve a vexing paradox. The first section concerns the antinomy between contingency and necessity in finite being. The second handles the tension between the dynamism of love and the absolute's essential simplicity. Whereas analogy solves the first paradox, it encounters steep hurdles when approaching the second.

Maréchal's approach to the first paradox centers on a controversial thesis. If philosophical realism is to establish metaphysics, precisely as a

5. John Henry Cardinal Newman, *Apologia Pro Vita Sua* (New York: Doubleday, 1989), 132, referring to Joseph Butler, *Analogy of Religion* (originally published in 1736).

6. Avery Dulles, SJ, "Criteria of Catholic Theology," *Communio* 22 (1995): 303–15, at 305.

7. The origin of the movement is usually attributed to Pierre Rousselot, SJ, *Intelligence: Sense of Being, Faculty of God*, trans. Andrew Tallon (Milwaukee, Wis.: Marquette University Press, 1999 [1908]).

8. Joseph Maréchal, SJ, *Le point de départ de la métaphysique*, 5 vols. (Brussels / Paris: Desclée de Brouwer / Éditions universelle, 1923–26; 2nd ed., 1944–49); see the one-volume redaction, *A Maréchal Reader*, ed. and trans. Joseph Donceel, SJ (New York: Herder and Herder, 1970).

universal science, the tension between necessity and contingency cannot be resolved on the basis of the *a posteriori* alone. The Jesuit emphasizes texts such as *In Meta.* IV, l. 6: "For the first principles are known through the very *light of the agent intellect.*" These principles include non-contradiction, the *a priori* law without which thought is impossible. But the Belgian is firmly committed to the classic hallmark of Thomist realism: namely, that nothing exists in the intellect unless it first obtains in sensibility. Accordingly, first principles, although virtually innate in the agent intellect, can only become explicit because, *a posteriori*, a particular datum of sense is assimilated, abstracted, and judged as real.[9]

Controversy

Other Thomists hotly contest Maréchal's thesis. These include John Knasas, a contemporary disciple of Étienne Gilson (1884–1978).[10] He argues that our knowledge of necessity and universality, of the infinite, and of God is strictly *a posteriori*. *Ens materiale* is encountered, he claims, not as a finite participation of the infinite, but as the commonality in real things. Sensuous data suffice to objectify being, which, strictly on the basis of this commonality, can only subsequently be affirmed as *esse subsistens*.[11] As for "the light of the agent intellect," this, he says, "is automatically able to abstract the notion of being from which the first principle follows." In support, he cites *In De An.*, a. 5, co., where Thomas observes that some believe the agent intellect to be "nothing but the … knowledge of the first … principles in us." This "is impossible," continues the Common Doctor, because these principles are known "through abstraction from the singular."[12]

In support of his own argument, the Walloon could cite exactly the

---

9. Donceel, *Maréchal Reader*, 143.

10. John F. X. Knasas, *Being and Some Twentieth-Century Thomists* (New York: Fordham University Press, 2003). For another critique, see Benedict M. Ashley, OP, *The Way toward Wisdom: An Interdisciplinary and Intercultural Approach to Metaphysics* (Notre Dame, Ind.: University of Notre Dame Press, 2006), esp. 44–54. See also Gerald A. McCool, SJ, *From Unity to Pluralism: The Internal Evolution of Thomism* (New York: Fordham University Press, 1989), 117–18, citing Jacques Maritain, *The Degrees of Knowledge*, trans. Gerald B. Phelan (New York: Scribner, 1959), 71–72, 107–8, 128–29; see also McCool, *Unity*, 161–62, citing Étienne Gilson, *Réalisme thomiste et critique de la connaissance* (Paris: Vrin, 1947), chap. 5.

11. Knasas, *Being and Some Twentieth-Century Thomists*, 54.

12. Ibid., 60.

same text. It does not deny that the ground of metaphysics grasped in the first principles can be explained only by a subtle synthesis of the intellect's *a priori* and *a posteriori* ranges. With due respect to some of Maréchal's critics, the crucial issue for him lies not so much in his eagerness to establish a dialogue with the Kantian ego. Nor does it lie in his creative evincing of a transcendental deduction to establish metaphysical realism, however important to his method this may be. It lies in providing a satisfactory answer to the basic question concerning how the human mind can know that which intrinsically transcends the limits of sensuous objectivation. The crucial issue, in short, concerns vindicating a rule considered since Socrates as absolutely fundamental to metaphysics: that like can be known only by like.

The history of philosophy manifests a replete sensitivity to this rule, although its application varies. Henry of Ghent, a contemporary of Bonaventure, agrees that the human intellect can know something of the object *a posteriori* through sensory intuition. Following Aristotle, Henry avers that this knowledge does not exclude the general influence of the first cause, without which no motion is possible. Henry reminds us, however, that knowing *what is true of an object* and knowing *precisely its truth* entail distinct, albeit interrelated, mental operations. Whereas knowing what is true of an object obtains by abstraction from the phantasm, knowing the object's truth as such requires an *a priori* constitutive of mind. As a card-carrying Augustinian, he finds a solution in "illumination."[13]

Kant also posits an intellectually immanent *a priori* as a condition for the possibility of truth. For him, the idea of God arises from the internal dynamics of the transcendental dialectic. It seeks a first cause of the categories, under which the transcendental analytic schematizes the appearances of the world intuited through the transcendental aesthetic.[14] Mind's internal dynamics thus lend great force for Kant to the teleological argument. Kant's *a priori*, however, demonstrates only that the idea of God is logically possible, not that it objectively exists.[15]

13. Henry of Ghent, *Summa quaestionum ordinariarium* I, 3, in *Medieval Philosophy: Essential Readings with Commentary*, ed. Gyula Klima (Malden, Mass.: Blackwell, 2007), 105.

14. Immanuel Kant, *Prolegomena to Any Future Metaphysics*, trans. Paul Carus, rev. James W. Ellington (Indianapolis, Ind.: Hackett, 1977), 88–89.

15. Immanuel Kant, *Critique of Pure Reason*, trans. Norman Kemp Smith (New York: St Martin's, 1965), 519–20 (A622–23/B650–51).

For his part, Maréchal uses the rule to warrant the following thesis. If the existence of God is to be constitutive of human intelligence, and if being is to be grasped precisely as analogous, then without an interplay with the *a priori* the *a posteriori* will never, of itself, demonstrate infinite being as anything more than regulative of thought. Analogy cannot be grounded in illumination because Thomist realism disavows it. Ironically, however, knowledge of God must be grounded, as Kant claims, in a transcendental dialectic. According to the Walloon, following Thomas, this dialectic affirms infinite being when the mind "corrects" its objective concepts.[16] This correction is also known as *excessus*; it holds high significance for Rahner in *Spirit in the World*.[17] But if Maréchal is to counter Kant's agnosticism, he must, as a metaphysician, further press a vital question: "How could we perform this correction since, not knowing God directly, we have no way of comparing him with his creatures?"[18] He discovers an answer in his creative analysis of the first principle, "Whatever is, is."

First Principle

This fundamental axiom of thought, according to the transcendental school, places "essence" in metaphysical unity with itself. In other words, the first principle explains how the subjective species, sensuously intuited as a particular datum from the world, can become, properly speaking, an object of thought. It explains how to resolve the paradox underscored by Thomas in *ST* I, qq. 84 and 86: namely, that our intelligence knows what is necessary and unchangeable, even as it knows the objects of experience that are dependent and variable.[19] If someone were to claim, Maréchal speculates, that the intelligible species and the object of thought are univocally one and the same, then the distinction between contingency and necessity would effectively collapse.[20] By itself, the species entails no necessity, either subjective or objective, precisely because

16. Donceel, *Maréchal Reader*, 144.

17. Karl Rahner, SJ, *Spirit in the World*, trans. William V. Dych, SJ (New York: Herder and Herder, 1968), 145, 209, 394–98; see also Thomas Sheehan, *Karl Rahner: The Philosophical Foundations* (Athens: Ohio State University Press, 1987), 205 and 226.

18. Donceel, *Maréchal Reader*, 144.

19. *ST* I, q. 84, a. 1, ad 3, and a. 3, co.; Donceel, *Maréchal Reader*, 94.

20. Donceel, *Maréchal Reader*, 92.

the species, as a mere accidental modality of thought, constitutes a "simple *pros ti*," a "what" that is merely directed *toward* objectivation. Only under the first principle can the species emerge in conscious knowledge as an essence. As Maréchal metaphorically opines, when the first principle "freezes" the species precisely in identity with itself, then whatever is (a species), *is* (known precisely as an essence). Because knowledge entails the dynamic self-unification of essence, Rahner, for his part, defines it as "the self-presence of being."[21]

On account of this freezing, the subjective species, which is only variable, assumes the necessity requisite of an authentic object of knowledge.[22] It is therefore contradictory to affirm that the first principle, precisely as *a priori*, can emerge from the variable species as intuited *a posteriori*. On the contrary, in order for any object to be judged precisely as real, existence itself must be implicitly affirmed. Because "whatever is, is," any proper object of knowledge must be endowed with "a supratemporal, unchangeable, absolute aspect."[23] Any object of knowledge must, in short, be "immutably determined [in] relation to the absolute norm of being."[24]

Other corollaries follow. On the one hand, the first principle is analytic. As an immutable law of logic, it forbids contradictions. On the other hand, it is also synthetic.[25] The Belgian undergirds this last claim by appealing to the transcendental argument of Socrates, also known as retorsion. St. Thomas himself uses it in *ST* I, q. 2, a. 1: "It is self-evident [*per se notum*] that truth exists, for he who denies its existence" admits that "it is true that truth does not exist; but if something is true, then truth must exist." Even when any radical doubt or denial is asserted or affirmed, the absolute is inescapably asserted and affirmed as the implicit condition of possibility of the doubt and denial. Retorsion represents another form of the first principle. In other words, "whatever is" (that truth does not exist), "is" (truly exists). For this reason, the Jesuit defines retorsion as "an authentic transcendental deduction of the ontological

---

21. Karl Rahner, SJ, *Hearer of the Word: Laying the Foundation for a Philosophy of Religion*, trans. Joseph Donceel, SJ (New York: Continuum, 1994), 28.
22. Donceel, *Maréchal Reader*, 93.
23. Ibid., 94.
24. Ibid., 93.
25. Ibid., 91.

affirmation."[26] In other words, because logical truth ineluctably entails ontological truth, the first principle, precisely as analytic, is synthetic.

As a synthetic *a priori*, the first principle demonstrates conclusively that relativism, phenomenalism, and agnosticism contain "a hidden contradiction."[27] In fact, the first principle throws the gauntlet down before all nonmetaphysical philosophies. Exposed as artificial, they are, as Hamlet might say, "Hoist with [their] own petar[d]."[28] If the *a priori* constitutes the inescapable condition of knowledge, then it follows that the real order, precisely as the objective ground of being, is ratified in every judgment made by the subject. Maréchal's recovery of retorsion in Aquinas thus lies at the core of his argument.

Retorsion

For his part, Knasas raises probing questions about the efficacy of retorsion. According to its proponents, retorsion, he argues, entails that "any attempt to doubt the framework [of a proposition] employs the framework and so nullifies the doubt." In other words, "real doubt of the framework presupposes the ability to mentally stand apart from the framework." Because this "is impossible," "one concludes that the framework is objective."[29] In response to this understanding, Knasas reminds us of the inescapable context of thought. We are aware, for instance, of how varied contexts can color even our best judgments. Consequently, he believes that retorsion may well be caught in one of the contextual frameworks of our thinking.[30] Because these "can be limited and distortive," the universality of claims established by retorsion is undermined. Retorsion, he continues, is most likely indicative merely of "how we have to think rather than the way reality is." It thus "fails to beat the Kantian at his own game."[31] Because retorsion does not establish metaphysical realism, the first principle may be analytic, as Maréchal claims, but certainly not synthetic. In response to the Transcendental Thomists who

26. Ibid., 96.
27. Ibid., 94.
28. William Shakespeare, *Hamlet*, act 3, sc. 4.
29. Knasas, *Being and Some Twentieth-Century Thomists*, 115.
30. Ibid.
31. Ibid., 116.

cite *ST* I, q. 2, a. 1, in which Thomas seems to use retorsion to demonstrate the self-evidence of truth, Knasas argues that presupposed in
this text is the fundamental *a posteriori* premise that, according to him,
grounds Thomist realism: "Thought is about the real."[32] As a result,
Thomas is immune to any criticism of retorsion, because he actually
does not employ it.

Let us respond by first quoting Maréchal himself. Precisely as a *performatory* contradiction, retorsion entails that:

When you say there is no truth, you affirm implicitly that to your present
negative statement there corresponds a certain objective disharmony between
thought in general and outside reality.... For to admit a relation of truth is tantamount to admitting, outside of your present and subjective thought, "something" which "controls" it, a norm with respect to which it is inevitably either
true or false.[33]

His claim is threefold. First, retorsion discloses the necessary conditions
for the possibility of asserting the proposition that denies truth. Second,
in so disclosing these, retorsion renders the proposition incoherent. This
incoherence does not obtain on the basis of the framework from which
the terms of the proposition emerge. On the contrary, it obtains on the
basis of the condition of possibility of any framework precisely as such.
Third, this incoherence immediately establishes the correspondence
theory of truth as *adequatio rei et intellectus*. The intellect must, in other
words, submit to an objective reality: in this case, a necessary norm imposed on it. Retorsion demonstrates, therefore, that when judgments are
made, being—the absolute—is implicitly opposed to the relative (the
specific terms of the proposition judged). In short, retorsion evinces the
first principle as a synthetic *a priori*, because it shows that at least some-
thing is known with certainty and hence unconditionally true.

Furthermore, Maréchal argues that "a merely logical contradiction
'in the terms' [of a proposition], independently of any ... concealed ...
presupposing, would be unable to yield us ... reality on the rebound. He
who tries to demonstrate the absolute necessity of being ... by analyzing
concepts ... would commit the ... error of the ontological argument."[34]

32. Ibid., 128.
33. Donceel, *Maréchal Reader*, 90.
34. Ibid., 210.

Knasas's objection contains this very error. If retorsion were equivalent to Anselm's response to the fool in *Proslogion*, we could surely agree with Knasas that it would hardly convince a Kantian. Anselm, we will recall, argues that his definition of God as "that than which a greater cannot be conceived" is synthetic. If it were not, it would only be analytic. But if it were, then the definition would be intrinsically contradictory. To be its definition, "God" entails extramental existence.[35] Disputing Anselm, Maréchal follows Thomas and agrees with Kant that only sensible experience can serve as the ground of knowledge.[36] Certainly Kant wanted to avoid Anselm's mistake in his own transcendental deduction of the *a priori* categories. Whatever its purported weaknesses, Kant's deduction, as retorsion, intends to be synthetic.[37]

The previous quotation from Maréchal receives support in Lonergan's insight that the question of "how the subject gets beyond himself to the known" is misleading. The subject knows himself in and through the first principle.[38] As both synthetic and analytic, it shows that other judgments are reasonable and possible for the relentless "task of adding increments to [our] merely habitual knowledge."[39] Advancing a similar position, Gaston Isaye (1903–84), another Transcendental Thomist, contends that in retorsion *we* do not possess the fact that we know and that being is intelligible to us. On the contrary, this fact possesses *us*, and it forms the ground of our every act as human persons.[40]

Before concluding this defense of retorsion, let us respond to Knasas's assertion that we could be deluded in our knowledge of the *a priori*. He means, in other words, that the *a priori* may arise merely from one contextual framework of our minds. It seems that this claim would effectively dispense with the principle of noncontradiction altogether. From his perspective as a logician of language, Otto Muck of Innsbruck University offers a confirmation. Building on the semantic theory of Paul Lorenzen of Erlangen University, his careful study, too detailed

---

35. Anselm of Canterbury, *Proslogion* IV.

36. See *ST* I, q. 2, a. 1.

37. Kant, *Critique of Pure Reason*, 305–7 (A306–9/B362–66).

38. Bernard J. F. Lonergan, SJ, *Insight: A Study of Human Understanding* (San Francisco, Calif.: Harper and Row, 1978), chap. 11.

39. Ibid., 278.

40. Martin X. Moleski, SJ, "Retorsion: The Method and Metaphysics of Gaston Isaye," *International Philosophical Quarterly* 17 (1977): 59–83, at 63.

to reproduce here, shows that the principle of noncontradiction constitutes an *a priori* norm systemically inherent in language as such.[41] The principle is not dependent on any special language. If it were, its origin could then be claimed to lie in some distinctive context or sequestered framework of our thinking. On the contrary, however, the rule is part and parcel of every context and framework. It cannot be denied without a performatory contradiction. Because its negation "is inadmissible" in any language, it grounds "the possibility of the coherence" for "the linguistic expression of any knowledge whatsoever."[42] In short, as *a priori*, the first principle imports ontological validity.

Abstraction

Let us now consider Maréchal's view of the role that abstraction plays in harmonizing the *a priori* and *a posteriori* ranges of the intellect. The Walloon draws attention to the Neo-Platonic motif of emanation and return in Thomas's anthropology. According to the Angelic Doctor, the soul is both the agent and the end or *telos* of sensibility. Just as any cause necessarily insinuates itself into its effects, so the soul emanates its influence into the material powers. But it does so in degrees.[43] Only at the level of the imagination's synthesis of the intuited datum does the intellect work with direct command on sensibility. Here the intellect serves as the imagination's "immediate principle" and "proximate end." Because the phantasm's unity *precisely within matter* depends on the intellect's direct insinuation into it, the datum is raised above the level of mere sensibility.[44] This elevation, however, does not constitute abstraction, however much it does constitute its necessary cause.

Abstraction itself obtains when the unified phantasm, imbued now with spirit, returns to the intellect. It becomes incorporated into "the term of the intellect's natural activity." As a result, the phantasm bathes in the "light of the agent intellect which is always in act."[45] In other

---

41. Otto Muck, SJ, "The Logical Structure of Transcendental Method," *International Philosophical Quarterly* 9 (1969): 342–62, at 356 and 359.

42. Ibid., 356.

43. Donceel, *Maréchal Reader*, 132, referring to *ST* I, q. 77, a. 4.

44. Donceel, *Maréchal Reader*, 133.

45. Ibid., 134.

words, the species and the light become one act under the intellect's finality. It must be emphasized, however, as both Maréchal and Rahner do, that the proper act of the intellect in relation to the phantasm never obtains in isolation from the phantasm.[46] The *a posteriori* is never abandoned in abstraction and judgment, precisely because the phantasm constitutes an intrinsic symbol. Such a symbol makes present in its empirical form another reality.[47] In other words, the phantasm serves as the necessary ontological medium between the intuited object and the consciously known object, and so as a medium of our affirmations of finite being and of absolute being. The phantasm is thus a fundamental ground of the analogy of being, its *sine qua non*.

Accordingly, precisely because the species is incorporated into the subject's own act, the question for Maréchal becomes: what accounts for the objectivation of the immanent object over against the intuiting, knowing subject? The answer can only be that the object is known as distinctly separate from the subject by contrast with the "speculative unity of being."[48] What is finite is consciously known precisely as such when it is projected against what is implicitly known as infinite by the subject—the *a priori* first principle, in other words. This *a priori* cannot be known as a concomitant result of knowing the species alone, because, argues the Jesuit, the highest ontological unity that conditions abstraction is only quantitative, not speculative.

Maréchal justifies this last claim by discerning precisely what contribution our intellect makes to the immanent species. He develops his argument on the basis of *ST* I, q. 84, a. 7, which states that the "quiddity of nature ... exists in corporeal matter." But, says the Belgian, the unity of material quiddities is grounded in quantitative being. As a result, although quiddity can be multiplied indefinitely as instances of their common universal concept, it cannot serve to unify the known object in the ontological order beyond an undetermined number.[49] According to Maréchal, Kant, for his part, stopped precisely here in his account of the object's unification. For the great Königsberger, the *a priori* relation

46. Ibid., 140. Rahner, *Spirit in the World*, 121; see Sheehan, *Philosophical Foundations*, 202.

47. Karl Rahner, SJ, "The Theology of the Symbol," in *Theological Investigations* 4, trans. Kevin Smyth (Baltimore, Md.: Helicon, 1966), 221–52, at 244.

48. Donceel, *Maréchal Reader*, 141.

49. Ibid.

of the categories to sensibility suffices for judgment. This relation, as we know, obviates metaphysics. Although the judgment in Kant cannot function without the governance of the transcendental dialectic, still, because God, soul, and world are concepts without percepts, the faculty of judgment does not unify beyond the numerical diversity of the categories on the one hand and the numerical diversity of those phenomena that they schematize on the other hand.[50] Hence, no phenomenon can be noumenally known or, properly speaking, conform to the first principle "whatever is, is."

Before summarizing my argument, I would like to offer a word in passing on Rahner's creative retrieval of emanation and return in Aquinas. It lays the foundation for his metaphysics of the *Realsymbol*. Like his Belgian mentor, Rahner understands the soul as a dynamic form that emanates itself in and through the body. The soul infuses the corporeal faculties such that, by means of them, it fulfills its own proper function. In reaching its perfection by means of the body, the soul returns to itself. It incorporates sensible data from the world into its own immanent activity. It thus constructs the raw material of intuition into a proper object of knowledge, whose truth only spirit can posit.[51] The body does not serve as a mere appendage of the soul, much less a hindrance to it. On the contrary, the body constitutes the symbol within which the soul mediates itself "immediately," as Rahner claims.[52] This means that the symbol (in this case, the body) contains intrinsically, and makes possible, what it, as an empirical medium, represents (in this case, the person's analogous knowledge of being). Morever, being itself—being pure and simple, as well as the being of substances—is "*realsymbolic*."[53] We will soon examine the theological use to which Rahner puts this claim.

Let us now review the conclusions that we have reached thus far. If quantitative being is the highest unity obtainable on the basis of the *a posteriori*; and if, as we have seen throughout our analysis, objectivation cannot obtain by this unity alone; then when Aquinas says that the first principle "comes from without to someone who, as it were, pos-

50. Ibid., 141–42.

51. Rahner, "Theology of the Symbol," esp. 232–33 and 246–47.

52. Ibid., 244.

53. See Stephen M. Fields, SJ, *Being as Symbol: On the Origins and Development of Karl Rahner's Metaphysics* (Washington, D.C.: Georgetown University Press, 2000).

sesses it by nature," it is reasonable to infer that this *a priori* is virtually immanent in the agent intellect without in any sense determining the absolute.[54] For its part, retorsion evinces this *a priori* as synthetic. It therefore follows that "whatever is, is," because every finite judgment implicitly affirms the infinite. The first principle thus contains the seeds of Maréchal's doctrine of analogy.

Analogy

Resolving the paradox of contingency and necessity, the first principle grounds the objectivation of the material world's quiddities. This obtains in an excessus that makes possible the certain affirmation of the existence of God. Because the analogy of being thus springs from objectivation, we must now probe into its conditions of possibility. Earlier it was mentioned that excessus requires the mind "to correct" its determined concepts. In explaining the definition of this term, we come to the heart of Maréchal's originality: his distinctive theory of the intellect's "dynamic finality."

The Belgian first proceeds phenomenologically. He notes that the human intellect experiences in every freshly intuited datum its dynamic capacity to expand. About this expansion, Aquinas himself observes: "Our intellect extends into infinity in knowing. This is shown by the fact that whatever finite quantity may be presented, our intellect can think of a greater one."[55] Although the knowing subject verifies this dynamism as a psychological necessity, logic also confirms it. The immanently assimilated phantasm is, by definition, relative; it is, after all, specific and determined.[56] But all determination, as Spinoza reminds us, entails negation.[57] Negation, however, must imply an implicit affirmation; determination must obtain against some background other than nonbeing.

According to the Jesuit, in our very knowledge of the relative, we implicitly gain access to a higher epistemic range. This can only be what

---

54. *In Meta.* IV, l. 6; *Maréchal Reader*, 143.

55. *SCG* I.43.7; *Maréchal Reader*, 164 and 166.

56. Donceel, *Maréchal Reader*, 144.

57. Baruch Spinoza (Letter 50 to Jelles), cited in G. W. F. Hegel, *Hegel's Logic*, trans. William Wallace (Oxford: Clarendon, 1975), 135.

is not relative, but absolute. For his part, Hegel would concur with Maréchal. For instance, Hegel criticizes Kant, who fails to grasp so fundamental an inference. "A very little consideration might show," Hegel says, "that to call a thing finite or limited proves by implication the very presence of the infinite and unlimited."[58] Accordingly, if nothing more than contingency can be sensuously intuited, and if our grasp of contingency implies the absolute, then, the Walloon concludes, thought constitutes "a movement" toward God (infinite being) as the intellect's final cause. It draws "us constantly 'beyond' that which may still be represented by [determined] concepts."[59]

Not satisfied, however, Maréchal wishes to establish the intellect's dynamic finality as an inescapable law of cognition. He wishes, therefore, to bring it under retorsion. As we know, doing so would establish it as a first principle of thought immune to denial. He begins by asserting that the intellect's dynamism establishes the empirical ground for the possibility of the existence of absolute being. In other words, because thinking begins with sensuous intuition, and because no intuited object can ever halt the mind's movement, the intellect's tendency toward the absolute is existentially necessary for every human subject. Against the Kantian criticism that the notion of the absolute generated by the mind could merely be some finite notion arising from cognition's inner workings, he responds that, because the notion is empirically grounded and subjectively necessary, the absolute must necessarily exist. Because the absolute is necessary in and through itself, it constitutes the universal ground of all possible being, including its own. Because the absolute is necessarily possible, insofar as thinking could not obtain without it, the absolute must objectively exist.

A performatory contradiction thus obtains when the absolute's real existence is denied. The denial is an affirmation that the absolute does not exist as extramental reality. But because the absolute's objective existence is a necessary condition for the possibility of every affirmation, the denial implicitly affirms the absolute's objective reality.[60] The Walloon thus supplies to the ontological argument what it lacks: an empirical

---

58. *Hegel's Logic*, 92.
59. Donceel, *Maréchal Reader*, 145.
60. Ibid., 183–85.

and existential ground. It follows that whatever is (God's psychological necessity), is (God's objective existence).

We can now see more clearly how the Jesuit's theory of objectivation follows from the finality of the dynamic intellect. As we noted in the previous section, the immanent species is detached from its unity with the subject's own epistemic act when it is projected against the speculative unity of being. The finite form, assimilated by the subject, is "referred to the proper end of" the mind's dynamism.[61] Because this end is infinite and absolute, the subject is able to acquire a new determination. The contingent datum is known precisely as such. It is "spun off," so to speak, by the mind as it ineluctably moves beyond finitude. To use Maréchal's own metaphor, the object is thus "frozen" in the real order as an entity eternally affirmed as true.

When the Belgian claims that the mind corrects its determined concepts and that it freezes the immanent object, he gives new meaning to excessus. This dialectical act results from the reciprocal action of two distinguishable finalities of the intellect that are actually inseparable. On the one hand, an "antecedent" finality affirms the object as existing independently of the subject. On the other hand, a "consequent" finality is nothing less than the absolute, which alone could confer on the intellect a lasting surcease.[62] But the consequent finality suffuses the antecedent finality. In other words, objectivation cannot obtain without the mind's supernatural end. It therefore follows that the contrast between finite and infinite that causes objectivation results from the tension between these two dovetailed finalities.[63] The finite is grasped as a subordinate end of a process whose adequate end can only be absolute. The hallmarks of truth, necessity and university, borne by every finite object antecedently affirmed, are derived, then, from the consequent finality.

In sum, analogy, to use another metaphor, can be defined as the dynamic "releasing" of the marks of absolute being in every finite judgment.[64] The *a posteriori* becomes our gateway, not only to the determined knowledge of created essences, but also to the unqualified field of first philosophy. We may in fact further conclude that the *a posteri-*

---

61. Ibid., 183.
62. Ibid., 149–51 and 164–65.
63. Ibid., 152, 162, 190–91.
64. See Rahner, *Spirit in the World*, 404–5.

ori becomes for the Walloon an intrinsic symbol of this range. If, as we recall, such a symbol makes present in its empirical form the invisible transcendent, then each and every judgment about the world is naturally endowed with the potential to lead us by *excessus* to God. In the finite datum, therefore, contraries meet. Because of Maréchal's help, this paradox should vex us no longer.

Developing his Jesuit confrere's doctrine of analogy, Rahner attempts to reconcile his own paradox. Given that an analysis of the conditions for the possibility of finite judgments enables us to affirm the existence of God, can we proceed to show, by metaphysics alone, that God is free, loving, and personal? These three terms imply each other. To be free means to act without constraint; to love means to desire an object spontaneously; these qualities, together with intelligence, define the essential distinctiveness of personhood. If Rahner's demonstration is successful, he would accomplish a breakthrough in Thomist philosophy. For his part, Aquinas is influenced by Aristotle, whose discussion of the prime mover makes clear that, however necessary divinity is, it cannot be the subject of love, if by love we imply that the infinite being desires something which it does not have.[65] This cannot be. The prime mover is pure actuality, immune to change, and perfect because it contemplates its own absolute self-knowledge. Thus spared love, the infinite reality, at least for Aristotle, is also spared freedom and personhood.[66]

Being as Free

Rahner begins his argument in *Hearer of the Word*, his extended essay in the philosophy of religion.[67] Knowing, he contends, entails volition or will as a necessary cause. Will, traditionally defined as the intellect's ap-

65. See, e.g., *ST* I, q. 20, a. 1; and the critique of Robert O. Johann, *The Meaning of Love: An Essay Towards a Metaphysics of Intersubjectivity* (Westminster, Md.: Newman, 1955), 7. For further analysis, see Stephen Fields, SJ, "Analogy in Aquinas and Denys the Pseudo-Areopagite," in "Thomas Aquinas and the Greek Fathers," ed. Michael Dauphinais, Roger W. Nutt, Andrew Hofer, OP (Naples, Fla.: Sapientia Press, 2019).

66. Aristotle, *Metaphysics* 1072b. For Aristotle, the prime mover is the object of love of all sublunary causes, which it draws to completion as a final cause. See also W. D. Ross's commentary in Aristotle's *Metaphysics* (Oxford: Clarendon, 1924), 1:cxxv–cliv.

67. My explication, which involves considerable interpretation, follows *Hearer of the Word*, chap. 7.

petite, implies yearning. It explains the intellect's dynamic drive toward its absolute term. As such, it also explains objectivation. Where there is volition, he continues, freedom is necessarily entailed.

It follows, therefore, that we can, and indeed must, freely will ourselves as contingent beings—at least implicitly. To refuse to do so flies in the face of an indubitable datum of human existence: the incompleteness of our knowledge. To acquire knowledge, we must, over time, ask questions and grope laboriously for answers. To find these, we must inquire, often without success, into the world that confronts us heteronomously as a brute given. To deny this claim only affirms it. Because our knowledge depends on external phenomena lodged in time and space, we find ourselves inescapably finite, contingent, and caused. In addition to these claims, Rahner, borrowing from Maréchal, asserts two further claims already familiar to us. First, it is undeniable that our very contingency serves as the ground of necessity and universality. Second, the analogy of being resolves the tension between our *a priori* and *a posteriori* knowledge. Collectively, these claims enable Rahner to conclude that, if freedom lies in the core of knowledge, then freedom must be intrinsic not only to finite reality but also to God, the infinite being.

An important corollary follows. Because we must will ourselves as contingent, doing so is tantamount to ratifying that we are posited, and do not posit ourselves. In other words, because we are by nature contingent, we are not by nature necessary. We could not have existed. The same applies to the universal cosmos of finite reality. That it, together with ourselves, does in fact exist implies that we are posited by a being who is not contingent but absolute.

Thus far the argument leaves us with little to quibble with. Its next inferences, however, are crucial. We must be posited freely by the absolute. Rahner has already shown that the absolute entails freedom. Accordingly, if the absolute did not posit us freely but necessarily, then we would be necessary, just as our cause is necessary. In that case, we would be posited necessarily by the absolute as beings who could or could not exist. This is a contradiction. If we were posited necessarily by the absolute, we would be beings who must exist. Because we are radically contingent, however, we could not have existed. If follows, he concludes, that it is absurd to claim that contingent beings can be posited necessarily by absolute being. Let us withhold a critique of Rahner's argument until after we have inquired into how he uses it to advance the Christian understanding of God.

Divine Kenosis

Rahner opines that, when facing the mystery of the incarnation, both faith and reason "blink and stutter." This fundamental revelation presents us with a paradox that seems outright contradictory. God, who is immune to change, assumes, in the human nature of Jesus, what God is not. Aiming to obviate an absurdity, theology has traditionally claimed that the change entailed in the doctrine occurs only "in the created reality," not in the divinity. Accordingly, "all change and history ... remain on [the finite] side of absolute gulf." God and the world of becoming are thus prevented "from mingling."[68] The integrity of God's infinite simplicity thus rests assured.

Rahner, however, finds this approach unsatisfactory. Strictly to divide the predicates "absolute" and "dynamic" between infinite and finite reality misses "by a hairsbreath" what is most important to the incarnation: namely, that human history really is God's own.[69] The doctrine's paradox is better stated as follows: "He who is unchangeable in himself can *himself* become subject to change *in something else*."[70] But according to Rahner, this statement itself presents a challenge. "Become" must be defined as a divine predicate without in any sense compromising the absolute's immutability.[71] The German claims to find the synthesis of this dialectic in his interpretation of St. Paul's famous text about the preexistent Word: "He emptied himself, taking the nature of a slave and being made like human beings" (Phil 2:7).

Rahner's interpretation relies on the argument previously discussed. If metaphysics shows that the core of infinite being is loving, free, and personal, then a basis is laid in reason for defining God's self-emptying. The kenotic text means that God "expresses himself" in, through, and

68. Karl Rahner, SJ, "On the Theology of the Incarnation," in *Theological Investigations* 4:105–20, at 113.

69. Ibid., 113n3.

70. Ibid., 113.

71. Ibid., 113–14n3.

because of the love that is also essential to his absolute simplicity. God's love consists of a "prodigal freedom" by which he gives himself away.[72] In creating the world from nothing, for instance, God freely empties himself by constituting what is "other" precisely as such. In so doing, God manifests his unity without compromising his "unoriginated origin."[73] Pure act does not entail stasis but dynamism; and for its part, the divine dynamism does not entail change. Furthermore, in the incarnation, what God has constituted as other than God is brought immanently into God.[74] God thus creates by taking otherness on; and he takes it on by filling it totally with himself. Accordingly, "the finite itself [is] given an infinite depth and is no longer a contrast to the infinite, but that which the infinite himself has become."[75] It will be apparent that Rahner uses the metaphysics of the *Realsymbol* to structure his theology of creation and redemption. He thus posits a panentheism that purportedly preserves the freedom of the divine transcendence, as well as the distinct integrity of creation, in which God is nonetheless immanent.

Critique

The first problem in Rahner's extended argument concerns his claim that, under contradiction, we contingent beings must be posited freely by the absolute person. This is questionable. Plotinus has shown us that no contradiction obtains in the absolute's necessary positing of contingent beings. As the intrinsic dynamism of goodness overflows from the One, it constitutes the subsequent grades of reality as images of their preceding archetypes. The very nature of goodness entails the sharing of its bounty. Each emanation intrinsically contains its immediate origin, but in a limited and restricted form. Accordingly, the material world of time and space emerges from the World-Spirit in its proper ontological order.[76]

72. Ibid., 114–15.

73. Ibid., 114.

74. Karl Rahner, SJ, *The Christian Commitment: Essays in Pastoral Theology*, trans. Cecily Hastings (New York: Sheed and Ward, 1963), 49.

75. Rahner, "Theology of the Incarnation," 117.

76. See, e.g., Plotinus, *Enneads* III.7. Hans Urs von Balthasar observes that, strictly speaking, no necessity or freedom can be predicated of the One, rising as it does so beyond reason and

The second problem concerns the vagueness of Rahner's claim that the absolute is free. This cannot mean that God either could or could not create, at least as we contingent persons understand an option to do some act or not. If God is immutable, he cannot be subject to a change of mind. We must therefore say that God, from all eternity, "decides" to create in a way that perfectly accords with his infinite goodness. But then how do we spare God's freedom in the face of the necessary emanation of goodness? We might appeal to the apophatic dimension of analogy. Maréchal reminds us, for example, that absolute predicates, while empirically grounded, defy objectivation. Accordingly, if we can reasonably assert, by analogy, that God is free, and hence personal, then no necessary contradiction seems to obtain in asserting a voluntary dimension to the goodness of the divine person. It is appropriate that reason cannot satisfactorily define this goodness. Nonetheless, if a finite person's goodness is free, it is not unreasonable to posit the same of God's. In sum, although we cannot prove under contradiction that God freely posits us contingent beings, we can still argue from our contingency that God's freedom and goodness are not contradictory.

A related problem in Rahner's argument emerges in another vague claim: that God's freedom entails love. He does not seem to mean *agapē*, the universally disinterested love that Aristotle and Aquinas predicate of divinity. On the contrary, he seems to mean *eros*, the extroverted engagement consistent with the kenotic text of Philippians. His use of this meaning echoes the fifth-century Dionysius, who defines *eros* as convertible with the divine beauty and goodness.[77] If the conjoining in the divine of freedom and goodness can be spared a contradiction, it is nonetheless certain that eros must entail necessity. Because *eros* is intrinsically dynamic, it must aim at an end, as Aristotle and Aquinas perceive, even if this end is freely "decided" from all eternity. Consequently, to be truly free, the divine love must be satisfied within itself. It must entail its own end. Otherwise, if the free motion of love immanent in God does

---

beyond will. *The Glory of the Lord*, vol. 4: *The Realm of Metaphysics in Antiquity*, trans. Brian McNeil, CRV, et al., ed. John Riches (San Francisco, Calif.: Ignatius Press, 1989), 280–313, at 287, citing *Enneads* V.3.13.

77. See Hans Urs von Balthasar, *Glory of the Lord*, vol. 2: *Studies in Theological Style*, ed. Joseph Fessio and John Riches (San Francisco, Calif.: Ignatius Press, 1984), 144–210, at 189, referring to Dionysius, *De divinis nominibus*, chap. 4.

not terminate in God as its own immanent goal, then it must terminate in a goal other than God. It must terminate therefore in finite being. If it does, then the gratuity of creation is vitiated. To avoid this conclusion, God must be seen to communicate his love to finite being precisely because he is perfectly satisfied. In this case, God's love would be utterly free and gratuitous. Because Rahner's argument does not deal with this problem, its use of the *Realsymbol* to work out a theology of creation and redemption does not, as it currently stands, spare God's freedom, immutability, essential simplicity, and sovereignty.

The last problem concerns Rahner's critique of theology's traditional division, in the incarnate Word, of the predicates "absolute" and "dynamic." Surprisingly, he does not mention the famous doctrine of the "exchange of predicates" (*communicatio idiomatum*) advanced in the patristic age. It claims that, because of the unity-in-diversity of the two unconfused natures, what can be positively asserted of one nature can be asserted of the other. Neither the human nor the divine nature is the subject of the exchange, but the one divine person of Christ. It is fitting, therefore, to affirm that Jesus, in Christ, is divine, although not in his human nature. It is also fitting to say that, in the crucifixion, God, in Christ, dies, although not in his own essence.[78]

The point is that the exchange does not inappropriately dichotomize the predicates applicable to each nature, as Rahner avers. On the contrary, it binds them together in one subject, while preserving "the distinctive character of each."[79] We might well argue, as a result, that this vital teaching of the tradition posits exactly what Rahner says it does not: namely, that God, immutable in himself, can himself become subject to change in something else. In other words, God, in Christ, changes, although not in his divine nature. To further blur the distinction between finite and infinite, as Rahner seems to wish, risks undermining Chalcedon's skillful integration of the analogy of being into the analogy of faith. Such an undermining could render the finite but a mere acci-

---

78. For more on the exchange, see J. N. D. Kelly, *Early Christian Doctrines* (San Francisco, Calif.: Harper and Row, 1978), chaps. 12–13; for a problematic interpretation of it, see Roger Haight, *Dynamics of Theology* (New York: Paulist, 1990), 139 and 220; this interpretation also appears in the author's *Jesus Symbol of God* (Maryknoll, N.Y.: Orbis, 1999).

79. *The Chalcedonian Decree* (451), in *Christology of the Later Fathers*, ed. Edward Rochie Hardy (Philadelphia: Westminster, 1954), 372–74, at 373.

dent of the infinite substance and thus inevitably devolve Christianity into an ontological idealism inimical to it.

Conclusion

Our study of Transcendental Thomism thus leaves us in the threshold of a perennial problem facing Christian theology: how can faith satisfactorily integrate into its beliefs a metaphysics that is philosophically consistent? On the one hand, I have favorably assessed Maréchal's development of what we might call an "ascending" analogy. Grounded in retorsion, it warrants absolute being on the basis of contingency. On the other hand, I have criticized Rahner's attempt to develop a "descending" analogy from the free and loving absolute to a created order that is redeemed. However problematic his results, Rahner, I must in all fairness admit, takes up the more challenging task. If we concede with him that metaphysics can warrant God as *eros*, then positing a cogent descending analogy still awaits a happy handling of the following aporias. First, the dynamism of God's *eros* must terminate in itself so as to spare the divine's essential simplicity. Second, the otherness of creation must be shown to spring from the divine love without constituting an accident of the divine substance. Third, the redemption must be intrinsically connected to creation without constituting a divine emanation required for the divine to reach its own perfection. It may well be possible to develop the metaphysics of the *Realsymbol*, in tandem with the exchange of predicates, to accomplish these tasks. Those who try will owe as much to the seminal genius of the intrepid German as he owes to the great Walloon's.[80]

---

80. For such an attempt, see Stephen M. Fields, SJ, "God's Labor, Novelty's Emergence: Cosmic Motion as Self-Transcending Love," in *Love Alone Is Credible: Hans Urs von Balthasar as Interpreter of the Catholic Tradition*, ed. David L. Schindler (Grand Rapids, Mich.: Eerdmans, 2008), 1:115–40.

5

Knowledge of *ens* as *primum cognitum* and the Discovery of *ens qua ens* according to Cornelio Fabro and Jan A. Aertsen

JASON A. MITCHELL

Two debated points in twentieth-century Thomism concern how we know being (*ens*) at the dawn of knowing and how we discover *ens qua ens* as the *subiectum* of metaphysics. In this essay, I would like to trace the development of Cornelio Fabro's (1911–95) thought on these two points and point out connections with the work of Jan A. Aertsen (1938–2016). Fabro's theories, I believe, offer convincing alternatives to the proposals of Jacques Maritain and Etienne Gilson on *ens* as *primum cognitum* and to the theory of *separatio* as developed by Louis-Bertrand Geiger. As we will see, the problem of our knowledge of being (*esse*) is common to both problems: how is *esse* known in the *primum cognitum* and what is the role of *esse* in the discovery of the *subiectum* of metaphysics?

Evolution of Fabro's Thought on
ens as *primum cognitum*

Cornelio Fabro gradually modifies his early position on *ens* as *primum cognitum* and speaks in the end of a synthetic apprehension of *ens* as plexus of content and act rather than a formal abstraction of *ens*. The most important stages in the evolution of his thought are as follows.[1]

In his first major work, *La nozione metafisica di partecipazione* (1939), Fabro holds that *ens* as *primum cognitum* is obtained by means of formal abstraction. He writes: "From the psychological point of view, we know that the first notion that the intellect forms is that of *ens*, and it is a notion evidently obtained by formal abstraction; but this is the most imperfect and confused notion and indicates the beginning and awakening of the intellectual life."[2] Further on, Fabro qualifies this abstraction as a "quasi-formal abstraction" and links it to the perception of the concrete.[3] Although he modifies his position in his later works, this early work already contains references to both the concrete and actual nature of *ens*. In this way, Fabro avoids the dangers of a purely formalistic conception of *ens*.[4] In Fabro's later works, he stresses the "actual aspect" (and not the formal aspect) of the *primum cognitum* and its reference to reality.

Three years later, in *Percezione e Pensiero* (1942), Fabro once again considers the initial notion of *ens* in relation to the perception of the concrete. Our grasping of *ens*, he argues, is prepared by the senses by

1. The theme of *ens* as *primum cognitum* in the work of Cornelio Fabro has been dealt with by several authors: Luis Romera, *Pensar el ser: Análisis del conocimiento del "Actus essendi" según C. Fabro* [Thinking Being: Analysis of Knowledge of *Actus Essendi* according to C. Fabro] (Bern: Peter Lang, 1994), 131–222; Christian Ferraro, "La conoscenza dell'*ens* e dell'*esse* dalla prospettiva del tomismo essenziale," *Doctor Angelicus* 5 (2005): 75–108; Adrián Lozano, *La primera captación intelectual como fundamento del proceso de abstracción del universal según Santo Tomás de Aquino: una interpretación desde Cornelio Fabro, Étienne Gilson, Jacques Maritain y Léon Nöel* [The First Intellectual Grasp as Foundation of the Process of the Abstraction of the Universal according to St. Thomas Aquinas: An Interpretation based on Cornelio Fabro, Etienne Gilson, Jacques Martiatin and Leon Noel] (Rome: Pontificia Università Lateranense, 2006), 71–106; Javier Pablo Olivera, *El punto de partida de la metafísica de Santo Tomás de Aquino, según Cornelio Fabro* [The Point of Departure of Metaphysics of St. Thomas Aquinas according to Cornelio Fabro] (Rome: Pontificia Università Lateranense, 2007).

2. Cornelio Fabro, *La nozione metafisica di partecipazione secondo s. Tommaso d'Aquino* [The Metaphysical Notion of Participation according to St. Thomas Aquinas], Opere Complete 3 (Segni: EDIVI, 2005), 136. All translations from non-English sources are mine.

3. Fabro, *La nozione metafisica di partecipazione*, 187.

4. Romera, *Pensar el ser*, 172–73: "In this early work, Fabro maintains the idea that an abstraction corresponds to the first notion (precisely because it is an intellectual notion), yet already manifests the relationship that it has with perception: because to know *ens* is to know the *ratio entis* of the real, which every man has and with which, thanks to sensible knowledge, we enter into contact at the noetic level. This last aspect, its relation to perception, is developed in other works, yet even in this first work, he highlights that being as existence is touched in sensibility, due to the 'present' characteristic that the known sensibly has, and due to the fact that such existence is grasped by understanding within or together with essence."

means of *experimentum*, the operation of experience by means of which the intellect stays in direct contact with reality. In the *primum cognitum* we grasp in a confused way both *something* and *existing*. The interplay between the senses, *experimentum*, common sense and the *cogitativa* means that this grasping and knowledge of *ens* is founded on sensible knowledge.[5] The continuity between the senses and understanding highlights the importance of the *conversio ad phantasmata*, for by means of this conversion our intellect knows the singular, and thus the *ratio entis*.[6]

In *Partecipazione e causalità* (1954–61), Fabro calls *ens* the *primum psychologicum*, referring to its temporal priority, and the *primum criticum-ontologicum*, referring to its constitutive priority with regard to all other notions of the intellect.[7] The confused notion of *ens* is the first notion, the proper-formal object of the intellect, the ultimate reference point for all concepts and the first and last (*prima conceptio et ultima resolutio*) in the *conceptual* reduction of the real.[8] With regard to the grasping of *esse* in the *primum cognitum*, Fabro notes that we experience *esse in actu* and not *esse ut actus*.[9]

In the 1960s, Fabro begins to use the term *apprehensio* instead of *abstractio* to refer to the *primum cognitum*.[10] In his oft-quoted article, "The Transcendentality of *ens-esse* and the Ground of Metaphysics" (1966), Fabro affirms that "the original apprehension of the *notio entis*, which precedes everything and is presupposed in everything, cannot be merely the effect of abstraction in the ordinary sense."[11] In addition, as the

---

5. Romera, *Pensar el ser*, 173–82.

6. Cornelio Fabro, *Percezione e pensiero* [Perception and Thought] (Segni: EDIVI, 2008), 380–82.

7. Originally given as the Cardinal Mercier Lectures at the University of Louvain in 1954, *Partecipazione e causalità* was published in 1960, while *Participation e causalité* was published in 1961. I will quote from the *Opere complete* Italian edition published in 2010.

8. Cornelio Fabro, *Partecipazione e causalità* [Participation and Causality], Opere complete 19 (Segni: EDIVI, 2010), 173. See also Romera, *Pensar el ser*, 135: "Thus, we are dealing with a first not only in the analytical order, in the sense that analyzing any object one ultimately finds the notion of *ens*; but also of a first, both on the psychological plane—since it is the first that comes to our intellect, it is the unveiling and awakening of our mind—and on the critical-ontological plane, since it is the fundament to which the critical problem remits and the basis of openness of the mind to reality, on which the metaphysical problem is sustained and has meaning."

9. Romera, *Pensar el ser*, 183.

10. Cornelio Fabro, "Per la determinazione dell'essere tomistico," in *Tomismo e Pensiero moderno* (Rome: Pontificia Università Lateranense, 1969), 264.

11. Cornelio Fabro, "The Transcendentality of *Ens-Esse* and the Ground of Metaphysics," *International Philosophical Quarterly* 6 (1966): 424.

notion of *ens* includes and embraces both essence (content) and *esse* (act), "the origin of the *notio entis* can in no wise be referred to the process which abstracts only essence."[12] As a synthesis of content and act, the *notio entis* is grasped in a certain form of "conjoint apprehension" of content on the part of the mind and of act on the part of experience.

Throughout the 1960s and 1970s Fabro hones his critique of those who stress the role of judgment in our initial knowledge of *ens*. *Ens*, he will argue, is the *transcendentale fundans* and the foundation of the first principles of the intellect.[13] One should not stop the *resolutio in fundamentum* at the first principles of the second operation of the intellect, but rather continue on and found such principles on *ens*. Fabro highlights that *esse participatum* is grasped in *ens per participationem* and thus there is a reference to *esse per essentiam* as foundation and principle in the *primum cognitum*. The apprehension of *ens* is the primary noetical foundation of all knowledge and, therefore, of our knowledge of God.[14]

Fabro affirms that we have a direct, immediate experience (or apprehension) of *ens* and that reflection on *ens* permits a certain content and act of being to emerge. Knowledge by abstraction, he writes, regards the "content," namely, the essence. The apprehension of *ens*, however, "is immediate and constitutes the first step in the apprehension of the real."[15] The act grasped in the initial apprehension of *ens* is *esse in actu*. To know *esse ut actus*, the metaphysician needs to pursue a resolution of act: from accidental acts to substantial acts and from these to *actus essendi*. This point is mentioned in a debate from 1973: "I did not say that *ens* is acquired from immediate perception, but from immediate apprehension. From *ens*, thus understood, one comes to *esse* ... by means of a resolutive and not abstractive process. Therefore, by a resolutive process, of a resolution to the principle, of act to act: from accidental acts to substantial act, from substantial act to entitative act."[16]

12. Fabro, "The Transcendentality of *Ens-Esse*," 424.

13. Cornelio Fabro, "L'*esse* tomistico e la ripresa della metafisica," *Angelicum* 44 (1967): 295–302.

14. Cornelio Fabro, *L'uomo e il rischio di Dio* [Man and the Risk of God] (Rome: Editrice Studium, 1967), 368–69.

15. Cornelio Fabro, "Il nuovo problema dell'essere e la fondazione della metafisica," *Rivista di filosofia neoscolastica* 66 (1974): 475–510, at 490.

16. Cornelio Fabro, "Dibattito congressuale," *Sapienza* 26 (1973): 371–432, at 403. See also Cornelio Fabro, *La svolta antropologica di Karl Rahner* [The Anthropological Turn of Karl Rahner] (Milan: Rusconi Editore, 1974), 56–57, 162–63, 173–76, 213–16.

Fabro's 1983 article entitled "Problematica del tomismo di scuola" is particularly enlightening as to his mature position regarding our apprehension of *ens*. The article is largely a critique of Maritain's position on the abstraction of *ens* in the line of essence. Arguing against Maritain, Fabro states that Aquinas does not speak of *intuitio* and much less of *abstractio* in reference to our knowledge of *ens*, "but simply of *apprehensio* which is the most obvious and immediate operation and, thus, the most important."[17] Fabro explains that the first object of intellectual knowledge refers to knowing things that are in act. To this corresponds, not a simple abstraction according to the essence, but rather a synthetic apprehension according to the act of being.[18] *Esse* is grasped within *ens*: "*Ens* expresses the primary and total concreteness since it embraces both act (*esse*) and content (*essentia*) in a more or less vague way or precisely according to the psychic development of the subject."[19]

Fabro's mature works, then, emphasize two aspects of our knowledge of the *primum cognitum*. On the one hand, he denies that this knowledge is of the order of abstract essences[20] and, on the other, he accentuates

17. Cornelio Fabro, "Problematica del tomismo di scuola," *Rivista di filosofia neoscolastica* 75 (1983): 187–99, at 198.

18. Romera, *Pensar el ser*, 331–32: "The *primum cognitum* is a plexus of content (essence) and act, which one can express with the formula *id quod habet esse*. It is not the mere apprehension of a form or of the most general formality, or directly knowing *actus essendi* as such. It is rather a plexus that includes a duality. From this we gather that the understanding is not initially of forms (*simplex apprehensio*), while in a second moment it will affirm existence (in judgment). On the contrary, it grasps in its origin the plexus of formal content (minimal) and of act, of actuation, of insertion in reality. As a participle, our author sustains that *ens* says act, the being in act of *esse*. This means that already in the first knowledge we have notice—even though confused—of the act of being; not insofar as it is properly act (as resolutive metaphysical notion of the real), but yes as regards the actual character of the real insofar as it is real. The understanding is not, we insist, initially formal, in order to later come to the real as such in a second moment; the intellect comes to the notion of the real from the beginning."

19. Fabro, "Problematica del tomismo di scuola," 198. Also notable in this period are Fabro's Thomistic theses and the fact that a large number of them (theses VI–XVIII) are dedicated to problems related to *ens* as *primum cognitum*. See also his *Introduzione a san Tommaso* (Milan: Ares, 1997), 159–65.

20. Cornelio Fabro, *La prima riforma della dialettica hegeliana* [The First Reform of the Hegelian Dialectic], ed. Christian Ferraro (Segni: EDIVI, 2004), 235: "The plexus *ens* cannot be grasped by way of some abstractive process, but is itself the primary nucleus and intelligible light which renders all understanding possible. [...] Every thing is and becomes intelligible insofar as it is and is presented as *ens*, i.e., with reference to *esse*. This reference to *esse* is participation: therefore, it is insofar as they participate in *esse* that beings (*entia*), things and essences all become intelligible and that *ens* is the first intelligible. Therefore constitutive point of departure for thought is not the concrete-formal (the determinate singular of formalistic Scholasticism), nor

the relationship that this knowledge has with the concrete singular and how this is a grasping of a concrete-transcendental existent in act.[21] As Luis Romera concludes: "The grasping of *ens* is neither an abstraction, nor an intuition; it is rather a simple and synthetic apprehension (of content and act) which is had thanks to the primary and constitutive convergence of the sensible and the intelligible. It is an intellectual apprehension, prepared for by the *experimentum*, made by the intellect in the act of perceiving the singular."[22]

Three Assessments of Fabro's theory

Jan A. Aertsen

There seems to be some confusion regarding Fabro's theory about *ens* as *primum cognitum* and our grasping of *esse* within that initial *cognitum*. In his *Medieval Philosophy and the Transcendentals* (1996), Aertsen considers three positions concerning our initial knowledge of *ens* and places Fabro together with Gilson in the second position, as they both hold that the conception of *ens* cannot be the result of abstraction.[23] Aertsen's placing of Gilson and Fabro together is perplexing, as their two proposals are notably different.[24] Aertsen opines that neither Fabro's position as presented in "The Transcendentality of *ens-esse*" nor that of the others is correct. I would argue, however, that Fabro's solution actually seems to be in substantial agreement with Aertsen's proposal: *ens* is initially "apprehended" by the intellect. Aertsen points out that Aquinas "clearly affirms that the concept of being belongs to simple apprehension" and that this stands in contrast to "the contention of 'Existential Thomism' that the concept of being is a judgment or proposition."[25] The difference between the interpretations of Fabro and Aertsen lies in the latter's preference for

---

the formal *a priori* or transcendental abstract or empty *cogito* of modern immanence, but rather *ens* which is the concrete transcendental."

21. Romera, *Pensar el ser*, 186.

22. Ibid., 332.

23. Jan A. Aertsen, *Medieval Philosophy and the Transcendentals: The Case of Thomas Aquinas* (Leiden: Brill, 1996), 175.

24. Romera, *Pensar el ser*, 113–18 and 126–30; Battista Mondin, "La conoscenza dell'essere in Fabro e Gilson," *Euntes Docete* 50 (1997): 85–115; Andrea Robiglio, "Gilson e Fabro. Appunti per un confronto," *Divus Thomas* 17 (1997): 59–76.

25. Aertsen, *Medieval Philosophy and the Transcendentals*, 179.

the term "simple apprehension" and Fabro's use of "synthetic apprehension" to refer to the grasping of the *primum cognitum*.

Luis Romera

Regarding how to improve upon Fabro's theory, Romera notes Fabro's lack of precision and clarity when dealing with the gnoseological nature of the *primum cognitum*. In his works, Fabro adequately deals with sensible knowledge, perception and *conversio ad phantasmata*, yet lacks a more detailed study on the nature and distinction of the intellectual operations and the function of the agent intellect.[26] Precision and clarity can be gained by identifying the *primum cognitum* as an intellectual *habitus*, present in every intellectual act of knowledge.[27]

Antonio Millán-Puelles

Another evaluation of Fabro's theory is found in A. Millán-Puelles's *La lógica de los conceptos metafísicos*, in which he considers Fabro's article, "The Transcendentality of *ens-esse*." Regarding Fabro's position that the notion of *ens* cannot be the mere effect of an ordinary abstraction proper to the grasping of the essence, Millán-Puelles asks whether there is really any abstraction that is limited to grasping the essence alone without reference to the act of being or whether there is any abstraction that truly isolates the essence from the notion of *ens*.[28] He proposes that we should speak of an "imperfect abstraction" of *ens* in contrast to a "perfect abstraction" proper to the species and genus.[29]

By way of conclusion, it is important to note at this point how Fabro's theory on the synthetic apprehension of *ens* as plexus of con-

---

26. Romera, *Pensar el ser*, 186.
27. Ibid., 215.
28. Antonio Millán-Puelles, *La lógica de los conceptos metafísicos*, Tomo I: *La lógica de los conceptos trascendentales* [The Logic of Metaphysical Concepts, vol. I: The Logic of Transcendental Concepts] (Madrid: RIALP, 2002), 157.
29. Antonio Millán-Puelles, *La lógica de los conceptos metafísicos*, Tomo II: *La articulación de los conceptos extracategoriales* [The Logic of Metaphysical Concepts, vol. II: The Articulation of Extra-categorial Concepts] (Madrid: RIALP, 2003), 288. A possible, speculative parallel could be drawn between Fabro's distinction (ordinary abstraction / synthetic apprehension) and that of Millán-Puelles (perfect abstraction / imperfect abstraction).

tent (essence) and act (*esse*) permits theorizing a gradual opening up, through reflection, to metaphysics. *Esse*, according to Fabro, is grasped in different ways: implicitly in the first notion, as existence in later reflection, at the beginning of metaphysics as common act of *ens*, throughout metaphysics as the actuating act of *ens* that is measured and specified by the substantial essence, and at the culmination of metaphysics as intensive, analogical notion, grasped against the backdrop of the *habitudo* between the participated *actus essendi* of the creature and the subsistent *esse* of God. In the section that follows I will deal primarily with Fabro's thought on the grasping of *ens qua ens* at beginning of metaphysics.

Fabro on the Discovery of *ens qua ens*

Fabro's theory regarding our discovery of the *subiectum* of metaphysics can be drawn out from a consideration of three different texts. The first text, taken from his early *La nozione metafisica di partecipazione*, speaks of the passage to metaphysics as a passage from physical contrariety to metaphysical contrariety. Here the emphasis lies on intensifying participated perfection in the passage from the problem of movement to the problem of being. The second text is taken from his unpublished *Metaphysica* course notes (1947–49) and concerns the "resolution of act" and the passage from accidental act and substantial form to the act of being. The third text, taken from one of his articles, refers to an initial, metaphysical notion of *esse* that is superseded by a methodological notion and which eventually comes to rest in an "intensive" notion. Gathering the three texts together will enable us to understand the convergence in Fabro's thought between a dialectic of participated perfection, a resolution-intensification of act, and the grasping of an initial, metaphysical notion of *esse* as aspects of the solution to the problem of the constitution of the *subiectum* of metaphysics.

Passage from Physical to Metaphysical Contrariety

In *La nozione metafisica di partecipazione*, Fabro speaks of a type of reflection which gives rise to the "metaphysical notion of being." This reflection, he writes, is conditioned by formal and total abstraction, but differs from both insofar as it is more properly a dialectical process of contrast involving analogical predication. All beings are said to have their own *ratio* of being (*ragione d'essere*), yet, concretely, each being has its own *mode* of being, which is diverse from all the others.[30] Universal, univocal notions such as "man" (species) and "animal" (genus) adequately inform the mind with the content proper to their notions; the analogical notion of being, however, is "intrinsically inadequate to inform the mind once for all, but rather needs to be explicated, time after time, in objectification."[31]

These points are developed at length in Fabro's presentation of "predicamental participation," namely, the four participations mentioned by Aquinas in his *In de Heb.*: individual-species, species-genus, subject-accidents, matter-form. Fabro tries to show how we can move from these participations (proper to the philosophy of nature) to transcendental-structural participation and the real composition of *essentia* and *esse*. This passage is characterized as the passage from *physical* contrariety to *metaphysical* contrariety: "[Movement] can be considered from a more vast and comprehensive point of view: namely, not only on the physical plane as a succession of contraries, but on the metaphysical plane of being, as a succession of '*more*' or '*less*' perfect, according to the ontological intensity of perfection."[32] Physical contrariety concerns the *opposition* of two terms in relation to movement; metaphysical contrariety concerns the *distinction* between the contraries according to a *magis et minus* in the order of being. The *magis et minus* of perfection appears when the terms of movement on the physical plane are considered *sub ratione entis*.[33] *Magis et minus* expresses different degrees of realization of the same "form," which is communicated or participated to various subjects according to varying intensive degrees of perfection. Metaphysical contrariety is found in every creature and understood as a gradation of perfection in the formal order and in reference to the supreme *ratio* of being.

The notion of *ens* is seen to be indicative of a perfection or formality which is transcendent and superior to all the perfections and formalities

30. Fabro, *La nozione metafisica di partecipazione*, 137.
31. Ibid.
32. Ibid., 161.
33. Ibid., 162.

to which it is applied. Being a plant, being a horse, and being a man are all particular modes of being, but are not convertible with one another. At the same time, all of these modes are "of being" and all are finite. Thus, in the light of the notion of being, I understand that this limitation of being "is not due to being, insofar as it is being, but only to the determined formality to which it is united and which specifies it."[34]

In synthesis, this first text holds that one enters into metaphysics after the consideration of movement in the philosophy of nature by seeing being as a "formality" which is common to all things but which is found in varying degrees of intensity. This necessitates another speculative science which goes beyond the problem of the foundation of movement and change (both accidental and substantial) and seeks the ultimate cause of the degrees of the perfection of being.

Reflection on Act

Fabro's second indication on the constitution of the *subiectum* of metaphysics is found in his unpublished *Metaphysica* course notes (1947–49). Here, he deals explicitly with the problem of the beginning of metaphysics and states that it is found in considering *ens* problematically and reflecting on it: "*something is*, a thing has *esse*, an essence participates or has *esse*: apprehending this is the beginning of metaphysics."[35] *Ens qua ens* does not express a particular mode of being, but rather the fundamental demand of any mode of being: *esse* belongs to a thing according to the measure of its own essence or nature.

In dealing with how we grasp the initial metaphysical notion of *ens* (*ens commune*), Fabro first notes that this notion is not *ens* as *primum cognitum*, but rather requires an understanding of the problem of the duality of "that which is" and "being" in *ens*.[36] The initial, metaphysical notion of *ens* arises from admiration and wonder and from the recognition of the insufficiency of the ordinary premetaphysical notion of *ens*.

34. Ibid., 137.

35. Cornelio Fabro, *Metaphysica*, unpublished manuscript in Progetto Culturale Cornelio Fabro dell'Istituto del Verbo Incarnato, 38. The manuscript corresponds to Fabro's metaphysics course given at the Pontifical Urbaniana University in Rome from 1947 to 1949 and can be found at Largo Barbarigo 1, 01027 Montefiascone (VT), Italy. It is slated for eventual publication in Fabro's *Complete Works*.

36. Ibid., 43.

Metaphysical wonder arises when we become aware of the problem of *esse* and seek an ulterior foundation of being (*ens*), not upon the essence alone, but rather in relation to the act of being (*esse*).

In *Metaphysica*, Fabro states that the first problems dealt with in and by philosophical reflection are those of multiplicity, change, and movement. In fact, the cause of wonder concerns the phenomena of change and multiplicity.[37] Change and multiplicity, however, must be considered as expressions or manifestations of being, explained, and given a solid foundation. Philosophical reflection on such phenomena (a reflection that Fabro calls "phenomenological reduction") concludes that: "Within being, there are things that change and things that remain the same; some things determine the thing in an absolute way in knowledge, others in an accidental way; some things pertain to being as intrinsic constitutive [principles], others come and go as properties without *ens* itself changing."[38] Based on this, being (*ens*) is first divided into the categories (substance and accidents) according to the "reductive" method.

Toward the end of the first book of his *Metaphysica*, Fabro proposes that the metaphysical reduction of potencies to act closes the phenomenological reduction and opens up to a metaphysical analysis of *ens qua ens*.[39] This is described as follows:

The division of being into act and potency investigates and penetrates with greater depth the preceding division of finite being, into substance and accident, and brings categorial being to the light of *ens qua ens*. The substance, which has accidents, is composed of act and potency and is shown to be finite, dependent, participated and created. For this reason, by means of potency and act one realizes the transition to the constitution of metaphysics.[40]

Metaphysics is "constituted" for Fabro by bringing categorial being (*ens* divided into subject and accidents; the material essence as composed of prime matter and substantial form) under the light of *ens qua ens* by means of the real distinction between act and potency and the recognition of the dependent and participated nature of finite being. When Fabro speaks of *separatio* as a method of metaphysics in his *Metaphysica*,

37. Ibid., 58.
38. Ibid., 63.
39. Ibid., 111.
40. Ibid., 118.

he does not refer to a demonstration of the existence of immaterial be-ing, but rather to the procedure proper to metaphysics of "distinguish-ing" (separating) the real or intentional oppositions we encounter in metaphysical reflection (in opposition to "abstraction"). In the *Epilogue* to *Metaphysica*, Fabro places *separatio* within the context of the ultimate reduction of participated *esse* to *esse per essentiam* and not within the context of an initial demonstration of immaterial being.

The Initial, Metaphysical Notion of *ens*

Throughout Fabro's works we find that he continually develops the theme of progressive stages in our knowledge of *ens* and *esse*. The discov-ery of *ens qua ens* corresponds to what he calls our initial, metaphysical knowledge of *ens-esse*. In an article entitled "La problematica dello *esse* tomistico" (1959), Fabro specifies that metaphysics begins with an initial notion of *esse* which is seen as the act of *ens* in an indeterminate sense. He writes:

There is an "initial notion" of *esse* (like that of *ens*), which is the act of *ens* in the most indeterminate sense, that which St. Thomas sometimes indicates as "*esse commune*": *esse* can indicate any realty or actuality, the essence (*albedo*) and *actus essendi*, the belonging both to the real order and the logical order. It is called an initial notion since it is by recognizing it, by reflecting on it, metaphysical reflection is begun.[41]

In his article on the ontological difference in twentieth-century Thomism, Alain Contat comments on the passage just quoted and suc-cessfully integrates it with Fabro's other texts on the passage of the mind from an initial notion of *esse* to the second "methodological-structural" notion of *ens-esse* and to the third "intensive" notion of *ens-esse*. Contat's synthesis of Fabro's thought brings out that there is a resolution into an act and correlative potency at every stage of the itinerary:

There is an initial *resolutio* of *ens* into the common notion of *esse commune* (a), complementary to the thing which has it; then one undertakes a methodologi-cal *resolutio* of *ens*, within its quadripartite division, into the Aristotelian couplet of *ousia* and *energeia*, interpreted by Fabro as the couplet of *quidditas* and *esse in*

---

41. Fabro, "La problematica dello *esse* tomistico," 107. See also Romera, *Pensar el ser*, 220–22.

actu (b); and finally, one comes to the ultimate metaphysical *resolutio* of *ens* into the twofold opposition between *Esse subsistens* and *esse inhaerens*, the latter of which is *esse ut actus* limited by *essentia*, i.e., intensive being (c).[42]

The third, intensive notion of *esse*, Contat argues, is obtained by means of a *formal* resolution of participated perfection and a *real* resolution of actuating causality according to the principles of the Fourth Way and the demonstration of creation. At the end of this resolution, the metaphysician understands that created *ens*, which receives its being from subsistent being, is *ens per participationem* and that *ens per participationem* is "composed of a participant and of a participated, which oppose one another as potency and act; thus, created *ens* is composed of two co-principles, essence and the act of being, correlated as potency and act."[43]

This leads to an interesting theoretical-speculative solution to the problem of how to understand Fabro's many arguments for the real distinction. Contat notes that while most are in agreement that the difference between the determination of *ens* and its actuality is "pre-announced" in the moment when thought reflects on its first object (*ens*), the real question hinges on the epistemological place in which one comes to the *certainty* of the real composition between essence and *esse* in finite *ens*. Contat writes: "When one reflects on the initial notion of *ens*, one is certain only of an alterity between a determination that one can conceptualize as form, and an actuality which transcends the plane of form, without yet being able to establish what both the determination and the actuality are, and, hence, much less what is the real extent of their distinction."[44]

For Contat, the syllogism found in the fourth chapter of *De Ente et Essentia* concludes apodictically that the being-in-act in reality is other than the essence or quiddity. The "logical" argument found in *De Ente*, he notes, is a *quia* demonstration, which focuses on the *fact* of the real composition. The *foundation* of the composition, however, is found by means of a *propter quid* demonstration. Such a demonstration seeks to

---

42. Alain Contat, "Le figure della differenza ontologica nel tomismo del Novecento," *Alpha Omega* 11 (2008): 77–129 and 213–50, at 119–20.

43. Contat, "Le figure della differenza ontologica," 121.

44. Ibid., 234.

clarify the nature of the difference and does this though a comparison of the modes of being proper to the creator and the creature in light of the doctrine of participation.[45] Based on Fabro's texts, Contat summarizes the three stages of our knowledge of the real distinction between essence and *esse* or ontological difference between *ens* and *esse* as follows:

> The ontological difference is revealed to the metaphysician in three original stages: it is *problematized* at the beginning of metaphysics, when the common notion of *ens* is objectivized; then the difference is *established*, but only by means of a *quia* argument, when, based on the quadripartition of *ens*, the notions of quiddity, the formal principle of the substance, and being-in-act, the condition of the reality of the substance, are confronted; and finally the difference is *led back to its proper fundament*, which is the participation of finite *ens* in Infinite Being, by means of the creation of a participated *esse*, when one defines the ontological status of the creature. Thus, we believe with Étienne Gilson and Cornelio Fabro that the properly metaphysical question about the being of *ens* is "resolved" in the *chiaroscuro* of the difference between participated being and Subsistent Being, which remains *penitus ignotum* to us in this life.[46]

Both Alain Contat and Mario Pangallo interpret Fabro as making a distinction between a *quia* demonstration and a *propter quid* demonstration of the real distinction.[47] Their interpretations, in my opinion, enable us to understand the relation between Fabro's early classifications of the various arguments for the real distinction (including the argument of *De Ente*) and his continual (almost exclusive) emphasis on the role of participation in the ultimate determination of the structure of created *ens*.

To summarize, in an initial stage of philosophical reflection, the problems of change and multiplicity are solved by means of the distinctions and connections made between substance-accidents, potency-act, individual-species, species-genus, and matter-form. These are themes

---

45. Ibid., 236–38.

46. Ibid., 238.

47. Mario Pangallo, *L'essere come atto nel tomismo essenziale di Cornelio Fabro* (Vatican City: Libreria Editrice Vaticana, 1987), 38. The phrase *ratio propter quid* is used by Fabro in *La nozione metafisica di partecipazione*, 233, in reference to the *quarta ratio* of *De substantiis separatis*, chap. 8. Fabro writes: "It is in the response to the 'quarta ratio' that participation is invoked, as usual, as the *ratio propter quid* of the composition of essence and the act of being, which substitutes the composition of matter and form, and with this the creature is sufficiently distinguished from God."

proper to the philosophy of nature. For Fabro, the *subiectum* of metaphysics (*ens qua ens*) is constituted in the passage from the opposition of the terms of movement to the metaphysical distinction between different degrees of perfection of a participated "form." The reduction of potencies to act and of accidental acts to more profound acts and the consideration of the finite, dependent, and participated nature of beings both lead to the constitution of the *subiectum* of metaphysics. Insofar as the principles involved in the problem of movement may be considered *sub ratione entis*, they can be said to form part of the beginning of metaphysical reflection. The discovery of *ens qua ens* may be characterized as an initial resolution of *ens* to *esse commune* as act of *ens*.

Aertsen on the Discovery of *ens qua ens*

In this last section, I would like to draw out some connections between Fabro's theory and that of Jan Aertsen on the role of *resolutio* (analysis) in the constitution of the *subiectum* of metaphysics. Beginning with his doctoral dissertation, *Nature and Creature* (1988), Aertsen argues that there is a resolution proper to physics, a resolution of *movement* to its intrinsic and extrinsic causes,[48] and a resolution proper to metaphysics, a resolution of *being* to its causes.[49] In physics, there is a progression of the "if" question (*an sit*) toward the "what" question (*quid sit*): a composed thing is reduced to the essence as cause of being. In the metaphysical order of questioning, however, the "if" question is directed to the *actus essendi* whereby a being is being and not nothing. This "to be" of things which enters into composition with the essence needs to be reduced to the cause of being, which is God. The first mode of questioning is connected to the predication model of *per se* and *per accidens*; the second mode of questioning is connected to the Platonic mode of predicating, that of *per essentiam* and *per participationem*, which is capable of reducing a multiplicity to unity at the level of being. In coherence with these modes of questioning and predicating, there is also an *alius mo-*

---

48. Jan A. Aertsen, *Nature and Creature: Thomas Aquinas's Way of Thought* (Leiden: Brill, 1988), 269–70.

49. Ibid., 271–78. See esp. 275: "In the resolution of being, certain principles of the reduction of movement are continued. Such a continuation is possible because the analysis of movement, too, came to the metaphysical."

dus causandi—creation—that corresponds to the metaphysical level.[50]

After making this distinction between questioning, predication, and causality, Aertsen investigates the three stages in the consideration of being outlined by Aquinas in various texts, such as *ST* I, q. 44, a. 2 and *De substantiis separatis*, chap. 9. Aertsen draws attention to the consideration of being as being and the metaphysical analysis that reduces that-which-is (*quod est*) to its being (*esse*). This consideration transcends the categorial level of becoming and particular causality.[51] (See table 5-1.) In the resolution of movement, Aertsen notes, there is a reduction to the intrinsic principle and terminus of matter and form which, as causes, relate to one another as potency and act. Movement is subsequently reduced to the extrinsic causes: the active principle, the agent, and the end: "The end is ruled by the law of synonymy and by perpetuity. That requires a hierarchy of movers characterized by an increasing degree of immobility. In this cosmic order the celestial bodies occupy a place of importance. Their movement is reducible to an ultimate, metaphysical cause, God."[52] Accordingly, the First Way *ex parte motus* does not extend beyond "being-moved" to "being," and requires a further resolution to come to the latter.[53] The intensification of the resolution no longer considers the cause of the movement of the mobile, but rather seeks the cause of its being. Here, though, we are dealing with creation, a metaphysical origin "out of nothing" that transcends every movement. According to Aertsen, the objects of metaphysics (being as being and the highest causes) are found by the way of resolution "after" physics.[54]

In *Medieval Philosophy and the Transcendentals* (1996), Aertsen takes up more directly the problem of the passage from physics to metaphysics. He first notes the limits inherent to L.-B. Geiger's view of *separatio*: "The majority of modern scholars are of the opinion that for Thomas transmateriality provides the entrée to the subject of metaphysics and the condition for the transcendental consideration of reality."[55] According to this interpretation, *separatio*, which is the intellectual operation proper to metaphysics, consists in a negative judgment that being is not

50. Ibid., 90.
51. Ibid., 199–201.
52. Ibid., 269–70.
53. Ibid., 271.
54. Ibid., 255.
55. Aertsen, *Medieval Philosophy and the Transcendentals*, 128.

TABLE 5-1.

	Physics (Nature)		Metaphysics (Creature)
Consideration of being	*ens tale*	*ens hoc*	*ens in quantum est ens*
Structure of being	substance – accidents	matter – form	essence – *esse*
(Efficient) causality	particular	more universal	universal
Becoming	alteration	generation	creation

necessarily material and it is this judgment that establishes the *subiectum* of metaphysics. However, as Aertsen writes:

The "separatistic" thesis implies, therefore, that being cannot be considered as being until the existence of an Unmoved Mover or a separate substance is proven. Such a view, however, seems to be at odds with Thomas's conception of metaphysics. In the prologue [to his *Commentary on Aristotle's Metaphysics*] transmateriality is not the exclusive criterion of metaphysical intelligibility. The "highest intelligibles," which first philosophy considers, are of three sorts: (i) the first causes; (ii) which is most universal, such as being and that which is consequent upon being; and (iii) that which is altogether separate from matter. The subject of metaphysics is *ens commune*, and what is sought in this science is the cause of principle of the subject. It is the universal cause of being which is altogether separate from matter, and knowledge of these immaterial substances is for Thomas the final end of metaphysical inquiry. Geiger's thesis reverses that order: knowledge of the transcendent and transmaterial being becomes the condition for the consideration of being in general.[56]

Aertsen holds that Aquinas uses the method of *resolutio* instead of the process of *separatio* to establish the *subiectum* of metaphysics.[57] Recalling the three phases of the consideration of being, he writes:

The third phase in the history of the question of being began when some thinkers (*aliqui*) raised themselves to the consideration of being-as-being (*ens in quantum est ens*). In this metaphysical consideration each thing is resolved (*resolvitur*) into that which is (*id quod est*) and its being (*esse*). The origin of being as such cannot be a "generation," because it no longer presupposes anything in that which is caused. It is *creatio*, for to produce being absolutely pertains to the essence of creation. These philosophers considered a causality of things, insofar

56. Ibid., 129.

57. Ibid., 130. According to Aquinas's Prologue to his *Commentary on Aristotle's Metaphysics*, transphysical things are discovered in the process of resolution (*in via resolutionis*).

as they are being (*entia*). These thinkers were therefore the only ones who have posited a universal cause of being, God.[58]

The transition to the third phase is a transition to the metaphysical consideration of reality, from the categorial to the transcendental level. It is a transition to the inquiry into the origin of being, taken in its generalness. Aertsen's analysis of Aquinas's commentaries on Boethius's *De trinitate* and Aristotle's *Metaphysics* "shows a shift from a theological conception of metaphysics, based on immateriality, to an ontological conception, based on commonness. The subject of first philosophy is not the first being, that is transcendent, but being in general and that which is consequent upon being."[59]

In his article "La scoperta dell'ente in quanto ente" (2004), Aertsen links Geiger's view to that of Averroes, for whom the end of the *Physics* is the natural transition to the beginning of metaphysics. This position holds that if one does not demonstrate the existence of God in physics, there would be no metaphysics.[60] Aertsen once again recalls the three phases of the history of philosophy and the metaphysical analysis proper to the third stage which reduces each thing to its "being." He concludes:

The object of metaphysics is discovered, not by means of the demonstration of the existence of immaterial beings, but by means of the continual analysis of material beings. Hylemorphism—the composition of form and matter—can explain the *type of being* that material beings possess, but does not explain their *being as such*. Therefore, another way of considering material things is necessary, and in this process one discovers the object of metaphysics. The radical comprehension of the question of the origin is decisive for the discovery of being as being. The origin of being as such surpasses the level of becoming (change, motion) in nature.[61]

By constituting the *subiectum* of metaphysics through this *resolutio*, the doctrine of creation (and divine governance) becomes the point of arrival of metaphysical inquiry and understanding *ens qua ens* means ultimately understanding it as created.[62]

---

58. Aertsen, *Medieval Philosophy and the Transcendentals*, 154.

59. Ibid., 157.

60. Jan A. Aertsen, "La scoperta dell'ente in quanto ente," in *Tommaso d'Aquino e l'oggetto della metafisica* [Thomas Aquinas and the Object of Metaphysics], ed. S. Brock (Rome: Armando Editrice, 2004), 36.

61. Aertsen, "La scoperta dell'ente in quanto ente," 46.

62. Miguel Peréz de Laborda, "Il ruolo della *compositio* in metafisica," in *Tommaso d'Aquino*

Conclusion

This essay has shown that in assessing twentieth-century Thomists like Cornelio Fabro we need to be attentive to the development of their thought and analyze and interpret their theories against the backdrop of the whole of their philosophical production. Fabro's and Aertsen's theories on the *primum cognitum* are shown to concur in emphasizing that we are dealing with an apprehension and not an intuition, abstraction, or a notion consequent upon a judgment of existence. They differ insofar as Aertsen calls this a "simple apprehension" and Fabro a "synthetic apprehension."

Fabro and Aertsen are also seen to converge in proposing analysis (*resolutio*) as the way in which the *subiectum* of metaphysics is discovered. Both authors agree in passing from the problem of movement to that of being as being not by means of a demonstration of transmateriality or a demonstration of God as first immobile mover, but rather by means of common resolution of things to their being (*esse*). For his part, Fabro emphasizes the possibility of constituting the *subiectum* of metaphysics either through a passage from physical contrariety to metaphysical contrariety by means of participated perfection or through a continuing of the resolution of act begun in philosophical consideration of the problem of movement. In terms of *resolutio*, there is for Fabro an initial analysis of *ens* to *esse commune* which consists in problematically considering their difference. Aertsen, by contrast, brings out more clearly the aspect of the change in questioning and predicating proper to metaphysics and the change from the study of particular causality to the metaphysical search for a radical origin of things.[63]

---

e l'oggetto della metafisica, 61. Aertsen's theory is shared by Rudi te Velde, who, in his *Aquinas on God* (Aldershot: Ashgate, 2006), argues that *resolutio* is not limited to a process within a science, but is also employed in the transition from physics to metaphysics: "Physics studies reality under a particular aspect, while metaphysics proceeds to a universal consideration of being as being by transcending the particular perspective of physics. This passing over from physics to metaphysics happens by way of *resolutio*" (54–55).

63. For more on the connection between *resolutio secundum rationem* and its three stages (subject-accidents; matter-form; essence-esse) and *resolutio secundum rem*, see Jesús Villagrasa, "La *resolutio* come metodo della metafisica secondo Cornelio Fabro," *Alpha Omega* 4 (2001): 35–66.

PART TWO

Philosophical Perspectives

6

Aquinas and the Categories
as Parts of Being

GREGORY T. DOOLAN

For Thomas Aquinas, the ten categories first identified by Aristotle are the ten supreme *genera, genera* that follow from ten fundamental modes of being (*modi essendi*).[1] Thus, we find him noting in a number of places throughout his writings that being (*ens*) is divided by (*per*), or into (*in*), these ten categories.[2] This language indicates that for Thomas the categories are, in some respect, parts of the whole that is being. In what

---

1. Thomas Aquinas, *De Ver.*, q. 1, a. 1, co., editio Leonina (hereafter, Leon.) (Rome: Leonine Commission, 1975), 22.1:5.116–23: "Sunt enim diversi gradus entitatis secundum quos accipiuntur diversi modi essendi et iuxta hos modos accipiuntur diversa rerum genera; substantia enim non addit super ens aliquam differentiam quae designet aliquam naturam superadditam enti sed nomine substantiae exprimitur specialis quidam modus essendi, scilicet per se ens, et ita est in aliis generibus." Although Thomas himself prefers to refer to the Aristotelian categories as the "predicaments" (*praedicamenta*), I will instead refer to them as "categories" because that is the term more commonly employed today. All translations from the Latin are my own.

2. There appears to be no distinction in meaning in his use of these different prepositions. For instances where he employs the preposition *in*, see, e.g., *In Sent.* I, d. 22, q. 1, a. 1, ad 2; *In Phys.* III, l. 5, n. 322; *In Meta.* V, l. 9, n. 885, and VII, l. 1, n. 1246. For instances where he employs the preposition *per*, see, e.g., *In Sent.* I, d. 19, q. 5, a. 1, ad 1; II, d. 34, q. 1, a. 1, co.; IV, d. 1, q. 1, a. 4, ad 1; *De Ente*, chap. 1; *SCG* III.8.13; *ST* I, q. 5, a. 6, ad 1; q. 48, a. 2, ad 2; *In Meta.* V, l. 9, n. 889; VII, l. 1, n. 1245; IX, l. 1, n. 1769; *De Malo*, q. 7, a. 1, ad 1. Thomas also at times refers to *ens* as divided "according to" (*secundum*) the categories. See, e.g., *In Meta.* V, l. 12, n. 930, and IX, l. 11, n. 1895. Because *esse* is the principle by which *ens* is *ens*, Thomas also at times speaks of *esse* as divided by the categories. See, e.g., *In Sent.* III, d. 6, q. 2, a. 2, co., and *Quodl.* IX, q. 2, a. 2, co.

follows, I will offer some considerations of how he views the traditional ten Aristotelian categories as such parts. To this end, my essay will
consist of three sections. In the first, I will examine what for Thomas it
means to say that being is "divided" into the ten categories. In the second section, I will briefly consider his account of the derivation of the
categories in an effort to discern whether he considers the traditional
list of ten to be an exhaustive list of all possible categorial parts of being.
Finally, in the third section I will examine whether he thinks that in
reality being must be manifested through all ten categories. As I intend
to show, for Thomas these categories are necessary parts of this universe
and, perhaps, any universe that God would create.

Being as Divided by the Categories

If we wish to understand what Thomas means when he says that being is "divided" into the categories, we need to identify what he thinks
is divided. To begin with, it is helpful to recall a frequent observation
by Thomas that the term "being" (*ens*) can be taken in two respects. In
one respect it signifies the truth of a proposition, which consists in a
judgment of composition. In this sense, even what does not really exist as such can be said "to be," as when a privation such as blindness is
said "to be" in the eye. In the second respect, "being" signifies the entity
of a thing (*entitas rei*). This is the sort of being that exists (or is capable
of existing) outside of the mind. And it is in this sense, Thomas tells us,
that being is divided into the ten categories.[3] His distinction provides us
with some clarity regarding what the categories divide. But still further
clarification is needed, because when he says that they divide being, the
being to which he is referring is not *a* being (*unum ens*), such as Socrates. Nor is it the first being (*primum ens*), God. Rather, he is referring

---

3. *ST* I, q. 48, a. 2, ad 2. See also texts cited in note 2, above. When commenting on Book V
of Aristotle's *Metaphysics*, Thomas identifies additional senses of being (*ens*). After distinguishing
between *ens per se* and *ens per accidens*, he identifies three senses of *per se* being: perfect being
(*ens perfectum*), being as true (*ens ut verum*), and being as divided by act and potency. "Perfect
being" lies outside the mind (*ens naturae*, or real being) and is divided by the categories; "being
as true" concerns the truth of a proposition and as such "is" only within the mind (*viz.*, as logical
being). Act and potency divide both real being (because it divides all of the categories) and logical
being (beacuse the mind can either actually or potentially know something). See *In Meta.* V, l. 9,
nn. 885–97.

to *being-in-general* (*ens commune*): the universal class to which all finite beings belong.[4]

To say that *ens commune* is divided into the categories is to acknowledge that in some way it possesses unity in itself—that in some way it is one. Commenting on Aristotle's *Metaphysics*, Thomas reminds us that the essential characteristic of unity is undividedness. And, following Aristotle, he identifies four principal senses in which things can be "one": as continuous in nature, according to form, as a singular thing, and as a universal.[5] It is this last sense that concerns us here; for as the very name *ens commune* indicates, what we are considering is a sort of universal.

Following this sense, a thing is said to be one according to a single *ratio*—a single "intelligible characteristic." As such, it is one insofar as it is understood—insofar as it is grasped by the mind according to a single apprehension of an undivided object. Consider, as examples, species such as *man* and *horse*; according to Thomas, such universals do not exist outside of the mind with a unity *as* universals. They are one only according to knowledge and concept (*secundum scientiam et notitiam*). Still, we should be careful here not to read Thomas as a nominalist, as though he viewed universals as mere mental fabrications. Although there is no nature in distinct singular things that is numerically one which we could call a species, he tells us that our intellect apprehends as one that characteristic that the individuals share in common.[6] Thus, what in reality is

4. Considering the subject matter of metaphysics, Thomas notes that "haec scientia consideret ens commune sicut proprium subiectum, quod quidem dividitur per substantiam et novem genera accidentium." *In Meta.* VIII, l. 1, n. 1682, ed. M. R. Cathara and R. M. Spiazzi (Turin: Marietti, 1950), 402. Earlier in his commentary, when considering the four senses of being (*ens*) outlined in *Metaphysics* V, he instead identifies *ens perfectum* as what is divided by the categories. I would argue, however, that these two accounts of what the categories divide are not in conflict, because the division of *ens perfectum* results in a division of *ens commune*. This conclusion follows by reduction: Thomas presents *per accidens* being as reduced to *per se* being; logical being as reduced to perfect being; and the division of being by act and potency as subsequent to the division of being into the categories (*In Meta.* V, l. 9, nn. 885–97; see also VII, l. 1, n. 1245–46; IX, l. 1, nn. 1768–69; IX, l. 11, n. 1895). Insofar as perfect being is primary among these four senses of being, then, we can conclude that the categories thereby divide *ens commune*. And inasmuch as *ens commune* is divided by the categories, so too is *esse commune*. See, e.g., *In Sent.* III, d. 6, q. 2, a. 2, co., and *Quodl.* IX, q. 2, a. 2, co. On the reduction of the different senses of being to being as divided by the categories, see Ralph McInerny, "Notes on Being and Predication," *Laval théologique et philosophique* 15 (1959): 236–74, at 273–74.

5. *In Meta.* X, l. 1, nn. 1921–34; Aristotle, *Metaphysics* X.1, 1052a15–b1.

6. *In Meta.* X, l. 1, n. 1930.

diverse in diverse individuals is made indivisible (and, hence, "one") as a universal in the apprehension of the intellect.

For Thomas, this account is no less true regarding *ens commune*. Without getting into the debates among Thomists regarding the formation of the concept of being, suffice it to say that in considering the really distinct individual beings that we experience, our intellect is capable of forming a concept of being—the intellect finds in these diverse beings the common *ratio* of being: "what is" (*quod est*). And forming the concept of being, we apprehend this unity that is a universal, which the metaphysician will come to recognize as being *qua* being, which Thomas terms being-in-general, *ens commune*.[7] Nevertheless, even though *ens commune* is undivided in *ratio*, our experience and understanding of diverse beings also shows us that it is somehow divisible; *ens commune* is a whole that in some way consists of parts.

Again, commenting on Aristotle's *Metaphysics*, Thomas explains what a "whole" (*totum*) is.[8] The common notion (*ratio*) of a whole consists in two characteristics. First, the perfection (or completion) of a whole is derived from its parts. If a part is missing, the whole is not complete. We could consider a dog such as Fido: if he lost an eye in a fight, his body (which consists of parts) would be incomplete—it would not be whole. Thus, quoting Aristotle, Thomas notes that something is called "whole" for which none of its parts is missing. The second characteristic of a whole is that those parts perfecting the whole are, in turn, united in it and made one. Thus Fido's parts not only complete his body, but they are all of *one* body insofar as they are contained in that body.

In light of these considerations, Thomas follows Aristotle in identifying two kinds of wholes: an integral whole and a universal whole.[9]

7. For summaries of the different accounts of the formation of the concept of being (both prephilosophical and philosophical) see Joseph Owens, "Aquinas on Knowing Existence," *Review of Metaphysics* 29 (1976): 670–90; Jan A. Aertsen, "Method and Metaphysics: The *via resolutionis* in Thomas Aquinas," *New Scholasticism* 63 (1989): 405–18; Jan A. Aertsen, *Medieval Philosophy and the Transcendentals: The Case of Thomas Aquinas* (Leiden: Brill, 1996), 170–93; John F. Wippel, *Metaphysical Themes in Thomas Aquinas* (Washington, D.C.: The Catholic University of America Press, 1984), 69–104, and *The Metaphysical Thought of Thomas Aquinas* (Washington, D.C.: The Catholic University of America Press, 2000), 23–62.

8. *In Meta.* V, l. 21, nn. 1098–1108.

9. Ibid., nn. 1099–1101. I am considering Thomas's treatment out of order here for the purposes of this essay. Elsewhere, Thomas identifies a third kind of whole, the sort that includes potential or power parts, such as the soul (*ST* I, q. 77, a. 1, ad 1; II-II, q. 48, a. 1, co.; *In De An.*, a. 19, ad 4).

An integral whole is one in such a way that none of its parts is the one thing. The most obvious case of an integral whole is something that consists of quantitative parts, as in my example of Fido's body. No one part of his body is the whole body. And in an integral whole, the whole is not predicable of any of the parts: neither Fido's eye nor his leg nor any other bodily part could be called his "body." By contrast, a universal whole is one in such a way that it *is* predicable of each of its parts. For example, the genus *animal* is a whole that contains the species *man* and *horse*, and it is predicable of each of them. The reason that it is predicable of such parts is that the parts are present in the universal whole in such a way that each *is* the whole. Thus, we can say that the species *man* is *animal*, and so too with *horse* and every other species of *animal*.

It is clear in the case of an integral whole that its parts (which Thomas terms "integral parts") perfect the whole, because without them the whole is lacking in some way. But what about the parts of a universal whole, which he terms "subjective parts"?[10] It seems, in fact, that what he at first listed as a general characteristic of a whole does not apply to a universal whole. Indeed, shortly after identifying it in the *Metaphysics* commentary, Thomas notes that only a quantified whole can be mutilated, or made imperfect, through the loss of a part: "For a universal whole cannot be said to be mutilated if one of its species were taken away."[11] As he makes clear elsewhere, subjective parts are not required for the perfection of a universal whole because the perfect *ratio* of the whole is found in every part, as the genus *animal* is found in the species *man*.[12]

It should be clear that for Thomas *ens commune* is a universal whole. Indeed, he tells us that the division pertaining to being is not the same as the sort pertaining to continuous quantity.[13] To say that being is divided into the ten categories does not mean that it is divided into tenths, like a pie. Rather, as a universal whole, it is divided in such a way that it is nevertheless predicable of each of its parts: "being" is predicable of

---

10. *In Meta.* V, l. 21, n. 1097. See also *ST* II-II, q. 48, a. 1, co., and q. 120, a. 2, co.

11. *In Meta.* V, l. 21, n. 1110: "Non enim totum universale potest dici colobon si una species eius auferatur" (286).

12. *In Sent.* IV, d. 16, q. 1, a. 1, qa. 3, s.c. 1, ed. M. F. Moos (Paris: Lethielleux, 1947), 4:771: "Partes subiectivae non requiruntur ad perfectionem totius universalis: quia in qualibet parte perfecta ratio totius invenitur, sicut perfecta ratio animalis in homine."

13. *In Meta.* X, l. 4, n. 1997.

each and every category. Still, even though it is a universal whole, *ens commune* is not divided in the same way as a genus is. Thomas is careful to explain that there are two ways in which universals are divided into their parts, and these two ways are based upon the mode of universality that is involved.[14]

A genus is one type of universal, which is divided into species by differences that are not entailed in the *ratio* of the genus. Thus, the genus *animal* is divided into the species *man, horse*, etc., and it is divided equally, which is to say, univocally. By contrast, another type of universal is not divided according to differences, but instead according to "diverse modes."[15] It is universal according to analogy. And it is in this way that being is divided into the categories; for as Thomas famously notes following Aristotle, being is not a genus.[16] Although it is truly predicated of each and every category, being is not predicated of each according

14. *In Sent.* II, d. 42, q. 1, a. 3, co., ed. Mandonnet (Paris: Lethielleux, 1929), 2:1057: "Duplex modus dividendi commune in ea quae sub ipso sunt, sicut est duplex communitatis modus. Est enim quaedam divisio univoci in species per differentias quibus aequaliter natura generis in speciebus participatur, sicut animal dividitur in hominem et equum, et hujusmodi; alia vero divisio est ejus quod est commune per analogiam, quod quidem secundum perfectam rationem praedicatur de uno dividentium, et de altero imperfecte et secundum quid, sicut ens dividitur in substantiam et accidens, et in ens actu et in ens potentia: et haec divisio est quasi media inter aequivocum et univocum." See also *In Sent.* I, d. 22, q. 1, a. 3, ad 2; *ST* II-II, q. 120, a. 2, co.

15. *In Sent.* I, d. 22, q. 1, a. 3, ad 2 (ed. Mandonnet, 1:538): "Aliter dividitur aequivocum, analogum et univocum. Aequivocum enim dividitur secundum res significatas; univocum vero dividitur secundum differentias; sed analogum dividitur secundum diversos modos. Unde cum ens praedicetur analogice de decem generibus, dividitur in ea secundum diversos modos. Unde unicuique generi debetur proprius modus praedicandi." We can infer that there are no universals of the purely equivocal precisely because they are divided according to diverse *res significatae* and share no commonality.

16. See e.g., *De principiis naturae* 6; *In De interpretatione* I, l. 8, n. 5; *In Meta.* I, l. 9, n. 139. The analogical character of being is one of two reasons Thomas cites for why *ens commune* is not a genus; the other reason is that, unlike a genus, *ens commune* includes all differences. On this point see, e.g., *In Meta.* III, l. 8, n. 433; *De Ver.*, q. 1, a. 1. Despite his conclusion that *ens commune* is not a genus, in a number of places Thomas nevertheless explicitly refers to it as such (see, e.g., *In Meta.*, Prooemium; *De Ente*, chap. 6; *SCG* I.28.8; *ST* I, q. 2, a. 3, co., *quarta via*; *De Malo*, q. 1, a. 1, ad 11). The reason Thomas will refer to being in this way is that he sometimes will use the term "genus" in an extended, or metaphorical, way to speak of analogical communities because they are like *genera* as regards their universality. In one location, he refers to "genus" taken in this sense as a metaphysical genus, contrasting it with both a natural genus and logical genus, which are univocal in character. See my "Substance as a Metaphysical Genus," in *The Science of Being as Being: Metaphysical Investigations*, ed. Gregory T. Doolan (Washington, D.C.: The Catholic University of America Press, 2012), 99–128. Regarding Thomas's use of the term "metaphysical genus," see *De spiritualibus creaturis*, a. 1, ad 10.

to a *ratio* that is entirely the same. Rather, each of the nine categories of accidents is called "being" with reference to substance, inasmuch as substance is the subject of the other categories. Thus, being is predicated according to a relationship of priority and posteriority.[17]

In this way, then, the universal whole that is *being-in-general* is divided into the categories as its subjective parts.[18] We might ask, then, whether being requires *all* of these parts. If we consider Thomas's observation that subjective parts are not required for the perfection of a universal whole, it seems that being does not need all of them. Does this mean that its division into the ten categories is merely contingent upon the structure of the universe as God has willed it? Could being be divided by other, different categories? Or by a shorter list? To begin to answer these questions, let us turn to a brief discussion of Thomas's account of the derivation of the categories.

The Derivation of the Categories

Thomas provides us with detailed accounts of this derivation in two of his works: the commentary on Aristotle's *Physics* and the commentary on Aristotle's *Metaphysics*.[19] Although these accounts are similar, there are some notable differences between them (see figure 6-1). Because the latter is Thomas's more mature presentation as well as the more metaphysical one, it will be my focus here.[20]

17. *De principiis naturis* 6.

18. *ST* II-II, q. 120, a. 2, co., Leon. (Rome: Leonine Commission, 1897), 8:470: "Pars autem subiectiva est de qua essentialiter praedicatur totum, et est in minus. Quod quidem contingit dupliciter: quandoque enim aliquid praedicatur de pluribus secundum unam rationem, sicut animal de equo et bove; quandoque autem praedicatur secundum prius et posterius, sicut ens praedicatur de substantia et accidente."

19. See *In Phys.* III, l. 5, nn. 321–24 (written 1268–69), and *In Meta.* V, l. 9, nn. 889–97 (written 1270–71). Dating of Thomas's texts follows Jean-Pierre Torrell's *Saint Thomas Aquinas*, vol. 1, *The Person and His Works*, rev. ed., trans. Robert Royal (Washington, D.C.: The Catholic University of America Press, 2005).

20. For scholarship on Thomas's derivation of the categories, see John F. Wippel, "Thomas Aquinas's Derivation of the Aristotelian Categories (Predicaments)," *Journal of the History of Philosophy* 25 (1987): 13–34, and *Metaphysical Thought*, 208–28; E. P. Bos and A. C. van der Helm, "The Division of Being over the Categories According to Albert the Great, Thomas Aquinas and John Duns Scotus," in *John Duns Scotus: Renewal of Philosophy* (Amsterdam: Rodopi, 1998), 183–96, at 187–89; Paul Symington, "Thomas Aquinas on Establishing the Identity of Aristotle's *Categories*," in *Medieval Commentaries on Aristotle's* Categories, ed. Lloyd Newton

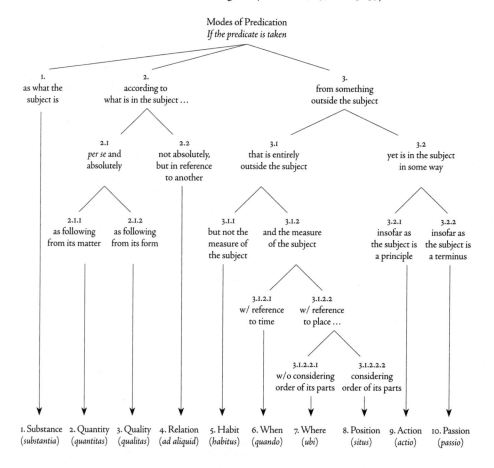

The Derivation of the Categories (*In Meta.* V., l. 9, nn. 889–97)

Modes of Predication
If the predicate is taken

1.
as what the
subject is

2.
according to
what is in the subject …

3.
from something
outside the subject

2.1
per se and
absolutely

2.2
not absolutely,
but in reference
to another

3.1
that is entirely
outside the subject

3.2
yet is in the subject
in some way

2.1.1
as following
from its matter

2.1.2
as following
from its form

3.1.1
but not the
measure of
the subject

3.1.2
and the measure
of the subject

3.2.1
insofar as
the subject is
a principle

3.2.2
insofar as
the subject is
a terminus

3.1.2.1
w/ reference
to time

3.1.2.2
w/ reference
to place …

3.1.2.2.1
w/o considering
order of its parts

3.1.2.2.2
considering
order of its parts

1. Substance
(*substantia*)

2. Quantity
(*quantitas*)

3. Quality
(*qualitas*)

4. Relation
(*ad aliquid*)

5. Habit
(*habitus*)

6. When
(*quando*)

7. Where
(*ubi*)

8. Position
(*situs*)

9. Action
(*actio*)

10. Passion
(*passio*)

FIGURE 6-1. The Derivation of the Categories in *In Meta.* V, l. 9, nn. 889–97, and *In Phys.* III, l. 5, n. 322

The Derivation of the Categories (*In Phys.* III, l. 5, n. 322)

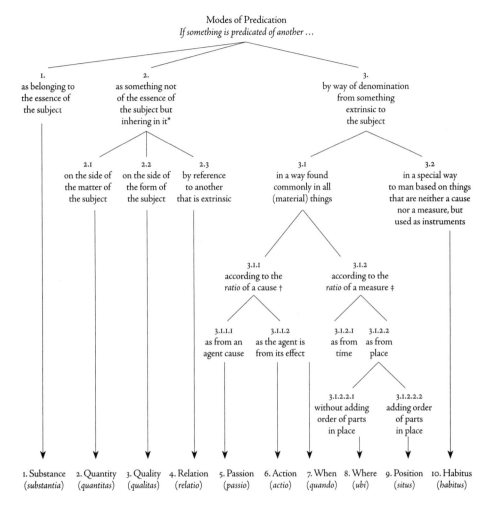

Modes of Predication
If something is predicated of another …

1.
as belonging to
the essence of
the subject

2.
as something not
of the essence of
the subject but
inhering in it*

3.
by way of denomination
from something
extrinsic to
the subject

2.1
on the side of
the matter of
the subject

2.2
on the side of
the form of
the subject

2.3
by reference
to another
that is extrinsic

3.1
in a way found
commonly in all
(material) things

3.2
in a special way
to man based on things
that are neither a cause
nor a measure, but
used as instruments

3.1.1
according to the
ratio of a cause †

3.1.2
according to the
ratio of a measure ‡

3.1.1.1
as from an
agent cause

3.1.1.2
as the agent is
from its effect

3.1.2.1
as from
time

3.1.2.2
as from
place

3.1.2.2.1
without adding
order of parts
in place

3.1.2.2.2
adding order
of parts
in place

1. Substance   2. Quantity   3. Quality   4. Relation   5. Passion   6. Action   7. When   8. Where   9. Position   10. Habitus
(*substantia*)   (*quantitas*)   (*qualitas*)   (*relatio*)   (*passio*)   (*actio*)   (*quando*)   (*ubi*)   (*situs*)   (*habitus*)

* Although Thomas does not explicitly divide this second mode of predication in terms of absolute and non-absolute inherence as he does in his later commentary on the Metaphysics, he nevertheless implicitly acknowledges here that basic division when he gives an example of fatherhood as a relation: "cum enim dico homo est pater, non praedicatur de homine aliquid absolutum, sed respectus qui ei inest ad aliquid extrinsecum."

† An extrinsic cause. Thomas notes here that matter and form are intrinsic causes, which are parts of the essence of a (material) being. Hence, predication based upon these causes pertains to the category substance. Although the final cause, like the agent cause, is extrinsic to the effect; since it only has the character (ratio) of a cause inasmuch as it moves the agent, it does not cause anything apart from the agent cause. Hence, Thomas concludes that the only extrinsic cause from which something is denominated is the agent cause.

‡ An extrinsic measure. If the subject is denominated by a measure that is intrinsic, the denomination pertains to the category quantity. He identifies these measures as the subject's length, width, and depth.

In his *In Meta.* V, l. 9, Thomas explains that the division of being into the categories is of the kind that lies outside the mind—real being as opposed to logical being. But how do we know that such being is divided into the categories that Aristotle identifies? Aristotle himself never offers a justification for his division; but Thomas now does. Going beyond a literal commentary of the text at hand, he offers a methodology for deriving the categories.

As he explains, the sorts of things that are said in the proper sense "to be" are the sorts of things that signify the different figures of predication. Reminding us that being is not a genus, Thomas notes that it cannot be divided by differences but is instead divided according to diverse modes of predication. Lest we think this is merely a linguistic or grammatical account of the derivation of the categories, Thomas is careful to note that these modes of predication themselves follow from diverse modes of existing (*modi essendi*), because in whatever way the term "being" (*ens*) is predicated, in just as many ways "to be" (*esse*) is signified. It is for this reason that Thomas commonly calls the categories "predicaments."

Following this approach, which he terms the method of predication (*modus praedicandi*), Thomas offers a detailed account of the derivation of the categories. He notes that some words signify "what a thing is" (or *substance*) as when we say, "A human is an animal." Some words signify "what sort" (or *quality*) as when we say, "A human is white." Some signify "how much" (or *quantity*), and so forth. I will not get into the details of how he derives each category (instead, see figure 6-1). Suffice it to say that according to Thomas, every mode of predication must signify a mode of existing (*esse*).[21]

Still, Thomas himself grants that in itself the method of predication is a logical methodology, because predication is the province of logic. It is not metaphysics that studies *genera* and species, but logic. This is so because a genus, such as a category, is not a real being (*ens naturae*) but only a being of reason (*ens rationis*), for a genus taken as such cannot

---

(Leiden: Brill, 2008), 119–44; Paul Symington, *On Determining What There Is: The Identify of Ontological Categories in Aquinas, Scotus and Lowe* (Piscataway, N.J.: Ontos, 2010); and Gregory T. Doolan, "Aquinas on the Metaphysician's vs. the Logician's Categories," *Quaestiones Disputatae* 4 (2014): 133–55.

21. *In Meta.* V, l. 9, nn. 889–97.

exist outside of the mind. Nevertheless, our concepts and words signify things in reality. And because there is this connection between predication and real being, he concludes that the method of predication can be employed in the service of metaphysics.[22] There are some limitations to its use as such a tool, but he thinks it is effective at least in this basic respect: namely, in identifying the fundamental modes of being.[23]

Considering Thomas's use of this tool, scholars generally agree that he views all ten of the traditional Aristotelian categories as real modes of being (a view not held by most of his later medieval counterparts). For Thomas, none of these categories is reducible to any of the others; rather each is a distinct, irreducible mode of being. Again, scholars also tend to agree that he views the list of ten categories as sufficient in number, exhaustive of all possible modes of (finite) being.[24] It seems that in Thomas's view, there could not be an eleventh category or further additional categories. This conclusion follows from his use of the method of predication, which, as he presents it, provides a list of modes of being that are mutually exclusive and jointly exhaustive. The list of ten categories is complete: they are all *per se* parts of being (*ens commune*), and being must be divided in terms of them. If that is the case, we might next ask if he considers them also to be necessary parts of the universe.

The Categories as "Parts" of the Universe

As we have seen, Thomas's use of the method of predication is intended to offer a quasi-deduction of the categories. But that does not mean that it is intended to prove what *in fact* exists. Consistently, Thomas avoids the path of the rationalist who argues from the mind to the world. Even though the method is a logical one, as he employs it the method presupposes experience of the world: an experience of beings *in* the categories—beings that we come to know and talk about. He does not try to

---

22. *In Meta.* IV, l. 4, n. 574; VII, l. 1, n. 1253; VII, l. 3, n. 1308.

23. One such limitation is that the logician is concerned with formal definition and not with act and potency. As a result, he treats genera as univocal which in reality are analogical. One such genus is the very category *substance*. On this point, see *Expos. de Trin.*, q. 4, a. 2. On the analogical character of the genus *substance*, see my "Substance as Metaphysical Genus," 99–128. See also my "Aquinas on the Metaphysician's vs. the Logician's Categories."

24. See note 20 above.

deduce the categories in a purely *a priori* way. Hence, for Thomas, simply to say that the categories are *per se* parts of being is not to say that they are necessary parts of this universe. What the method of predication reveals is that they are *per se* parts of the universal whole that is *ens commune*: the concept of being-in-general. As such, the method in itself does not on its own tell us what is actually existing—or even what must exist—but tells us only what is absolutely possible inasmuch as it does not violate the principle of noncontradiction.[25]

With that said, I would contend that another line of Thomas's reasoning does suggest that all ten categories are indeed in some sense necessary parts of the universe. This is the picture we get if we consider his observations regarding the perfection of the universe, observations in which he maintains that certain parts of the universe were necessarily created by God. This statement will no doubt seem surprising if we consider what he has to say about God's freedom and power.

According to Thomas, not only is God free to create or not to create, but he is also free to create a different universe, and it is in his power to do so. Thus, he could create a universe with only angels.[26] And if he did create such a universe, there would be nothing existing, for example, in the categories *position* or *place*: these modes of existence would remain uninstantiated. Again, God could create a universe with only accidents. Even though Thomas holds that it belongs to an accident to exist within a substance, he also notes that it is within God's power to cause an accident to exist independently of any substance, as occurs in the case of the Eucharist.[27] Following this account, it seems to be within God's power to create a universe with no beings in the category *substance* (as curious as such a universe would be). And again, following from Thomas's metaphysics, God is free to create either of these alternate universes.

25. Regarding Thomas's identification of the principle of noncontradiction as the standard for determining absolute possibility, see e.g., *De Pot.*, q. 1, a. 3. One might object that the method of predication could at least tell us what exists with hypothetical necessity, for one might argue that *if* accidents exist, so must substance. Nevertheless, this line of reasoning does not hold up if we consider that Thomas considers it to be within God's power to create accidents that do not in fact depend upon substances, as occurs in the case of the Eucharist. See *In Sent.* IV, d. 12, q. 1, a. 1, qa. 1, ad 1, and *ST* III, q. 77, a. 1, ad 2.

26. Thomas indicates at least the possibility of a universe with only two angels in *In Sent.* I, d. 44, q. 1, a. 2, ad 6. See note 32 below.

27. See note 25 above.

To my knowledge, Thomas never explicitly answers the question whether this given universe or any universe God might create must contain instantiations of each of the ten categories. Nevertheless, I believe he offers an implicit answer to this question in his various discussions about the parts of the universe. On a number of occasions, he considers the universe as an integral whole, noting that certain parts are essential for its perfections. In the *Summa contra Gentiles*, for example, he tells us that "it pertains to divine providence that the grades of being [*gradus entium*] that are possible be fulfilled .... But being [*ens*] is divided by the contingent and the necessary, and this is a *per se* division of being. If therefore divine providence were to exclude all contingency, not all the grades of beings would be preserved."[28] In addition to the contingent and necessary, elsewhere he identifies the grades of beings in terms of the incorporeal and the corporeal, and the simple and the composite.[29] In each case, the implication is the same: the universe without these grades would be imperfect. As God did not create an imperfect universe, he must necessarily have created it with these essential parts.

In making these claims, Thomas is not arguing that every possible *species* must be created for the universe to be complete. Cajetan, commenting on one of Thomas's arguments for the existence of angels, clarifies this point by drawing a distinction between the grades of beings (*gradus rerum*) and the special modes (*modi speciales*) of these grades. As he explains, for Thomas the grades of being are determined by various degrees of act and potency. Hence there is a finite number of them. The supreme of these is most like God, and this is the grade of intellectual being. As regards the special modes (or species) of beings, there is again only a finite number as created, although as regards logical possibility and God's power, the number of possible species is infinite.[30]

28. SCG III.72.3, Leon. (Rome: Leonine Commission, 1926), 14:214: "Ad divinam providentiam pertinet ut gradus entium qui possibiles sunt, adimpleantur, ut ex supra dictis patet. Ens autem dividitur per contingens et necessarium: et est per se divisio entis. Si igitur divina providentia excluderet omnem contingentiam, non omnes gradus entium conservarentur."

29. *ST* I, q. 48, a. 2, co.; SCG III.72.3; *ST* I, q. 22, a. 2, co.; *De Pot.*, q. 3, a. 16, co.

30. Cajetan, *Commentaria, Summa theologiae* I, q. 50, a. 1, Leon., 5:4–5: "Unde perfectio universi exigit quidem continentiam omnium graduum creabilium, sed non omnes creaturas creabiles. Et ideo ex perfectione universi optime infertur gradus intellectualis." I am grateful to Fr. Lawrence Dewan for drawing my attention to Cajetan's commentary on this article. For Dewan's own discussion of this text, see "Thomas Aquinas and Being as a Nature," *Acta Philosophica* 12 (2003): 123–35, at 134.

If we follow Cajetan's reading, the perfection of the universe does not require the creation of any given species such as dog, oak tree, or rhinestone; it does, however, require the creation of at least some species of material beings and, similarly, some (or at least one) immaterial being. For, as Cajetan explains, "the perfection of the universe requires that it contain all grades of creatable things, but not all creatable creatures."[31] Still, this notion appears to be at odds with Thomas's doctrine of divine freedom: how is it that there can be necessary parts of the universe if it is within God's power and freedom to create a universe without them?

Thomas provides an answer to this question, among other places, in *De Pot.*, q. 3, a. 16, where he makes clear that although certain things are necessarily created, this necessity is a suppositional (or hypothetical) necessity, not an absolute one. There is no absolute necessity for God to create any kind of being because he need not create at all. But given the supposition that he does create, Thomas concludes that God must create certain things in a certain way. For example, if he creates man, God must create man as an animal that is rational, having both body and soul, otherwise what he creates would not be man. Similarly if God makes a universe at all, Thomas concludes that it must have certain essential parts, just as a house requires certain parts for it to be complete and to be a house, such as walls and a roof. And given that he has willed to make *such* a universe (*tale universum*)—by which I take Thomas to mean one like this given universe—it was necessary that God produce many and diverse creatures as its parts, some of which are simple, some composed, some corruptible, some incorruptible: in short, the grades of being mentioned before.[32] And this hypothetical necessity, Thomas tells us, follows from the intended form of the universe, which form he thinks we can infer from experience of the universe in which we live.[33]

---

31. Cajetan, *Commentaria, Summa theologiae* I, q. 50, a. 1, Leon., 5:4–5.

32. Thus, Thomas notes, "quamvis angelus absolute sit melior quam lapis, tamen utraque natura est melior quam altera tantum: et ideo melius est universum in quo sunt angeli et aliae res, quam ubi essent angeli tantum: quia perfectio universi attenditur essentialiter secundum diversitatem naturarum, quibus implentur diversi gradus bonitatis, et non secundum multiplicationem individuorum in una natura." *In Sent.* I, d. 44, q. 1, a. 2, ad 6 (ed. Mandonnet, 1:1020–21).

33. *De Pot.*, q. 3, a. 16, co., ed. M. Pession (Turin: Marietti, 1953), 87: "Sed supposito quod tale universum producere voluerit, necessarium fuit quod tales et tales creaturas produxerit, ex quibus talis forma universi consurgeret. Et cum ipsa universi perfectio et multitudinem et diversitatem rerum requirat, quia in una earum inveniri non potest propter recessum a complemento bonitatis primae; necesse fuit ex suppositione formae intentae quod Deus multas creaturas et

Thomas is careful to note, however, that this necessity does not stem from a limitation of God's power. Nor is it due to a demand of God's goodness, as the Neo-Platonists would hold. God is free to create or not to create, and (presumably) he is also free to create a universe without some of the grades of being. Instead, Thomas concludes, this hypothetical necessity is due to the order of God's wisdom: acting in light of it, God creates a universe that is perfect with all of its essential parts. Knowing what is best, God does what is best.[34] Thomas does not mean by this that the universe is a sort of Leibnizian "best possible world"; rather, as he notes in reply to an objection within the same article, "the universe that has been made by God is best as regards those things that exist, but not as regards those things that God can make."[35] God could always make this universe better, not by the addition of grades of being, but by the addition of new and different species.

Let us grant Thomas's position that all of the grades of being are necessary parts of this created universe. What follows for him, I would argue, is that all of the categories of being are also, by extension, necessary parts—perhaps not all as essential parts, but at least as something akin to properties or necessary accidents entailed by those that are.[36] Consider that one of the grades of being he identifies is corporeal being. If such being is an essential part of the universe, it follows that the category *substance* must be instantiated. And if there are bodily substances, there must also be quantities, as the category *quantity* follows upon the matter of such substances. Again, there must also be physical *qualities*

---

diversas produceret; quasdam simplices, quasdam compositas; et quasdam corruptibiles, et quasdam incorruptibiles."

34. Ibid.

35. *De Pot.*, q. 3, a. 16, ad 17: "Universum quod est a Deo productum, est optimum respectu eorum quae sunt, non tamen respectu eorum quae Deus facere potest" (90). Thomas addresses the topic of the "best possible world" a number of times throughout *De Pot.* See, e.g., *De Pot.*, q. 1, a. 5, ad 14–15; q. 3, a. 6, ad 26; q. 5, a. 1, ad 14. He also offers an *ex professo* consideration of this topic in the early *In Sent.* I, d. 44, q. 1, a. 2. On this topic, see Oliva Blanchette, *The Perfection of the Universe according to Aquinas* (University Park: Pennsylvania State University Press, 1992), 98–105 and 137–40.

36. My claim that Thomas implicitly views all the categories as necessary parts of the created universe is not to claim that he thinks each category must be instantiated at every given moment. Speaking in general about the necessary parts of the universe, he draws an analogy from the development of the human body, noting that the heart is formed in the embryo before any of the other organ parts. Similarly, the necessary parts of the universe need not have all existed together at its beginning, even though they must exist together at some later point in time for the world to be perfect and complete (*De Pot.*, q. 4, a. 2, ad s.c. 3).

possessed by them, such as colors, heat, and textures. Similarly, there must be *relations* between the aforementioned substances, and these substances have to exist at a certain *time, place,* and in a certain *position.* As corporeal beings are mobile beings, they will inevitably perform *actions* and suffer *passions.* The existence of corporeal substances, then, together with their ensuing accidents, ensures that each of the categories of being is manifested in the universe, with the exception of that one curious category, *habit* or *equipment* (not to be confused with the habit that is a quality).

This category, in Thomas's view, constitutes a real mode of being that is predicated of a subject as something extrinsic to it, but not as a measure of the subject.[37] As he presents it, the category is uniquely predicable of man alone, who as a rational being is able to "have" things in a way that other beings cannot.[38] Thus, for Thomas, a condition such as "being clothed," "being shod," or "being armed" is a real mode of existence that has its being dependent upon the existence of man.[39] For this last category to be a necessary part of the universe, therefore, man would have to be as well. And, indeed, Thomas holds this to be the case. He tells us that man is an essential part of the universe because of his rational soul as well as his body that is ordered to the perfection of his nature. With his immaterial form, man is unique in the physical order.[40] As Eleonore Stump puts it, the human soul is a metaphysical amphibian, "occupying

37. *In Meta.* V, l. 9, n. 892.

38. *In Phys.* III, l. 5. In this text, he notes that this category can, by extension, be predicated of other animals: "non secundum quod in sua natura considerantur, sed secundum quod in hominis usum veniunt; ut si dicamus equum phaleratum vel sellatum seu armatum" (ed. P. M. Maggiolo [Turin: Marietti, 1954], 159).

39. Thomas does not appear to go beyond these traditional examples in any of his writings, lending the impression that the category *habitus* only concerns the having of clothing items or weaponry. Indeed, his account in *In Phys.* III, l. 5, of the derivation of this category focuses on man's need and ability to preserve and protect himself by having items. Elsewhere, however, he gives a more general account of the category, presenting it as a distinct mode of existence because such "having" is a medium between the haver and what is had, "prout scilicet unum est ornans vel tegens, et aliud ornatum aut tectum." *ST* I-II, q. 49, a. 1, co. (309). As I read Thomas, this sort of "having" could extend to any sort of material object that a human being might make use of on his person, for example, wearing a decorative hat, having a cup in hand, using a tool like a hammer, or playing a musical instrument like a flute. For a detailed consideration and defense of the category *habitus* according to Thomas, see Mark K. Spencer, "The Category of Habitus: Artifacts, Accidents, and Human Nature," *The Thomist* 79 (2015): 113–54.

40. *De Pot.*, q. 5, a. 10, co.

a niche in both the material and the spiritual realm."[41] Consequently, for Thomas, humans constitute a distinct grade of being. And inasmuch as human beings are an essential part of the universe that will inevitably act in accord with their natures as rational beings, their existence ensures that the category *habitus* is part of the universe as well.[42]

So much for this given universe. But what of other possible universes? As I have noted, following Thomas's metaphysics, it seems to be within God's power to create a universe populated by a single angel or by accidents alone. In other words, God *could* create a universe in which only some of the categories of being are instantiated. And the reason this would be within God's power is that there is nothing logically contradictory about such worlds. Thus, in Thomas's terms, they are absolute possibilities. But *would* God create such worlds? Thomas does not seem to offer a definitive answer either way. If, however, we follow what he has to say regarding the perfection of *this* universe, the goodness of God's creative act, and the order of his wisdom, the implication appears at least that it would be unfitting for God to do so.

According to Thomas, every agent makes something like itself. Because God is the most perfect agent, it belongs to him to make something most perfectly like himself; and because no single species of finite being is perfectly like him, God created a multiplicity of beings. Discussing this created universe, Thomas notes in SCG that "it was necessary that there be a multiplicity and variety in created things for this reason: that there be found in them a perfect likeness of God according to their own manner."[43] Indeed, any universe God might create would be a likeness of God; viewing the issue from this perspective, then, we find in Thomas's writings the implication that any universe without all of the grades of being (and by extension all the categories of being) would be an unfitting likeness.

---

41. Stump, *Aquinas* (London: Routledge, 2003), 200; see also 17.

42. One objection to this conclusion might be that if man had never fallen from original sin, there would be no need for clothing or arms, and hence this category would not be instantiated. If, however, my hypothesis in note 39 above is correct—i.e., that the category of *habitus* for Aquinas extends to the having of other sorts of material objects as instruments of art—then even in a prelapsarian state there would be occasion for the instantiation of this category.

43. SCG II.45.2, Leon., 13:372: "Oportuit igitur esse multiplicitatem et varietatem in rebus creatis, ad hoc quod inveniretur in eis Dei similitudo perfecta secundum modum suum."

Conclusion

For Thomas, the ten Aristotelian categories are much more than logical intentions. As we have seen, these fundamental *genera* grasped by the mind refer back to fundamental modes of *esse*—modes of existing. And these modes are not merely parts of *ens commune*: they are also necessary parts of this created world. The reason that being manifests itself fully through all ten categories is that God makes the world as fully like himself as possible. Though God is not himself contained in any of the categories, Thomas tells us that he is nonetheless present in *all* of them as its measure and cause.[44] Thus, each of these parts of being—each of these finite modes of *esse*—is, in an imperfect way, like God; and the whole of created being, consisting of all of these parts taken together, is more perfectly like that infinite being who itself is subsisting *esse*.

44. *De Pot.*, q. 7, a. 4, ad 7. See also *In Sent.* I, d. 8, q. 4, a. 2, ad 3. Regarding God's presence in the genus *substance*, see my "Substance as a Metaphysical Genus," 119–27.

7

The Ontological Status of Artifacts

JAMES M. JACOBS

A perennial problem encountered in teaching Thomistic philosophy is that one is inclined to use classroom objects, such as desks, as examples of substances. The problem is that according to Thomistic metaphysics, artifacts clearly are not substances. In this essay, I hope to show that this common error arises due to the foundational Thomistic principle of the analogy of being: artifacts have activity similar to substances, but have a dependent, analogous mode of being. Natural substances reveal their essence through united activity; the united activity of artifacts, however, must be imposed on the materials by man through coordinated social practice. I will argue that this mental determination of the use of artifacts, which is ultimately an intentional reality, is the source of the artifacts' apparent ontological unity, and so the basis for their analogical similarity to natural substances. Although this thesis is grounded in Thomas's metaphysics, my argument develops those principles in light of the role of human culture, employing the insights of two quite different contemporary Thomists: John Deely and Alasdair MacIntyre. Hence, this argument is a sort of "creative retrieval" of Thomistic metaphysics enacted in order to help us understand the true ontological status of artifacts in a world increasingly dominated by manmade technology.[1]

1. The idea of a "creative retrieval" of Thomism is central to the work of the late W. Norris Clarke, SJ; see *Person and Being* (Milwaukee, Wis.: Marquette University Press, 1993), 1–5.

That Thomas does not consider artifacts to be substances is clear from his presentation of the ladder of being, for there he identifies as substances elements and inorganic compounds (such as complex molecular structures formed by nature), but skips from there to plants and animals.[2] Moreover, Thomas specifically states that artifacts are not substances. Thus, he says in his *In Meta.*, "some things are not substances, as is clear especially of artificial things."[3] As he succinctly explains in the *Principles of Nature*, "all artificial forms are accidental forms [for] art works only on what has already been put into existence by nature."[4] Thus, artificers simply rearrange existing substances, introducing new shapes (as bronze is formed into a statue) or new relations (as the parts of an ax are put together).[5] Because "art works upon materials furnished by nature" which already exist as substances,[6] this new shape or

---

Leo XIII, in *Aeterni Patris*, Encyclical Letter, August 4, 1879, recognizes that Thomas's metaphysics contains seeds for this kind of future development: "The Angelic Doctor pushed his philosophic conclusions into the reasons and principles of the things which are most comprehensive and contain in their bosom, so to say, the seeds of almost infinite truth" (par. 18); available at vatican.va.

2. See, for example, *Summa Contra Gentiles*, trans. Anton C. Pegis, James F. Anderson, Vernon J. Bourke, and Charles J. O'Neil (Notre Dame, Ind.: University of Notre Dame Press, 1975 [1955]), II.68 and IV.11. This position is affirmed in recent analyses of Thomistic metaphysics. For example, see Benedict M. Ashley, OP, *The Way toward Wisdom: An Interdisciplinary and Intercultural Introduction to Metaphysics* (Notre Dame, Ind.: University of Notre Dame Press, 2006), 224: "Below the level of life, distinct substances can also be identified, although chiefly at the level of single atoms or molecules that are intermixed with atoms or molecules of other species to form 'minerals.'" Another example can be found in Eleonore Stump, *Aquinas* (London: Routledge, 2003), 39–59. However, she also claims, "It may be that if Aquinas had known some of the products of contemporary technology, he would have found the distinction between substance and artifact harder to make crisp and clear" (44). I hope my argument can show how Thomas's principles avoid such confusion.

3. *In Meta.* VII, n. 1680, trans. John P. Rowan (Notre Dame, Ind.: University of Notre Dame Press, 1995 [1961]). Thomas makes this straightforward claim in many texts.

4. *The Principles of Nature*, chap. 1, in *Aquinas on Matter and Form and the Elements: A Translation and Interpretation of the* De Principiis Naturae *and the* De Mixtione Elementorum *of St. Thomas Aquinas*, trans. Joseph Bobik (Notre Dame, Ind.: University of Notre Dame Press, 1998). Cf. *In Phys.*, VII, l. 5, n. 915, trans. Richard J. Blackwell, Richard J. Spath, and W. Edmund Thirkel (Notre Dame, Ind.: University of Notre Dame Press, 1995 [1961]): "And a form is said to be that which gives specific being to an artifact. For the forms of artifacts are accidents."

5. *In Phys.* I, l. 12, n. 108: "Still other things come to be by composition, e.g., a house; and other things come to be by alteration, as those things whose matter is changed, either by nature or by art.... But it must be noted that artificial things are here enumerated along with those things which come to be simply (even though artificial forms are accidents) because artificial things are in some way in the genus of substance by reason of their matter."

6. *In De An.* II, l. 1, n. 218, trans. Kenelm Foster, OP, and Silvester Humphries, OP (Notre

relation must be an accidental form because, as Thomas explains, "whatever comes to a thing after it is complete in its being [as a substance], comes to it accidentally since it is outside that thing's essence."[7] This accidental form cannot be considered a substantial form because "in order that many things may become one actual thing, it is necessary that all should be included under one form, and that each one should not have its own form by which it would exist in act."[8] But the substances out of which an artifact is made retain their own form, thereby denying real unity to the artifact. Thomas illustrates this difference by contrasting an artifact to the way in which a soul truly unites disparate parts into one entity: "For since the body of a human being or of any other animal is a natural whole, it will be called one because it has one form; and by this one form it is completed in a way far different from the mere aggregation or assembling of parts that is found in a house and in other artifacts."[9] Thomas concludes, therefore, that artifacts are aggregates of substances, and not independent substances themselves.

Norris Clarke illuminates this by highlighting the fact of the transcendental unity of substantial being. Clarke begins by emphasizing the fact that activity is the self-revelation of being,[10] for as Thomas says, "All things created would seem, in a way, to be purposeless, if they lacked an operation proper to them; since the purpose of everything is its operation."[11] Thus, the unity of a being is made manifest to man in the unity of the activity by which the essence of the thing is revealed.[12] This is why

---

Dame, Ind.: University of Notre Dame, 1951): "Art works upon materials furnished by nature, giving these, moreover, a merely accidental form, such as a new shape and so forth; so that it is only in virtue of their matter, not their form, that artificial bodies are substances at all; they are substances because natural bodies are such. Natural bodies therefore are the more properly called substances, being such through their form as well as through their matter."

7. SCG II.58.6. In fact, Thomas argues that if an artifact loses that accidental form, it in no way changes the substances that composed it; see In De An. II, nn. 235–37.

8. In Meta. VII, l. 13, n. 1588; see also VIII, l. 3, n. 1719.

9. De Anima, trans. James H. Robb as Questions on the Soul (Milwaukee, Wis.: Marquette University Press, 1984), 10. See also Summa Theologiae, trans. Fathers of the English Dominican Province (Allen, Tex.: Christian Classics, 1981 [1911]), I, q. 76, a. 8: "Now the substantial form perfects not only the whole, but each part of the whole. For since a whole consists of parts, a form of the whole which does not give existence to each of the parts of the body, is a form consisting in composition and order, such as the form of a house; and such a form is accidental."

10. W. Norris Clarke, SJ, The One and the Many: A Contemporary Thomistic Metaphysics (Notre Dame, Ind.: University of Notre Dame Press, 2001), 31–34.

11. ST I, q. 105, a. 5, co.; see also SCG III.113.1.

12. See De Ver., q. 10, a. 1, trans. Robert William Mulligan, SJ, James V. McGlynn, SJ, and

Thomas argues for the unicity of substantial form in organic substances despite the variety of operative powers, for these activities are subordinated to the single operational unity of the substance.[13] It is this unity that is notably lacking in artifacts with readily interchangeable parts. Thus, Clarke argues that if there is not a single focused center of controlling activity, then there is not a single substance, but an aggregate united by some extrinsic consideration (for example: location, goal, time, etc.).[14] Thomas articulates this point clearly: "For the unity that accounts for [substantial unity] is not extrinsic to the nature of the thing ... as happens in the case of things which are one by art, in which the binding ... is entirely extrinsic to the nature of the things which are joined together."[15]

While this lack of ontological unity best exemplifies why artifacts are not substances, it is nevertheless obvious that an artifact does have a sort of united activity, otherwise it would not be functional; it does have a kind of unity that surpasses that of a mere pile or random amalgam of substances. (It is for this reason that we cannot define artifacts simply in terms of an accident of relation or location, for we need to explain why that relation subsists in a functional unity, and these categories merely beg the question.) We therefore need to discern the principle by which an artifact has an analogous mode of unity which is greater than that of a random amalgamation, yet less than a real natural substance.

As mentioned, this operational unity is convertible with, and revelatory of, the entity's being. Consequently, we must now make a digression to consider how natural substances are constituted as a single united being; we can then apply those principles to the analogical unity of artifacts. While some recent analyses of artifacts approach this question

---

Robert W. Schmidt, SJ, as *Truth* (Indianapolis, Ind.: Hackett, 1994 [1954]): "The essences of things are unknown to us, but their powers are revealed to us by their acts."

13. See the fundamental statement of this principle in *De mixtione elementorum* (in Bobik, *Aquinas on Matter and Form and the Elements*, 103–26); see the diverse applications of this principle to the human soul in *ST* I, qq. 75–78.

14. Clarke, *The One and the Many*, 65–68. Thomas argues for this extrinsic mode of unity in *ST* I-II, q. 17, a. 4, co.: "Nothing prevents certain things being distinct in one respect, and one in another respect.... Now 'one' is predicated in the same way as 'being.' And substance is being simply, whereas accident or being 'of reason' is a being only in a certain respect. Wherefore those things that are one in substance are one simply, though many in a certain respect." See also *In Meta.* VII, l. 4, n. 1340, where Thomas argues that unity applies primarily to substance, and only secondarily to accidents.

15. *In Meta.* V, l. 7, n. 851; see also V, l. 8, n. 870.

primarily in terms of matter-form composition,[16] this approach raises many perplexities concerning common-sense judgments about the unity and continued existence of artifacts over time.[17] Thus, we must seek a different solution.

This true solution can be found in the existential principle of unity behind matter-form composition. For Thomas, matter and form are principles which explain the fact of change in the world.[18] As principles, matter and form are not things,[19] and so their existence as principles must be explained by some prior metaphysical principle. Moreover, form and matter only explain *change*; this knowledge is at the first degree of abstraction in which the proximate causes of coming-to-be in the physical universe are understood.[20] The question of *being* is more profound; it is a properly metaphysical question, to which Thomas provides a metaphysical answer: form and matter are united by the act of existence which constitutes their substantial unity.

For one thing to be another's substantial form, two requirements must be met. First, the form must be the principle of the substantial being of the thing whose form it is.... The second requirement then follows from this, namely, that the form and the matter be joined together in the unity of one act of being.... And

16. See, most notably, Christopher M. Brown, *Aquinas and the Ship of Theseus: Solving Puzzles about Material Objects* (London: Bloomsbury Academic, 2005). In addition, the same author has a pair of related articles: "Souls, Ships, and Substances: A Response to Toner," *American Catholic Philosophical Quarterly* 81 (2007): 655–68, and "Artifacts, Substances, and Transubstantiation: Solving a Puzzle for Aquinas's View," *The Thomist* 71 (2007): 89–112. These discussions, however, by and large end up reiterating the conclusions we have already seen; thus, Brown says, "Artefacts [sic] too are material objects that Aquinas does not regard as substances. Many contemporary philosophers would find such a view counterintuitive" (*Ship of Theseus*, 98). Despite my differences, I have benefited greatly from Brown's research.

17. Brown himself admits this; see *Ship of Theseus*, 130–43. Brown's conclusion to this analysis is that for Aquinas, an artifact is identical if and only if it has the same accidental configuring form (of order/composition) that configures the same matter uninterrupted in time (133). He admits that this is a very restrictive idea of artifact identity, but claims that it presents no problem for Aquinas because artifacts are not substances in any case. It is only because our intuitions assume they are substances that this seems severely restrictive. I will argue that this analysis can be improved with a discussion of the proper mode of existence of artifacts, as well as a correlative analysis of their final causality, as this best illustrates their unity.

18. *Principles of Nature*, chap. I, in Bobik, *Aquinas on Matter and Form and the Elements*, 1–14.

19. On this point, see John Goyette, "St. Thomas on the Unity of Substantial Form," *Nova et Vetera* 7 (2009): 781–90.

20. See *Expos. de Trin.*, q. 5, aa. 1–3, trans. Armand Maurer as *The Division and Methods of the Sciences: Questions V–VI of the Commentary on the* De Trinitate *of Boethius*, 4th rev. ed. (Toronto: Pontifical Institute of Mediaeval Studies, 1986).

this single act of being is that in which the composite substance subsists: a thing one in being and made up of matter and form.[21]

Or, more succinctly, he says, "Being itself is the proper act, not of matter, but of the whole substance ... and being [*esse*] is that whereby the substance is called a being [*ens*]."[22] The question of existential unity cannot be accounted for by form alone, as the form itself must be given existence and united to the matter.[23] Indeed, Thomas says that, as principles united by *esse*, form and matter must be concreated and ontologically proportioned to one another.[24] Thus, it is clear that it is the act of existence that constitutes the co-principles in an existential and active unity as one substantial whole.

But if the act of existence is what constitutes real substantial unity, it is also crucial to understand that this act of existence is communicated to a substance by essence, for Thomas defines essence as that through which and in which a thing has being.[25] This is because for any essence that is not simply existence, that essence must be in potency to existence, and this potency limits the act of existence to a determinate mode of being,[26] thus making the substance a specific kind of being. Moreover, as the act of existence for a material composite being constitutes both its form and its matter, the defining essence of these beings necessarily includes both principles.[27] The essence, then, communicates the unique delimited act of existence that constitutes and defines the individual entity, giving the substance its actuality, its quiddity, its unity in operation, and its concomitant intelligibility.[28]

21. SCG II.68.3.

22. SCG II.54.3 and 6.

23. *ST* I, q. 3, a. 4: "Secondly, existence is that which makes every form or nature actual.... Therefore existence must be compared to essence, if the latter is a distinct reality, as actuality to potentiality."

24. See *ST* I, q. 45, a. 4, co. ("Ita magis debent dici concreata quam creata"), and SCG II.80–81.7–8 ("Formam igitur et materiam semper oportet esse ad invicem proportionata et quasi naturaliter coaptata").

25. See *De Ente*, chap. 1.4, trans. Armand Maurer as *On Being and Essence*, 2nd ed. (Toronto: Pontifical Institute of Mediaeval Studies, 1968).

26. *De Ente*, chap. 4.8: "Everything that receives something from another is potential with regard to what it receives, and what is received in it is its actuality." The limitation of act by receptive potency is a pillar of Thomistic metaphysics; see, for example, SCG I.43.5.

27. *De Ente*, chap. 2.3: "It remains, then, that in the case of composite substances the term 'an essence' signifies the composite of matter and form."

28. This, of course, is just an affirmation of the convertibility of the transcendentals.

Yet a problem emerges: if the essence constitutes a particular individual substance, how can it simultaneously be a universal quiddity such that it can define a species? Thomas resolves this problem, characteristically, with reference to the nature of existence. The essence itself has necessary defining qualities (man is rational, political, animal, etc.), but is neither, in itself, individual nor universal; it is existentially neutral.[29] The mode of existence is determined by whether it is real or intentional: if the essence exists in matter as a determinate individual, it is singular, yet if the essence exists in the mind, it is abstracted from the designated matter, and so is universal. This correlation between the essence's real subsistence and its intentional presence in the mind are the necessary foundation for science, by which universal principles are known, in spite of the factual particularity and contingency of real substances.

Thus, because we can know universals, it is clear that not all knowledge or predication has to do with real essences. Indeed, following Aristotle, Thomas says that *being* is used in two ways: to indicate categorical modes of being which really exist, as substance or accident; and in any way so as to make a proposition true.[30] The primary meaning of being is the real being indicated by the categories.[31] But the other kind of being, as for example privations, must use being in an analogous sense: the "being" of a privation is entirely dependent on the fact of predication, so it is a kind of dependent mode of being due to its lack of an independent act of existence.[32] This dependency on mental predication is akin to the intentional existence of universal natures abstracted from real essences. Therefore, universalized essences do not exist in themselves (as they do for Plato), yet they have a mode of being that is dependent on the predicating mind and so allow us to have scientific knowledge of material individuals.

29. This argument is made in *De Ente*, chap. 3.

30. See, for example, *De Ente*, chap. 1.2: "We must realize (with the Philosopher) that the term 'a being' in itself has two meanings. Taken one way it is divided by the ten categories; taken in the other way it signifies the truth of propositions. The difference between the two is that in the second sense anything can be called a being if an affirmative proposition can be formed about it, even though it is nothing positive in reality. In this way privations and negations are called beings .... But in the first way nothing can be called a being unless it is something positive in reality."

31. *De Ente*, chap. 1.3. In 1.5, Thomas specifies that among categorical beings, substances have priority over accidents because accidents are modes of being dependent on substances.

32. This dependency of privation on real being is just a further modulation of the dependency of accident on substance, for there are multiple levels of dependency defining the analogy of being.

There are, then, two mind-dependent modes of existence: privations and universals. These purely intentional beings are intelligible because they are grounded in some real being, and are referred to real being through abstraction or negation. But John Deely has argued that, in addition to these, there are other mind-dependent modes of being that play an important role in the constitution of intelligible human experience.[33] Deely's analysis of the role of signs in cognition overcomes the idea that being is restricted to *ens reale*, as the signs that are necessary for intelligence exist in a purely mind-dependent fashion.[34] In addition to those that are directly referrable to real beings (negations and universals), he suggests other mind-dependent beings that are primarily constituted in the mind as purely intentional. For example, fictions have a mode of existence that is mind-dependent: I can meaningfully affirm that Hamlet is the melancholy Dane, or that Santa is a jolly old man, and yet not affirm anything about their existence outside the mind. More significant, though, are those intentions constituted for the sake of organizing the human environment, such as cultural realities like political borders and offices of authority.[35] A political border is nothing visible from space, and yet in human intercourse it is real, with an active presence analogous to a real being's activity. In what way, then, are these intentional beings real? As being is communicated and defined by essence, I suggest that these have a kind of analogical essence which, as mind-dependent, I will call an intentional essence. As mind-dependent, the act of existence for these intentional essences lies in their being understood.[36] It is the act of understanding these intentional essences that gives them a real, active presence in the world. Because they lack real essences, they have no essential definition; they have nominal definitions by which they are recognized in human intercourse, but these have no reality outside the intersubjectivity by which their mind-dependent essences are constituted.

33. See in general John Deely, *Four Ages of Understanding* (Toronto: University of Toronto Press, 2001), and *The Impact on Philosophy of Semiotics* (South Bend, Ind.: St. Augustine's Press, 2003).

34. See SCG IV.11. See also Jacques Maritain's essay "Sign and Symbol" in *Ransoming the Time*, trans. Harry Lorin Binsse (New York: Scribners, 1941), 217–54, esp. 220–22 and 232–33.

35. These are examples that Deely cites; see the discussion in *The Impact on Philosophy of Semiotics*, 23–29.

36. SCG IV.11.6: "The act of being of the intention understood consists in its very being understood."

Man, therefore, can create intentional essences to organize the world. This is how practical reason orders material substance and determines the being and truth of artifacts:

Note, however, that a thing is referred differently to the practical intellect than it is to the speculative intellect. Since the practical intellect causes things, it is a measure of what it causes. But, since the speculative intellect is receptive in regard to things, it is, in a certain sense, moved by things and consequently measured by them. It is clear, therefore, that … natural things from which our intellect gets its scientific knowledge measure our intellect. Yet these things are themselves measured by the divine intellect … just as all works of art find their origin in the intellect of an artist. The divine intellect, therefore, measures and is not measured; a natural thing both measures and is measured; but our intellect is measured, and measures only artifacts, not natural things.[37]

Practical reason measures things by the forms conceived in the mind of the artisan.[38] As mentioned above, however, the craftsman cannot create a real substance with a real essence; rather, he uses already existing substances as instruments to an end, and so the artifact does not have real existential unity. It has an intentional unity arising from that conceived form accidentally uniting those substances;[39] it is this intentionality that is the extrinsic source of unity for the artifact and so acts as the essence of the artifact.[40] This is, in part, what Thomas means in affirming that "the speculative intellect by extension becomes practical."[41] By understanding the nature and potentiality of substances, man can harness the power of nature to accomplish an end he desires. Indeed, it is because the intentional essence constitutes the existence and truth of

37. De Ver., q. 1, a. 2; cf. ST I, q. 14, a. 8, ad 3.

38. De Pot., q. 7, a. 1, ad 8, trans. English Dominican Fathers as On the Power of God (Westminster, Md.: Newman Press, 1952 [1932]): "Now whereas a thing may be in the intellect as the thing which we understand, and as the species whereby we understand, art-forms are in the intellect as that whereby we understand: because it is through conceiving the form of his art-work that the craftsman produces that work in matter."

39. De Pot., q. 10, a. 2, ad 11: "The will imprints on the artifact the form which in the logical order was understood before it was willed, wherefore it is a likeness first of the intellect, though secondly of the will."

40. In Meta. V, l. 1, n. 762: "But while all principles agree in the respect just mentioned, they nevertheless differ, because some are intrinsic and others extrinsic, as is clear from the above. Hence nature and element, which are intrinsic, can be principles. … 'And mind,' i.e., intellect, and 'purpose,' i.e., a man's intention, are said to be principles as extrinsic ones."

41. ST I, q. 79, a. 11, s.c.

the artifact that we can know it more fully than any natural substance, whose ultimate truth rests in God's mind.[42]

This constituting of artifacts in the mind of man is a kind of similitude of the divine act of creation.[43] Only God can give the true act of existence, as only he whose essence is existence can communicate being to something that does not exist.[44] Nevertheless, man can give a similitude of the act of existence in constituting artifacts as extrinsically unified wholes through the intentional operation of practical reason. Moreover, in these cases, it is man's mind that is the rule and measure for the truth of the thing made, because it is man who constitutes the intentional essence of the artifact.

The intentional nature of these essences is made clear when we understand that this imposed unity is ordered by final causality, for it is this proposed purpose that motivates the artificer to organize the world in a certain way. Artifacts, for Thomas, exist to be used;[45] accordingly, it is the intended operation that defines the artifact.[46] Recall that natural substances exist for the sake of their operation; however, because artifacts have no inherent natural operation, they rely for this on the creative intent of the artificer.[47] In fact, Thomas argues that the nature

42. Thus, Thomas's famous claim that man can never know the essence of a fly. See also Josef Pieper, *In Defense of Philosophy: Classical Wisdom Stands up to Modern Challenges*, trans. Lothar Krauth (San Francisco, Calif.: Ignatius Press, 1992), 78: "We are dealing with the fundamental and unalterable difference between things made by man and things not made by man, between *res artificiales* and *res naturales*, that is: between those things that have received their identity from human ingenuity and are therefore totally knowable, and those things that have received their identity from a divine thought and are for this reason forever beyond our full comprehension; for no finite power will ever penetrate so deep as to reach the archetypes that dwell in the mind of God."

43. See Etienne Gilson, *The Arts of the Beautiful* (Normal, Ill.: Dalkey Archive Press, 2000 [1965]), 69–109, esp. 78.

44. See *ST* I, q. 44, a. 1.

45. Most artifacts are restricted to use (*uti*); however, we must acknowledge that significant field of artifacts that are made to be enjoyed (*frui*): the fine arts. This points out the difference between the servile arts and the liberal arts, between *techne* in the production of artifacts to be used, and *poiesis* which produces things as objects of enjoyment in themselves insofar as they embody the transcendental beauty. Indeed, it is in the fine arts that we most closely participate in God's free creation of the universe, and because it embodies beauty, it appeals equally to the intellect and will as an intrinsic good, and so is of a greater objective importance than merely useful technical innovations.

46. See *ST* III, q. 19, a. 1: "But the operation which belongs to the thing, as moved by another, is not distinct from the operation of the mover; thus to make a bench is not the work of the axe independently of the workman." See also *ST* III, q. 62, a. 1, ad 2.

47. See *In Phys.* II, l. 1, n. 142.

of the artifact depends more on the person who determines how an artifact is to be used than on the person who actually makes it, because use
follows from form while making is from matter.

Therefore, although each is architectonic, i.e., the art which uses and the productive art, they nevertheless differ. For the art which uses is architectonic insofar as it knows and passes judgment on the form, whereas the other, which is
architectonic as productive of the form, knows the matter, i.e., passes judgment
on the matter. [Aristotle] makes this clear by an example. The use of a ship pertains to the navigator, and thus the art of the navigator is an art which uses, and
hence it is architectonic with respect to the art of the ship builder, and knows
and passes judgment on the form. He says that the navigator knows and judges
what the shape of the rudder should be. The other art, however, i.e., the art of
the ship builder, knows and judges from what wood and from what kind of
wood the ship should be made. It is clear, therefore, that the art which produces
the form directs the art which makes or disposes the matter. However the art
which uses the completed artifact directs the art which produces the form.[48]

Thus, it is use, or final causality, that ultimately gives intentional unity to the elements aggregated in an artifact. As Thomas succinctly puts
it, "In the case of some things (for example, a house and a bed) [the es-
sence] is 'that for the sake of which a thing exists,' i.e., its goal [or end]."[49]
Because the form of an artifact (in the mind of the artificer) cannot be a
new substantial form, the intended use uniting the material substances
becomes the defining element, the intentional essence, constituting its
mind-dependent mode of united being.[50]

48. *In Phys.* II, l. 4, n. 173. See also *In Meta.* I, l. 1, n. 26: "Hence the shipbuilder is a superior
artist compared with the one who prepares the wood; and the navigator, who uses the completed
ship, is a superior artist compared with the shipbuilder."

49. *In Meta.* VII, l. 17, n. 1658.

50. It is worth noting at this point that Thomas does not consider certain natural compounds
brought about at the instigation of a human agent to be artifacts. The primary example of this is
bread, as there is a natural chemical constitution of the compound that could in fact happen in
nature even apart from any human intervention; see *ST* III, q. 75, a. 6, ad 1: "There is nothing to
prevent art from making a thing whose form is not an accident, but a substantial form; as frogs
and serpents can be produced by art: for art produces such forms not by its own power, but by
the power of natural energies. And in this way it produces the substantial forms of bread, by the
power of fire baking the matter made up of flour and water." Cf. *In Meta.* I, l. 15, n. 238: "Therefore
... natural things, can both be and come to be because of such proximate causes as those just
mentioned, i.e., artificial ones; so that, just as artificial things come to be as a result of proximate
agents, so also do natural things." This would appear to have important applications to contemporary biotechnology. See the discussion of these passages in Michael Rota, "Substance and Artifact

If an artifact is defined purely by an intentional essence dependent on the artificer, the very real problems of nominalism and relativism arise. It seems as if objects of practical reason are constituted in truth independent of any truly objective standard. But if this were the case, any work of art is merely what the artificer says it to be, and so the ironical work of the Dadaists becomes the standard for all practical reason. This is where it is important to make a clear distinction between fictions and cultural realities. While in one sense both are fictive, in that they are created by man, we must recognize that cultural realities are not *mere* fictions, for in ordering man's relation to the world they exercise a mode of active presence not shared by arbitrary intentional constructs. Thus, cultural realities, in ordering the world, are active as uniting cultural activity; although they are intentional, there is a shared intersubjective affirmation of the people ordered by that intentional essence. A border is real for those who recognize the reality of the political divisions it represents. Similarly, inasmuch as artifacts are primarily tools ordered to social utility, they must be defined by the culturally agreed-upon ordering of natural substances and their active powers to a determined end. The active unity of these realities is present only when there is an intersubjective acceptance of the mind-dependent orientation to use.

This practical, communal understanding of culture can be illuminated by Alasdair MacIntyre's analyses of practice and tradition. MacIntyre defines a practice as a "coherent and complex form of socially established cooperative human activity through which goods internal to that form of activity are realized."[51] He also specifies that these practices take on full significance only in the context of a tradition, a social structure made intelligible by its orientation to a *telos* or end representing the good to be achieved by that practice.[52] While MacIntyre's focus is on the role of moral virtue as a practice necessary for human happiness, it is important to see that Thomas also recognizes the necessary role of artifacts for attaining the common good. Thomas says that society orders man to happiness by procuring three things: peace, virtue, and the material

---

in Thomas Aquinas," *History of Philosophy Quarterly* 21 (2004): 240–59, and Brown, "Artifacts, Substances, and Transubstantiation."

51. Alasdair MacIntyre, *After Virtue*, 2nd ed. (Notre Dame, Ind.: Notre Dame University Press, 1984), 187.

52. Ibid., 204–12.

wealth to support the first two ends.[53] Thus, man establishes intentional, communal social structures to encourage the development of
moral virtue, as well as the common ordering of material substance as
artifacts for material wealth which frees man from servile labor so that
he might better attain his true spiritual end. Therefore, it is the intersubjective end of the common good as achieved in social practice that
acts as the stable extrinsic criterion for the essence of an artifact. This
is true whether the thing made is primarily intentional—like a political
border or office—or whether it is a material artifact used in the context
of a complex social practice. Cultures are distinguished, then, by their
practices, both moral and material. (As will be seen, cultures can also
be evaluated in light of the extent to which these practices achieve the
final end of society, human happiness.) These shared practices enable a
culture to define its corresponding artifacts in a more or less objective
fashion. Moreover, implicit in this is the fact of a kind of hierarchical
subsidiarity of practices, so that specialized fields within a larger society
have their own cultural organization and corresponding artifacts (not all
of which are broadly understood).[54] Thus, the truth of any artifact is
best understood from within the practice in which its use is defined, and
in which its use in relation to the end of society is most clearly known.[55]

The human world, then, is not simply a physical environment, but
is rather that environment shaped to meet human needs by means of
our intentional ordering of it. Mind-dependent realities are, then, part

---

53. *De Regimine* I.16, trans. R. W. Dyson, in *St. Thomas Aquinas: Political Writings*, Cambridge Tests in the History of Political Thought (Cambridge: Cambridge University Press, 2002),
42–45.

54. That the intentional unity of existence of an artifact is determined by its use within
a specialized practice is easily seen by looking at common experience; specialized instruments
(hardware, electronics, medical) are often incomprehensible to those outside these practices.

55. Brown, replying to criticisms of *The Ship of Theseus*, cites Norris Clarke and revises his
original thesis to a position similar to this: an artifact is an extrinsic unity which is "a function
of the beliefs, attitudes, and practices that a community of rational agents takes up relative to a
substance or a collection of substances" ("Reply to Toner," 661). Thus, he argues that the unity
over time depends on the use the community makes of it. Following this, I would also offer this
solution to the traditional problem of the ship of Theseus. Just as use of artifacts is culturally
defined, so are the ideas of continuity and ownership. The obvious objection would arise when
different societies had conflicting ideas; but here again I refer to MacIntyre, and suggest that
conflicting ideas would precipitate a kind of epistemic crisis, which would require a refinement
in the idea of the continuity of the artifact. On the idea of an epistemic crisis, see *Whose Justice?
Which Rationality?* (Notre Dame, Ind.: University of Notre Dame Press, 1988), 349–69.

of our experience: intentional essences like political borders help to organize society for the common good of its citizens; again, and more mundanely, this practical activity can organize material substance into artifacts in order to help man perform a practice that is pertinent not just for his survival but for the achievement of the perfection of human nature. The ontological unity of these artifacts is fully grasped only by those who participate in the social practice in which they are defined.

This foundation of the truth of an artifact in cultural practice, though, does not fully answer our concern with relativism, for it leaves open the significant problem of cultural relativism. It is here that the profound breadth of Thomas's metaphysics, subsuming man's relation to reality and especially to God, places artifacts in a truly objective context, thereby eliminating any potential cultural relativism.

First, Thomas is clear that an artifact is not simply any aggregate of independent substances, but is rather an ordered aggregate that allows man to make use of the natural powers of the substances involved. Thomas makes a distinction between three ways in which compounds might be united: first is mere aggregation, where independent substances are brought together without any ordering (such as a pile); second is a coordinated, or ordered, aggregation, and this is what constitutes the unity of an artifact; third is a mixture, where constituent elements are bound so as to form a new compound being with an intrinsic form.[56] Thus, the unity of a substance, even as an intentional essence, relies on the objective fact of matter suitably disposed and ordered to the end. Thus, as long as an artifact is able to serve the same end, it is the same thing; this allows for interruptions in serving this function due to needing repair. If the community no longer accepts the thing as serving that end, then the remains merely "used to be" that artifact.

Second is the fact that artifacts are elements of a practice, but these practices are (as MacIntyre makes clear) necessarily ordered to a *telos*, the ultimate end of human happiness.[57] Therefore, artifacts can be used

56. This mode of composition explains why bread is not an artifact for Thomas; see note 50 above. Thomas outlines these distinctions in a number of places, for example *In Meta.* V, l. 3, n. 779, *SCG* IV.35, and *ST* III, q. 2.

57. See the analysis related to the moral question of use is in Yves Simon, *The Definition of Moral Virtue*, ed. Vukan Kuic (New York: Fordham University Press, 1986), 19–29, in which he distinguishes between the value of the instrument, one's ability to use the instrument, and one's actual use of it.

or abused when judged in light of this ultimate goal. Some practices (contraception comes to mind) can thereby be seen to be naturally aberrant, and such practices must eventually yield to the greater rationality of other practices rightly ordered to the common good, and in which the artifact reveals its true usefulness.[58]

This last point brings us to the ultimate criterion for the place of artifacts in creation: divine providence. All things are subject to providence by which creation is ordered to the universal good.[59] But Thomas insists that man has a unique role to play in disposing of providence: "Now among all others, the rational creature is subject to Divine providence in the most excellent way, in so far as it partakes of a share of providence, by being provident both for itself and for others."[60] Man is provident in perfecting human culture, creating practices and institutions by which his own powers are ordered to the perfection of the universe.[61] Artifacts, then, can be trans-culturally evaluated according to the extent to which they actually fulfill the order of universal providence. Just as the truth of human speculative reason is finally measured by the ontological facts of natural existence—being, in first act, as created by God—so the truth of human practical reason is finally measured by the ultimate good for which all artifacts, and all cultural realities, are invented: creation as providentially ordered by God to second act, the perfection of the universe itself.[62]

58. As Ashley comments, "The goal of human life is the contemplation of ultimate reality.... Thus also the technologies and fine arts are subordinate to ethics, since their purpose is to serve the good life and, if unethical, are destructive of human existence" (*The Way toward Wisdom*, 120–21). See also 314: "For any technology to prove truly useful to human life, it must meet true human needs and not false ones."

59. See *ST* I, q. 22, a. 1: "It is necessary to attribute providence to God. For all the good that is in created things has been created by God.... In created things good is found not only as regards their substance, but also as regards their order towards an end and especially their last end, which ... is the divine goodness."

60. *ST* I-II, q. 91, a. 2.

61. See *SCG* II.46.

62. Note, again, the difference between speculative and practical reason. The ontological grounding of truth makes one speculative theory more objectively adequate than others. This is why Kuhnian scientific revolutions are not merely relativistic, alternative interpretations of the physical universe. Science is really objective and thus is trans-culturally true. Practical reason, on the other hand, is a question of prudence. The nature of cultural practices as means to an end allows for real diversity inasmuch as the goal can be achieved in a variety of ways; nevertheless, there is a final objectivity based upon the adequacy of any construct with respect to human perfection. It is the confusion of this variability of means with the necessity of end that has led

Thus I conclude that the use of artifacts is an intrinsic element in completing providence and so must be judged with reference to providence. Man's development of cultural practices becomes a necessary part of divine government of the universe: "Now it is a greater perfection for a thing to be good in itself and also the cause of goodness in others, than only to be good in itself. Therefore God so governs things that He makes some of them to be causes of others in government."[63] In recognizing the necessary role of culture and artifacts in providence, Aquinas takes seriously the reality of secondary causes, especially man's causal role in establishing a communally mind-dependent mode of being for artifacts, analogous to the unity of natural substances, for the sake of the perfection of the universe. To understand this is particularly important today, when man is drowning in an ever-growing sea of artifacts; as technology further invades our lives, understanding the ontological dependence of artifacts on man's own mind might ensure that they always serve the human good instead of man enslaving himself to the technology he creates.

---

relativists over the years to assume that ethics is merely a question of custom, for they fail to see the teleological criterion of all acts.

63. *ST* I, q. 103, a. 6.

8

The Transcendentals, the Human Person, and the Perfection of the Universe

ALICE M. RAMOS

In the past twenty years excellent studies on the transcendentals have been published, among them Jan Aertsen's masterful book *The Transcendentals and Medieval Philosophy: The Case of Thomas Aquinas*. Aertsen points to the correlation between *anima* and being, between the transcendental openness of *anima* to all being, which makes the human being capable not only of knowing being (*capax entis*) but also capable of knowing God (*capax Dei*). For Aertsen, the anthropological motif of Aquinas's doctrine of the transcendentals converges with the theological motif. Aertsen also points to the connection between the transcendentals and morality, the former providing the metaphysical basis for the latter.[1]

My interest in this essay lies not only in these connections suggested by Aertsen, but also and more especially in the role played by the human person in the perfection of the universe, in the return of all things to their source. Given the intellectual creature's place in the universe,

1. See Jan Aertsen, *The Transcendentals and Medieval Philosophy: The Case of Thomas Aquinas* (Leiden: E. J. Brill, 1996), 431. I am using portions, here and elsewhere in this essay, of my book *Dynamic Transcendentals: Truth, Goodness, and Beauty from a Thomistic Perspective* (Washington, D.C.: The Catholic University of America Press, 2012), 1–8.

the human person is responsible both for actualizing his own nature and for bringing everything else in the universe to perfection. In accomplishing this task I maintain that the person also brings about what may be called an intensification of the transcendentals, such that those aspects of being which are said to be convertible with being and which are participated to a greater or lesser degree in all created beings acquire a higher level of actuality. We can thus say, for example, that although the human person is created true by that *ipsum esse subsistens* that is identical with its understanding,[2] the person will through his proper operations maximize the degree of his own truth and will bring everything else to the actualization of their truth, and also of their goodness and beauty. To intensify the degree of participation in the transcendentals requires then a dynamic conception of the transcendentals rather than a static one, which is the standard consideration of the transcendentals as aspects inseparable from being.

Such a conception is made possible in part through an understanding of the human person as image of the first efficient and exemplary cause who is also the final cause of all created beings' becoming fully what they are, which is a matter of imitating God in the operations appropriate to them. The human person as *imago Dei* is a being intimately related to the wise and loving God who created him and destined him to freely return to his creator. Aquinas's account of the human person as *imago Dei* is not static and ahistorical but is rather a dynamic and active conception of human nature. In having originated from a true and good God, the human person is naturally inclined to the true and the good; in his pursuit of truth and goodness he is, whether he knows it or not, actually pursuing God. Human perfection cannot therefore be separated from union with God or religious fulfillment.[3] God as the exemplary and final cause of the *imago* is the measure of the human person in being and in activity and in his return to the source.[4]

In this dynamic consideration of the human person and of the transcendentals, I am indebted not only to Aertsen's work on the transcendentals but also to the work of Joseph De Finance. In his magnificent

---

2. See *De Ver.*, q. 1, a. 2.

3. See J. Augustine DiNoia, OP, "*Imago Dei—Imago Christi*: The Theological Foundations of Christian Humanism," *Nova et Vetera* 2 (2004): 267–78.

4. See my *Dynamic Transcendentals*, 1–2.

book, yet to be translated and fully studied, *Être et agir dans la philosophie de Saint Thomas*, or *Being and Action in the Philosophy of Saint Thomas*, De Finance emphasizes the radical dynamism of being in terms of the tendency of a created being to its own perfection, its tendency to action, and its return to its origin or beginning, a return which is the conversion or turning back of the effect to the cause.[5] This tendency to the perfection of a creature's nature and its reversion to the cause also constitute the perfection of its participation in being and thus in the transcendentals, such that the creature would not only become more of what the creature already is and as such would be all it could be, but would also be more true, more good, and more beautiful, as well as more one or united, because of its union with the source from where all being and the transcendentals originate. In this essay I will especially draw from the work of De Finance concentrating on the actualization of the intelligibility or truth of created beings.

While De Finance does not specifically speak of an intensification of the transcendentals, everything that he says regarding the metaphysics of *esse* and the metaphysics of action in Aquinas points in that direction. According to De Finance the Thomistic doctrine of being (as act) and of participation does not simply give an account of the existence of beings but also aims at justifying their action.[6] Created beings not only proceed from the subsistent being that is God, they also tend toward him, they return to him and are ordered to him;[7] they turn back by nature to the cause from which they originate, for in their likeness to the source lies the perfection of the effects. While the *ipsum esse subsistens*, from whom all created beings originate, is one with and identical to the divine intellect, the divine will, and divine action, this is obviously not the case in created beings. The reception of being or *esse* in a quiddity separates being from its perfection, disconnects or disjoins being from action, existence from thought.[8] The expansiveness of being as act is thus limited by the essence receiving and participating in the act of being. In order to provide a remedy for this limitation, the first level of act of a being—a

---

5. Joseph De Finance, *Être et agir dans la philosophie de Saint Thomas* (Rome: Presses de l'Université Grégorienne, 1965), 250n95.

6. Ibid., 159.

7. Ibid.

8. Ibid., 136.

being's being what it is—exists in view of second-level acts, that is, a being's ability to become more of what it is through the exercise of its particular powers. The second perfection of a created being will thus be realized through the being's proper operations, by means of which it will attain a greater degree of actuality and thus acquire a greater similitude to God who is being itself, pure act.

Now if it is the case that the ultimate end toward which all creatures move is to be like God, and in God there is no distance between his essence and his being, because in him there is an identity of essence and being, then in the creature which distances itself from the creator in not being Being itself but in participating in being through essence, it can be said that the creature's essence is limiting and restricting the expansiveness of the act of being, and that the act of being itself, which is the creature's act of all acts, perfection of all perfections, attempts through the creature's operations to make the essence somehow conform more fully to itself. Although it is true that there exists a proportion, a relation of fitness, between a thing's essence and its act of being, which proportion is constitutive of the thing's first perfection, it is also the case that this initial perfection is ordered to further perfection; the conforming of the essence to the act of being in and through the being's proper activities would in the end bring about a greater actualization of the being and its transcendental aspects and would also bring the creature closer to the source of being itself.[9]

Created beings are thus ordered to their proper operations; the latter proceed from the substantial form, which Aquinas calls the principle of being, because it is the form that enables the subject to receive being. The operations are, as Aquinas puts it, "the end of created things."[10] For this reason, it can be said that the order of the universe is not realized in a mere harmonious scale of forms, but rather is really revealed in the tendency of the many to oneness, to the One.[11] This tendency can be explained as an internal response to the call of being: it is the act of being, in effect, as a separated perfection, which gathers everything in

9. See my "Beauty and the Perfection of Being," *Proceedings of the American Catholic Philosophical Association* 71 (1997): 255–68.

10. See *ST* I, q. 105, a. 5, co.: "Operatio est finis rei creatae." See also De Finance, *Être et agir*, 117.

11. De Finance, *Être et agir*, 214.

itself and which takes the essence to itself. But the tendency to unity is explained not only through an internal finality, but also through the external finality to being, that is, through a movement of return to the beginning. This return is possible due to the very separated character of the *esse* of the creature. Being is not a mere component of what is, but rather an "excess," a "plus," which (thus understood) leads to a consideration of being as "a reference to God."[12] This is why, I think, De Finance insists on the completion of a being in its relation *ad extra*, such that no being can complete itself without transcending itself and thus being in communion with others and ultimately in communion with God.[13]

If in Aquinas's thought creatures proceed from God, then they are to return to him, and this return is effected by all beings through and in their proper operation; their operation enables them to actively assimilate themselves to the principle from whence they proceeded and also to perfect their own intelligibility. Created being cannot find its perfection in itself because it proceeds from a free act of love and of understanding on the part of God. As De Finance sees it, a participated being can only complete itself by adhering to its principle, by fulfilling the idea eternally present in the mind that created it.[14] The divine mind and God's creative freedom then order the return of creatures to their source. If created being proceeds freely from or through an idea, it is this idea which will, as it were, terminate the return, for the divine idea is not only the exemplary cause of things but also their final cause. The movement toward God cannot therefore be seen simply as an initiative on the part of the creature, as is so often the case when we consider the desire for God on the part of the human person, but rather as first and foremost an initiative on the part of God who attracts the creature and converts or orders the creature to himself.[15]

Operation in a created and consequently mutable being is movement: it is, therefore, the actualization of a potency. The more actual the created being is, the more intelligible it will also be. The act can be said

---

12. See Frederick Wilhelmsen, *El Problema de la trascendencia en la metafísica actual* (Pamplona: EUNSA, 1963), 42. Cf. Wilhelmsen, *The Metaphysics of Love* (New York: Sheed and Ward, 1962), 87–89. See also Étienne Gilson, *Le Thomisme*, 5th edition (Paris: Vrin, 1957), 54.

13. De Finance, *Être et agir*, 251.

14. Ibid., 176.

15. Ibid., 176–77.

to be the *truth* of the potency, its reason for being, and thus its very end. The operation then constitutes the second stage of the metaphysical movement; because of it, the being is completed and attains to its truth, as De Finance puts it.[16]

Now, the importance of the operation does not in any way contradict the primacy of being, because the latter is the most excellent act, the greatest perfection. De Finance points out, however, that being is an act not only in its dimension of actuality, but also in its active dimension, in what I think De Finance refers to as *virtus essendi* or active energy, which is possessed fully by God and only in part by creatures.[17] But this active dimension of being is not realized directly through the operating substance, but rather in a second act, by means of the operative potency of being. The human soul is for example an act by its essence, but if the very essence of the soul were the immediate principle of its operation, then everyone who has a soul would be continually realizing in act his proper operations. According to Aquinas, the soul, as a form, is not an act ordered to an ulterior act, because it is the ultimate term of generation. Consequently, that it be in potency with respect to another act does not characterize it according to its essence, insofar as it is a form, but rather according to its potency. The soul is the subject to its potency and, therefore, is termed a first act ordered to a second act. Only in God who is pure act is the operation identified with his substance. When a created being operates, it moves and is actualized. In order for a created being to be able to operate, or move itself, it must possess some potency, that is, that in the created being we can distinguish his being, which is act, from his operation, which is the actualization of a potency. This generally is referred to as the relationship between the substance and the accidents: the substance is the final cause of the accidents and also, in a certain measure, the efficient cause. The operation is, however, the emanation of being, the expression of being, but as a second act, it consists in the determination of the being, in its perfection.[18] Because of the operation, the realization of the being along the line of its being is brought about. By situating in the operation the completion of

16. Ibid., 241–42.
17. Ibid., 52.
18. Ibid., 216.

the being, Thomistic ontology acquires a specifically dynamic character. Things realize themselves; they acquire their ultimate perfection to the extent to which they act. The operation thus emerges, according to De Finance, as "the keystone for the intelligibility of being."[19]

By considering the substance as the end of the operation, it is evident that the substance is not an inert, closed reality, but rather a dynamic, open reality, capable of realizing itself. If the operation is considered as being distinct from the essence and the *esse*, and so is placed in the order of the accidents, it cannot be said that the second act is superadded to the first act, that it constitutes another reality, overloading, as it were, the substantial form or the substance. On the contrary, the second act permits the substance to be truly itself, being, in a certain way, more.[20] The union that exists between the substance and its operation, between the agent and its action, is according to De Finance closer than the union between the substance and the accidents. For De Finance there is a perfect existential unity between the agent and its action such that one and the same *esse* completes both the substance and its action.[21] Operations, actions, proceed from the substance, and consequently, express or manifest it. Operations perfect the substance, unify and simplify it; for this reason, it cannot be said, in any way, that they overload the substance. If we consider, for example, intellection, it is evident that the activity of understanding does not, in any way, overload the substance. The intellect in act is what it should be.[22]

We observe then how being and action complement each other and how they are ordered one to the other. The being exists thanks to the first and with a view to the second. In action and not simply as a consequence of it, the substance increases its participation in being, and in the transcendentals as well, becoming thus more true, more good, more beautiful, and more united. By operating or acting, created being tends toward its own perfection and ultimately to the conversion, to the return, to the beginning.[23] In this way, we observe the double dimension

19. Ibid., 247.
20. Ibid.
21. Ibid., 248.
22. Ibid., 249–50.
23. Ibid., 250. See also my "Activity and Finality in Saint Thomas," *Angelicum* 68 (1991): 231–54, at 238.

of operations, of actions: action expresses being because it emanates, emerges, from it; but, at the same time, it determines the being perfecting it. Action is thus the unfolding of the fullness which constitutes the being and also the remedy, as it were, for its indigence. Being, the most excellent of acts, even though it find itself received in an essence, and consequently limited by the latter, tends beyond itself. By means of action, the interior richness of the being and also its final determination are then expressed.[24]

By being ordered to the end through the action that is proper to each agent, the action may be termed not only as the end of the agent but also as its good. Aquinas observes that by tending to the end which is their good, created beings are ordered to God who is their supreme end and good. God is then the end of the created beings as that which each being should attain for itself in its own way according to its operations.[25] When they act and move, the ultimate end pursued by beings is likeness to God;[26] they imitate God according to the operations that are proper to them.[27]

Likeness to God is reached in the most perfect manner only in man, as he is a being that understands and loves.[28] Nevertheless, intellectual apprehension is not the only way of returning to the beginning. Infrarational beings that do not properly act as movers unfold, so to say, the image of divine attributes, by keeping their own perfection, that is, by maintaining the form that is proper to them and their specific place.[29] In keeping with what Aquinas himself says, De Finance points out that when each thing seeks its own being it is above all seeking being itself.[30] There are, in addition, other beings that are not only moved by natural movements but that also move others. They attain to likeness with God in two ways: by maintaining their own form and their own being, and also by being the cause of others. According to Aquinas, causality or transitive action is the appropriate way through which corporeal beings imitate God. Because God is the supreme cause, beings which through

24. See my "Activity and Finality in Saint Thomas," 238.
25. SCG III.17–18.
26. SCG III.19.
27. SCG III.20.
28. See ST I, q. 93, a. 4, co.
29. SCG III.22. See my "Activity and Finality in Saint Thomas," 242.
30. De Finance, Être et agir, 166.

their own operation become the cause of others, thus tend to divine likeness. That beings are the causes of others shows us that, as effects, they
are like God not only with respect to their being but also with respect to
their causing other beings.[31] While there are some creatures that cause
others of their same type and so act for the good of the species and
not simply for their own individual good, there also exists an equivocal
agent, namely the heavens, which by causing seek the good of the genus.[32] As Aquinas sees it, "A thing which tends to become the cause of
others tends toward the divine likeness, and nonetheless it tends toward
its own good."[33] For according to Aquinas, "God, who is most perfect in
goodness and who diffuses his goodness in the broadest way, must be in
his diffusion the archetype of all diffusers of goodness."[34]

Now intellectual creatures tend toward God and reach their end in a
different way. If the end of everything that exists is its proper operation
because this constitutes the being's second perfection, then the proper
operation of the intellectual substance consists in the act of understanding. What is most perfect in this operation is the ultimate end. To know
God, who is the most perfect intelligible object, by an act of understanding is therefore the ultimate end of every intellectual substance.[35] The
creature that is most like God is the intellectual one, precisely because
of its intellectual nature. And it is especially like God when it understands in act, because God is always understanding in act. The intellectual creature is like God even more when it knows God himself. By
understanding God, the intellectual creature draws closer to knowledge
of all creatures because, as Aquinas says, "God understands all things in
the act of understanding himself."[36]

The act of understanding is an immanent action, very different from
transitive action. Immanent action is characterized by a certain infinity.

31. See my "Activity and Finality in Saint Thomas," 242–43.
32. Ibid., 243. See SCG III.22: "If, therefore, the movement of the heaven is directed to man
as the last end of this genus: it is evident that the end of the heavenly movement is directed to
man as its last end in the genus of things subject to generation and movement."
33. SCG III.24: "Hinc etiam patet quod unumquodque tendens ad hoc quod sit aliorum
causa, tendit in divinam similitudinem, et nihilominus tendit in suum bonum."
34. Ibid.: "Deus, qui est in bonitate perfectissimus et suam bonitatem communissime dif-
fundens, in sua diffusione sit exemplar omnium bonitatem diffundentium."
35. SCG III.25.
36. Ibid.: "Nam ipse Deus intelligendo se intelligit omnia alia." See also my "Activity and
Finality in Saint Thomas," 244–45.

The true and the good, objects of the intellect and the will, have the unlimited scope of being, of which they are aspects. The being of the intellectual creature is finite and does not therefore coincide with this potential infinity. Action in this sense always refers being to another. Action opens the intellectual being such that it can participate in the value, as it were, of other beings. Action is essentially an openness toward the other, such that it makes possible communion with the other. For De Finance, transitive action is existential, because it seeks to produce an existing thing, whereas mind (the intellect) is existential because its end is to grasp an existence; for a spirit-endowed being such as man the grasping of an essence in intellection is only of interest in its relation to *esse*.[37]

According to Aquinas intellectual creatures have more affinity with the whole, because by their understanding they can become all things, encompassing thus through their cognitive power the totality of being, while the other substances only participate individually in being. As Aquinas says, "The spiritual soul ... possesses a potency unto the infinite."[38] The universe would be incomplete without intellectual creatures and without them would not reach its perfection. If in material beings there is a kind of imperfection due to the limitation of their own individuality, then this imperfection is in a sense compensated for when material things are being known by man, for "all things are somehow in the higher immaterial substances as in universal causes."[39] Because according to Aquinas all things are perfected when they return to their origin, and because the principle of the production of creatures is, as Aquinas says, the intelligence of God, then this return to the origin is made possible by means of intellectual substances.[40]

It can perhaps be said that the intellectual creature returns all things to their origin when he knows them, because there is thus reproduced in him the form of the divine intelligence. What was intelligible in potency for man becomes intelligible in act as it is for God, when man's intelli-

37. De Finance, *Être et agir*, 313.

38. *ST* I, q. 76, a. 5, ad 4: "Anima intellectiva, quia est universalium comprehensiva, habet virtutem ad infinita."

39. *In De An.* II, l. 5, n. 283: "Unde in substantiis superioribus immaterialibus sunt quodammodo omnia, sicut in universalibus causis." See Oliva Blanchette, *The Perfection of the Universe according to Aquinas* (University Park: Pennsylvania State University Press, 1992), 270.

40. *SCG* II.46. See also II.23–24 and my "Activity and Finality in Saint Thomas," 248.

gence knows things actually. Things, created true by the divine intelligence, can thus be known by human intelligence. Upon knowing, man turns as it were to divine intelligence, which is the principle and source of the multiplicity of beings.[41]

So that the universe could reach a more finished perfection, it was fitting that there exist creatures who could return to God not only by a likeness of nature, but also by a likeness of operation. And because what is proper to God is his understanding and his willing, it was fitting that there exist intellectual creatures who would act in the same manner as God with respect to himself.[42] Man is likened to God in his action, because not only is it a matter of the same type of action but also of the same mode of acting.[43] So man, like God, can contain within himself corporeal creatures in an intelligible mode. What is superior contains thus what is inferior not according to extensive quantity, but rather according to intellection, which permits the immaterial possession of the form of another, the immaterial union of one being with another.[44] The perfection of the universe is therefore actualized in human reason, while reason itself finds its perfection in its knowledge of the universe and of its first principle.

Now, following Aristotle, Aquinas tells us that because the first maker of the universe is the divine intelligence, the ultimate end of the universe is then the good of the intelligence which is the truth, and the truth as the origin of all truth. As Aquinas puts it, "The first truth is the ultimate end. So, the ultimate end of the whole man, and of all his operations and desires, is to know the first truth, which is God."[45] This return to God on the part of the intellectual creature requires that man freely direct himself to the good of his intellect, namely, the truth. Moral rectitude is therefore necessary for man to reach his contemplative end, his union with that *ipsum esse subsistens* who is his own understanding, with that divine idea that is his measure in being and in truth. When man's will is also directed by intelligence, when the will loves in effect the

41. See my "Activity and Finality in Saint Thomas," 249.

42. SCG II.46.

43. Ibid.

44. Ibid.

45. SCG III.25: "et per consequens ultimus finis primum verum. Est igitur ultimus finis totius hominis, et omnium operationum et desideriorum eius, cognoscere primum verum, quod est Deus."

truth, the true good, then in each upright action of man, that is, in each action in conformity with the truth, there is concomitantly effected a return to the beginning, that is, to the origin of all truth, to divine intelligence.[46] It is in this way that through his actions man will become more true and will also intensify the truth of everything else in the universe.

46. See my "A Metaphysics of the Truth of Creation: Foundation of the Desire for God," *Proceedings of the American Catholic Association* 69 (1995): 237–48. This article, slightly revised, is included in my *Dynamic Transcendentals*, 11–26.

9

Thomas Aquinas, the Analogy of Being, and the Analogy of Transferred Proportion

STEVEN A. LONG

Since roughly the 1960s it has become common for authors to argue that Thomas Aquinas relies most pronouncedly upon the analogy of causal participation or of proportion as the foundational metaphysical analogy (one thinks prominently of Montagnes,[1] but also of Klubertanz,[2] or earlier Ramirez[3]), and that he dropped his earlier reliance upon the analogy of proper proportionality as the analogy of being in his work subsequent to *De Ver.* This essay argues the following points:

(1) that the Aristotelian response to Parmenides in terms of the analogical division of being by act and potency is the discovery of the analogy of being;

---

1. See, e.g., Bernard Montagnes, *The Doctrine of the Analogy of Being according to Thomas Aquinas*, trans. E. M. Macierowski, ed. Andrew Tallon (Milwaukee, Wis.: Marquette University Press, 2004).

2. George P. Klubertanz, SJ, *St. Thomas Aquinas on Analogy: A Textual Analysis and Systematic Synthesis* (Chicago: Loyola University Press, 1960).

3. Santiago Ramirez, OP, *Edicion de las Obras Completas de Santiago Ramirez, OP*, Tomo II, *De analogia*, ed. Victorino Rodriguez, OP (Madrid: Institute de Filosofia "Luis Vives," 1970). Of course, Ramirez's famed article from 1954 included at the end of vol. 4 of *De analogia*—arguing that *In Sent.* I, d. 19, does not articulate the teaching later offered in *De Ver.*—is earlier than 1960. I believe his earlier views—when he suspected proper proportionality was in some way more fundamental than other forms of analogy—to be closer to the mark than his later views.

(2) that it is an analogy of proper proportionality, a likeness of diverse *rationes* of act as limited by potency;

(3) that this account is also necessary because God has no determined relation or proportion to the creature, and because all perfections predicated of God incomprehend God and are exceeded by God;

(4) that if one speaks of analogy of proportion, only an analogy of transferred proportion—the language of Thomas in *De Ver.*—is possible between creature and creator, that is, an analogy that is "one-way" thus excluding proportion in the strict sense which is "two-way";

(5) that consequently such analogy must be retranslatable into the analogy of proper proportionality which both involves no definite real determined relation obtaining between the things having something in common analogically, and is also an analogy of intrinsic attribution; and

(6) that the relation of createdness and causal participation reflects causal wisdom proceeding from the analogy of being, but is itself secondary and derivative *vis-à-vis* that primal analogy of being—that is, the causal relations of createdness and participation *presuppose* the prior analogy of being as the likeness of diverse *rationes* of act as limited by potency.

The Aristotelian Provenance of the Analogy of Being

The first point to be observed is the Aristotelian provenance of this teaching, and the origin of this teaching in the need for a response to the metaphysical challenge of Parmenidean monism (from Parmenides's *On Nature*). Aristotle's answer is worked out in the *Physics* but it is in part a response to a metaphysical argument and actually implicitly of metaphysical value. Parmenides argued that being is unitary, unlimited, and immobile. It is unitary because it is wholly identical with itself; it is unlimited because outside being there is nothing that could limit it; and it is immobile because being cannot become nonbeing nor derive from it, and so being is unchangeable. Aristotle, of course, looked up and saw birds flying, and knew that the Parmenidean account denying manyness, limit, and change of being must be incorrect. If we were garden-variety analytic philosophers we could stop here. But Aristotle realized that although the *relation* of being and nonbeing is purely notional, the distinction between being and nonbeing is a metaphysical and real distinction.

Of course any putative "relation" of being and nonbeing is a conceptual relation, because nonexistent beings do not have real relations. But the *distinction* between being and nonbeing is a real distinction because it is founded on the real character of being; that is, the difference between nonbeing and being is *being*, and being is real. Just as one might say that, even had creation never occurred, it would be true that God's nature is not a created nature by virtue of the reality of the divine nature itself, or that one's sister is by virtue of her real humanity not a square root, so likewise one may say that being is, by virtue of its real character, not nonbeing. Thus understood, the principle of noncontradiction articulates a real distinction. Far from being merely a logical principle, it is first and with a priority both epistemic (we begin with knowledge of things that exist, not with mere concepts) and real (the principle concerns *being*); the principle of noncontradiction is a metaphysical principle.

But this means that one must reconcile this principle—that being is not nonbeing—with the intelligible perception of manyness, limit, and change. Aristotle of course argues that there is a principle of being which is not act and which is not merely nonbeing or negation, but rather potency or capacity that is always founded upon act. Thus, being is understood as act as limited by potency; and the analogy of being is that of the likeness of diverse acts as limited by potency. Indeed, for Aristotle potency and act divide every order of being.[4] As he argues in *Metaphysics* XI, 1065b15–16: "Hence there are as many kinds of motion and change as there are of being. Now because each class of things is divided by potentiality and actuality, I call motion the actualization of what is potential as such."[5] The language of this division of being by potency

---

4. Thus Aristotle's words from the first paragraph (sometimes translated as two paragraphs) of XI.9: "One thing is actual only, another potential, and others both actual and potential; and of these one is a being, another a quantity, and another one of the other categories. Motion is not something apart from things themselves; for a thing is always changed according to the categories of being, and there is nothing that is common to these and in no one category. And each belongs to all its members in a twofold way, for example, this particular thing; for sometimes this is the form of a thing and sometimes its privation. And with regard to quality, one thing is white and another black; and with regard to quantity, one is perfect and another imperfect; and with regard to motion in space, one thing tends upwards and another downwards, or one is light and another heavy. Hence there are as many kinds of motion and change as there are of being. Now since each class of things is divided by potentiality and actuality, I call motion the actualization of what is potential as such."

5. Compare Hugh Treddenick's translation (available at perseus.tufts.edu/hopper/text?doc=Perseus%3atext%3a1999.01.0052) with that of W. D. Ross.

and act is the *analogy of proper proportionality*. As Aristotle wrote in the
Metaphysics:

Our meaning can be seen in the particular cases by induction, and we must not
seek a definition of everything but be content to grasp the analogy, that it is as
that which is building is to that which is capable of building, and the waking
to the sleeping, and that which is seeing to that which has its eyes shut but has
sight, and that which has been shaped out of the matter to the matter, and that
which has been wrought up to the unwrought. Let actuality be defined by one
member of this antithesis, and the potential by the other. But all things are not
said in the same sense to exist actually, but only by analogy—as A is in B or to
B, C is in D or to D; for some are as movement to potency, and the others as
substance to some sort of matter.

In short, the language of being is that of the likeness of diverse *rationes* of act as limited by potency. It is the language of proper proportionality: as A is to B, so is C to D. St. Thomas famously took this up in *De
Ver*. and, some would argue, in his *Sentences* commentary.

Thomas's teaching on analogy in the *Sentences* is clear, but as all will
allow, the *Sentences* is a work from many of whose teachings Thomas
later distances himself, while about those teachings that he elsewhere
further develops, one often finds the *Sentences* articulating merely the
earliest or most inchoate stage. Hence for purposes of the present consideration it is reasonable to stress more heavily the teaching from *De
Ver*. It is however well to note that whereas in the *Sentences* one does
not find Thomas accounting for the limitation of received perfections
owing to potency, from *De Pot*. onward his account of participation presupposes and is formally dependent upon the doctrine of the analogical
division of being by potency and act. This is a point that Klubertanz
makes in his fine book *St. Thomas Aquinas on Analogy* and is a point of
profound relevance to those who today suppose that the analogy of being may simply be identified with an analogy of participation.[6] Indeed,
in the *Sentences* itself the relation of createdness is treated as a quasi-
accident *following upon* the gift of being,[7] as "a certain relation of having

---

6. Klubertanz, *Aquinas on Analogy*, 27–29.

7. *In Sent*. II, d. 1, q. 1, a. 2, ad 4, where he speaks of creation passively (because taken *actively*
creation signifies merely the divine essence with a conceptual relation to the creature): "If, however, it [i.e., creation] is taken passively, then it is a certain accident in the creature and it signifies
a certain reality which is not in the category of being passive properly speaking, but is in the

being from another following upon the divine operation."[8] But surely the relation of having being from another is founded upon *habens esse*, which accordingly is ontologically prior to the relation of createdness. This is a point of formal significance which will be considered more thoroughly below.

De veritate, Analogy of Proper Proportionality, and "Transferred Proportion"

To return to *De Ver.*, here we find Thomas introducing the analogy of proper proportionality with a standard mathematical example, but quickly moving to genuine analogy of proper proportionality exemplified by the proposition that understanding is to the mind as sight is to the eye. Whereas the comparison of diverse proportions immediately suggests a mathematic example, it also resolves into one univocal mathematical proportion—for example, if we say that 3:6 as 25:50, this resolves into 1:2. But Thomas turns to genuine analogy of proper proportionality with the proportionality obtaining between sight:eye and truth:mind, because this does not resolve into one univocal object and yet there is a likeness of diverse *rationes*. It is clear that the mind and the

---

category of relation. Creation is a certain relation of having being from another following upon the divine operation. In the same way, sonship is in Peter insofar as he receives human nature from his father, but it is not prior to Peter himself, but rather follows upon the action and motion which are prior. The relation of creation, however, does not follow upon motion, but only upon the divine action, which is prior to the creature" (Si autem sumatur passive, sic est quoddam accidens in creatura, et sic significat quamdam rem, non quae sit in praedicamento passionis, proprie loquendo, sed quae est in genere relationis, et est quaedam habitudo habentis esse ab alio consequens operationem divinam: et sic non est inconveniens quod sit in ipso creato quod educitur per creationem, sicut in subjecto; sicut filiatio in Petro, inquantum recipit naturam humanam a patre suo, non est prior ipso Petro; sed sequitur actionem et motum, quae sunt priora. Habitudo autem creationis non sequitur motum, sed actionem divinam tantum, quae est prior quam creatura).

8. All Latin quotations are taken from the *Corpus Thomisticum, S. Thomae de Aquino opera omnia*, made available online by the University of Navarre at unav.es/filosofia/alarcon/amicis/ctopera.html#OM. This is not because the author fails to value the Leonine texts, but because (1) no sufficient difference in the cited material exists to weigh against relying on the editions cited, and (2) the editions cited are accessible to students who have neither the funds to afford Leonine folios nor proximity to libraries that possess them. The Leonine Commission was founded to make these texts available for theological and philosophic use, and while computerized versions of Leonine texts are slowly being released, at the present moment—and in the judgment of the present author—the Navarre site may rightfully boast of having the most easily accessible collection of Thomas's texts.

eye, and understanding and sight, are simply different, yet there is a likeness of diverse *rationes* of act. Thomas writes, speaking of the analogy
of proper proportionality, that "To this kind belong all attributes which
include no defect nor depend on matter for their act of existence, for
example, being, the good, and similar things."[9]

It is because the analogy of proper proportionality can avoid all implication of any strict determined relation of God to the creature that all
analogy of creature to God must finally be, as it were, "translatable" back
into the analogy of proper proportionality. Thomas writes, comparing
analogy of proportion (the first type of analogy) to analogy of proportionality (the second type of analogy):

We find something predicated analogously of two realities according to the first
type of agreement when one of them has a relation to the other, as when being
is predicated of substance and accident because of the relation which accident
has to substance, or as when healthy is predicated of urine and animal because
urine has some relation to the health of an animal. Sometimes, however, a thing
is predicated analogously according to the second type of agreement, as when
sight is predicated of bodily sight and of the intellect because understanding is
in the mind as sight is in the eye.

In those terms predicated according to the first type of analogy, there must
be some definite relation between the things having something in common
analogously. Consequently, nothing can be predicated analogously of God and
creature according to this type of analogy; for no creature has such a relation
to God that it could determine the divine perfection. But in the other type of
analogy, no definite relation is involved between the things which have something in common analogously, so there is no reason why some name cannot be
predicated analogously of God and creature in this manner.[10]

---

9. *De Ver.*, q. 2, a. 11, co., unequivocally referring by context to the analogy of proper proportionality: "At other times, however, a term predicated of God and creature implies nothing in its
principal meaning which would prevent our finding between a creature and God an agreement of
the type described above. To this kind belong all attributes which include no defect nor depend
on matter for their act of existence, for example, being, the good, and similar things" (Quandoque
vero nomen quod de Deo et creatura dicitur, nihil importat ex principali significato secundum
quod non possit attendi praedictus convenientiae modus inter creaturam et Deum; sicut sunt
omnia in quorum definitione non clauditur defectus, nec dependent a materia secundum esse, ut
ens, bonum, et alia huiusmodi).

10. *De Ver.*, q. 2, a. 11: "Unde et secundum modum primae convenientiae invenimus aliquid
analogice dictum de duobus quorum unum ad alterum habitudinem habet; sicut ens dicitur de
substantia et accidente ex habitudine quam accidens ad substantiam habet; et sanum dicitur de
urina et animali, ex eo quod urina habet aliquam habitudinem ad sanitatem animalis. Quando-

Thus Thomas not only affirms that this (analogy of proper proportionality) is the type of analogy appropriate for speaking of transcendental and pure perfections. He also holds that the analogy of proper proportionality must frame all other analogies of creature to God. Of course he acknowledges a likeness of the creature to God, but a likeness that is exceeded by still greater unlikeness. As Thomas puts it in *De Ver.*:

As Dionysius says, God can in no way be said to be similar to creatures, but creatures can in some sense be said to be similar to Him. For what is made in imitation of something, if it imitates it perfectly, can be said to be like it absolutely. But the opposite is not true; because a man is not said to be similar to his image, but the converse. But if the imitation is imperfect, then it is said to be both like and unlike that which it imitates: like insofar as it resembles it; unlike insofar as it falls short of a perfect representation. Thus it is for this reason that sacred scripture denies that creatures are similar to God in every way. It does sometimes grant that creatures are like God and sometimes denies this. It concedes the similarity when it says that man is made in the likeness of God, but negates it when it is said in the Psalms, "O God Who is like unto thee?"[11]

Later in *De Ver.*, Thomas makes it very clear that although the creature is truly and determinately ordered to God, God has no determined real relation to the creature.[12] Hence there can be no strict analogy of proportion. Whereas the difference from the nickel to the dime is the same as that distance from the dime to the nickel, it is not true that as the creature is really and determinately ordered to God, so God is really and determinately ordered to the creature.

Man is conformed to God since he is made to God's image and likeness. It is true that, because man is infinitely distant from God, there cannot be proportion between him and God in the proper sense of proportion as found among quantities, consisting of a certain measure of two quantities compared to each

---

que vero dicitur aliquid analogice secundo modo convenientiae; sicut nomen visus dicitur de visu corporali et intellectu, eo quod sicut visus est in oculo, ita intellectus in mente. Quia ergo in his quae primo modo analogice dicuntur, oportet esse aliquam determinatam habitudinem inter ea quibus est aliquid per analogiam commune, impos- sibile est aliquid per hunc modum analogiae dici de Deo et creatura; quia nulla creatura habet talem habitudinem ad Deum per quam possit div- ina perfectio determinari. Sed in alio modo analogiae nulla determinata habitudo attenditur inter ea quibus est aliquid per analogiam commune; et ideo secundum illum modum nihil prohibet aliquod nomen analogice dici de Deo et creatura."

11. Ibid., ad 1.

12. *De Ver.*, q. 23, a. 7, ad 9.

other. *Nevertheless, in the sense in which the term proportion is transferred to signify any relationship of one thing to another* [secundum tamen quod nomen proportionis translatum est ad quamlibet habitudinem significandam unius rei ad rem aliam] *(as we say that there is a likeness of proportions in this instance: the pilot is to his ship as the ruler to the commonwealth), nothing prevents us saying that there is a proportion of man to God, since man stands in a certain relationship to Him inasmuch as he is made by God and subject to Him* [emphasis added].[13]

Or it could be said that although there cannot be between the finite and the infinite a proportion properly so called, still there can be proportionality which is the likeness of two proportions. We say that four is proportioned to two because it is the double; but we say that four is proportionable to six because four is to two as six is to three. In the same way, although the finite and the infinite cannot be proportioned, they can be proportionable, because the finite is equal to the finite, just as the infinite is to the infinite. In this way there is a likeness of the creature to God, because the creature stands to the things which are its own as God does to those which belong to Him.[14]

It is not uncommon to find that this passage is read as suggesting two different solutions, whereas it appears to provide one solution that is expressed in two semantic formulations. According to the *first semantic formulation*, we might speak of an analogy of "transferred proportion," in which we temporarily suspend the normal requisite of determinate proportion and simply acknowledge that the creature has a relationship to God, so that the relation of creature to God may be viewed as an analogy of one to another. That is, the creature truly is really ordered and related to God, and when we affirm this truth it is impossible to

---

13. Ibid.

14. *De Ver.*, q. 23, a. 7, ad 9: "Ad nonum dicendum, quod homo conformatur Deo, cum sit ad imaginem et similitudinem Dei factus. Quamvis autem propter hoc quod a Deo in infinitum distat, non possit esse ipsius ad Deum proportio, secundum quod poportio proprie in quantitatibus invenitur, comprehendens duarum quantitatum ad invicem comparatarum certam mensuram; secundum tamen quod nomen proportionis translatum est ad quamlibet habitudinem significandam unius rei ad rem aliam, utpote cum dicimus hic esse proportionum similitudinem, sicut se habet princeps ad civitatem ita gubernator ad navim, nihil prohibet dicere aliquam proportionem hominis ad Deum, cum in aliqua habitudine ipsum ad se habeat, utpote ab eo effectus, et ei subiectus. Vel potest dici, quod finiti ad infinitum quamvis non possit esse proportio proprie accepta, tamen potest esse proportionalitas, quae est duarum proportionum similitudo: dicimus enim quatuor esse proportionata duobus, quia sunt eorum dupla; sex vero esse quatuor proportionabilia, quia sicut se habeat sex ad tria, ita quatuor ad duo. Similiter finitum et infinitum, quamvis non possint esse proportionata, possunt tamen esse proportionabilia; quia sicut infinitum est aequale infinito, ita finitum finito. Et per hunc modum est similitudo inter creaturam et Deum, quia sicut se habet ad ea quae ei competunt, ita creatura ad sua propria."

do so without linguistically seeming to imply that God is really ordered and related to the creature. But this latter is false. Hence, we must affirm the former, and then perform the mental act whereby we negate the latter. The latter realization removes all strict or genuine proportion inasmuch as strict proportion requires determined and real reciprocal relation. If proportion involves the relation of a part to a whole, or definite determined relation, then it is inapplicable to the "relation" or "proportion" of creature to God because God has no definite determined relation or proportion to the creature. Thus the term proportion is "transferred" from its normal and strict signification in order to refer to the real ordering (relation/proportion) of creature to God, and this analogy of "transferred proportion" must necessarily be retranslated into analogy of proper proportionality (precisely because there *is* no strict proportion of God to the creature). That seems clear enough. But what is his illustration of such analogy?

It is true that, because man is infinitely distant from God, there cannot be proportion between him and God in the proper sense of proportion as found among quantities, consisting of a certain measure of two quantities compared to each other. Nevertheless, in the sense in which the term proportion is transferred to signify any relationship of one thing to another (as we say that there is a likeness of proportions in this instance: the pilot is to his ship as the ruler to the commonwealth), nothing prevents us saying that there is a proportion of man to God since man stands in a certain relationship to Him inasmuch as he is made by God and subject to Him.[15]

In short, Thomas's illustration is an analogy of proper proportionality: "as we say there is a likeness of proportions in this instance: the pilot is to his ship, as the ruler to the commonwealth." This passage is Thomas's *illustration* of what he is speaking about in the case of transferred proportion, that is, we speak of the order of the creature to God, and the creature's likeness to God, realizing that this must always be *retranslatable* in terms of the analogy of proper proportionality because God is never in a real determined relation to the creature. The pilot is not a political ruler; and the ship is not a commonwealth (although these are closer than any similar comparison of creature to God); and the analogy of creature to God is an analogy of *transferred* proportion

15. Ibid.

because it never implies strict proportion and so its intelligibility formally presupposes the analogy of proper proportionality.

As for the *second semantic formulation* of the same answer, he continues to say: "Or it could be said that although there cannot be between the finite and the infinite a proportion properly so called, still there can be proportionality which is the likeness of two proportions." And what does this lead to? It leads to the judgment that: "although the finite and the infinite cannot be proportioned, they can be proportionable, because the finite is equal to the finite, just as the infinite is to the infinite. In this way there is a likeness of the creature to God, because the creature stands to the things which are its own as God does to those which belong to Him."

But this, too, is proper proportionality. *In other words, recognition of the real ordering of the creature to God and of the creature's real relationship to God is acceptable insofar as no determined relation of God to the creature is imported*, which is to say: as long as the propositions can be formulated fundamentally in terms such as "the creature stands to the things which are its own as God does to those which belong to Him."

Thus the semantic difference between the two formulations amounts only to whether one is willing, given these provisos, to extend the term "proportion" to the creature's real ordering toward, and likeness with respect to, God, given that properly speaking "proportion" implies reciprocal relation and here that is not and cannot be the case. Inasmuch as the ordering of creature to God so denominated must be retranslatable into proper proportionality in order to respect the divine transcendence—because God is not proportioned to, or really ordered to, the creature, howsoever true it is that the creature is really ordered to God—all real ordering and proportion of God to creature must be denied. Thus the semantic formulation is of significantly lesser importance than the realization that when we affirm the creature's real determined relation to God, we do not—despite the seeming linguistic *sequitur*—affirm the real determined relation of God to creature.

The term "proportion" is dangerous inasmuch as it denotes reciprocal relation, and while the creature has a real determined relation and order to God, God has no real determined relation or order to the creature. But if we retain the term "proportion" solely for the creature's real ordering to God, this is *retranslatable* into analogy of proper proportionality "because the creature stands to the things which are its own as God does to those which belong to Him." This *permits* the affirmation of the real causal ordering of creature to God, without implying real ordering of God to the creature (the divine causing of created effects *does not even attain the status of an accident in God*, nor is it *essential* to the divine perfection or *a necessary emanation*, which is why God is with respect to creation *free*).

The Persistence of This Teaching
in the *Summa Theologiae*

It is common for the objection to be raised that because Thomas nowhere repeats his express teaching from *De Ver.*, he must have abandoned it. One's disposition to accept this will be in large measure a function of whether one considers the teaching of *De Ver.* to be strategically crucial. Thomas has told us in *De Ver.* that the analogy of being, true, and good—essentially, the *analogia entis*—is an analogy of proper proportionality. He has also taught that analogies of transferred proportion—where we transfer the term "proportion" from its normal "two-way" usage to a "one-way" usage—emphasize the creature's real ordering and relationship to God, but require the understanding that such analogies must (because the real proportioning and ordering is only "one-way") be retranslatable into analogies of proper proportionality. They must be retranslatable into analogies of proper proportionality because God has no real determined relation to the creature.

Thus analogy of transferred proportion enables us to speak of the relation of creature to God analogically as a relation of one to another, without implying any determinate proportion of the infinite divine perfection to created perfection: God has no determined relation to the creature. This same insight obtains for the analogy of effect to cause, for although the creature is really related to God as an effect, God is not really, but only conceptually, related to the creature as creator (this is what Thomas refers to in *ST* I, q. 13, a. 7, co., and ad 4 as a "temporal predicate" that pertains only conceptually to God, and pertains exclusively because of something that is true about the creature).

As has already been noted, this type of analogy of transferred proportion is expressly countenanced in *De Ver.* on the express supposition that it be *articulable as an analogy of proper proportionality*. Hence there is no reason why Thomas should not unfold these analogies of one to another, or of effect to cause, in later works. In *De Ver.* he has told us that the analogy of being, true, and good is an analogy of proper proportionality, and all causal reasoning to God proceeds from, and presupposes, this *analogia entis* as its foundation. Nowhere does Thomas ever deny this fundamental affirmation, and never does he revisit the teaching of *De Ver.* because he has no reason to alter his view of the metaphysical truth that the analogy of being is an analogy of proper proportionality according to diverse *rationes* of act as limited by potency.

But does not Thomas state in *ST* I, q. 13, a. 6, co., that "In names predicated of many in an analogical sense, all are predicated because they have reference to some one thing; and this one thing must be placed in the definition of them all"? And does he not use as an example the analogy of attribution of health, urine, etc.? The answer is yes. But *first*, one must note that in any analogy of effect to cause, or of creature as really related to God as one to another, the created effect is really attributed to God. It is of this type of analogy—the chief theological analogy of the real attribution of the created effect to the uncreated divine cause—that Thomas is principally speaking when he defines analogy in this way. Simply put, of course it is true that the effect is always *attributed* to the cause. But *secondly*, that the teaching of *De Ver.* is retained becomes most clear by noting that in the immediately preceding article (a. 5), Thomas states that perfections that are predicated of God signify God as "incomprehended" by these perfections and as "exceeding" these perfections. That is to say, God exceeds that which is predicated of Him, and does so by no mere finite degree, but infinitely. This is simply and absolutely to say what he says earlier: *there is no genuine or strict proportion*.

It follows that any analogy of proportion that Thomas affirms can only be what he has earlier called an analogy of transferred proportion, in which we use the term "proportion" (because the creature is really ordered to God) but realize that this is not a proportion in the proper sense of the term (because God is not really and determinately ordered to the creature and the divine perfection is absolutely and infinitely *disproportionate* to the creature). This latter insight then moves one to realize that the analogy of *transferred proportion* must, to be metaphysically rigorous and to respect the divine transcendence, be reformulated in the language of proper proportionality. Article 5 affirms thus again that God has no determined real relation to the creature, that the divine perfection is not merely a function or bound variable determined by or in relation to or in dependence upon the creature. Surely this is his plain teaching in the *Summa Theologiae*, as I have suggested already in pointing toward the teaching of Thomas in q. 13, a. 7,[16] which it is now fitting to quote:

Since therefore God is outside the whole order of creation, and all creatures are ordered to Him, and not conversely, it is manifest that creatures are really related to God Himself; whereas in God there is no real relation to creatures, but a relation only in idea, inasmuch as creatures are referred to Him. Thus there is nothing to prevent these names which import relation to the creature from being predicated of God temporally, not by reason of any change in Him, but by reason of the change of the creature; as a column is on the right of an animal, without change in itself, but by change in the animal.

And it is Thomas himself who connects this insight with analogical discourse regarding God. Hence his words in ad 2 of the same article: "For it was above explained (13, 2), in treating of the divine names, that more is contained in the perfection of the divine essence than can be signified by any name." And, likewise, in ad 3: "the perfection of the divine essence is greater than can be included in any name." Need one observe that he does not mean "greater by a finite degree"? What is clearer than the proposition that an infinite excess is not a "proportionate" excess, unless we mean to refer to proper proportionality, that is, as God is to what is his own, so is the creature to what is its own, without implying any real determined relation between God and creature? For God's perfection is infinite, and the creature's is finite.

Perfections predicated of God do not comprehend God and are exceeded by God, and are exceeded by God by no mere finite degree but rather infinitely. This is to say: properly speaking, there is no metaphys-

16. Cf. *ST* I, q. 13, a. 7, co., and ad 4; also III, q. 16, a. 6, ad 2; and, of course, I, q. 13, a. 5, co.

ical analogy of proportion, but only what he has already described in
De Ver. as an analogy of *transferred proportion*. Likewise, one finds this
teaching also in *De Pot.*, q. 7, a. 10, ad 9, where Thomas argues: "If by
proportion is meant a definite excess, then there is no proportion in
God to the creature. But if proportion stands for relation alone, then
there is relation between the Creator and the creature: in the latter really, but not in the former."[17] Indeed, in *ST* I, q. 28, a. 2, ad 1, we find
Thomas teaching that "nothing that exists in God can have any relation
to that wherein it exists or of whom it is spoken, except the relation of
identity; and this by reason of [propter] God's supreme simplicity."[18]
But the proper name of God is not "cause of Prof. Long"—"cause" is
said of God owing to the real dependence of the creature upon God and
its real relation to God, not because being the cause of the creature is
essential to God (to the contrary, creation is free precisely because the
divine perfection *cannot be augmented*, is actually infinite, and God wills
necessarily only the divine perfection). We cannot, laboring under the
epistemic limitations of created likenesses, easily judge rightly of that
divine reality that is so transcendently perfect that for God to *cause* signifies no change whatsoever in the divine perfection but rather signifies
only the being of the effect as ordered to God.

Presuming we mean by "analogy of being" to refer to the real, we can
hardly designate as the analogy of being an analogy whose whole claim
to be a "proportion" is *fundamentally conceptual rather than real*. Any putative analogy of strict and proper proportion of creature to creator, of
effect to cause, or of one to another with respect to creature and God,
would affirm that the divine perfection is proportionate to finite perfection (which is false), that God has a real determined relation to the
creature (which is false), that perfections affirmed of God comprehend
God, and that God does not absolutely and infinitely exceed the distinct
rationes of these perfections (which is false). Thus, when the theologian
uses the language of analogy of proportion, he does so only by transferring this term from its strict signification which requires a two-way

17. "Ad nonum dicendum, quod si proportio intelligatur aliquis determinatus excessus, nulla
est Dei ad creaturam proportio. Si autem per proportionem intelligatur habitudo sola, sic patet
quod est inter creatorem et creaturam; in creatura quidem realiter, non autem in creatore."

18. "Nihil autem quod est in Deo, potest habere habitudinem ad id in quo est, vel de quo
dicitur, nisi habitudinem identitatis, propter summam Dei simplicitatem."

reciprocal relation (if one is half of two, then two is twice one) to the signification of a "one-way" real relation, a use that presupposes and implies for its intelligibility the need to retranslate all such affirmations of proportion into the analogy of proper proportionality which does not imply any determined real relation or proportion between the things having something in common analogically. It presupposes and implies this need to retranslate into proper proportionality because causal reasoning proceeds from the evidence of being, which is analogous according to proper proportionality; and because if we say the creature is to God as "one" to "another" we must understand that this "other" has no proportion to the first, infinitely exceeds it, and that hence the likeness is one of proper proportionality, a likeness of *differing rationes*. Any understanding which were to suppose that there were a determined real relation of God to the creature—or that the divine perfection is really some finite augmentation in relation to the perfection of the creature—would simply be an error.

If God has no determined real relation to the creature, then it follows that all the proposed analogies of proportion must tacitly be understood as presupposing the divine transcendence and as translatable into the analogy of proper proportionality. In the analogy of effect to cause, for example, God is not really related to the creation as cause, but only conceptually, because "to create" is not of the essence of God and whatever is really predicated of God is predicated by way of identity with the divine simple substance (but God is not compelled by his substance to create; creation is free). The foundation of the causal relation of the creature to God is the being of the creature (nonexistent creatures have no real relations to God); and the creature's relation to existence is founded in the active power of God with a conceptual relation to the creature. Thus we have real analogy of effect to cause, but not vice versa. It is not a true analogy of proportion and nothing can make it so but revising our sense of the term "proportion"—literally *transferring* the language of "proportion" to a unique case that exhibits only a one-sided or partial real proportion but not a true proportion in the sense of a determined real relation of those things having something in common analogically. Thus "transferred," the proportion need not retain all the normal aspects of proportion, as God being really and essentially "cause"—which is to say, really related to the creature as bound to bring about the creature—is not retained, whereas the creature as really and essentially "caused" is retained in the analogy of created effect to uncreated cause.

This is simply what Thomas calls the analogy of *transferred proportion*, a transference of a term that in its strict sense implies reciprocality (if one is half of two, then two is twice one) but here retains only the real proportioning and ordering of the creature with respect to God but not vice versa. This is tantamount to "as the creature is to what is its own, so is God to what is his" with solely the following difference: that the affirmation of the ordering of the creature to God represents an insight of supervenient causal wisdom with respect to the analogy of being. But this supervenient insight is built on the analogy of being and does not escape its limitations absolutely speaking. There is no kicking away of a ladder whilst one is standing on it that has happy results.

Soon after *De Ver.*, writing in *SCG* Thomas will make clear (in speaking of the *lumen gloriae* and the proportion of human intellect to beatific vision) that by "proportion" of creature to God he means "any relation of one thing to another."[19] The "transferred proportion" is now simply "proportion" because what else could a cultivated theologian mean by the term other than a one-way real relation or ordering? Proportion in the strict sense, as a determined commensurate relation, is ruled out by metaphysical wisdom: God has no real relation to the creature. But used in this new way, "proportion" is simply "transferred proportion" with the adjective dropped for convenience. There is no new teaching. There is a different mode of expression that refuses to weary the reader with needless repetitions of fundamental metaphysical

---

19. See *SCG* III.54: "Now, the proportion of the created intellect to the understanding of God is not, in fact, based on a commensuration in an existing proportion, but on the fact that proportion means any relation of one thing to another, as of matter to form, or of cause to effect. In this sense, then, nothing prevents there being a proportion of creature to God on the basis of a relation of one who understands to the thing understood, just as on the basis of the relation of effect to cause. Hence the answer to the sixth objection is clear" (Proportio autem intellectus creati est quidem ad Deum intelligendum, non secundum commensurationem aliquam proportione existente, sed secundum quod proportio significat quamcumque habitudinem unius ad alterum, ut materiae ad formam, vel causae ad effectum. Sic autem nihil prohibet esse proportionem creaturae ad Deum secundum habitudinem intelligentis ad intellectum, sicut et secundum habitudinem effectus ad causam. Unde patet solutio sextae obiectionis).

predispository judgments of which any cultivated theologian is already aware and has already made. It is not the task of the theologian to focus solely upon the metaphysical framing of truths about God, but to articulate those truths. The creature is really ordered to God as effect to cause. Once it is understood that God absolutely transcends all relation and proportion to the creature, the use of "proportion" and "relation" to pertain to the ordering of creature to God is reasonable and necessary. The predispository role of the analogy of being as an analogy of proper proportionality renders this possible precisely because it implies no real determined relation of God to creature, and so permits one to affirm that as the creature is to its own, so is God to what is his. This too is necessary lest one take from the use of proportion in its transferred sense the erroneous judgment that God is really determined in relation to the creature rather than absolutely transcendent.

Analogy of Proportionality as Impoverished and Agnostic?

This brings one back to the contemporary claim that analogy of proportion is more properly fundamental to Thomas's thinking than is proper proportionality. This claim seems to arise following upon two questions. First, is not the causal analogy of participation a metaphysically richer and more instructive doctrine than that of proper proportionality? Second, does not analogy of proper proportionality imply a nearly Maimonidean agnosticism?

As to the first, there is no need to derogate the analogy of causal participation. But the analogy of being does not do our causal reasoning for us. More fundamentally, the creature's relation of createdness, and its causal relation of participation, are founded upon the being of the creature. There is no real relation of God to the creature, and actively considered, as Thomas teaches, creation designates only the divine nature. Passively considered, the relation of createdness is a quasi-accident founded upon the being of the creature as received from God. The analogy of being is not the analogy of causal participation, because prior to the existence of the creature it has no causally participatory relation to God: its being is ontologically, although not temporally, prior to this relation. In the *Sentences*, Thomas speaks of creation passively, because taken *actively* creation signifies merely the divine essence with a conceptual relation to the creature:

> If, however, it is taken passively, then it is a certain accident in the creature and it signifies a certain reality which is not in the category of being passive properly speaking, but is in the category of relation. Creation is a certain relation of having being from another following upon the divine operation. It is, thus, not inappropriate that it be in the created thing, which is brought into being through creation, as in a subject. In the same way, sonship is in Peter insofar as he receives human nature from his father, but [sonship] is not prior to Peter himself, but rather follows upon the action and motion which are prior. The relation of creation, however, does not follow upon motion, but only upon the divine action, which is prior to the creature.[20]

Because nonexistent beings do not have real relations, *whatever the analogy of being is, it is ontologically prior to the relations of createdness and of causal participation* even if the latter are temporally simultaneous with the former. The analogy of being as the likeness of diverse *rationes* of act as limited by potency is prior to the analogy of participation and indeed is its foundation, the very basis upon which the causal inference to God as first cause is made. It is no derogation to the doctrine of participation to note that it articulates a sapiential causal wisdom whose foundation is the being common to substance and the categories, a being which comprises diverse *rationes* of act as limited by potency. What the analogy of transferred proportion articulates that is distinct from, but implicitly subject to, the analogy of proper proportionality is the creature's real ordering and likeness to God. But because God has no real proportion or ordering to the creature, the one-way analogy of transferred proportion must be always understood in the light of the analogy of being and as retranslated into the analogy of proper proportionality.

Nor, as regards the second question, is the analogy of proper pro-

---

20. *In Sent.* II, d. 1, q. 1, a. 2, ad 4: "Si autem sumatur passive, sic est quoddam accidens in creatura, et sic significat quamdam rem, non quae sit in praedicamento passionis, proprie loquendo, sed quae est in genere relationis, et est quaedam habitudo habentis esse ab alio consequens operationem divinam: et sic non est inconveniens quod sit in ipso creato quod educitur per creationem, sicut in subjecto; sicut filiatio in Petro, inquantum recipit naturam humanam a patre suo, non est prior ipso Petro; sed sequitur actionem et motum, quae sunt priora. Habitudo autem creationis non sequitur motum, sed actionem divinam tantum, quae est prior quam creatura."

portionality Maimonidean, precisely because it is not a requirement of the valid affirmation of a perfection of God that we directly cognize the mode in which this perfection is true of God (which would require of us the beatific vision). One may know by causal inference that every transcendental or pure perfection is more properly spoken of God than of creatures, and is identified with God as pure act, without knowing the perfection directly as it is thus found in God. The perfections affirmed of God are not synonyms, nor do they mean only that God is the *cause* of perfections in creatures. Rather, what is designated by these perfections truly exists in God, but we have no direct and natural cognition of the unique mode in which these perfections exist in God and as identified with his simple substance. We know the truth of the proposition that the diverse *rationes* of all the transcendental and pure perfections—lacking potency in their definitions—may rightly be affirmed of the one and unique *actus purus* unlimited by any potency, who is God. And these are not synonyms because they are distinct *rationes* (what is intended by justice is not the same as what is intended by mercy or truth or being). Yet the varied perfections designated are present in God formally and supereminently as identified with the divine simple substance. This does not mean that we have direct cognition of the way these exist as identified with God in his simple substance. To know that X is so does not require direct knowledge of *the mode* in which it is so, although of course we can describe this mode by indicating that all the perfections are identified with the divine simple substance, and that they incomprehend God and are exceeded by God while truly and positively being said of God. The reluctance of some contemporaries to affirm cataphatic knowledge of God is chiefly a function of their failure to understand that the mode of this cataphatic affirmation is the analogy of proper proportionality, which permits simultaneous intrinsic attribution (God truly is wise, is good, is just, is merciful) without placing God in a determined real relation to the creature. Thus this analogy of proportionality also includes the judgment that these are found in God as proportioned to one in whom there is no limit of potency and as identified with the divine simple substance, and so not in any proportion to the finite creature.

Thus these perfections are in God in a way which wholly transcends our natural cognition. But this is far from meaning that being, true, good, wisdom, love, mercy, and justice are said of God merely as the cause of these in creatures, because everything designated by these diverse *rationes* is identified with the divine simple substance and is simply and positively true of, and proportionate to, God himself. It is this remotion from all potency that renders the divine mode in which these perfections exist in God to wholly transcend the natural cognition of all created intellects).

Conclusion

There are of course many other objections to the proposition that the analogy of being is that of proper proportionality. But the analogy of being as the likeness of diverse *rationes* of act as limited by potency stands immediately proximate to the principle of noncontradiction and is developed to reconcile this principle with the manyness, limit, and change manifest in being. This analogy of being is the evidentiary source of causal reasoning to God and of the doctrine of participation; and only the analogy of proper proportionality formally retains both intrinsic attribution and respect for the absolute divine transcendence by refusing to treat the divine perfection as existing in a determined relation or proportion to finite creatures. No valid analogy to God can finally avoid the need to be retranslated into analogy of proper proportionality if the intelligibility of our knowledge of God and the divine transcendence are to be respected, or the evidentiary foundation in the analogy of being of our causal reasoning to God is to be affirmed.[21]

21. I have, since writing this essay, published a more recent essay (in the volume deriving from the 2017 meeting of the Pontifical Academy of St. Thomas Aquinas) addressing further implications of my analysis. The more recent essay explains the valid role of analogical proportion in the strict sense solely within finite being but not as extending to God, while placing this limited analogical proportion within the more fundamental analogy of proper proportionality, and denying that between creature and God there can be any other than an analogy of transferred proportion (that is, a use of the term "proportion" for any relation of one to another, since God has no real relation to the creature and stands in no determinate reciprocal real relation to the creature). See Steven A. Long, "The Order of the Universe," in *Dio creatore e la creazione come case commune*, ed. Serge-Thomas Bonino and Guido Mazzotta (Vatican City: Urbanania University Press, 2018), 117–36.

PART THREE

Theological Perspectives

10

A Metaphysics of Human Nature
in the Christology of Aquinas

PAUL GONDREAU

Not long ago in a short entry from *Crisis Magazine*, the Thomist scholar Romanus Cessario, anticipating the theme of this present volume, wrote the following: "Aquinas's discussion of the metaphysics of the Incarnation ranks among the best in this genre of Christian literature. Aquinas locates the supreme moment of alliance between God and man in the hypostatic union. In the person of the Son, a human nature comes together with the divine nature, without either one thereby suffering division or mixture."[1] The purpose of this essay is to verify the "human side" of this claim, that is, to show that in Aquinas's Christology one encounters a stout anti-docetic and metaphysically-charged adherence to Christ's full human consubstantiality. For, even if Aquinas holds to the orthodox Christian belief in the Word become flesh first and foremost as an object of revealed faith, at the same time and in a second speculative move the Dominican master brings a robust metaphysics of human nature, indebted in large measure (though not exclusively) to Aristotle, fully to bear on this revealed mystery of God made man. By an act of faith Thomas believes in the incarnation, but by philosophy he has more

---

1. Romanus Cessario, "The Spirituality of St. Thomas Aquinas," *Crisis Magazine* 14 (July/ August 1996): 14–16.

than a faint idea of what it means to be a man, and thus of what it means for God to be a man. And it is here where Aquinas makes one of his unique, and lasting, contributions to western Christology.

So while much can be said of the metaphysics of the divinity of Christ in Aquinas's thought, especially regarding the person/nature distinction (wherein, for instance, Thomas affirms God's absolute immutability by stressing that the union occurs in the person, the person of the Word, and not in the nature, with the result that the divine nature suffers no change through its being joined to a human nature),[2] we shall restrict our consideration to the metaphysics of Christ's full humanity. To this end, this essay will focus on three metaphysical notions that are foundational to the Christology of Aquinas: Christ's hylemorphically constituted humanity (to which a brief consideration of Christ's male sexuality is appended); Christ's full human affectivity; and the instrumental causal role that Christ's assumed humanity plays in our salvation.

Christ's Hylemorphically Constituted Humanity

"Nothing implanted in our nature by God," writes Aquinas in *ST*, "was lacking in the human nature assumed by the Word of God."[3] With this expression, Thomas confirms in the most explicit terms possible the fact that Christ's human nature is fully consubstantial with our own.

2. "Because human nature is united to the Word, so that the Word subsists in it, and not so that his [divine] nature receives therefrom any addition or change, it follows that the union of human nature to the Word of God took place in the person, and not in the nature." Aquinas, *ST* III, q. 2, a. 2. See also *ST* III, q. 1, a. 1, ad 1, where, in the very opening article of the *Tertia Pars* of the *Summa*, that is, at the very outset of his comprehensive treatment of Christ, Aquinas wastes no time in dispelling the illusion that the incarnation implies a change in God: "The mystery of the Incarnation was not completed through God being changed in any way from the state in which he had been from eternity, but through his having united himself to the creature in a new way, or rather through having united it to himself." Finally, see *ST* III, q. 2, a. 1, co., and ad 3, and *In Ioh.* I, l. 7, n. 172: "The statement, 'the Word was made flesh' [Jn 1:14], does not indicate any change in the Word, but only in the nature newly assumed into the oneness of a divine Person.' And the Word was made flesh' through a union to flesh. Now a union is a relation. And relations newly said of God with respect to creatures do not imply a change on the side of God, but on the side of the creature relating in a new way to God."

3. *ST* III, q. 9, a. 4. See as well *ST* III, q. 18, a. 2: "The Son of God assumed human nature together with everything that pertains to the perfection of human nature"; and, from the beginning of Thomas's writing career, *In Sent.* III, d. 14, a. 3, qa. 3, s.c. 1: "Christ assumed everything natural that follows upon human nature."

Here, of course, Aquinas shows his adherence to that which the Conciliar tradition (of which Thomas enjoyed unique firsthand knowledge for his day), and specifically the Nicene-Constantinopolitan profession, makes clear when it declares the Son of God to have "become incarnate" (σαρκωθέω) and "become man" (ἐνανθρωπέω).[4] For Aquinas, this means that the Son of God assumed a fully integral human nature endowed with everything that belongs to the essence of this nature.

To delineate precisely what God has "planted" in our nature, and what therefore accrues to the Word's assumed humanity, Aquinas turns to an Aristotelian-inspired metaphysics of human nature. For him, only a sound Aristotelian (i.e., philosophical) conception of human nature allows for a sufficiently penetrating grasp of Christ's consubstantiality with our humanity. To this end, Thomas affirms that the humanity assumed by Christ is hylemorphically composed of matter and form, that is, of a body and a rational soul: "Now it belongs to the essence of the human species for the soul to be united to the body," writes Aquinas, "hence, one must say that in Christ a soul was united to his body."[5]

Christ's Possession of a Genuine Human Body

While orthodox Christian thought affirms the same, implicit in the church's condemnation of Arianism and Apollinarianism (both of which deny a full human soul in Christ) and in her rejection of various forms of docetism, all of which deny the reality of Christ's material body (as in the second-century gnostic, Valentinus, who held that Christ had assumed a heavenly body), Aquinas's Aristotelian-inspired metaphysics of human nature makes him an unparalleled champion of Christ's hylemorphically constituted humanity. When writing on the issue of Christ's body, Aquinas unloads the most anti-docetically charged state-

---

4. DS 150 for the conciliar profession. It is well known that Thomas's stay at the papal court in Orvieto in 1261–65 gave the Dominican privileged access to the conciliar decrees of the early church, an access that was practically unheard of in his day. For enlightening studies on this, see C. G. Geenen, "The Council of Chalcedon in the Theology of St. Thomas," in *From an Abundant Spring: The Walter Farrell Memorial Volume of 'The Thomist'*, ed. staff of *The Thomist* (New York: P.J. Kenedy, 1952), 172–217.

5. *ST* III, q. 2, a. 5. For the composition of the human being, see also *ST* I, q. 76, aa. 1 and 4, and a. 6, ad 1, where Thomas writes: "the same essential form makes man an actual being, a body, a living being, an animal, and a man."

ments found in his entire *opera*. In the two articles from *ST* III that treat
this issue (q. 5, aa. 1–2), Aquinas affirms Christ's possession of a "true
body" (*verum corpus*) no fewer than nine times, and he repudiates (a total of fourteen times) the view that Christ's body was purely "imaginary"
(*imaginatum*) or "illusory" (*phantasticum*), or even "heavenly" (*caeleste*).
Sticking closely to the testimony of the risen Christ in Luke 24:39 ("a
spirit has not flesh and bones as you see that I have"), Thomas insists
that Christ's body is "carnal and earthly" (*corpus carneum et terrenum*),
that is, composed of "flesh and bones and blood" (*caro et ossa et sanguis*).
In vain would one look for semi-docetic tendencies banishing Christ's
possession of the body to the realm of the pure abstract in the writings
of this Dominican friar.

In these same two articles, Aquinas discloses the fundamental soteriological reason for his anti-docetic adherence to the reality of Christ's
embodied humanity: because this flesh and these bones were beaten and
broken for our salvation. The mystery of Christian redemption hinges
on the reality of the tortuous crucifixion and death of Christ's body. As
Thomas, resonating in unison with the patristic voice, writes: "if Christ's
body was not real but illusory, he underwent no real death … from which
it follows that the true salvation of the human race has not been accomplished."[6] The realism of Christian salvation succeeds or fails with the
realism of Christ's humanity, to which a body (and a soul) are integral.

On a side note, one should see in the background here Aquinas's
reliance upon the soteriological principle, employed in the patristic age
to great effect: "What was not assumed by the Word was not healed by
him."[7] Without the Word's assumption of a body and a soul, the soteriological purpose of the incarnation falls flat.

In addition to the soteriological concerns, Thomas's adherence to the

6. *ST* III, q. 5, a. 1. See as well *SCG* IV.29 and *In Ioh.* V, l. 5, n. 791. Among the Church
Fathers, no one appreciated more the soteriological stakes of affirming the full reality of Christ's
material body than Ignatius of Antioch, as in *Ad Trall.*, chaps. 9–10, and *Ad Smyrn.*, chap. 2.

7. Though Thomas prefers to cite Damascene's use of this principle—see his *De fide orth.* III,
chap. 6, in *De fide orthodoxa: Versions of Burgundio and Cerbanus*, ed. E. M. Buytaert (St. Bonaven-
ture, N.Y.: Franciscan Institute, 1955), 188—it originates with Origen and is possibly rooted in
Irenaeus's theory of recapitulation. Other Fathers who employ the principle include Athanasius,
Basil, Cyril of Jerusalem, Gregory of Nazianzus, Gregory of Nyssa, Ambrose, Augustine, and
Cyril of Alexandria. For passages in Aquinas, see, e.g., *ST* III, q. 5, a. 4; *In Ioh.* I, l. 7, n. 168; *SCG*
IV.81; and *In Sent.* III, d. 2, q. 1, a. 2, obj. 1.

reality of Christ's "carnal and earthly" body ensues upon another deeply held conviction: that of the fundamental goodness of material reality. In this connection, G. K. Chesterton, holding in mind Aquinas's determined efforts to counter the ever-present human tendency to demean the physical, rightly dubs Aquinas "St. Thomas of the Creator."[8] Aquinas's metaphysical instincts keep him close to all modes of being, no matter how "low grade" or inferior, because all issue from the creative handiwork of God. To be sure, as this Dominican student of Aristotle knows full well, one never finds form existing apart from matter, as matter is that which form actualizes. And because matter is for the sake of form (as the lower is for the sake of the higher), Aquinas in one magnificent passage does not hesitate to affirm that the human body, because of its dignity of being fitted for a rational form, stands apart from all other bodies as the most excellent expression "of the divine art" (*ab arte divina*).[9] Looked at purely physically or in its very material design, such as in its ability to stand upright and erect indefinitely (unique among the animal kingdom) or in the unique manner of sexual union ("face to face"), the human body gives witness to the rational soul to which it is ordered and substantially joined. Aquinas the theologian has little difficulty ascribing this artistic masterpiece of God's to the humanity of Christ.

Christ's Possession of a Genuine Human Soul

Because form does not exist apart from matter and is itself the "the principle of the life of the body, as its form," to quote Aquinas's remarks on

8. G. K. Chesterton, *Saint Thomas Aquinas* (Garden City, N.Y.: Image Books, 1956), 119. Among those who have insightfully highlighted this aspect of Aquinas's thought, Josef Pieper merits first mention for his *Guide to Thomas Aquinas* (San Francisco, Calif.: Ignatius Press, 1991), 120–33. See also Jean-Pierre Torrell, *Saint Thomas Aquinas*, vol. 2: *Spiritual Master*, trans. Robert Royal (Washington, D.C.: The Catholic University of America Press, 2003), 252–75, which argues how Aquinas's anthropology, indebted to Aristotle, stands against the various Platonic currents of his day.

9. *ST* I, q. 91, a. 3. And as Thomas makes clear in q. 93, a. 4, the human form (soul) bears the very image of God: "Since man is said to be to the image of God by reason of his intellectual nature, he is the most perfectly like God according to that in which he can best imitate God in his intellectual nature. Now the intellectual nature imitates God chiefly in this, that God understands and loves himself." Or in III, q. 4, a. 1, ad 2, he writes: "The likeness of the image [of God] is found in human nature, in as much as it [i.e., human nature] is capable of God, namely, by attaining to him through its own operation of knowledge and love."

Christ's humanity,[10] to affirm a full human body in Christ is to affirm Christ's possession of a full human soul. Formulating his response to the Arian and Apollinarian heresies, the former of which denies outright a human soul in Christ and the latter of which denies a rational or intellectual soul (but not an animal soul) in Christ, Thomas drives his metaphysics of human nature further by declaring, along with his favorite Aristotelian-inspired patristic author, John Damascene (d. 749): "'The Word of God assumed a body and an intellectual and rational soul,' since the body ... is not truly human flesh if it is not perfected by a human, i.e., rational, soul.... For man is what he is on account of his reason."[11]

This means that Christ's soul was endowed with all the powers of a rational soul, including a human mind or intellect and an intellectual appetite or will. As is well known, Aquinas offers an extensive treatise on Christ's human knowledge in *ST* III, qq. 9–12. Yet he also gives top treatment to Christ's human will, especially given its role in our salvation, as "by his free [human] will Christ willed the salvation of the human race" and offered up his life in expiation of human sin.[12] Hence, Thomas's aversion to monothelitism, the heresy denying a human will in Christ. The Third Council of Constantinople, with the help of that other Aristotle-inspired patristic author, Maximus the Confessor (d. 662), had condemned monothelitism in 680–81.

---

10. *ST* III, q. 5, a. 3, ad 2.

11. *ST* III, q. 5, a. 4, and q. 19, a. 2. See also Damascene, *De fide orth.* III, chap. 6 (ed. Buytaert, 188). For Arianism, Thomas Weinandy notes in *Does God Suffer?* (Notre Dame, Ind.: University of Notre Dame Press, 2000), 175n5, how Arius's error consists in his conceiving of the Person of the Word as having united himself not to a human body and a human soul *together* (i.e., to an integral human nature) but to a human body *alone*, in such a way that the Word takes the place of a human soul and thus joins himself to a body after the manner of the soul's union with the body. It is for this reason that Arius denies the Word's divinity; he thinks that the nature possessed by the Word would itself have undergone suffering and passibility, which we would otherwise attribute to the soul. Apollinarius comes close to Arius's view of Christ's human soul, but his position has greater nuance: Christ possesses a *psychē* (animal soul), but not a *nous* (rational soul), as this latter was replaced by the *Logos*, the Word. That is, Christ's soul, endowed with animal or sensitive powers, could be the subject of animal-like passions (i.e., suffering and passibility), but not rational thought and choice. For more on these two ancient heresies, see Aloys Grillmeier, *Christ in Christian Tradition: From the Apostolic Age to Chalcedon (451)*, trans. J. Bowden, 2nd ed. (Atlanta: John Knox Press, 1975), 1:219–32 (for Arianism) and 329–43 (for Apollinarianism).

12. *ST* III, q. 18, a. 6. Later in his treatment of Christ's priesthood in q. 22, a. 2, co., and ad 1, Thomas affirms that it is as a man that Jesus offers up his life "of his own free will" (*seipsum voluntarie*) for the expiation of human sin.

The philosophically driven psychology of Christ goes further. Because the intellectual or rational soul subsumes the powers or capacities for operation of the lower grades of soul (namely, the sensitive or animal grade, and the vegetative grade), Christ's soul, Aquinas affirms, possesses full human affectivity, that is, a sub-rational animal-like ordering to bodily goods (sensitive appetite), from which arise the passions or emotions.[13] Thomas asserts: "the Son of God assumed together with the human nature that which belongs to the perfection of animal nature."[14] While the term "animal nature" may today carry a pejorative sense (a holdover from seventeenth-century rationalism), Aquinas's objective metaphysical regard for human nature, and by extension for Christ's human nature, leads him to esteem "animal nature" as simply expressive of the goodness of God's creative will. And this leads to a consideration of Christ's human affectivity, because for Thomas there is no more evident manifestation of the "perfection of animal nature" in Christ than his possession of a sensitive appetite, the seat of human emotion. But first let us say something about that other expression of the perfection of his animal nature, and more particularly of his embodied nature: Christ's male sexed nature.

Christ's Assumption of a Male Sexed Nature

Aquinas's metaphysically-charged esteem for the perfection of animal nature in Christ stands out most strikingly in the passing remarks he offers on the male sex that Christ assumes. In a little known yet highly revealing passage in his commentary on the *Sentences*, Aquinas takes the occasion of a discussion, initiated by Augustine, on the fittingness of Christ's male sex to examine whether Christ had to assume any particular sex at all (*Utrum Christus debuerit sexum aliquem accipere*).[15]

13. See *ST* III, q. 19, a. 2; and, for the human soul in general, *ST* I, q. 78, a. 1. See also Aristotle, *De anima* II.3–4, 414a28–415b28; and, for those authors who appropriate this aspect of the Stagirite's thought and who have an influence on Thomas, Nemesius of Emesa, *De natura hominis*, chap. 14 (ed. Verbeke-Moncho, 91–92); Damascene, *De fide orth.* II, chap. 12 (ed. Buytaert, 118–19); and Albert the Great, *De homine*, q. 67, a. 2.

14. *ST* III, q. 18, a. 2. See as well *In Iob*, on 6:4.

15. *In Sent.* III, d. 12, q. 3, a. 1, s.c. and qa. 1. In *De div. Quaest. 83*, q. 11 (CCSL 44A.18), Augustine states that God became a man (male) because this represents the "more honorable sex" (*sexus honorabilior*), a view that Thomas endorses in *ST* III, q. 31, a. 4, ad 1. Peter Lombard takes this issue up for discussion in *In Sent.* III, d. 12, ch. 4 (ed. Brady, 83), from which it passes to the

Driven by an objective metaphysics of human nature and by soteriological concerns, Aquinas has little difficulty affirming such a concrete
consequence of the incarnation, albeit one of such an obviously delicate
consideration. Genuine human consubstantiality *must* mean the Word's
assumption of a sexed nature:

Christ had to be like his brethren in all things natural, as Heb 2:17 says. *Yet sex
is natural to man.* Therefore, he had to assume a sex.... [Further] Christ came to
restore [or redeem] human nature by his very assumption; and for this reason it
was necessary that he assume everything following upon human nature, namely,
all the properties and parts of human nature, among which is sex; and therefore
it was proper for him to assume a particular sex.... *He assumed a sex not in order
to use it but for the perfection of nature.*[16]

"Sex is natural to man" (*sexus est de naturalibus hominis*). With this
short locution, so rarely uttered in the history of patristic or medieval thought, Aquinas invites his reader to look upon sexuality as part
and parcel of God's creation.[17] Cognizant of the biblical witness (cf.
Gn 1:27: "male and female God created them") and of an Aristotelian-
inspired metaphysics of human nature, Thomas appreciates the fact that
sexuality represents an essential property of our animal-like bodies, that
is, of our concrete materiality or animality.[18] Put another way, to possess an individuated human nature is to own an embodied sexed nature.
Aquinas sees sex as so integral to our nature, we should note, that he
insists we shall retain it even in the resurrected state.[19]

---

thirteenth-century *Sentences* commentaries. Yet only Aquinas adds the query on whether Christ
had to assume any sex at all.

16. *In Sent.* III, d. 12, q. 3, a. 1, qa. 1, sol. 1, co. and ad 2; emphasis added. While Thomas does
not pick up the matter again in the *Summa*, we know from this passage in his *In Sent.* that he does
clearly imply Christ's sexed humanity when he again asserts, "nothing implanted in our nature by
God was lacking in the human nature assumed by the Word of God" (*ST* III, q. 9, a. 4).

17. For texts in which Aquinas affirms the integral role of sexuality in God's creation of man,
see *ST* I, q. 98, a. 2—where Thomas takes to task the views of Gregory of Nyssa in *De hominis
opificio* 17 (PG 44:189) and John Chrysostom in *In Genesim*, hom. 16 (PG 53:126)—as well as
SCG III.126; *De Ente*, chap. 5; and *In Sent.* II, d. 20, q. 1, a. 2. We should note that Thomas in
some ways inherits this regard for human sexuality from Albert the Great.

18. This is covered in detail in my essay, "The 'Inseparable Connection' between Procreation
and Unitive Love (*Humanae Vitae*, §12) and Thomistic Hylemorphic Anthropology," *Nova et
Vetera* 6, no. 4 (2008): 731–64, at 738–42.

19. "The diversity [of sex] is becoming to the perfection of [our human] species.... Wherefore ... (human beings) shall rise again of different sex. And though there be difference of sex,
there will be no shame in seeing one another, since there will be no lust to invite them to shameful

In order, then, to keep the bottom from falling out of a fully integral incarnated humanity and of the salvation of the whole of human nature (note the unmistakable echo of the soteriological principle in Thomas's line, "Christ came to restore human nature by his very assumption"), Aquinas is unabashed in his recognition of that which the tradition has otherwise been loathe to acknowledge, save at the time of the Renaissance (whose artistic representations, inspired by what one scholar terms an "incarnational theology," draw deliberate attention to Christ's male sexuality): Christ was a male individual in the fullest sexed sense of the term.[20] Long a champion of "no more docetism" before this slogan became fashionable in twentieth-century theology (from the Greek δοκέω, "to seem," docetism alleges that Christ only appeared to have come in the flesh, and thereby denies Christ's full humanity), Thomas has an esteem for the full consubstantial realism of the humanity of Christ that runs deep.[21] He knows that Jesus is no generality, he is not "humanity," as is no human being.

It goes without saying that Aquinas stakes out a position here on

deeds which are the cause of shame." *ST* Suppl., q. 81, a. 3 (this is taken from *In Sent.* IV, d. 44, q. 1, a. 3, qa. 1). Thomas offers this same argument on sex "belong[ing] to the perfection of nature" as the reason for its inclusion in our glorified risen bodies in *SCG* IV.88: "[The risen] will, therefore, have all the members of this sort [i.e., sexual members], even though there will be no use for them, to re-establish the integrity of the natural body."

20. We have Leo Steinberg's *The Sexuality of Christ in Renaissance Art and in Modern Oblivion*, 2nd rev. ed. (Chicago: University of Chicago Press, 1996), to thank for bringing to light the "incarnational theology," to use John O'Malley's term in his "Postscript" to this work (213–16, at 213), that inspired much of Renaissance art. With ample evidence, Steinberg shows that many Renaissance paintings of the infant Christ and of the dead Christ depict a veritable *ostentatio genitalium*, that is, a deliberate viewing of Christ's genitals (as when the infant Christ's clothes are deliberately removed to reveal his genitals), with the goal of making manifest his full humanity. Supplying images for support, Steinberg writes: "In many hundreds of pious, religious works, from before 1400 to past the mid–16th century, the ostensive unveiling of the Child's sex, or the touching, protecting or presentation of it, is the main action.... And the emphasis recurs in images of the dead Christ, or of the mystical Man of Sorrows" (3).

21. Docetism has ravaged Christianity since its very inception in various, sometimes diluted or masked forms. Already in the Johannine and Pauline writings of the New Testament, one can see clear anti-docetic retorts: 2 Jn 7, for instance, warns that "many deceivers ... will not acknowledge the coming of Jesus Christ in the flesh," while Jn 1:14 and Col 2:9 announce, respectively, that "the Word became flesh" and that "in Christ the fullness of the Godhead dwells bodily." For its part, Heb 2:14–16 attests that Christ "partook of the same nature" as "the children of flesh and blood" and as "the stock of Abraham." As for Aquinas, Jean-Pierre Torrell does not hesitate to assert in *Le Christ en ses mystères: La vie et l'oeuvre de Jésus selon saint Thomas d'Aquin* (Paris: Desclée, 1999), 1:188, that Thomas affirms "wherever possible that Christ is a man fully subject to the laws of humanity."

Christ's male sexed humanity that might offend modern sensibilities. Some contemporary theologians, for instance, scandalized by the "naive physicalism" of giving weight to the particularity of Jesus' maleness, are fearful that such focus "collapses the totality of the Christ into the human man Jesus," and so wish that discussion on this topic would simply "fade away."[22] These theologians, in other words, want to warn us that if we accentuate Christ's maleness, as does Aquinas in his *Scriptum*, we do so at the theological peril of women. Such accentuation, on their account, can only obscure the way Christ's redemptive accomplishments extend to all without distinction: male and female, Jew and Gentile, slave and free man, "for you are all one in Christ Jesus" (Gal 3:28).

Such concerns, while not entirely without merit, arise from a mindset that is wont to pit the particular against the universal. More generally, this is the mindset that is troubled by the "scandal of particularity," as it is sometimes called, which is part and parcel of the larger Christian story of salvation. The scandal of particularity refers to the irony that a salvation of universal import should be bound up in, because accomplished through, not only a particular history of a particular people, namely, the Jewish people, but especially a particular member of this Jewish people: Jesus of Nazareth, who is himself God "particularized," embodied, in a human individual.[23] To many it seems scandalous that the God of all peoples should bind himself to one particular people, the Jews, thereby raising them above all other peoples, and should unite himself substantially to one particular human individual, to a man, to the male Jesus, thereby granting him "the name which is above every name," to quote St. Paul (Phil 2:9).

With that said, I think it safe to say that Aquinas, who, as one schol-

---

22. Thus, the charge of the feminist theologian Elizabeth A. Johnson, "The Maleness of Christ," in *The Special Nature of Women?* / *Concilium* 6 (1991): 108–15, at 113 and 115. Eleonore Stump repeated this same charge during the discussion portion of a paper I presented on Aquinas's thought at a conference at Blackfriars Hall, University of Oxford, in March 2006.

23. The scandal of particularity is touched upon in many authors. For instance, C. S. Lewis broaches the notion in *Mere Christianity*. Normally, it is used in reference to God's becoming a member of the Jewish race, as when Karl Barth stresses in *Church Dogmatics*, IV.1, ed. G. W. Bromiley and T. F. Torrance (Edinburgh: T and T Clark, 1961), §59 (166–67), how the universality of the Son of God is revealed in the particularity of the Son's assumption of Jewish flesh (Barth bemoans the "all too generalised views of the man Jesus" which lose sight of "the simple truth that Jesus Christ was a born Jew"), or when William N. Ewer whimsically pens in a rhyme: "How odd of God, / to choose the Jews."

ar notes, stands out for his pronouncing upon Christ's humanity at all points in light of the doctrine of the hypostatic union, that is, as subsisting in a divine Person,[24] would insist that the perceived divide between the universal and the particular can be easily overcome. This in turn will sidestep the fear that focusing on Jesus' male sex will lead to an implosion of the "totality of Christ." For Aquinas would point out that the incarnation *unites* the particular with the universal. How so? The concrete reality of Christ's humanity is joined to a divine hypostasis, the one divine Person of the Son. Put more directly, the particulars of the incarnation (Jesus' maleness, his Jewishness, his body and soul, etc.) subsist in a divine Person who, as God, transcends all particulars and all limits of time and place. The whole of God and the whole of his infinite power, a power that cannot be quantified or temporally constrained in any way, are at work in every existential particularity of the life of Jesus.

The reality of God's accomplishing our redemption through his assumed manhood presses us to say more. If the universal (namely, salvation of the human race) does not occur through the particular—that is, through the man Jesus, the son of Mary and Joseph of Nazareth and whose historical male body was put to death on a cross in Palestine nearly two thousand years ago only to come to life again three days later—it does not occur at all: "Christ gives life to the world through the mysteries that he accomplished in his flesh," writes Aquinas, for whom "flesh" always signifies the particular.[25] We must ever be on our guard, Thomas would seemingly wish to warn us, against recycled forms not only of docetism, but also of Gnosticism, that other ancient heresy which proposes universal (spiritual) salvation with no necessary, immediate link to historical particularity.

The Jewishness of Jesus, a favorite topic of current biblical scholarship, provides a fine illustration of universal salvation being linked to the historical particularities of Jesus' humanity. If we stress the fact that

---

24. Ghislain Lafont, *Structures et méthode dans la "Somme théologique" de saint Thomas d'Aquin* (Paris: Les Éditions du Cerf, 1996), 355–59.

25. *In Ioh.* VI, l. 4, n. 914. Similarly, in V, l. 5, n. 791, Aquinas writes: "through the mysteries Christ accomplished in his flesh we are restored not only to an incorruptible life in our bodies, but also to a spiritual life in our souls." More generally, Aquinas likes to say it is the humanity of Christ that leads us to God, as in the prologue to the entire *ST* itself: "Christ, who, as man, is our way to God"; or again in *In Ioh.* VII, l. 4, n. 1074: "the humanity of Christ is the way that leads us to God." See as well *ST* III, q. 9, a. 2.

Jewishness is inseparable from the historical reality of the incarnation, it does not follow from this that we are slighting non-Jews and calling into question St. Paul's claim in Galatians 3:28 that there is "neither Jew nor Gentile" in Christ. In the same way, laying stress on Jesus' maleness does not of itself undercut the place of women in the "totality of Christ." If God became human, then he *had* to become one of us in all the existential particulars that being genuinely human requires. "The Christian faith can never be separated from the soil of sacred events," writes Joseph Ratzinger (the future Pope Benedict XVI), "from the choice made by God, who wanted to speak to us, to become man, to die and rise again, in a particular place at a particular time."[26]

Indeed, the same St. Paul who claims there is neither male nor female in Christ also, through his use of the term *kenosis* when discussing the incarnation in his celebrated "Hymn to the Philippians" (Phil 2:6–11), exalts the soteriological import of the existential particulars of the God-man. *Kenosis*, on the Apostle's account, signifies the fact that the Son of God freely emptied himself of his divine condition in order to embrace our human condition in all its particulars. *Kenosis* in the Pauline sense, in other words, implies God's self-emptying embrace of a true flesh-and-blood embodiment, and thus of such things as subordination to human parents and to the Mosaic Law, or subjection to the penal demands of Roman law regarding the execution of criminals. *Kenosis* is predicated on God's becoming a Jew, a Nazarene, a man "in all the singular parts" of being a man, to use Aquinas's phrase.[27]

It is, then, a great paradox of the faith: the universal is realized through the particular. Universal reconciliation of humanity with God is achieved only because God became the individual man Jesus of Nazareth. To aver the existential particulars of the incarnate Christ, including his male sex, is to affirm the indispensable means through which we arrive at the doctrine where "there is neither male nor female" (Gal 3:28). As Jesus is no generality, so neither is the means of our redemption a mere generality.

---

26. Joseph Ratzinger, *Theology of the Liturgy: The Sacramental Foundation of Christian Existence*, in *Collected Works*, ed. Michael J. Miller, trans. John Saward, Kenneth Baker, SJ, Henry Taylor, et al. (San Francisco, Calif.: Ignatius Press, 2014), 11:101.

27. *De Ver.*, q. 26, a. 10.

As regards the soteriological principle, it is because the Son of God took on a particular sex, the male sex, that the redemption of our sexuality, universally considered, is made possible. To call this "naive physicalism" is to misconstrue fundamentally the realism of the incarnation and instead veer toward a semi-docetic Christology, toward an abstract Christ, as well as toward a Gnostic-like bias against the body. Such is the value that a sound metaphysics can provide theology, or, more specifically, soteriology.

Christ's Full Human Affectivity

On affirming Christ's possession of a full human affectivity, and thus his being subject to human affections or emotions, Aquinas knows no rival.[28] He is not the first to broach the issue—John Damascene and Peter Lombard, and to a lesser degree Augustine, had previously charted the course—but he goes further than anyone else. He assigns the matter more attention than any other thinker, patristic or medieval (though Damascene deserves honorable mention), and he drives the discussion deeper than all others. For him, one simply fails to come to terms with Christ's full humanity until one appreciates that which the Gospels make quite plain: Jesus is a man subject to movements of passion, even intense ones, such as sorrow and fear (as in the Garden of Gethsemane), compassion (as for his disciples who seemed like sheep without a shepherd), joy (as at the Last Supper), and, most reported by the Evangelists, anger (such as that directed against the scribes and Pharisees, or even on occasion against the Apostles).

It is undoubtedly Aquinas's metaphysics of human nature, coupled with his anti-docetic adherence to the realism of Christ's humanity, that leads him to drive forward the discussion on Christ's human affectivity. Thomas understands that to be human is to own a sensitive appetite, and to experience the subsequent movements of this appetite. Drawing upon the famous axiom of Pope St. Leo the Great (d. 461), namely, "Each form [in Christ] accomplishes in concert with the other what is appropriate to it, the Word performing what belongs to the Word,

---

28. For much more on this, see my *The Passions of Christ's Soul in the Theology of St. Thomas Aquinas* (Münster: Aschendorff, 2002).

and the flesh [or the human nature] carrying out what belongs to the flesh," Aquinas insists upon the full operation of Christ's sensitive appetite: "Christ allowed all the powers of his soul to do and undergo what was proper to them."[29] This lays the theological groundwork for full-blown passions in the God-man: "He took on a true human nature with all its natural affections."[30] The passions enter into the essential makeup of the human being and the normal function of our ordering to bodily goods. To be human is to feel sad, angry, joyful, and hopeful at times. A true man, Jesus undergoes the same: "the Lord [exhibited passions]," Thomas writes in his commentary on John's Gospel, "to prove the truth of his human nature, since the passions certainly pertain to every human being."[31]

This view would put Aquinas on a collision course with Stoic philosophy. For the Stoics, the passions count as mere "sicknesses of the soul."[32] As such, then, they merit contempt and complete eradication from the moral life. The goal of the moral life, on the Stoic account, is *apatheia*, indifference to one's emotional states.

Yet for Thomas, who wages a relentless lifelong polemic with the Stoic view (which on one occasion he denounces as *valde inhumanum*, "excessively inhuman"), the passions are in themselves morally neutral, as they belong to the animal-like side of our nature, whereas moral value accrues to reason and will.[33] The passions can even assist in the work of virtue.

---

29. *ST* III, q. 18, a. 5. As for Leo the Great's axiom, see his *Tomus ad Flavianum* (DS 294): "Agit enim utraque forma cum alterius communione quod proprium est. Verbo scilicet operante quod Verbi est et carne exsequente quod carnis est." John Damascene, who was clearly influenced by Leo's *Tome*, reproduces the equivalent of this axiom all throughout his *De fide orth.* III, chaps. 19–20 (ed. Buytaert, 256–60). Though Thomas does cite Leo's axiom itself (cf. *ST* III, q. 19, a. 1), he prefers Damascene's use of it, as here in *ST* III, q. 18, a. 5, but also in q. 14, a. 2; q. 46, a. 6; and *In Sent.* III, d. 15, q. 2, a. 2, sol. 2, ad 2.

30. *ST* III, q. 21, a. 2.

31. *In Ioh.* XII, l. 5, n. 1652.

32. For Stoic texts indicating a contempt for the passions, see Cicero, *De finibus* III, 20; *De Tuscul. Quaest.* I, chap. 80; III, chaps. 4 and 10; IV, chaps. 5–6; Virgil, *Aeneid* IV, 449; and Seneca, *De clem.*, 7; *Moral Epistles* IX, eps. 5, 9, 85; and *De constantia sapientis*, chap. 7, in *L. Annaei Senecae Opera omnia quae supersunt*, ed. F. E. Ruhkopf (Augustae Taurinorum: Ex typis Iosephi Pomba, 1833), 1:348: "Non est autem fortior nequitia virtute; non potest ergo laedi sapiens .... Quod si laedi nisi infirmior non potest ... iniuria in sapientem virum non cadit."

33. *In Ioh.* XI, l. 5, n. 1535. See as well *ST* I-II, q. 59, a. 3, where Thomas denounces the Stoic view as "unreasonable" (*hoc irrationabiliter dicitur*). For an analysis of the influence of Stoicism on Thomas's thought, including the morality of the passions, see E. K. Rand, *Cicero in the Courtroom of St. Thomas Aquinas* (Milwaukee, Wis.: Marquette University Press, 1946); Gerard Verbeke,

Aquinas nowhere makes this clearer than when he inserts an extensive treatise on the passions—the longest treatise in the entire *Summa*—near the beginning of the *moral* part of the *Summa* (I-II, qq. 22–48). Entirely without precedent, such a tactical maneuver sends the clear message that the passions play an indispensable role in the pursuit of moral excellence and holiness, a necessary first step in our striving for happiness, in our attaining the highest good (*summum bonum*). By being inclined internally to bodily goods, we are already on the road, as it were, to the highest good. We are set on a trajectory, even if only in its initial stages, that has as its ultimate endpoint God himself. It bears insisting: the life of spiritual and moral excellence, including that of Jesus, is not bereft of the enjoyment of earthly and bodily pleasures. Such a perspective grants Thomas the objectivity needed to give an honest reading to the New Testament's account of Christ's human affectivity.

Still, Aquinas remains clear on the singular moral quality of Christ's experience of emotion. Christ's sinlessness exempted him from the crippling effects of original sin on human affectivity, effects that otherwise touch every human being. A vast topic explored throughout Aquinas's entire *opera*, the moral quality of Christ's emotions is at every turn affirmed as one that is wholly devoid of disordered movements: "the passions were in Christ otherwise than in us," goes Thomas's preferred expression.[34] Nonetheless, it is the very disparity between the moral quality of Jesus' passions and our own that allows Christ, a real man subject to real movements of affectivity, to act as "the supreme model of perfection" (*summum exemplar perfectionis*), to quote Aquinas's commentary on John 12:6, after whom we can mold our affective lives.

Bolstered, in fact, by the profession of the Second Council of Constantinople (553) that Jesus was "not troubled by the passions of the soul nor the desires of the flesh," Aquinas does not delay in introducing the Aristotelian notion of rational by participation in his opening remarks

---

The Presence of Stoicism in Medieval Thought (Washington, D.C.: The Catholic University of America Press, 1983), 1–19; and Michel Spanneut, "Influences stoïciennes sur la pensée morale de S. Thomas d'Aquin," in *The Ethics of St. Thomas Aquinas: Proceedings of the Third Symposium on St. Thomas Aquinas' Philosophy*, ed. L. J. Elders and K. Hedwig (Vatican City: Libreria Editrice Vaticana, 1984), 50–79.

34. *ST* III, q. 15, a. 4. For the same wording, see *In Ioh.* XII, l. 5, n. 1651; *Comp. Theol.*, chap. 232; *De Ver.*, q. 26, a. 8; and *In Sent.* III, d. 15, q. 2, a. 2, sol. 1.

on Christ's sensitive appetite in *ST* III, q. 18.[35] In short, "rational by participation" refers to the view that through the work of moral virtue, the passions, which can otherwise "talk back" to our higher faculties of reason and will, learn to speak "the same voice" as reason and will, to use Aristotle's language, and thus assist, rather than foil, our striving to live virtuously.[36] Because the sensitive appetite must give its consent to the will's command that it carry out the judgment of right reason, it follows that this lower appetite can act as an *active principle*, as a *source*, of virtuous behavior. Moral virtue converts the very emotions themselves into virtue-oriented movements, with the result that we act with pleasure and promptness, and find ease, not burdensome toil, in living virtuously. For this reason, Aquinas does not hesitate to assert that the lower appetite, our animal-like inclination to bodily goods, has the capability of becoming, in its very act, "rational by participation."[37] And if this is true anywhere, it is nowhere more true than in the case of Christ's moral life, as Aquinas makes plain.[38]

35. For Aristotle, the sensitive appetite "participates in reason to some extent." *Nicomachean Ethics* I.13, 1102b13–14. In its twelfth anathema (DS 434), Constantinople II condemns Theodore of Mopsuestia's view that, to quote the Council (which isolates certain elements of Theodore's position from their original context), Christ experienced "troubling passions and desires of the flesh and became better by his progress in good works." For Thomas's exhaustive knowledge of Constantinople II's teaching, see M. Morard, "Une source de saint Thomas d'Aquin: le Deuxième Concile de Constantinople (553)," *Revue des sciences philosophiques et théologiques* 81 (1977): 21–56. For Aquinas's citing the very wording of the Council, see *ST* III, q. 18, a. 1.

36. On Aristotle's account, one can say of the fully virtuous person that "every act [of his lower sensitive appetite] harmonizes [*homophonia*, 'is of one voice'] with reason." *Nicomachean Ethics* I.13, 1102b29.

37. Aquinas, *Ethica* I, l. 13, n. 242; trans. C. I. Litzinger (Notre Dame, Ind.: Dumb Ox Books, 1993). Thomas outlines this position in much greater depth in three principal *loci*: *ST* I-II, q. 56, a. 4; *De Virt.*, a. 4 ("Whether the irascible and concupiscible appetites can be the subject of virtue"), which was written just after the completion of the *Prima Secundae Pars* of the *Summa*; and *In Sent.* III, d. 33, q. 2, a. 4, qa. 2. The classic study of this issue is found in M.-D. Chenu, "Les passions vertueuses. L'anthropologie de saint Thomas," *Revue philosophique de Louvain* 72 (1974): 11–18, and his "Body and Body Politic in the Creation Spirituality of Thomas Aquinas," *Listening* 13 (1974): 214–32. For another excellent read on this issue, see William Mattison, "Virtuous Anger? From Questions of *Vindicatio* to the Habituation of Emotion," *Journal of the Society of Christian Ethics* 24 (2004): 159–79; and Bonnie Kent, *The Virtues of the Will: The Transformation of Ethics in the Late Thirteenth Century* (Washington, D.C.: The Catholic University of America Press, 1995). This issue is also the subject of my "The Passions and the Moral Life: Appreciating the Originality of Aquinas," *The Thomist* 71 (2007): 419–50.

38. *ST* III, q. 18, a. 2. We should note that the judgment of right reason on the appropriateness or inappropriateness of a given movement of passion is made in light of the truth of the human person and of how the sensible good in question is ordered to our highest good. For this

In the background of this view on the sensitive appetite becoming rational by participation stands the Aristotelian notion of *principatus politicus*.[39] By this term Aristotle, and Thomas after him, liken the type of relationship that exists between our highest faculties, reason and will, and our lower sensitive appetite to an association of governance. Although reason and will retain a natural "power to command" (*imperium*) our lower animal-like ordering to bodily goods, this power is not absolute. The sensitive appetite retains its own quasi-autonomy, as it were. This explains why emotions can "talk back" to our highest faculties, in that they can disobey (or obey) reason and will's *imperium*. We can contrast this to the situation of our bodily limbs, which always carry out the commands of reason and will. The hand, the foot, the arm, and the neck will always observe what the mind commands of them and would never, on their own, resist the commands of reason and will. The relationship between our bodily limbs and reason and will better approximates the political model of a despotic association.

Principatus politicus means, then, that the lower appetite and the emotions which arise from it can be likened to free subjects who participate in limited ways, namely, through their free consent, in the governance of a sovereign, the sovereign in this case being reason and will. Today we would say constitutional monarchy best corresponds to the type of political model to which Aquinas wishes to compare the "power to command" (*imperium*) exercised by reason and will over the sensitive appetite.

In likening the sensitive appetite to a free subject under a sovereign,

---

the virtue of prudence is indispensable, because prudence allows right reason to know when a particular inclination to some sensible good falls in line with our ordering to the first good. For an excellent study on right reason as the rule and measure of human acts, see Laurent Sentis, "La lumière dont nous faisons usage. La règle de la raison et la loi divine selon Thomas d'Aquin," *Revue des sciences philosophiques et théologiques* 79 (1995): 49–69. Also, it is through moral virtue that such consent on the part of the lower appetite occurs. Thomas, with Aristotle, knows full well that it is possible to do the virtuous good, yet without the consent of the sensitive appetite. This defines the continent person, i.e., the person who acts virtuously but only after waging a struggle against disordered bodily desires. See Aristotle, *Nicomachean Ethics* I.13, 1102b17–19, and III.2, 1111b15; and Aquinas, *Ethica* VII, l. 9, n. 1443. There is also the case of the incontinent person, i.e., the person who succumbs to his disordered bodily desires and thus acts contrary to his principles, contrary to what he knows he ought to do. In short, it is only in the fully virtuous individual where the sensitive appetite can be said to be rational by participation; see Aquinas, *Ethica* I, l. 13, n. 239, and VII, l. 9, nn. 1453–54.

39. The classic text from Aquinas affirming this comes in *ST* I, q. 81. a. 3, ad 2; and from Aristotle in *Politics* I.5, 1254b2–5.

Thomas does not mean to suggest that the lower appetite is "free" in the same univocal sense as the rational appetite (the will), our power of free choice. At the same time, it is not merely a metaphorical use of the term "free," either. Aquinas truly believes that the dynamic interplay between our higher faculties and our lower ones is such that, through the work of moral virtue, reason and will penetrate into the sensitive appetite and endow it with a real, albeit derived and partial, sharing in rationality and freedom. It bears repeating: the lower appetite, our animal-like inclination to bodily goods, on Thomas's account, has the capability of becoming rational (and thus free) by participation. Christ provides the supreme example of this.

Of final note on the issue of Christ as the model of integrating emotion into the true human good, we should mention that highlighting Christ's exemplarity is consistent with the prominent role that the notion of *imitatio Christi* (Christ as exemplar to emulate) enjoys in Aquinas's Christology, as evidenced by the Dominican's penchant for the line, "Christ's action is our instruction."[40] On Thomas's account, Christ alone provides an infallible model of human conduct, as he is the God-man who enjoys perfect moral rectitude.[41] Lest one think sinlessness jeopardizes Christ's full human consubstantiality, Aquinas, distinguishing a metaphysical sense of our nature from a postlapsarian, historical, or existential one (the latter of which necessarily implies sin), quickly points out: "Christ ought not to have assumed the defect of sin, since the truth of human nature is not proved by sin, as sin does not belong to human nature, a nature that has God for its cause."[42] Hardly turning Christ into any less of a true man, sinlessness in reality allows Christ to embody in his own Person all that it means to be genuinely human.

40. See *ST* III, q. 40, a. 1, ad 3: "Christi actio fuit nostra instructio." For more on this expression, see Richard Schenk, "*Omnis Christi actio nostra est instructio*: The Deeds and Sayings of Jesus as Revelation in the View of Thomas Aquinas," in *La doctrine de la révélation divine de saint Thomas d'Aquin*, ed. L. Elders (Vatican City: Libreria Editrice Vaticana, 1990), 103–31; and Jean-Pierre Torrell, "«Imiter Dieu comme des enfants bien-aimés». La conformité à Dieu et au Christ dans l'oeuvre de saint Thomas," in his *Recherches thomasiennes* (Paris: J. Vrin, 2000), 325–35.

41. "The example of a mere human being would not be an adequate model for the entire human race to imitate.... And so we were given the example of the Son of God, which cannot err and which meets the needs of all human beings." *In Ioh.* XIII, l. 3, n. 1781; for the same see *SCG* IV.54. See also *ST* III, q. 40, a. 2, ad 1: "Our Lord gave an example of perfection as to all those things which of themselves relate to salvation."

42. *ST* III, q. 15, a. 1; here Thomas explicitly relies upon Damascene, *De fide orth.* III, chap. 20 (ed. Buytaert, 259). See also *ST* I, q. 98, a. 2: "what is natural to man was neither acquired

Christ's Humanity as the Instrumental
Cause of His Divine Personhood

Continuing to employ thoroughly metaphysical language, Thomas teaches that Christ's human actions are not only fully human "in their nature" (in keeping with Chalcedon's distinction of natures), but also expressive of Christ's divine personhood "in their mode" (with respect to Chalcedon's unity in hypostasis or in person).[43] The Council of Chalcedon in 451 confessed, on the one hand, a unity of Person in Christ (as owing to the profession of the Council of Ephesus twenty years earlier) and, on the other, a distinction in natures with their respective properties or predicates, with the key phrase reading: "one and the same Christ, Son, Lord, only-begotten, acknowledged in two natures which undergo no confusion (ἀσυγχύτως), no change (ἀτρέπτως), no division (ἀδιαιρέτως), no separation (ἀχωρίστως)."[44] The distinction in natures implies, for instance, that the Son of God knows in a truly human way with his human mind and that this human knowledge is in no way confused or intermingled with what he knows in his divine mind. But the unity in person means that the one who acts humanly, the one who knows humanly, is none other than the Person of God the Word. The divine Person of the Word is always the acting subject of Christ's human actions.

It is one thing, then, to speak of Christ's human nature and of the attributes of that nature, another to speak of the hypostatic mode or manner in which this human nature subsists—and acts. Because it sub-

---

nor forfeited by sin." For more on the distinction between the metaphysical and existential or historical senses of human nature, see the seminal study on original sin by M.-M. Labourdette, "Aux origines du péché de l'homme d'après saint Thomas d'Aquin," *Revue thomiste* 85 (1985): 357–98, at 366–70.

43. For more on this, see Thomas Joseph White, "The Voluntary Action of the Earthly Christ and the Necessity of the Beatific Vision," *The Thomist* 69 (2005): 497–534. White additionally shows that Aquinas's distinction in nature and mode in Christ follows in the line of Damascene (*De fide orth.* III, chap. 14) and, through Damascene, of Maximus the Confessor (*Disp. Cum Pyrrho* [PG 91:293A]). White takes his inspiration from Jean Miguel Garrigues, "La conscience de soi telle qu'elle était exercé par le Fils de Dieu fait homme," *Nova et vetera* (French edition) 79 (2004): 39–51, and "L'instrumentalité rédemptrice du libre arbitre du Christ chez saint Maxime le Confesseur," *Revue thomiste* 104 (2004): 531–50; and Hermann Diepen, "La psychologie humaine du Christ selon saint Thomas d'Aquin," *Revue thomiste* 50 (1950): 515–62.

44. DS 302.

sists not in a human person (as with all other human beings) but in a divine Person, Christ's human nature possesses a unique mode of being, and thus enjoys a unique mode of acting.[45] In terms of nature, Christ's human actions are identical to ours. But in terms of the subject of those actions, in terms of the Person whose actions they are, Christ's human actions are unique—they have their own mode. The actions of Christ's humanity are the personal actions not of a human person but of the Son of God: "to the hypostasis alone," Aquinas writes, "are attributed the operations and the natural properties, and whatever belongs to the [human] nature [of Christ] in the concrete."[46]

This profoundly metaphysical understanding casts Christ's humanity in a whole new causal light. If, as Jean-Pierre Torrell reports, Bonaventure sees in Christ's humanity "no proper causality" with respect to the accomplishments proper to his divinity, this is not so for Aquinas.[47] Following Damascene, Thomas turns to the Aristotelian notion of efficient causality (or, more specifically, of principal and instrumental causality) to affirm how Christ, as a man, can "cause" human salvation. Only God, or, in Jesus' case, the divine Person of the Word, can of course cause salvation. However, given what I just noted about Christ's unique mode of being, the Word can produce effects proper to him as God *through* the active or free-willed mediation of his assumed humanity.

Considering this fact in light of the notion of efficient causality, then, Aquinas can affirm that *both* God the Word *and* the humanity of Christ produce our salvation, *but in different respects*: the Word, the acting subject of Christ's humanity, by way of "principal" efficient cause (the One who is proportioned to the effect or to the production of human salvation as such, the cause which operates by the power of its own

45. As Aquinas writes in *ST* III, q. 2, a. 2, ad 3: "We must bear in mind that not every individual in the genus, even in rational nature, is a person, but that alone which exists by itself.... Therefore, although (Christ's) human nature is a kind of individual in the genus of substance, it has not its own personality, because it does not exist separately, but in something more perfect, namely, in the Person of the Word." For more on Aquinas's conception of the hypostatic union, see Jean-Hervé Nicolas, *Synthèse dogmatique: De la Trinité à la Trinité* (Fribourg: Éditions Universitaires, 1985), 301–58.

46. *ST* III, q. 2, a. 3.

47. See Jean-Pierre Torrell, "La causalité salvifique de la résurrection du Christ selon saint Thomas," *Revue thomiste* 96 (1996): 179–208; here Torrell has in mind Bonaventure, *In Sent.* IV, d. 43, a. 1, q. 6, co. and ad 4 (ed. Quar., 895).

form), and the humanity of Christ by way of conjoined or assumed (not separated) "instrumental" efficient cause (the Word's chosen channel or medium through which he produces human salvation, even if not proportioned to the effect as such). Because the principal cause and the instrumental cause operate at two different levels, each causes the action completely. As Thomas explains in a key passage from *SCG*: "When the same effect is attributed to a natural cause and to the divine power, it is not as though the effect were produced partly by God and partly by the natural agent: but the whole effect is produced by both, though in different ways, as the same effect is attributed wholly to the instrument, and wholly also to the principal agent."[48]

Without contradiction, then, we can and must affirm that human salvation is produced completely by God the Word and completely by the humanity of Christ, just as Michelangelo's *David* is produced both completely by Michelangelo, as principal cause, and completely by his chisel, as instrumental cause. Indeed, as Torrell points out, it is the constant teaching of Aquinas that an instrumental cause always leaves its mark, truly modifying the action of the principal efficient cause (as the type of chisel used by Michelangelo would have played a role in the quality and style of his carving).[49] Moved by the divine Person of the Word (like a brush moved by a painter), Christ's humanity truly produces or causes human salvation. The Son of God acts as savior of the human race *through* his assumed embodied human nature, not apart, around, or in abstraction from it. Among his Scholastic contemporaries, only Aquinas teaches that Christ's humanity acts as the conjoined "instrument" (*organum*) of his divinity, and this only later in his career (*De Ver.* marks the decisive turning point).[50]

---

48. *SCG* III.70. For the same idea as it pertains to the Bible's being authored both by God and by human beings, see Charles Morerod, *The Church and the Human Quest for Truth* (Ave Maria, Fla.: Sapientia Press, 2008), 33–37.

49. Jean-Pierre Torrell, *Saint Thomas Aquinas: Spiritual Master*, 128–31, esp. 130. For texts in Aquinas (provided by Torrell), see *ST* III, q. 62, a. 1, ad 2; *ST* I, q. 45, a. 5; and esp. *SCG* IV.41.

50. For Aquinas's definitive position on this matter, see *ST* III, q. 19, a. 1, co. and ad 2; and *In Ioh.* VI, l. 6, n. 959 (the definition of instrumental causality comes in *ST* I, q. 45, a. 5); for Damascene's remarks, see *De fide orth.* III, chaps. 15 and 19 (ed. Buytaert, 239 and 258). For the position of Thomas's contemporaries (all of whom were familiar with Damascene) on the matter, see Albert the Great, *De resurrectione*, tr. 2, q. 1, sol. (ed. Colon., 26:259); and, again, Bonaventure, *In Sent.* IV, d. 43, a. 1, q. 6, co. and ad 4 (ed. Quar., 895).

Conclusion

Tomes could be written on the role of metaphysics in Aquinas's Christology. In this short essay, I have attempted to place the spotlight on three metaphysically charged aspects of Thomas's teaching on Christ's full human consubstantiality: Christ's hylemorphically constituted humanity; Christ's full human affectivity; and the instrumental causal role that Christ's humanity plays in our salvation. By singling out, among the countless metaphysical themes and notions of Aquinas's Christology, these three, I have attempted adequately to show that the adage "being (or metaphysics) first" could not more resoundingly ring true than in Thomas's treatment of the humanity of Christ. It is no exaggeration to say that, on Aquinas's account, without a thoroughly forged metaphysics of human nature, one is at best ill-equipped to understand properly the doctrine of God made man, and at worst positively inclined to espouse heretical Christological error.

II

Angelic Corporeality

A Case of Metaphysical Manuduction in
Albertus Magnus and Thomas Aquinas

FRANKLIN T. HARKINS

In his 2003 essay on reason and faith in Aquinas's *Summa Theologiae*, Rudi te Velde noted that for Thomas theological science "is conceived against the background of a metaphysical picture of reality, in which the human intellect and its mode of apprehending the truth is positioned in distinction to the intrinsic truth of reality."[1] The human intellect comes to know the truth of reality "from the bottom up," by reducing what is more known to it—namely, sensible effects—to the intelligible causes of those effects.[2] Within this metaphysically grounded epistemology, *manuductio* is the key term according to which Thomas understands the relationship between philosophy or reason, on the one hand,

---

1. Rudi A. te Velde, "Understanding the *Scientia* of Faith: Reason and Faith in Aquinas's *Summa Theologiae*," in *Contemplating Aquinas: On the Varieties of Interpretation*, ed. Fergus Kerr, OP (London: SCM Press, 2003), 55–74, at 73. On Aquinas's metaphysics, see John F. Wippel, *The Metaphysical Thought of Thomas Aquinas: From Finite Being to Uncreated Being* (Washington, D.C.: The Catholic University of America Press, 2000), as well as the various essays of Wippel reprinted in *Metaphysical Themes in Thomas Aquinas* (Washington, D.C.: The Catholic University of America Press, 1984) and *Metaphysical Themes in Thomas Aquinas II* (Washington, D.C.: The Catholic University of America Press, 2007).
2. Te Velde, "Understanding the *Scientia* of Faith," 73.

and sacred doctrine or the truths of faith, on the other.[3] Although Thomas uses the word only three times in the *Summa Theologiae* and only ten times in his entire written corpus, *manuductio* captures well his understanding that the human intellect is more easily led by rationally intelligible things to those truths that are beyond the grasp of reason.[4] Stated differently, for Aquinas metaphysical manuduction is precisely what enables God's own self-revelation to be accessible to and ultimately useful for human comprehension. Without it, divine revelation would be altogether inefficacious and completely in vain. In the present essay, I seek to demonstrate that the teachings of Aquinas and his own master, Albertus Magnus, on the embodiment and corporeal life-functioning of angels illustrate well this basic notion of metaphysical manuduction that both theological masters shared.

Beginning with Alexander of Hales in roughly 1220, Scholastic theologians became increasingly interested in questions of metaphysics and embodiment in their treatment of angels.[5] Mid-century regent masters of theology at Paris and Oxford—including Alexander of Hales, Richard Fishacre, Richard Rufus of Cornwall, Albert the Great, Thomas Aquinas, and Bonaventure—variously drew on scriptural and patristic writings in combination with Aristotelian philosophy to construct a basic metaphysics of angels according to which these inherently incorporeal creatures assume bodies not because they themselves need bodies in order to fulfill their divinely ordained ministries, but rather simply so that we humans—rational, corporeal, and sensible creatures—might understand the purposes for which they have been sent. Because the relationship between angels and their bodies is strictly occasional and extrinsic, aiming at human instruction, bodily functions of life natural to human beings such as eating, engaging in sexual intercourse, and generating offspring are not, properly speaking, natural to angels.

Questions of angelic bodies and bodily functioning were, of course, by no means new in the thirteenth century. In fact, when Scholastic

---

3. See ibid., 74.

4. See ibid. *Manuductio* is found in *ST* I, q. 88, a. 2, obj. 1; II-II, q. 81, a. 7, co., and q. 82, a. 3, ad 2.

5. Marcia Colish, "Early Scholastic Angelology," *Recherches de théologie ancienne et médiévale* 62 (1995): 80–109, at 109. A fuller treatment of the following discussion can be found in Franklin T. Harkins, "The Embodiment of Angels: A Debate in Mid-Thirteenth-Century Theology," *Recherches de théologie et philosophie médiévales* 78 (2011): 25–58.

masters grappled with such questions, they did so on account of and in conversation with the preceding theological tradition, particularly in its myriad scriptural and patristic manifestations.[6] The canonical scriptures of both Judaism and Christianity reveal angels, as divine messengers, engaged in a variety of apparently bodily activities in their interactions with humans. For example, Gabriel announces the birth of Christ to the Virgin Mary in the opening chapter of Luke's Gospel. Moreover, according to Genesis 18, angels appeared in human form to Abraham, shared a meal with him, and announced that he and his wife Sarah, both very advanced in age, would have a son. Even more intriguingly, in Numbers 22 an angel speaks to the Mesopotamian soothsayer Balaam through the mouth of his donkey to make Balaam aware of God's opposition to his plan to curse Israel. Finally, as we will see, Genesis 6:1–4, together with its subsequent interpretive tradition, had perhaps the most decisive influence on Scholastic considerations of angelic embodiment and embodied life-functioning: this was certainly the case for questions of sexual relations and reproduction. In Genesis 6:1–4, according to some ancient Jewish and Christian interpreters, demons or fallen angels came to earth, desired the beautiful women they found there, engaged in sexual intercourse with them, and thereby produced the giant offspring called Nephilim. According to this reading, which is found in the Second Temple Jewish text known as 1 Enoch, these lustful demons also introduced humankind to the magical arts and other forbidden knowledge, further examples of the great wickedness that led God to regret having created humans and to send the Flood to destroy them.[7]

---

6. For an overview of angels and demons in scripture and patristic thought, see Serge-Thomas Bonino, OP, *Les anges et les démons. Quatorze leçons de théologie catholique* (Paris: Parole et silence, 2007), 15–71. For an inventory of scriptural and patristic texts dealing with angels and demons, see Giorgio Agamben and Emanuele Coccia (eds.), *Angeli: Ebraismo, Cristianesimo, Islam* (Vicenza: N. Pozza, 2009), 55–133, 599–647, 763–998. As its title indicates, this substantial work provides an impressive collection of traditional Jewish, Christian, and Islamic texts on angels and demons.

7. See, e.g., Annette Yoshiko Reed, *Fallen Angels and the History of Judaism and Christianity: The Reception of Enochic Literature* (Cambridge: Cambridge University Press, 2005); *The Fallen Angels Traditions: Second Temple Developments and Reception History*, ed. Angela Kim Harkins, Kelley Coblentz Bautch, and John C. Endres, SJ (Washington, D.C.: Catholic Biblical Association of America, 2014); and James C. VanderKam, "1 Enoch, Enochic Motifs, and Enoch in Early Christian Literature," in *The Jewish Apocalyptic Heritage in Early Christianity*, ed. James C. VanderKam and William Adler (Assen: Van Gorcum, 1996), 33–101. For a recent translation of 1 Enoch, see George W. E. Nickelsburg and James C. VanderKam, *1 Enoch: A New Translation Based on the Hermeneia Commentary* (Minneapolis, Minn.: Fortress Press, 2004).

It is noteworthy, however, that the ancient Christian exegetes to whom Scholastic masters looked as authorities in their theological work tended to reject this angelic interpretation of Genesis 6—which they understood as the "Jewish" interpretation—in favor of euhemeristic alternatives.[8] In *De civitate Dei*, for example, Augustine understands the "sons of God" and the "daughters of men" as human representatives of the metaphorical city of God and the city of man, respectively, rather than reading the former as fallen angels who illicitly mated with human women. Augustine also aims to blunt the preternatural aspects of interpretations like that found in Enochic literature by noting that, according to the scriptural text, there were giants (which Augustine takes simply to be humans with unusually large bodies) on the earth both before and after the "sons of God" mated with the "daughters of men."[9]

Peter Lombard's systematic treatment of angels in distinctions 2–11 of *Sentences* II provided a rich theological context within which subsequent thinkers were able to revisit scriptural texts on angels and demons such as Genesis 6. Scholastic theologians-in-training spilled much ink commenting on distinction 8 in particular, where Lombard asks whether angels have bodies naturally united to them or whether they are incorporeal creatures who assume bodies at particular times simply to carry out specific services commanded by God.[10] As has been suggested, mid-thirteenth-century masters generally opted for the latter position, although they developed their views in divergent theological contexts and with varying degrees of certainty. For example, Albert the Great, who delivered his *Sentences* lectures before becoming a master at Paris in 1245,[11] maintains: "The Fathers seem to think different things concerning this [question], and it is not clear to me which position I

---

8. See Reed, *Fallen Angels*, 190–232.

9. Augustine, *De civitate Dei* XV.22–23, ed. Bernardus Dombart and Alphonsus Kalb (Turnhout: Brepols, 1955), 487–92. The basic contours of the non-angelic, Sethite reading of Gn 6:1–4 promulgated by Augustine can be found in the third-century Pseudo-Clementine *Recognitions* and in the *Chronicle* of Julius Africanus (ca. 160–ca. 240). See VanderKam, "1 Enoch," 76–81 and 84, who observes: "It is abundantly clear that in the fourth century the so-called Sethite interpretation commended itself more and more to expositors. The result was that soon it completely drove the older angelic understanding from the field" (84).

10. Peter Lombard, *Sententiae in IV libris distinctae* II, d. 8, c. 1, ed. Ignatius Brady, OFM (Grottaferrata: Editiones Collegii S. Bonaventurae ad Claras Aquas, 1971–81), 1:365–67.

11. Rega Wood, "Early Oxford Theology," in *Mediaeval Commentaries on the Sentences of Peter Lombard*, ed. G. R. Evans (Leiden: Brill, 2002), 1:289–343, at 310n83.

should teach, and I admit that I do not know."[12] He proceeds to side
with many "Catholic doctors" who hold that whereas angels do not have
their own natural bodies, they do assume bodies "according to the will
and ordination of God."[13] According to Albert, an angel's adjoined
body, which he uses to carry out the divine purpose, can be either organic (i.e., he can operate through a donkey or a serpent, for example)
or formed exclusively according to his mission (as was the case with
the bodies of the three visitors to Abraham).[14] Roughly contemporary
with Albert's *Sentences* commentary is the commentary of the English
Dominican Richard Fishacre, the first Oxford theologian to comment
on Peter Lombard's collection, likely producing his work between 1241
and 1245.[15] Fishacre resolves the question of angelic bodies in much
the same way as Albert: "Therefore we say that they [i.e., angels] do not
have bodies naturally united to them, but [rather] for a great diversity
of ministries they produce bodies for themselves and clothe themselves
with them, just as we make and clothe ourselves with garments. Since,
however, there is no union between me and my garment, it is not natural
to me."[16]

But here a philosophical conundrum arises: namely, if angels are naturally incorporeal, spiritual creatures (as prominent Christian theologians through the centuries had taught), is not their assumption and use
of a material bodies necessarily unfitting, even problematic? Is there not
a fundamental disproportionality between an angel and a body? After
all, Aristotle teaches that the operation of a purely intellectual creature

12. Albertus Magnus, *Commentarium in II librum sententiarum*, ed. P. Jammy, t. 15: *Commentarii in II. et III. Lib. Sentent.* (Lyon: Claudii Prost. et al., 1651), d. 8, a. 1, sol. (94): "Videntur Pa-
tres de huiusmodi diversa sensisse, nec mihi perspicuum est unde alterutrum doceam, et nescire
me fateor." The English translations of all Latin texts in this essay are my own.

13. Albertus Magnus, *Comm. in II*, d. 8, a. 2, sol. (95).

14. Ibid., ad 1 (95).

15. See R. James Long and Maura O'Carroll, SND, *The Life and Works of Richard Fishacre
OP: Prolegomena to the Edition of his Commentary on the Sentences* (Munich: Verlag der Bayerischen Akademie der Wissenschaften, 1999), 39–48; and R. James Long, "The Beginning of a
Tradition: The *Sentences* Commentary of Richard Fishacre, OP," in *Mediaeval Commentaries on
the Sentences*, 1:345–57.

16. Richard Fishacre, *In secundum librum sententiarum*, d. 8, ed. R. James Long (Munich:
Verlag der Bayerischen Akademie der Wissenschaften, 2008), "Utrum omnes angeli corporei
sint," sol. (161): "Propterea dicamus quod non habent corpora sibi naturaliter unita, sed pro di-
versitate ministeriorum diversa sibi componunt et induunt corpora, sicut nos nobis vestimenta.
Cum tamen nulla sit unio inter me et vestimentum meum, nec sit mihi naturale."

can neither depend on nor derive from a body.[17] Furthermore, the Aristotelian principle that the simpler way is better implies that angels, who certainly are able to operate without bodies, should in fact do precisely that.[18] Albert addresses these objections in his *Summa Theologiae* I, q. 75, where he treats questions of angelic bodies and their operations in considerable detail. "It must be said," Albert begins the solution of a. 1, "that on this question the Philosopher is able [to say] little or nothing. And therefore we must rely wholly on the authority of the saints and the biblical writings."[19] Scripture clearly teaches, he proceeds to explain, that angels perform their ministries in bodies "on account of our material understanding" (*propter nostrum materialem intellectum*). Because we are corporeal creatures and, as such, are instructed more easily concerning heavenly things by means of corporeal likenesses, it is "fitting for us" (*conuenientia ad nos*) that angels assume bodies.[20] And indeed, the bodies assumed by angels indicate to us humans what they have come to do concerning us. If they come to protect us from ambush, Albert explains, they assume the forms of agents of war, as in 2 Kings 6:17: "Behold, the mountain was full of horses and chariots of fire all around Elisha." Or in Tobit 5, Raphael appeared as a young man ready for walking in order to teach Tobit that he would lead his son Tobias safely to Media.[21]

This seems quite reasonable. But why an angel spoke through the mouth of Balaam's donkey in Numbers 22 still remains inexplicable. Because the tongue of a donkey is certainly not the necessary instrument for the formation of speech, objection 6 makes clear, this angel did not need to assume the organized body of an donkey. Albert responds to this objection by maintaining that angels with respect to themselves in no way need bodies and the natural faculties of these bodies in order to carry out particular functions; they can utter articulate expressions,

---

17. Albert the Great, *Summa theologiae*, ed. P. Jammy, t. 17: *Prima Pars Summae Theologiae* (Lyon: Claudii Prost. et al., 1651), I, q. 75, mem. 1, obj. 2 (426).

18. Ibid.

19. Ibid., sol. (427): "Dicendum quod in quaestione hac parum potest Philosophus vel nihil: et ideo omnino innitendum est auctoritatibus Sanctorum et Scripturae Bibliae."

20. Ibid., mem. 1, ad 1 (427): "Licet enim quantum est de natura sua incorporei sint et simplices, nullam habentes inclinationem vel proportionem ad corpus: tamen quia nos corporei sumus et corporalibus similitudinibus facilius instruimur de caelestibus, ex convenientia ad nos, ut scilicet nobis congruant, utile est eos assumere corpora."

21. Ibid., sol. and ad 1 (427).

for example, without forming them by means of a tongue (e.g., they can speak through burning bushes or clouds, as scripture attests). But with respect to us they do need bodies, in order that we might be taught in the way that is "most fitting" for us.[22] And we are most accustomed to hearing and understanding language produced by means of the corporeal mouths of animals, albeit ordinarily the mouths of rational animals.

Genesis 6:1–4, together with other canonical texts in which angels appear to eat and speak (e.g., Gn 18 and Tb 12:19), provided the occasion for Scholastic theologians to reflect on the embodied life-functions of angels. Can angels with their assumed bodies walk, speak, eat, engage in sexual intercourse, and generate offspring? Aquinas addresses such questions in several of his works, from his early *Sentences* commentary to his mature *Summa Theologiae*.[23] In the *Sentences* commentary, Aquinas explains that the relationship between an angel and his assumed body is a metaphysically loose and extrinsic one, which has consequences for corporeal function on the part of the angel: "It must be said that ... angels do not pour life into their assumed bodies, but rather merely movement: and therefore it must be held that no operations which accompany a living body inasmuch as it is living can pertain to angels in their assumed bodies, but only those which accompany a mobile body inasmuch as it is movable, such as moving, pushing, dividing, and things of this sort."[24] Embodied angels, according to Thomas, can perform only those functions of life that require motion and only to the extent that those functions can be accomplished by simple motion. He explains, for example, that an angel is not able to truly eat by virtue of the fact that he cannot perform all of the operations that are essential

22. Ibid., mem. 1, obj. 6, and ad 6 (427–28).

23. For introductions to the *Sentences* commentary and *ST*, see respectively: Jean-Pierre Torrell, OP, *Saint Thomas Aquinas*, rev. ed., trans. Robert Royal (Washington, D.C.: The Catholic University of America Press, 2005), 1:36–47; Adriano Oliva, *Les débuts de l'enseignement de Thomas d'Aquin et sa conception de la sacra doctrina, avec l'édition du Prologue de son commentaire des* Sentences (Paris: Vrin, 2006), 187–287; and Jean-Pierre Torrell, OP, *Aquinas's Summa: Background, Structure, and Reception*, trans. Benedict M. Guevin, OSB (Washington, D.C.: The Catholic University of America Press, 2005).

24. Aquinas, *In Sent.* II, d. 8, q. 1, a. 4, sol. 1: "Respondeo dicendum, quod, ut praedictum est, angeli corporibus assumptis vitam non influent, sed tantum motum: et ideo considerandum est quod omnes operationes quae sequuntur corpus vivum, inquantum vivum, non possunt angelis in corporibus assumptis convenire; sed tantum illae quae consequuntur corpus mobile inquantum hujusmodi, ut movere, impellere, dividere, et hujusmodi" (211–12).

to eating: namely, cutting food with the teeth, swallowing it with the throat, digesting it in the stomach, and converting it into fuel for the body. Whereas the embodied angel can chew and swallow his food, his body simply does not have the capacity of a truly living body to process food and incorporate it into that selfsame body. Thomas is quick to point out, however, that "by some power of the angel" the swallowed food is dissolved into previously inactive or unformed matter.[25]

It is important to note here, in the context of Aquinas's denial of true eating among the angels, his relatively strong view of food *vis-à-vis* the human body and human nature. In commenting on *Sentences* II, d. 30, Thomas discusses three opinions on the question of "whether food passes over into the truth of human nature."[26] According to the first position, that of Peter Lombard, food is not converted into the truth of human nature at all; rather the truth of human nature consists completely in the original seminal material that the individual received from his or her parents. On Thomas's reading of this position, food simply protects the flesh from being consumed by vital heat rather than either augmenting or restoring the body.[27] The second position maintains that the human body possesses a primary seminal component that is fixed and endures throughout one's life, but that the rest of the body (i.e., the secondary component) consists of material that is subject to wastage and renewal. On this account, food is converted into the truth of human nature only secondarily, that is, only with respect to this second component.[28] The third position, that of Aristotle and Averroes, holds that food truly and completely becomes the truth of human nature precisely because there is no material part of the body that is fixed and permanent; rather, all bodily matter is susceptible to wastage and restoration.[29] Aquinas claims this third view as his own, thereby highlighting the indispensable role

25. Ibid.
26. Ibid., d. 30, q. 2, a. 1, sol. (778–87). For an analysis of Aquinas's treatment here, see Philip L. Reynolds, *Food and the Body: Some Peculiar Questions in High Medieval Theology* (Leiden: Brill, 1999), 361–71, on which the following summary depends.
27. Aquinas, *In Sent.* II, d. 30, q. 2, a. 1, sol. (778).
28. Ibid. (780–84).
29. Ibid. (784–85). Thomas does make clear that whereas, according to this position, no material part of (i.e., no matter in) the human body is permanent, the form and species of the human is permanent. Instructive here is Aristotle's analogy of the stoking of a fire: as the fire burns up logs, one adds new logs to replace them, but the form of the fire always remains (Reynolds, *Food and the Body*, 369).

of eating to both nourishment and nature among humans. Finally, it is significant, as a prelude to our consideration of his teaching on demonic reproduction, that Thomas also follows Aristotle in maintaining that human semen is entirely a byproduct of food and the digestive process.[30] Because angels do not really eat and nourish their bodies, they are wholly unable to produce sperm.

Thomas's refusal to admit that angels truly eat accords with the *Summa fratris Alexandri*, which had earlier arrived at a similar conclusion regarding angelic eating by a different route. The *Summa fratris Alexandri* has been traditionally attributed to Alexander of Hales, a synthesis perhaps begun and redacted by Alexander but completed by others in the Franciscan school after his death.[31] The author of the *Summa fratris Alexandri*, following Augustine, distinguishes between the necessity and the power of eating. Whereas angels do not eat out of any necessity of nourishing their assumed bodies (which are constituted of air, it must be recalled), they do truly eat inasmuch as eating pertains to the power of revealing God to those humans with whom angels share meals.[32] As one of the objections affirms, it is an abomination (*nefas*) to believe that in angels food moves into the stomach and is expelled through the intestines (i.e., that these divine messengers digest and defecate).[33] The precise words of the archangel Raphael to Tobit, "I *appeared* [*videbar*] to eat with you, but I use invisible food" (Tb 12:19), provide compelling scriptural evidence in support of the view of the *Summa fratris Alexandri*—and Aquinas—that angels eat only insofar as they chew and swallow their food (i.e., divide and move it locally).[34]

30. Aquinas, *In Sent.* II, d. 30, q. 2, a. 2, sol. (790–94). Cf. Reynolds, *Food and the Body*, 371–76.

31. On the dating and authenticity of the *Summa fratris Alexandri*, see M. Gorce, "La somme théologique d'Alexandre de Hales est-elle authentique?," *New Scholasticism* 5 (1931): 1–72; Christopher M. Cullen, "Alexander of Hales," in *A Companion to Philosophy in the Middle Ages*, ed. Jorge J. E. Gracia and Timothy B. Noone (Malden, Mass.: Blackwell, 2003), 104–8; and especially the prolegomena to the Quarrachi edition: *Alexandri de Hales Summa Theologica*, ed. Pp. Collegii S. Bonaventurae, t. 4 (Quarracchi: Ex Typographia Collegii S. Bonaventurae, 1948), LIX–LXXXI. Although the questions of Alexander himself likely served as one source for the material that came to constitute the first three books of the *Summa fratris Alexandri* which were compiled prior to Alexander's death in 1245, so many questions of authorship and authenticity remain unanswered that we certainly cannot assume that Alexander is the author or even compiler of the entire *Summa*.

32. *Summa fratris Alexandri* II, pars 1, inq. 2, tract. 3, sect. 2, q. 2, tit. 2, mem. 2, cap. 2, a. 2, co. (245–46).

33. Ibid., obj. 2 (245). Cf. Mt 15:17.

34. Ibid., obj. 1 and ad 1 (245–46); emphasis added. See Aquinas, who invokes Tb 12:19 to

Thomas's teaching on angelic eating (or non-eating, more properly) is in line with that of his master, Albert. On whether angels are able to eat, Albert affirms: "They seem to truly eat because Abraham the Patriarch, who was spiritual and probably had discernment, offered them food and they ate."[35] A second objection Albert raises is that it is not fitting or suitable for angels, who are heralds of divine truth, to deceive humans by merely appearing to eat when in fact they are not actually eating.[36] On the other hand, to believe that angels digest and incorporate food before excreting waste is absurd![37] Albert answers simply that angels do not truly eat. But neither do they deceive us in appearing to eat, he explains, since they intend such corporeal actions to refer to "some spiritual and moral [reality]."[38] The three angelic visitors to Abraham, for example, appeared in anthropomorphic bodies in which they seemed to eat in order to show forth the ministry of the triune God and his communion with us humans. Abraham served his guests food, Albert explains, because he did not recognize that they were angels with such a purpose until after the meal. That he did not recognize their angelic nature and ministry right away is "not unfitting [for a patriarch], nor does it demonstrate less sanctity [on his part]," Albert teaches.[39]

Let us turn, lastly, to the question of whether angels can procreate or generate offspring. Here Aquinas's thinking is guided by the aforementioned principle that angels can perform only those life-functions that require simple movement. Furthermore, it is this metaphysical hermeneutic that helps Thomas navigate the contested intellectual terrain between the strictly human Sethite interpretation of Genesis 6 represented by Augustine, on the one hand, and the angelic Enochic one, on the other. In the *Scriptum*, Aquinas writes:

---

support his argument concerning angelic eating in *ST* I, q. 51, a. 3, ad 5 (ed. P. Caramello [Turin: Marietti, 1952], 1:260); and *De Pot.*, q. 6, a. 8, co., in *Quaestiones disputatae et quaestiones duodecim quodlibetales*, Editio Quinta Taurinensis (Turin: Marietti, 1931), 1:211.

35. Albert the Great, *Comm. in II*, d. 8, a. 5, obj. 1: "Videbantur autem vere comedere: quia Abraham patriarcha qui spiritualis erat, et probabile est quod discretionem habuerit, obtulit eis cibos et illi comedebant" (97).

36. Ibid., obj. 2 (97).

37. Ibid., s.c. (97).

38. Ibid., ad 2 (98).

39. Ibid., ad 1 (98): "Ad id autem quod obiicitur de Abraham, dico quod recognouit quidem ministerium Trinitatis in eis figurari, sed non recognouit esse Angelos usque post mensam: et hoc non est inconueniens, nec minorem sanctitatem ostendens."

Some say that demons in their assumed bodies are in no way able to procreate; and that "the sons of God" do not signify angels [acting as] *incubi*, but rather the sons of Seth, and that "the daughters of men" signify those who descended from the race of Cain. But because the contrary is held by many, and [because] what seems true to many cannot be entirely false according to the Philosopher … it can therefore be said that by their [i.e., the demons'] action generation is completed inasmuch as they can put human semen in a place appropriate to the corresponding matter, just as they can also bring together the seeds of other things in order to bring certain effects to fruition …. So only what is local motion is attributed to them, not however generation itself, the beginning of which is not the power of the demon or of the body assumed by him, but rather the power of that one whose semen it was. Hence the one born is not the demon's, but rather is the son of a certain human.[40]

Although Thomas here does not reject the Sethite reading, he appears to give greater credence to what he understands as the more popular angelic interpretation found in 1 Enoch. Just as canonical scripture reveals that angels eat and speak, so too the sacred text depicts the fallen angels engaging in sexual relations with women and thereby producing offspring. For Thomas, however, the embodied demon acts merely as an angelic instrument of what is essentially human generation.

In *ST* I and in *De Pot.*, both of which were composed in 1265–68, Thomas further explains what appears to be angelic intercourse as recounted in Genesis 6. In *ST* I, q. 51, a. 3 (which asks simply whether angels in assumed bodies exercise the functions of life), Aquinas briefly describes the succubus-incubus theory, which relies on Augustine's doctrine of seminal reasons: just as demons artificially collect and bring together the seeds of things in combinations that enable these seeds to naturally produce certain effects, so too can they move human semen

---

40. Aquinas, *In Sent.* II, d. 8, q. 1, a. 4, sol. 2: "Ad id quod secundo quaeritur, dicunt quidam quod daemones in corporibus nullo modo generare possunt; nec per filios Dei angelos incubos significari dicunt, sed filios Seth, et per filias hominum eas quae de stirpe Cain descenderunt. Sed quia contrarium a multis dicitur, et quod multis videtur non potest omnino falsum esse, secundum Philosophum, in VII *Ethic.*, cap. xiv, et in fine *De somn. et vig.*, ideo potest dici quod per eorum actum completur generatio, inquantum semen humanum apponere possunt in loco convenienti ad materiam proportionatam, sicut etiam semina aliarum rerum colligere possunt ad complendum aliquos effectus, ut in praecedenti distinctione dictum est; ut attribuatur id tantum eis quod est motus localis, non autem ipsa generatio cujus principium non est virtus daemonis, aut corporis ab eo sumpti, sed virtus illius cujus semen fuit; unde et genitus non daemonis, sed alicujus hominis filius est" (212).

from a man into a woman in order that offspring might be generated. Such simple local motion, which for Thomas clearly is the purview of embodied angels, is achieved when the wicked angel assumes a female body in which he receives the man's semen in ordinary intercourse (thereby acting as succubus), before then assuming a male body from which he deposits the same semen into a human woman through another sexual encounter (in which he acts as incubus).[41]

In light of Thomas's treatment, we might well ask why angels *appear* to have bodies like humans in which they *appear* to perform certain natural human operations if, in fact, they neither have bodies nor naturally function in them in the same way that humans do. Do angels in assumed bodies deceive, whether intentionally or not, the humans with whom they interact? Is divine scripture, in which we read about angels performing various functions of life, less than completely trustworthy? Aquinas anticipates these important questions in the first objection of q. 51, a. 3, where he notes that it is not fitting that "angels of truth" should feign possessing living bodies and engaging in natural human behaviors. It is not contrary to the truth, Thomas explains in replying to the objection, that scripture describes certain intelligible realities under sensible figures as this is done not for the purpose of demonstrating that these intelligible realities are sensible, but rather so that the properties of intelligible things might be better understood according to likeness. "In this way it is not incompatible with the truth of the holy angels," Aquinas argues, "that the bodies assumed by them seem to be living humans, although they are not. For they [i.e., the bodies] are assumed only so that the spiritual properties and operations of the angels might be indicated through the properties and operations of the human."[42]

Although this question in *ST* provides no further explanation of how human properties and functions manifest the spiritual properties and operations of angels, Thomas appears to offer an example to the careful reader of *De Pot.*, q. 6, a. 8: namely, the generation of offspring.

41. Aquinas, *ST* I, q. 51, a. 3, ad 6 (260), and *De Pot.*, q. 6, a. 8, ad 5 (212).
42. Aquinas, *ST* I, q. 51, a. 3, ad 1 (260): "Ita non repugnat veritati sanctorum angelorum quod corpora ab eis assumpta videntur homines, licet non sint. Non enim assumuntur nisi ut per proprietates hominis et operum hominis spirituales proprietates angelorum et eorum spiritualia opera designentur." Thomas further explains here that it would be less fitting if angels were to assume true humans, as their properties would then lead us to humans rather than to angels.

The seventh objection points out that if angels in assumed bodies merely transferred human semen from a human male to a human female in
order to facilitate natural human reproduction, the offspring said to be
generated by demons would be proportionate to the power of the seed
and thus would be no taller and stronger than those produced according
to the normal mode of human reproduction. But Genesis 6:4 clearly
teaches that "giants" were born when the sons of God had intercourse
with the daughters of men.[43] In response to the objection, Thomas
makes perfectly clear that because the offspring produced by a demon
acting as succubus-turned-incubus is generated by the power of the human seed, he is not the son of the demon but rather of the human male
whose semen the demon transferred. He proceeds to explain, then, how
giants can be produced: "And nevertheless it is possible that stronger
and bigger humans could be produced in such a way because demons,
wishing to appear miraculous in their deeds, are able to actively contribute to this by observing the designated positions of the stars and the
disposition of the man and woman, and particularly if the seeds that are
used as instruments achieve a certain increase of power through such
use."[44] It is by such magical arts as astrology, according to Thomas, in
combination with the power of natural human semen that demons are
able to facilitate the generation of giants. It is through this operation
of procreation—an operation that remains ultimately a natural human
action even in this extraordinary case—that the spiritual properties and
operations of the demons are demonstrated: that an offspring is generated is a naturally human operation, a function of the power of the human
father and mother; that this offspring is a giant is a demonic operation,
a consequence of joining the power of the human seed with that of the
magical arts.

43. Aquinas, *De Pot.*, q. 6, a. 8, obj. 7 (211): "Praeterea, secundum hoc, ex tali semine homo
non generaretur nisi secundum virtutem humani seminis. Ergo illi qui dicuntur a daemonibus
generari, non essent majoris staturae et robustiores aliis qui communiter per semen humanum
generantur; cum tamen dicatur Genes. VI, 4 (aliis verbis), quod cum *ingressi essent filii Dei ad
filias hominum illaeque genuerunt, nati sunt gigantes, potentes a saeculo, viri famosi.*"

44. Ibid., ad 7 (212): "Et tamen possibile est quod per talem modum homines fortiores
generentur et majores; quia daemones volentes in suis effectibus mirabiles videri, observando
determinatum situm stellarum, et viri et mulieris dispositionem, possunt ad hoc cooperari. Et
praecipue si semina, quibus utuntur sicut instrumentis, per talem usum aliquod augmentum
virtutis consequantur." On this passage, see also Henry C. Lea, *Materials toward a History of
Witchcraft*, ed. Arthur C. Howland (New York: T. Yoseloff, 1957), 1:155–56.

In conclusion, we have surveyed the teaching of Albert and Thomas on angelic embodiment and corporeal life-functioning as one particularly illustrative example of metaphysical manuduction. For our Scholastic masters, angels, inherently incorporeal and spiritual creatures, assume bodies not on account of any necessity on their part, but rather in order to successfully instruct humans concerning the divine will. It is, as Albert teaches, "on account of our material understanding" that angels take bodies to themselves and appear to perform various life-functions in them. Although Aristotle had suggested that embodiment is wholly unnecessary and indeed inappropriate for a purely rational creature, Albert and Thomas gleaned from scripture that angels sometimes *appear* to function in bodies because it is "fitting for us." They *seem* to eat, as in Genesis 18 and Tobit 12:19, and to engage in sexual intercourse and generate offspring, as in Genesis 6. But particular details in these texts, read through the lens of certain traditional philosophical assumptions about angels, revealed to our theologians that angels do not truly eat, have sex, and reproduce in the way humans do. Rather, angels act in anthropomorphic ways, as Aquinas makes clear, in order to indicate their own spiritual properties and operations through human attributes and actions. In this way, through angelic intermediaries, God instructs us humans precisely according to our capacity to comprehend.

Finally, let us add a brief postscript related to recent trends in Aquinas studies as described by Otto-Hermann Pesch several years ago. In his essay entitled "Thomas Aquinas and Contemporary Theology," Pesch rightly pointed out that the question of Thomas's theological methods, and especially the relationship of reason and faith, constitutes an engaging topic in recent Aquinas studies, particularly as scholars have come to appreciate what Pesch calls "Thomas Aquinas without Thomism."[45] At the same time, in comparison with the 1930s and 1940s Thomas's teaching on the Trinity, Christology, and angels has been "relegated to the shadows" of contemporary scholarship. Pesch explains: "The many specific arguments [that Aquinas propounds on these topics] ... strike today's reader as more frustrating than stimulating, not so much perhaps from slothful thinking on the reader's part as because ... precisely

---

45. Otto-Hermann Pesch, "Thomas Aquinas and Contemporary Theology," in *Contemplating Aquinas*, 185–216, at 195–96.

for *theological* reasons, they are not felt to permit going into as much detail as Aquinas does because there are no compelling grounds for doing so in the documented traditions of faith."[46] Whereas we could formulate many responses to this affirmation, our foregoing analysis leads us to one in particular: namely, we have surely seen that a brief survey of Thomas's (and Albert's) doctrine of angelic embodiment indicates quite "compelling grounds" for studying their teaching on such theological topics, perhaps especially for scholars interested in the theological methods of Albert and Thomas. Contrary to those who might assume that the bodily behavior of angels constitutes an obscure, even irrelevant, theological topic, Albert and Thomas teach us that proper reflection on such realities can—"on account of our material understanding" and by way of metaphysical manuduction—teach us much about God, divine accommodation, and our own limited ability to know the things that surpass human reason.

46. Ibid., 198.

12

Aquinas and the Grace of *auxilium*

SHAWN M. COLBERG

Saint Thomas Aquinas's mature theology of grace reflects a deep continuity with preceding High Scholastic depictions of grace while also
introducing consequential and distinctive development of their most
basic insights. His later works receive High Scholastic emphases on
sanctifying grace (*gratia gratum faciens*) as establishing a supernatural
habitus or created form in the recipient, which equips the person to act
in meritorious ways, while also pairing the language of habitual grace
with that of helping grace, or more properly, divine *auxilium*.[1] This *auxilium* actualizes potential habits in an actor through divine movement,
thus expanding the categories for grace to include greater stress on efficient causality, including the way in which God can be said to cause
grace. Thomas's use of *auxilium* provides a critical advance over con-
temporaneous accounts of grace, including Thomas's earlier treatment
in the *Sentences* commentary which aligned the notion of sanctifying

This article was previously published in *Modern Theology* 32, no. 2 (2016): 187–210 (© John T.
Wiley and Sons Ltd, 2016), and is reprinted here with permission from the publisher. I am grateful
to *Modern Theology* for their permission, as well as to the editors of this volume, who sponsored a
conference for which I produced the original draft.

1. In terms of Thomas's systematic works, the increasing attention to divine *auxilium* is most
present in *ST*, which was written during the last seven years of his life (1267–74). Important
metaphysical antecedents having to do with God's causation, however, are established in the
SCG (completed 1264–65).

grace almost wholly with habitual grace.[2] Taken together, the language of habitual grace and divine *auxilium*, set out especially in the *Summa Theologiae*, provide Thomas with a wider and more precise conceptual canvas on which to depict the saving movement of the graced wayfarer into life with God. Thomas's increasing appreciation of *auxilium* parallels and complements a stronger metaphysical commitment to God as efficient and final cause of all movements in the cosmos, especially the movement of the elect to glory.

The present study will exposit Thomas's treatment of *auxilium* in *ST*'s treatise on grace, and to that end it will trace the way that his teaching on *auxilium* (1) informs his parsing of the effects of grace in justification and sanctification, (2) coheres with his overarching doctrine of God and divine providence, and (3) further illumines the concrete life of the believer, a life rooted in the sacraments and the ongoing work of the divine Persons. Emerging from this study is the categorical importance of *auxilium* for the way in which Thomas presents God as an actor in the created world, and in the case of human salvation, as a dynamic cause of progress toward divinization or final union with God. Appreciating the use of *auxilium* distinguishes Thomas from his contemporaries and illustrates, for modern readers, a distinctive double-emphasis on formal and efficient perfection—both tending toward final perfection—which

2. The dating of *In Sent.* is not altogether straightforward. According to Emery, the work was not yet complete when Thomas began his work as *magister* in 1256; he returned to commenting on the first book of the *Sentences* in 1265–66 before leaving off to begin work on *ST*. See "Brief Catalogue of the Works of Saint Thomas Aquinas," in Jean-Pierre Torrell's *Saint Thomas Aquinas*, trans. Robert Royal (Washington, D.C.: The Catholic University of America Press, 1996), 1:332. The foundational studies of grace with important implications for the understanding of *auxilium* include Henri Bouillard's *Conversion et grace chez S. Thomas d'Aquin. Etude historique* (Paris: Aubier, 1944) and Bernard J. F. Lonergan's *Grace and Freedom: Operative Grace in the Thought of St. Thomas Aquinas*, ed. J. Patout Burns (London: Darton, Longman and Todd, 1971). A highly accessible summary of the insights of Bouillard and Lonergan, among others, can be found in Joseph P. Wawrykow's *God's Grace and Human Action: 'Merit' in the Theology of Thomas Aquinas* (South Bend, Ind.: University of Notre Dame Press, 1995), esp. 34–55. Wawrykow also offers a useful introduction to Aquinas's mature teaching on grace in "Grace," in *The Theology of Thomas Aquinas*, ed. Rik Van Nieuwenhove and Joseph P. Wawrykow (South Bend, Ind.: University of Notre Dame Press, 2005), 192–221. While Lonergan's landmark work affirms the centrality of operative *auxilium* in Thomas's thought and Wawrykow's work situates its indispensability for understanding Thomas's approach to merit, this study extends their insights to the economy of salvation more generally and argues that, properly understood, one can see divine *auxilium* as an ordering principle in Thomas's presentation of Christian doctrine in *ST*.

informs most theological loci in Thomas's mature thought, including his
doctrine of God, treatments of nature and grace, and exposition of the
sacraments. The study thus argues that an expanded awareness of the
role of divine *auxilium* adds greater insight into Thomas's systematiza-
tion of theological loci.

Auxilium in the Treatise on Grace

Given Thomas's tripartite division of *ST*, one might expect him to place
the treatise on grace in either the *Prima* or *Tertia Pars* inasmuch as grace
might be said to belong to God's act of creation/governance or to the
way in which humankind returns to God through Christ. While Thomas already lays critical groundwork for an understanding of divine *auxilium* in the *Prima Pars*, he situates the treatise on grace at the end of the
Prima Secundae, centered in the middle of the second part. He specifies
the purpose of the *Prima Secundae* thus:

> Because, as the Damascene states, it is said that man is made in God's image, in-
> asmuch as image signifies an *intelligent being, having a free-will and self-movement*;
> now that we have treated of the exemplar, namely God, and of those things which
> proceed from divine power according to God's will, it remains for us to consider
> his image, that is, man, inasmuch as he too is the principle of his operation, as
> having free will and power over his actions.[3]

The *Secunda Pars* takes up a study of human nature as the image of
God. For Thomas, part of what is significant about human nature—in
addition to its rationality and freedom—is the distinct end to which
God has called the elect: eternal beatitude.[4] Thomas describes this end

---

3. *ST* I-II, q. 1, Prooemium. "Quia, sicut Damascenus dicit, homo factus ad imaginem Dei
dicitur, secundum quod per imaginem significatur *intellectuale et arbitrio liberum et per se potes-
tativum*; postquam praedictum est de exemplari, scilicet de Deo, et de his quae proceesserunt ex
divina potestate secundum eius voluntatem; restat ut consideremus de eius imagine, idest de homine, secundum quod et ipse est suorum operum principium, quasi liberum arbitrium habens et
suoruum operum potestatem." All quotations in the body of the text are my own, and the Latin
citations of *ST* are taken from *Summa theologiae* (Ottawa: Impensis Studii Generalis OP, 1941–
45). For the sake of economy, in the notes I use the English translation of the *Summa* in *Summa
Theologica*, trans. Fathers of the English Dominican Province (New York: Benzinger, 1947).

4. Thomas sets the horizon of the *Secunda Pars* in the first five questions, which pertain to
the final beatitude of humankind and the general means by which it is reached; the questions
which follow in the *Prima Secundae* and *Secunda Secundae* keep the goal of beatitude in mind for

as beyond the natural powers of human nature; it is a *super*natural end. Therefore, after treating many aspects that lie within the natural capacities of human nature, including those that may be thought of as infused habits given to human nature (*ST* I-II, qq. 1–105), he turns to that principle—grace—which restores those natural powers damaged by sin and helps human beings reach their special end.[5] In the Prooemium to the treatise on grace (I-II, qq. 109–14), Thomas writes: "It follows that we ought to consider the exterior principle of human acts, namely God, insofar as we are helped by him to act rightly [*recte*] through grace."[6] As integral to the successful return of human beings to God, Thomas situates the treatise on grace at the center of the *Secunda Pars* which piv-

---

the discussion of virtue, vice, and proper human action. Importantly, Thomas first approaches the question of final beatitude in *ST* I, q. 12, where he concludes that the blessed can see God when grace elevates nature and unites it to God's self. Thomas thus establishes eternal beatitude as the end to which human nature is naturally and supernaturally oriented.

5. *ST* I-II, qq. 106–8 pertain to the "Law of the Gospel" which Thomas also refers to as the New Law; q. 106 defines the New Law; q. 107 relates it to the Old Law; and q. 108 describes "what the law contains." In q. 106, Thomas summarizes that "it is the grace of the Holy Spirit, given through faith in Christ, which is predominant in the law of the New Covenant, and that in which its whole power consists" (q. 106, a. 1, co.). The Holy Spirit as source of grace, and so, *auxilium*, becomes a foundational theme in the questions preceding the treatise on grace proper, in I-II, qq. 109–14. In his treatment of the *Summa*'s order, Torrell comments on the coherence of the questions on the law with the questions on grace; he writes: "But God has reserved himself the right to intervene in salvation history. Thus, he promulgated two kinds of law: the *Old Law*, which Thomas examines in minute detail (qq. 98–105), and the *New Law*, which Thomas identified with the grace of the Holy Spirit (qq. 106–8). The whole of this treatise with its three subdivisions deserves to be known better. It is a magnificent apologia for the law. While Thomas highlights the great educative value of the law for personal freedom and stresses its necessary role in service to the common good, he also radically relativizes it, because its usefulness is only pedagogical and disappears once its service is completed." Jean-Pierre Torrell, *Aquinas's Summa: Background, Structure, and Reception*, trans. B. Guevin (Washington, D.C.: The Catholic University of America Press, 2005), 34. Brian Davies extends Torrell's insight to the *Secunda Secundae* and *Tertia Pars*; he writes: "[Thomas] takes the New Law to be what we are talking about insofar as we believe that God is at work to bring people to *beatitudo* and not just *felicitas*. He takes the New Law to be God acting in Christ to lift us to levels of virtue not acknowledged in the writings of philosophers such as Aristotle. And it is the New Law that Aquinas is chiefly concerned with in 2a2ae. Here he turns to theological virtues and gifts of the Holy Spirit in more detail than he has so far done in the *Summa Theologiae*, and in 3a he goes on to focus on the person of Christ, to try to say what it might mean to call Christ divine, and to explain (as far as he thinks he can) what the Incarnation amounts to when it comes to the benefit of human beings." Davies, *Thomas Aquinas's* Summa Theologiae: *A Guide and Commentary* (Oxford: Oxford University Press, 2014), 212–13.

6. *ST* I-II, q. 109, Prooemium. "Consequenter considerandum est de exteriori principio humanorum actuum, scilicet de Deo, prout ad ipso per gratiam adiuvamur ad recte agendum."

ots the discussion of human nature toward attaining eternal beatitude.[7] What follows in the *Secunda Secundae* will make sense in light of human nature enhanced by grace by outlining the manner in which the graced wayfarer may approach God as final end. Grace constitutes a hinge on which the movement of human beings turns in the second part, broadly moving the discussion from a study of a primarily intrinsic means of progression to an extrinsic-intrinsic means.[8]

Thomas frames the treatise on grace with a telling first question:

7. Speaking of the structuring of the second part, Torrell writes: "It is profoundly significant that the treatise on grace comes at the end of the *Prima Secundae*, and it is easy to understand the reason. This volume begins with the final end that man pursues in all his actions [*ST* I-II, qq. 1–5], and everything that follows is an examination of the means that allow him to attain this end. The a priori condition that has been assumed but until now not examined, is that an act must be proportionate to the end that one wishes to attain. Now since this end is beatitude—the enjoyment of God in perfect communion of knowledge and love—it is completely disproportionate to human capabilities. By definition, this kind of happiness is connatural only to God. God, therefore, must provide man not only with the wherewithal to act in view of this end and to have his desire inclined to it, but also with the means which human nature itself can be raised to the heights of that end. This is what the created gift of grace responds to, and with this Thomas concludes the *Prima Secundae*: God 'equips' man in such a way as to allow him to attain by his free and virtuous acts the end to which he calls him. What follows in the Second Part examines these acts in detail" (*Summa*, 35).

8. This study does not intend to argue that grace is the primary structuring theme in *ST* nor does it mean to suggest that I-II, qq. 109–14 is the complete teaching on grace. For such a debate, see Thomas O'Meara's "Grace as a Theological Structure in the *Summa Theologiae* of Thomas Aquinas," *Recherches de théologie ancienne et médiévale* 55 (1988): 130–53, and Romanus Cessario's "Is Thomas's *Summa* Only about Grace?," in *Ordo sapientia et amoris*, ed. Carlos-Josaphat Pinto de Olivera (Fribourg: Universitatsverlag Freiburg Schweiz, 1993), 197–207. Rather, the present study sees I-II, q. 109 adding a dimension to Thomas's treatment of the way in which human beings attain eternal beatitude which is then progressively expanded in the *Secunda Secundae* and *Tertia Pars*. Davies speaks of the treatise on grace thus: "I speak here of 1a2ae, 109–114 being a *general* discussion of grace because in 2a2ae Aquinas deals with *particular* theological virtues brought about by grace, and in 3a turns in some detail to the grace of Christ (grace resulting in people because of the life, death, and resurrection of Christ) and the means by which certain religious practices can be thought of as causes of grace" (223). Inasmuch as Marie-Dominique Chenu's proposal of an *exitus-reditus* schema of the *Summa* has some bearing on understanding its order, which is not an uncontroverted claim, the treatise on grace may reasonably be thought to act as an important locus for shifting the larger thematic discussion from one of going forth to one of return. Thinking of qq. 109–14 as providing the condition of the possibility for speaking of humanity's *reditus ad Deum*, one can reasonably think of the treatise as pivotal. For further exploration of Chenu's argument, see chap. 11 of his *Toward Understanding Saint Thomas* (Chicago: Henry Regnery, 1964). A helpful list of sources and summary to varying debates on the order of the *Summa* may be found in Brian V. Johnstone's "The Debate on the Structure of the *Summa theologiae* of St. Thomas Aquinas: From Chenu (1939) to Metz (1998)," in *Aquinas as Authority: A Collection of Studies Presented at the Second Conference of the Thomas Instituut te Utrecht, December 14–16, 2000*, ed. Paul van Geest, Harm Goris, and Carlo Leget (Leuven: Peeters, 2002), 187–200.

ST I-II, q. 109, "On the necessity of grace." Each of its ten articles asks whether a certain human act or accomplishment is possible apart from grace, and in all but one instance, Thomas answers with a resounding no. Among the most compelling propositions are "whether one can do any good without grace" (a. 2), "whether one can merit eternal life" (a. 5), "whether one can dispose oneself for grace" (a. 6), and "whether one can rise from sin, avoid it, or persevere apart from grace" (aa. 7, 8, and 10). In each of these critical aspects of human life, Thomas stipulates that grace is necessary. Question 109 therefore sets both a rhetorical and conceptual footing for the treatise with an insistence on prevening grace for any meaningful human progress on the journey to God.[9]

Immediately in q. 109, a. 1, Thomas introduces two related lines of thinking which substantiate human dependence on grace. He argues first that all created things depend upon God in order to act or move. God as unmoved mover sets all created things in motion, reducing the potency of their form to act in order to achieve a given end.[10] The language resonates with Thomas's doctrine of God, particularly his empha-

---

9. Thomas sets the movement to eternal life in the context of a journey where the elect progress as wayfarers on the way to eternal life or final perfection. See *ST* II-II, q. 24, a. 4, co., for a particularly concise affirmation of the Christian life as a journey wherein viators progress to union with God in which they become comprehensors. In discussing the effects of divine ordination on human merit, Wawrykow summarizes this conception: "When speaking of merit [in I-II, q. 114], Thomas repeatedly refers to the life of a Christian as a 'journey' or 'movement.' The basic idea here is that the Christian life can be viewed as a journey in which one who is in grace moves further away from sin and draws nearer to God through the good actions/merits which one performs. Eventually, the Christian will attain in this way the ultimate destination of this journey, God himself. And yet, as portrayed by Thomas in this question, it is at first glance a rather odd journey, for the journey itself is controlled principally not by the traveler, but by God" (*God's Grace*, 267n13). The primary agency of God on the journey can, indeed, be seen in the placement of the treatise on grace as the beginning of the discussion of those "extrinsic principles" by which human beings are moved to right action, action which will lead to union with God as the proper terminus of the elect.

10. Thomas defines movement very broadly to include the act of intelligence. He writes: "Now every use implies movement, taking movement broadly, so as to call thinking and willing movements, as is clear from the Philosopher (*De Anima, iii.*4). Now in corporeal things we see that for movement there is required not merely the form which is the principle of the movement or action, but there is also required the motion of the first mover.... But it is clear that as all corporeal movements are reduced to the first motion of the heavenly body to the first corporeal mover, so all movements, both corporeal and spiritual, are reduced to the simple First Mover, Who is God." This position shares patent parallels with Thomas's ontological proofs for God's existence (I, q. 2) as well as his affirmation that all beings participate in God's *esse* (I, q. 44); the latter not only suggests possessing a certain similitude of the divine by virtue of the thing's creation but also an intrinsic act of existing which is caused by God.

sis on God's nature as *ipsum esse*; it is that very being whose nature is pure act who moves the potential habits in created natures into action.[11] Thomas writes: "But we see in corporeal things that for movement [*motum*] not only the form which is the principle of the movement or action is required, but the motion of the first mover is also required."[12] Applying this to created intellects, Thomas reasons that human beings cannot think or know any truth without this movement: "Therefore we ought to say that for the knowledge of any truth whatsoever man needs *auxilio divino* so that the intellect may be moved by God to its act."[13] An appropriate divine motion—a premotion—is required for human beings to use their capacities as rational, freethinking persons.[14] The applica-

11. For the metaphysical implications of participating in the divine *esse*, see John Wippel's *The Metaphysical Thought of Thomas Aquinas* (Washington, D.C.: The Catholic University of America Press, 2000), 114–21. Wippel explains: "On the other occasions, Thomas refers to such entities as participating in the First Act, or the First *Esse*, or the First Being, and as he often adds, by similitude or imitation. This does not imply that they have a part of God's being. It rather means that in every finite substantial entity there is a participated likeness or similitude of the divine *esse*, that is, an intrinsic act of being (*esse*), which is efficiently caused in it by God. On still other occasions, when Thomas refers to such entities (or natures) as participating in *esse*, he seems to have in mind immediately the *esse* which is realized within such entities as their particular acts of being (*actus essendi*)" (121). Lonergan adds: "In this position it is easy to discern the origin of the Thomist analogy of the principle of operation. God is His own virtue; His essence, His potency, His action in the sense of principle action – all are one" (*Grace and Freedom*, 85).

12. *ST* I-II, q. 109, a. 1, co.: "Videmus autem in corporalibus quod ad motum non solum requiritur ipsa forma quae est principium motus vel actionis; sed etiam requiritur motio primi moventis."

13. Ibid.: "Sic igitur dicendum est quod ad cognitionem cuiuscumque veri, homo indiget auxilio divino ut intellectus a Deo moveatur ad suum actum." Wawrykow notes that, while Thomas sometimes elides the term *auxilium* with habitual grace, he consistently reserves a narrow sense of the term which means nothing other than God's application of persons to their acts, and in the case of acts which make one pleasing to God, one may speak of *auxilium* as a sanctifying grace. Wawrykow writes: "For auxilium in this [narrow] sense, see such texts as I-II 109, 1c, where he calls it *divinum auxilium*, I-II 109, 2c (*divinum auxilium*), I-II 109, 3c (*auxilium Dei moventis, auxilium Dei*), I-II 109, 4c (*auxilium Dei moventis*), I-II 109, 5 ad 3 (*auxilium gratiae*), and 109, 6c (*auxilium gratuitum Dei interius animam moventis*)" (*God's Grace*, 171n52).

14. Lonergan provides a careful historical overview of the development in Thomas's understanding of the Aristotelian doctrine of premotion; see *Grace and Freedom*, 63–91, esp. 72–76. For the present study, it is enough to note that Thomas adopts the notion of divine "premotion" to explain how divine causation unfolds in the cosmos. Lonergan writes: "On the other hand, the Aristotelian premotion understood by St. Thomas affects indifferently over the mover or moved, agent or patient; explicitly it is the *vel ex parte motivi vel ex parte mobilis*; and what it brings about is not some special participation of absolute being but, again explicitly, some relation, disposition, proximity that enables mover to act upon moved" (71). Lonergan will subsequently add that Thomas synthesizes premotion with the notion of "application" which implies that God—as

tion of divine premotion certainly includes the *concursus generalis* initially effected by the first mover as well as subsequent motions according
to the plan of divine providence; so in cases where the intellectual or
other movement of persons fall within their natural capacities, they are
moved naturally in what might loosely be called divine *auxilium*. The
term, however, is here used to denote God's movements in the order of
grace insofar as God applies *auxilium* to bring about sanctifying and supernatural effects.[15] Thomas anticipates the role of *auxilium* already in
his discussion of the will. He writes: "But nevertheless, God sometimes
moves some [people's wills] specially to the willing of something determinate, which is [willing] the good; just as in those whom he moves by
grace, as shall be said below in I-II.109.2."[16] Importantly, Thomas does
not restrict *auxilium* to an initial or singular movement by God. He
writes: "It should be said that we always need *divino auxilio* for every
thought, inasmuch as God moves the understanding to act; for actually
to understand anything is to think, as is clear from Augustine."[17] With
regard to knowing any truth, particularly the articles of faith, Thomas
suggests that God renders such knowledge actual "according to the plan

---

outside of the created order—applies motion to bring about the effects of the divine will through
the work of providence in the economy (79).

15. That the application of *auxilium* is needed in the natural movements is clear. Thomas
writes: "But it is clear that as all corporeal movements are reduced to the motion of the heavenly
body as to the first corporeal mover, so all movements, both corporeal and spiritual, are reduced
to the simple First Mover, Who is God. And hence no matter how perfect a corporeal or spiritual
nature is supposed to be, it cannot proceed to its act unless it be moved by God; but this motion
is according to the plan of providence, and not by necessity of nature, as the motion of the heavenly body" (*ST* I-II, q. 109, a. 1, co.).

16. *ST* I-II, q. 9, a. 6, ad 3. "Sed tamen interdum specialiter Deus movet aliquos ad aliquid
determinate volendum, quod est bonum: sicut in his quos movet per gratiam, ut infra (q. 109
a.2) dicetur."

17. *ST* I-II, q. 109, a. 1, ad 3. "Ad tertium dicendum quod semper indigemus divino aux-
iliio ad cognitandum quodcumque, inquantum ipse movet intellectu ad agendum: actu enim
intelligere aliquid est cogitare, ut patet per Augustinum." God "moves the understanding to act"
which underscores the role of premotion rooted in a larger sense of divine application; God
acts as the efficient cause of actual understanding by way of such motion. Importantly, Thomas
also connects his idea of *auxilium divinum* to the action of the Holy Spirit moving a person to a
particular act (in this case, the act of faith); moreover, he distinguishes such action from habitual
graces infused into the recipient. Thomas writes: "Every truth by whomsoever spoken is from
the Holy Ghost as bestowing the natural life, and moving us to understand and speak the truth,
but not as dwelling in us by sanctifying grace, or as bestowing any habitual gift superadded to
nature" (*ST* I-II, q. 109, a. 1, ad 3).

of His providence."[18] Even at the outset of the treatise on grace, Thomas's reader can observe him connecting the movements of grace to God's larger providential ordering of the cosmos and specific order of the elect to eternal life.

In a. 1, Thomas introduces a second argument, namely, that for those things which are beyond the capacity of a given nature, something must be superadded to the form (*naturae superadditam*), thereby raising its natural potency. Thomas uses the example of water which cannot by nature heat something else unless the formal power of fire is added to it. In the same way, human nature cannot ascertain truths beyond its nature except "by the light of faith or prophecy which is called the light of grace inasmuch as it is superadded to nature."[19] Thomas subsequently classifies such superadded forms as gifts of habitual grace (*gratiae habitualis donum*) because they inform human nature and dispose it to virtuous and, at times, surpassing goods.[20] In instances where a divine truth surpasses human reason—for instance that God is triune—a habitual grace (here the gift of faith) must be added to human nature. Guided by the premises that (1) human beings depend on divine movement for any action and (2) anything beyond the natural capacities of human beings requires the superadded habitual form, Thomas sketches the categories of divine *auxilium* and habitual grace for the subsequent nine articles which follow in q. 109. Each of those topics will require divine motion and, potentially, some formal perfection that either heals or elevates the soul such that Thomas is loathe to speak of any graced action without affirming both *auxilium* and habitual graces as causes. Habitual graces anticipate habitual action, and their actualization relies on divine *auxilium*. Thomas writes: "Much more therefore does God infuse certain forms or supernatural qualities into those he moves towards the attain-

---

18. *ST* I-II, q. 109, a. 1, co.: "secundum suae providentiae rationem."

19. Ibid.: "Altiora vero intelligibilia intellectus humanus cognoscere non potest nisi fortiori lumine perficiatur, sicut lumine fidei vel prophetiae; quod dicitur *lumen gratiae*, inquantum est naturae superadditum."

20. Notably, Thomas does not begin to use the term "habitual grace" until q. 109, a. 6; thereafter he uses it as the preferred term for the grace which heals and elevates nature. For example, at the outset of the corpus he writes: "The preparation of the human will for good is twofold: the first, whereby it is prepared to operate rightly and enjoy God; and this preparation of the will cannot take place without the habitual gift of grace [*habituali gratiae dono*] which is the principle of meritorious works, as stated above."

ment of supernatural good, or they may be moved by him sweetly and promptly to the attainment of eternal good."[21] Both categories inform the work of grace in the recipient.

One can turn to almost any of the remaining articles of q. 109 to see these categories of grace applied to questions of human action, including the second article where Thomas asks "whether a person does any good apart from grace." In the *respondeo* he adds further conceptual refinement by distinguishing between prelapsed and postlapsed human nature. Even in the prelapsarian state, Thomas argues that the person naturally could not do an act of "surpassing good" (*bonum superexcedens*); such acts arise from "infused goods."[22] An elevating habitual form is needed as well as divine motion to move persons to do goods of a surpassing nature. As for the postlapsed human person, sin corrupts his nature so that he is unable to perform properly those goods inherent to his nature.[23] Fallen human beings require habitual graces that heal their natural yet corrupted forms; in these ways, Thomas subdivides the effects of habitual grace into healing and elevating graces.

Whether habitual grace heals or elevates form, Thomas stipulates the necessity of divine motion. At the conclusion of q. 109, a. 2, he writes: "Yet beyond this, in both states, man needs the divine *auxilium* so that he may be moved to act well."[24] Thomas subsequently adds de-

---

21. *ST* I-II, q. 110, a. 2, co.: "Multo igitur magis illis quos movet ad consequendum bonum supernaturale aeternum, infundit aliquas formas seu suaviter et pompte ab ipso moveantur ad bonum aeternum consequendum." Earlier in the *respondeo* Thomas codifies the working distinction between habitual grace and *auxilium* set over the course of q. 109. He writes: "Now it was stated that man is aided by God's gratuitous will in two ways: first, inasmuch as man's soul is moved by God to know or will or do something, and in this way the gratuitous effect in man is not a quality, but a movement of the soul; for 'motion is the act of the mover in the moved' [*moventis in moto est motus*]. Secondly, man is helped by God's gratuitous will, inasmuch as a habitual grace is infused by God into the soul; and for this reason, that it is not fitting that God should provide less for those He loves, that they may acquire supernatural good, than for creatures, whom He loves that they may acquire natural good."

22. An act of surpassing good might be defined as one which is selfless or not obviously and rationally pertinent to one's own good. The ability to love one's enemies, for instance, might exemplify a type of surpassing good which a person will only do if his nature is informed by a habitual infusion of grace.

23. Thomas allows that human beings in a state of sin are not "shorn of every natural good" and so can still "by virtue of its natural endowments, work some particular good, as to build dwellings, plant vineyards, and the like" (*ST* I-II, q. 109, a. 2, co.).

24. *ST* I-II, q. 109, a. 2, co.: "Ulterius autem in utroque statu indiget homo auxilio divino ut ab ipso moveatur ad bene agendum."

tail to this position in a. 6, where he asks "whether one may prepare oneself for grace." He reasons that all created or infused habits remain in potency unless something reduces them to act. The reduction cannot be accomplished by further infusions of habitual grace—requiring an infinite sequence—but must instead be actualized by the application of divine motion.[25] He writes: "We ought to presuppose a gratuitous *auxilium* of God, who moves the soul interiorily or inspires the good wish."[26] This inward movement of the soul is not merely a residual effect of God's general "first movement"; it connotes God's discrete movement that actualizes a person's particular virtuous action, in this case, preparation for conversion.[27] Thomas thus maintains his metaphysics by insisting that divine premotion applies all things to specific ends as a reflection of the divine will and its execution in providence. By decisively rejecting the possibility that sinners can of themselves prepare for grace, at least in part on the grounds that wayfarers cannot move themselves from potency to act, Thomas firmly defines sanctifying grace as unfolding both through habitual gifts and divine movement.

As with almost every question of any length in *ST*, Thomas structures q. 109 pedagogically, laying down vital conceptual information, such as the definitions and classifications of grace, in the early articles and then employing it to answer more practical or distinct questions in the latter part. In this instance, having outlined the importance of *auxilium* for moving the wayfarer to action, Thomas asks in aa. 9–10 whether the wayfarer, once possessed of grace, can maintain himself in that state of grace. Here one might expect Thomas's affirmations of ha-

---

25. Without divine *auxilium*, Thomas will liken a person with habitual grace to a soldier who is capable of seeking victory but motionless without the command of the leader of the army prompting him to act (*ST* I-II, q. 109, a. 6, co.).

26. *ST* I-II, q. 109, a. 6, co.: "Sed oportet praesupponi aliquod auxilium gratuitum Dei interius animam moventis, sive inspirantis bonum propositum."

27. In his discussion of Bouillard's scholarship on grace, Wawrykow points to the way in which Thomas uses *auxilium* in the order of salvation to bring about specific effects. He follows Lonergan's criticisms of Bouillard, noting that the latter has been justly criticized for failing to recognize the movement of the grace of *auxilium* as something distinct from the general movement of God in creation, and so, the larger category of habitual grace. Wawrykow notes that Thomas recognizes instances where God causes discrete acts of feeling, thinking, or willing to be received in the natural faculties of the recipient through the effects of *auxilium*; this leads Wawrykow to conclude: "Thus, to the extent that Bouillard incorrectly identifies divine motion and habitual grace as one and the same sanctifying grace and does not recognize that divine motion may also refer to actual grace, his analysis of Thomas on grace cannot be endorsed" (*God's Grace*, 41).

bitual grace and God's initial inspiration of the wayfarer to be adequate graces for maintaining the proper *status*; perhaps it is enough for God to set the saving process in motion. On the contrary, Thomas notes that habitual grace heals the soul but does not reorder it to a prelapsed state, particularly in the flesh; it does not capacitate a person so as to avoid all venial sin or to withstand the effects of concupiscence. Rather, the gift of *auxilium*, given as discrete applications which reduce corresponding potencies to actions, moves a person to act righteously, and as such, its repetition is needed to maintain the state of grace. I quote Thomas in his entirety:

Therefore regarding the first mode of help, man in a state of grace does not need another help of grace, such as another infused habit. Nevertheless he needs the help of grace according to another mode, namely to be moved by God to act rightly. And the reason for this is twofold. First, by the general reason, as said above [a. 1] that no created thing is able to put forth any act, except by virtue of the divine motion. Secondly, for this special reason on account of the condition of the state of human nature. For although healed through grace as to the mind, it nevertheless remains corrupted and infected in the flesh, through which it serves *the law of sin* as is said in Romans 7:25. A certain obscurity [darkness] of ignorance also remains in the intellect according to which it is written in Romans 8:26: *We do not know not what we ought to pray for.* Because of various turns of events, and because we do not know ourselves perfectly, we cannot fully know what is expedient for us, according to Wisdom 9:14: *The thoughts of mortals are timid and our counsels uncertain.* And for that reason we need to be protected and guided by God, who knows everything and is able [to do] everything. And for that reason also, for those born again as children of God in grace, it is fitting to say: *Lead us not into temptation,* and *Thy will be done on earth as it is in heaven,* and whatever else is contained in the Lord's Prayer pertaining to this.[28]

28. *ST* I-II, q. 109, a. 9, co.: "Quantum igitur ad primum auxilii modum, homo in gratia existens non indiget alio auxilio gratiae quasi aliquo alio habitu infuso. Indiget tamen auxilio gratiae secundum alium modum, ut scilicet a Deo moveatur ad recte agendum. Et hoc propter duo. Primo quidem, ratione generali: propter hoc quod, sicut supra (a. 1) dictum est, nulla res creata potest in quemcumque actum prodire nisi virtute motionis divinae. Secundo, ratione speciali, propter conditionem status humanae naturae. Quae quidem licet per gratiam sanetur quantum ad mentem, remanet tamen in ea corruptio et infectio quantum ad carnem, per quam *servit legi peccati,* ut dicitur ad Rom. 7,25. Remanet etiam quaedam ignorantiae obscuritas in intellectu, secundum quam, ut etiam dicitur Rom. 8,26 *quid oremus sicut oportet, nescimus.* Propter varios enim rerum eventus, et quia etiam nosipsos non perfecte cognoscimus, non possumus ad plenum scire quid nobis expediat; secundum illud Sap. 9,14: *Cogitationes mortalium timidae, et incertae providentiae nostrae.* Et ideo necesse est nobis ut a Deo dirigamur et protegamur, qui omnia novit et omnia potest. Et propter hoc etiam renatis in filios Dei per gratiam, convenit dicere, *Et ne no*

The indispensability of divine *auxilium* comes to the fore in the discussion on perseverance with Thomas acknowledging that even after the reception of healing and elevating habitual graces, one cannot maintain oneself in a state of grace given the effects of sin. The ongoing provision of divine *auxilium* is critical to the wayfarer's progress in a state of grace. In the specific effect of perseverance, *auxilium* promotes order in the intellect and will, and in doing so, it moves the wayfarer to persist when tempted by false or private goods that appeal to the lower appetites.[29] Temptation constitutes a very real threat insofar as the deleterious effects of sin persist even in the converted sinner whose sensual appetites remain disordered and for whom ignorance of the divine will persists.[30] To substantiate the consequent need for *auxilium*, Thomas draws on Paul's conclusion in Romans 7:25 that, even for the justified, the mind serves the "law of God" while the flesh serves the "law of sin."[31] Thomas additionally appeals directly to passages from the Lord's Prayer that petition God to "lead" and "deliver" persons away from temptation and evil. Similar references are made by Saint Augustine in his late anti-Massilian works which Thomas here echoes.[32] In *On the Gift of*

---

inducas in tentationem, et Fiat voluntas tua sicut in caelo et in terra, et cetera quae in oratione Dominica continenetur ad hoc pertenentia."

29. Importantly, Thomas argues that the provision of *auxilium* that effects perseverance is distinct from habitual grace or other auxilia such as the preparation for grace. In fact he goes so far as to say that "To many grace is given to whom perseverance in grace is not given" (*ST* I-II, q. 109, a. 10, co.). This would seem to imply that God may introduce persons into the life of grace who fail to reach their intended end because they do not receive this further *auxilium*. For example, in *ST* I-II, q. 109, a. 10, ad 3, Thomas draws from Augustine and stresses the necessity of perseverance by suggesting that the prelapsed Adam had the capacity or habit to persevere while he lacked the gift of perseverance. This latter gift is made available through the grace of Christ.

30. In I-II, q. 85, on the effects of sin, Thomas argues that sin "wounds" human nature by disordering the natural order of intellect, will, and lower appetites; in a. 3, co., he writes: "Again, there are four powers of the soul that can be the subject of virtue, as stated above (Q. 61, A. 2), viz. the reason, where prudence reside, the will, where justice is, the irascible, the subject of fortitude, and the concupiscible, the subject of temperance." In q. 109, Thomas carries a sense of this disorder over even to the justified wayfarer whose irascible will and concupiscence remain unconformed to the movement of the intellect and will.

31. Torrell dates Thomas's completion of the *Prima Secundae* to 1271 at the end of the second Parisian regency, while Thomas's final lectures on Rom 1–8 were likely given in 1272–73 (*Summa*, 340). Regardless of when Thomas commented on Romans for the last time, his mature teaching on grace is notably more indebted to Paul's appreciation of sin's effects on human nature. Henri Bouillard notes with some effect the increasing appreciation of Paul in Thomas's late works; see Bouillard, *Conversion*, 135–50.

32. Late in his career (ca. 427), Augustine received inquiries from Prosper of Aquitaine and

Perseverance, for example, Augustine writes: "For this indeed the saints, who do the will of God, also pray, saying the Prayer, 'Thy will be done.' Since it has already been accomplished in them, why do they still ask that it be done, unless that they may persevere in that which they have begun to be?"[33] Thomas's mature insistence on *auxilium* thus illustrates not only critical metaphysical insights about God as cause but also advancing theological insights that stem from Thomas's greater familiarity with the late Augustine and ongoing exposition of the Pauline corpus. These theological insights insist that sin is such that habitual grace, by itself, is an inadequate theological category for understanding the ongoing agency of God in the conversion, sanctification, and progress of the graced wayfarer to eternal life.

---

a bishop named Hilary concerning the *initium* of conversion, with the suggestion that human beings can initiate their faith and God then supplements this initial movement. In response, Augustine composed a work that has come to modern readers as two separate treatises: *On the Predestination of the Saints* and *On the Gift of Perseverance* (ca. 428). In the latter, Augustine makes direct appeal to the Lord's Prayer as an indication that persons naturally implore God to complete, through grace, what they cannot do solely through human efforts. Augustine cites Cyprian's *De dominica oratione* directly, and he offers an extended discussion of the ways in which the Lord's Prayer suggests a gift of divine perseverance in sections 2.2–13.33. Augustine makes similar references, though with less exposition, to the Lord's Prayer in *On the Predestination of the Saints* (8.15). For Augustine's anti-Massilian works, see *On the Predestination of the Saints* and *On the Gift of Perseverance* in *Four Anti-Pelagian Writings,* trans. J. A. Mourant and W. J. Collinge (Washington, D.C.: The Catholic University of America Press, 1992), 181–337. Thomas explicitly cites *On the Gift of Perseverance* in the treatise on grace at I-II, q. 112, a. 3, co., where he reframes the Scholastic maxim "facienti quod in se est, Deus non denegat gratiam" (do what is in yourself and God will not deny grace). By Thomas's time, the *facienti* was widely deployed in medieval presentations of grace, the preparation for grace, and the possibility of congruent merit of the first grace. Thomas cites Augustine's *On the Gift of Perseverance* in an effort to show that God's grace precedes any effort by the elect to move toward justification. He writes: "But it may be considered, secondly, as it is from God the Mover, and thus it has a necessity—not indeed of coercion, but of infallibility—as it regards what is ordained to by God, since God's intentions cannot fail, according to the saying of Augustine in his book on the Predestination of the Saints (*De Dono Persev xiv*) that *by God's good gifts whoever is liberated, is most certainly liberated*" (*ST* I-II, q. 112, a. 3, co.). Scholars in the past century have argued that Thomas encountered Augustine's anti-Massilian works sometime in the 1260s prior to his completion of the treatise on grace. For a discussion of ways in which Thomas may have mediated the late Augustine, see Wawrykow, *God's Grace,* 269–76, especially n16 and n18, as well as Max Seckler's *Instinkt und Glaubenswille nach Thomas von Aquin* (Mainz: Matthias Grünewald, 1961), 90–98. Wawrykow also treats of the Augustinian influence on Thomas in "Perseverance in 13th-Century Theology: the Augustinian Contribution," *Augustinian Studies* 22 (1991): 125–40.

33. Augustine, *On the Gift of Perseverance* 3.6.

The Role of *auxilium* in Justification
and Sanctification

Having emphasized *auxilium* as a category for explaining the effects of grace on the wayfarer in *ST* I-II, q. 109, Thomas considers the divisions of grace in q. 111. In the second article he takes up the language of Augustine, repeated by Peter Lombard, and subdivides the distinction between habitual grace and divine *auxilium* according to the difference between operative and cooperative grace.[34] Thomas notably redefines earlier Scholastic uses of this distinction which had become nearly synonymous with the categories of prevenient and subsequent grace.[35] He begins the *respondeo* with the assertion that God's grace can be distinguished as (1) operative and cooperative habitual grace and as (2) operative and cooperative *auxilium*. Operative effects cause the mind to be moved with God as the sole mover, and cooperative effects cause the mind to be moved and to move with God so that both are genuine operators in the movement.[36] When applied to divine *auxilium*, the distinc-

---

34. Lonergan provides an overview of Augustine's treatment of grace as operating and cooperating and its transmission through Lombard as part of the historical backdrop to his study; see *Grace and Freedom*, 2–13.

35. Of Thomas's distinction between operative and cooperative grace in the *Scriptum* (*In Sent.* II, d. 26, q. 1, a. 5), Lonergan writes: "In treating of the unity of sanctifying grace both St. Bonaventure and St. Thomas in their *Commentaries on the Sentences* had raised the objection that grace was both operative and cooperative, both prevenient and subsequent. The answer they gave was that this distinction did not imply a multiplicity of graces but only a multiplicity of effects from one and the same sanctifying grace" (*Grace and Freedom*, 35). One can see an illustration of multiplied effects in Bonaventure's *Breviloquium* where, in the fifth part, "On the Grace of the Holy Spirit," Bonaventure devotes chaps. 4–6 to the ways in which grace "branches out" in virtues, the gifts of the Holy Spirit, the beatitudes, and the spiritual senses. He maintains a strong sense of such virtues or gifts as effects of a singular sanctifying grace. Lonergan later notes the overarching development in Thomas's thought: "Third, there is development with regard to the prevenient action of grace on free will: in the *Commentary on the Sentences* and the *De veritate*, the free acts that take place in justification are informed by the infused grace; in the *Contra gentiles* the prevenience of grace is pressed in terms of *motio moventis* and *motus mobilis*; in the *Summa theologiae* this terminology is developed on the analogy of Aristotelian physics and the motion of free will as well as its information is attributed to the simultaneously infused habitual grace" (*Grace and Freedom*, 61). This final development in the *ST* allows Thomas to conceive of both habitual grace and *auxilium* as operative and cooperative.

36. Thomas writes: "Hence in that effect in which our mind is moved and does not move, but in which God is the sole mover, the operation is attributed to God, and it is with reference to this that we speak of operating grace. But in that effect in which our mind both moves and is moved, the operation is not only attributed to God, but also to the soul; and it is with reference to this that we speak of co-operating grace" (*ST* I-II, q. 111, a. 2, co.). Because of the centrality of this

tion suggests that Thomas sees God's movement or efficient causation as divisible into separate instances: some *auxilia* simply move the recipient to act while others allow for authentically cooperative responses. This permits Thomas to classify the variety of human actions on the journey with greater precision, and to that end, he introduces particular instances of these effects. He first specifies that operative *auxilium* moves the mind in the experience of conversion or justification: "But there is a double act in us. First [there is] an interior [act] of the will. And in regard to that act, the will is a thing moved, and God is the mover; and especially [*praesertim*] when the will begins to will good which before had willed evil."[37] Thomas points to the conversion of the sinner as a special instance (*praesertim*) of operative *auxilium* because it constitutes that moment in which the sinner is redirected toward a new object of apprehension.

The commentary tradition has diverged on whether the conversion of a sinner—inclusive of the will's movement toward God as object of love—is operative from its outset to its term or whether it initiated operatively and concluded cooperatively.[38] Critical to the divergence is the meaning of the *duplex actus* of the will in conversion which is not immediately symmetrical to Thomas's earlier discussions of the will's action in *ST* I-II, qq. 8–17, where he elucidates three dimensions to the will's action: willing the end, the choice of means for attaining the end, and the execution of the end.[39] The three dimensions include an initial,

---

passage, I also include the Latin: "In illo ergo effectu in quo mens nostra est mota et non movens, solus autem Deus movens, operatio Deo atribuitur: et secundum hoc dicitur *gratia operans*. In illo autm effectu in qou mens nostra et movet et movetur, operatio non solum attrbuitur Deo, sed etiam animae: et secundum hoc dicitur *gratia cooperans*."

37. *ST* I-II, q. III, a. 2, co. "Est autem in nobis duplex actus. Primus quidem, interior voluntatis. Et quantum ad istum actum, voluntas se habet et mota. Deus autem ut movens: et praesertim cum voluntas incipit bonum velle quae prius malum volebat."

38. Thomas's response to an objection in the same question occasions some of the difficulty. He writes: "One thing is said to cooperate with another not merely when it is a secondary agent under a principal agent, but when it helps to the end intended. Now man is helped by God to will the good, through the means of operating grace. And hence, the end being already intended, grace cooperates with us" (I-II, q. III, a. 2, ad 3).

39. I here feature Wawrykow's summary of I-II, qq. 8–17. Wawrykow explores the asymmetrical relationship between I-II, qq. 8–17, and q. III, a. 2, offering a reasonable resolution in *God's Grace*, 174–76. Lonergan takes up the interpretive question in detail in *Grace and Freedom*, 121–38, noting the difference between the *duplex actus* of I-II, q. III, a. 2, and the *triplex actus* of I-II, qq. 8–17, at 132–33. Importantly, Thomas does elsewhere speak of a twofold act of the will in I-II, q. 19, a. 6, co., where he writes: "Now, in a voluntary action, there is a twofold action, namely, the

intermediate, and final act of the will with the initial seeming to fit an interior act and the final seeming to fit with an exterior act, though even the status of the final act is disputed by some.[40] In the case of conversion, determining the status of the choice of means is especially significant insofar as it identifies the agent or agents in the act.[41] Scholars in favor of identifying a cooperative dimension to the act of conversion elicit a series of texts from other parts of *ST* to support the necessarily contingent action of the will in its choice of means.[42]

A decisive text affirming the operative character of conversion, taken here to be include the choice of means and coextensive with justification, is the Prooemium to *ST* I-II, qq. 113–14, where Thomas writes: "We ought now to consider the effects of grace, and first of the justification of the ungodly, which is the effect of operating grace; and second of merit, which is the effect of co-operating grace."[43] Thomas here includes the entire sequence of justification under the heading of operative grace.

---

interior action of the will, and the external action: and each of these actions has its object. The end is properly the object of the interior act of the will: while the object of the external action is that on which the action is brought to bear." This division, less interested in the discrete interior acts of the will and more on the initial interior act of the will and the subsequent external action, approximates to I-II, q. 111, a. 2. If the parallel holds, one could argue that operative *auxilium* actualizes the interior act of the will as love or desire for union with God while cooperative *auxilium* facilitates the free choice of the will to select those things conducing to that end.

40. In fact, even the status of the interior act (as moved by God alone) is subject to some debate in *Summa* commentaries. Lonergan notes that Cajetan advanced an opinion, later amplified by John of St. Thomas, that the interior act might also be considered free because the will retains the ability to reject divine motion (Lonergan, *Grace and Freedom*, 131–32). Twentieth-century Thomists including Norbert del Prado, in *De Gratia et Libero Arbitrio: in qua Explanantur Sex Quaestiones de Gratia Dei ex D. Thomae Summa Theologica*, vol. I (Fribourg: Ex Typis Consociationis Sancti Pauli, 1907), and Santiago Ramirez in *De Gratia Dei* (San Esteban: Salamanca, 1992), sought to fortify this reading.

41. Wawrykow notes: "The significance of this question is great. Since merit is the effect of cooperative grace, when we ask whether choice of means is the effect of operative *auxilium* or of cooperative *auxilium*, we are in effect defining the limits of human merit" (*God's Grace*, 174–75).

42. Such passages include I, q. 83, a. 3, co.; I-II, q. 13, a. 3, co.; and III, q. 85, a. 5, co. *ST* III, q. 85, a. 5 seems especially forceful; Thomas writes: "Secondly, we may speak of penance, with regard to the acts whereby in penance we cooperate with God operating." Working from the fourfold sequence of justification outlined in I-II, q. 113, a. 6, Thomas here distinguishes six movements related to the act of penance which begin in divine operation and terminate in cooperation. Notably, Thomas does not link these steps explicitly to *auxilium*.

43. *ST* I-II, q. 113, Prooemium. "Deinde considerandum est de effectibus gratiae (cf. q. 109 introd.). Et primo, de iustificatione impii, quae est effectus gratiae operantis; secundo, de merito, quod est effectus gratiae cooperantis."

While one might argue that even cooperative movements begin under the heading of operative grace—and so justification may include cooperative dimensions—Thomas does not classify merit in that way, instead distinguishing it as a discrete effect of cooperative grace over and against justification as an effect of operative grace.[44] Later in his discussion of the movement of the free will in justification, Thomas writes: "Hence in him who has the use of free will, the motion to justice by God does not occur without a movement of the free will; but God so infuses the gift of justifying grace that God simultaneously moves the free will to accept the gift of grace, in those who are capable of such movement."[45] Even as God infuses the habitual gift of justifying grace, God moves the free will to accept the gift; while conceptual room is left to classify such movement as cooperative, the stress seems to fall on God's primary and probably sole agency. What is clear is that the *initium* of the conversion is a result of God's operative *auxilium* alone; the *praesertim* of Thomas's discussion in q. 111, a. 2 specifies the moment *cum voluntas incipit bonum velle quae prius malum volebat*. Even if the will can be said to cooperatively participate through the choice of means, such an act depends on movement where the mind is *mota et non movens*.[46] Without

44. Worth noting in Thomas's discussion of justification in *ST* I-II, q. 113 is his clear stipulation that an operative infusion of habitual grace, parsed as the gift of faith (a. 4), makes possible a movement of the free will. The stipulation seems to resurface the same question visited by Lonergan and others of *ST* I-II, q. 111, a. 2, yet Lonergan does not cite these texts (q. 113, aa. 3–4) in *Grace and Freedom*.

45. *ST* I-II, q. 113, a. 3, co. "Et ideo in eo qui habet usum liberi arbitrii, non fit motio a Deo ad iustitiam absque motu liberi arbitrii; sed ita infundit donum gratiae iustificantis, quod etiam simul cum hoc movet liberum arbitrium ad donum gratiae acceptandum, in his qui sunt huius motionis capaces."

46. Lonergan suggests that the force of other statements in *ST* lead him to conclude that the internal act of the will includes the middle term, leaving some space to think of conversion as cooperative. Lonergan defends this reading of Thomas by arguing that Thomas sees *auxilium* not as separate operative and cooperative auxilia but as "a single grace that is both *operans* and *cooperans*" (136). Important for our purposes is Lonergan's clear conclusions that *auxilium* possesses both operative and cooperative dimensions and that *auxilium* is indispensable (1) for conversion and (2) for ongoing upright willing that conduces to the end of eternal life. Lonergan summarizes, beautifully: "Hence, while St. Augustine is content to affirm his *operator incipiens*, St. Thomas has to take a broader view to consider the beginnings of the spiritual life not as unique but as a single instance of a more general law.... The general law is that man is always an instrument; that his volitional activity deploys in two phases; that in the first phase he is governed, *mota et non movens*, while in the second he governs *et mota et movens*; that the first phase is always a divine operation while in the second the theorem of cooperation necessarily follows" (136–37).

finally attempting to resolve a longstanding interpretive difference on the possibly cooperative dimension of conversion, one can confidently affirm that Thomas identifies two critical points at which operative *auxilia* indispensably effect forward progress in the wayfarer's journey: conversion and perseverance. In both cases, operative *auxilium* can be reasonably understood as God's application of motion interiorly on the recipient which actualizes a particular end and from which cooperative movements may follow. Both points on the journey typify development in Thomas's mature theology of grace and notably acknowledge that the habitual forms established by grace cannot themselves convert or sustain the wayfarer; nor are the cooperative effects of God's movement wholly adequate.

Having noted the indispensable role of operative *auxilium*, Thomas also affirms cooperative *auxilium* in those moments when the wayfarer makes an exterior act that proceeds freely from his inspired will. Referring to the second part of the *duplex actus* he writes:

> But there is another exterior act; and since it is commanded by the will, as was shown above (I-II.17.9) it follows that the operation of this act is attributed to the will. And also because God helps us in this act, both by confirming the will interiorly so that it reaches the act, and by providing outwardly the faculty of operating, it is with respect to this it is called cooperating grace. Whence after the words set down above in the *Sed contra* Augustine subjoins: *He operates so that we may will; and when we will, He cooperates so that we may perfect.* And therefore if grace is taken for God's gratuitous motion whereby He moves us to meritorious good, it is fittingly divided into operating and cooperating grace.[47]

Thomas identifies as effects of cooperative *auxilium* all those movements in which the will freely consents to God's initial movement. In such instances, provisions of *auxilium* fortify an impetus or movement of the will itself (already having been set in motion by prevenient operative *auxilia*) so that cooperative *auxilium* increasingly actualizes the poten-

---

47. *ST* I-II, q. 111, a. 2, co.: "Alius autem actus est exterior; qui cum a voluntate imperetur, ut supra (q. 17 a.9) habitum est, consequens est us ad hunc actum Deus no adiuvat, et interiius confirmando voluntatem ut ad actum perveniat, et exterius facultatem operandi praebendo; respectu huius actus dicitur gratia cooperans. Unde post praemissa verba (in Sed contra) subdit Augustinus: *Ut autem velimus operatur: cum autem volumus, et perficiamus nobis cooperator.* Sic igitur si gratia accipiatur pro gratuita Dei motione qua movet nos ad bonum meritorium, convenienter dividitur gratia per operantem et cooperantem."

cy of the will for right action. The mind is not merely moved but also moves (*mens nostra et movet et movetur*), and as such, it becomes a secondary and consequential agent so that it is also an identifiable operator in the movement. This can perhaps best be identified in acts of charity, that is, free acts of love undertaken for God or others. While such acts arise out of a habitual disposition to love, the movement of the will toward the object of love is facilitated by *auxilium*.

In *ST* I-II, q. 114, Thomas will stress the centrality of charity as the root virtue which underlies all meritorious action, and inasmuch as free choice is part and parcel of charity, all merit depends on God's gratuitous motion which effects cooperation in the recipient.[48] Here again the structure of *ST* is compelling. Following the treatise on grace, Thomas will outline a substantial treatise on charity itself (II-II, qq. 23–27) as well as the other virtues which are directed according to charity; the *Secunda Secundae* becomes practicable in light of the cooperative effects of divine *auxilium* which strengthen and inspire the will to love and so merit rewards from God, realizing the horizon of beatitude set down at the outset of the *Prima Secundae*. Along with habitual grace that instills the forms or habits necessary for particular acts on the journey, *auxilium* thus shapes the key experiences of justification and ongoing sanctification. Thomas applies strong commitments about divine transcendence and motion as the cause of all that occurs in the cosmos, particularly in the effects of predestination.[49]

48. In *ST* I-II, q. 114, a. 4, co., Thomas writes: "Hence the merit of everlasting life pertains first to charity, and secondly, to the other virtues, inasmuch as their acts are commanded by charity. So, likewise, it is manifest that what we do out of love we do most willingly. Hence, even inasmuch as merit depends on voluntariness, merit is chiefly attributed to charity."

49. Because of the study's focus on *auxilium*, it does not rehearse, in detail, the operative and cooperative dimensions of habitual grace. In short, operative infusions of habitual grace are those which create in the recipient the possibility of habitual action. Infusing such possibilities does not require the cooperation of the recipient. Think here, for example, of the habitual gift of faith which was not available, for example, to Paul prior to his conversion. Thomas associates the effects of operative habitual grace with healing and sanctifying the soul's form or nature. Cooperative infusions of habitual grace incline one to action with which one freely chooses to cooperate. Think here, for example, of the habitual gift of charity which inclines one to choose freely to love; as such, it serves as the principle of merit. Thomas thus concludes in *ST* I-II, q. 111, a. 2, co.: "But if grace is taken for the habitual gift, then again there is a double effect of grace, even as of every other form; the first of which is 'being,' and the second, 'operation'; thus the work of heat is to make its subject hot and to give heat outwardly. And thus habitual grace, inasmuch as it heals and justifies the soul, or makes it pleasing to God, is called operating grace; but inasmuch as it is the principle of meritorious works, which spring from the free-will, it is called cooperating grace."

The Role of *auxilium* in Thomas's Doctrine of God

Having noted the particular gains of divine *auxilium* in Thomas's treatise on grace, it is helpful to locate its role in the larger plan of *ST*, including its doctrine of God. This is readily accessible in the treatment of divine providence and predestination in the *Prima Pars*. That a sinner's conversion is an operative effect of grace is remarkable. The exclusion of cooperative human agency, and therefore human merit, from conversion implies that God alone calls and justifies the sinner. Such an affirmation rests on a larger conception of divine providence and God's immediate governance of the cosmos. In *ST*'s treatment of providence, Thomas associates providence and predestination with the preceding discussion of divine nature, specifically, with God's self-communication and manifestation of divine goodness through creation. God freely wills to create things which participate in divine goodness such that all things manifest goodness according to their natures. When taken as a whole, the cosmos manifests divine goodness in its variegation and the ends toward which things attain.[50] God creates with intention, that is, with a final end in view, and Thomas argues that God directs and governs all things toward their ordered ends.[51] This governance, broadly discussed, falls under the heading of providence, and with specific regard to human ends, it falls under the heading of predestination. For the present study,

---

50. Thomas explains in *ST* I, q. 19, a. 2, co.: "It pertains, therefore, to the nature of the will to communicate as far as possible to others the good possessed; and especially does this pertain to the divine will, from which all perfection is derived in some kind of likeness. Hence if natural things, insofar as they are perfect, communicate their good to others, much more does it appertain to the divine will to communicate by likeness its own good to others as much as possible. Thus, then, God wills both himself to be, and other things to be; but himself as the end and other things as ordained to that end; inasmuch as it befits the divine goodness that other things should be partakers therein." As goodness itself (derived from the position that God is *ipsum esse*), God communicates goodness in the act of creation, and all created things exist for this end: to manifest divine goodness. God thus creates with "intention," ordering the cosmos in all its variety to maximally demonstrate goodness. For a detailed treatment of Thomas's connection between God's creative plan and grace, see Wawrykow, *God's Grace*, 149–64. See also Harm Goris, "Divine Foreknowledge, Providence, Predestination, and Human Freedom," in *The Theology of Thomas Aquinas*, 99–122.

51. For helpful treatments of final causality and its relation to creation, see Corey L. Barnes, "Natural Final Causality and Providence in Aquinas," *New Blackfriars* 95 (2014): 349–61, and David B. Burrell, "Act of Creation with its Theological Consequences," in *Aquinas on Doctrine: A Critical Introduction*, ed. Thomas Weinandy, OFM Cap., Daniel Keating, and John Yocum (London: T and T Clark, 2004), 27–44.

such governance depends, importantly, on divine motion for its effects.

In *ST* I, q. 22, on providence, Thomas affirms that God intends all created things for a specific end, and as such, all things fall under the ordered government by which God directs the cosmos. To that end Thomas speaks of providence in two respects: (1) the eternal order of providence and (2) the execution of the plan, both of which underscore the category of final causality.[52] God has immediate providence inasmuch as God's plan or intention exists eternally in the divine mind. Habitual grace to some extent mirrors this because it pertains to the natural and supernatural forms which God provides; it reflects divine wisdom and its ordering of the cosmos, and in the economy of salvation habitual grace is that which heals or elevates nature so that it can attain eternal beatitude. As for the execution of the plan, which Thomas calls governance (*gubernatio*), God remains intimately involved in its prosecution which includes the agency of secondary causes. He writes: "As to the second, there are certain mediations of God's providence; because he governs inferior things through superior things, not on account of any defect in his power, but on account of the abundance of his goodness, so that God communicates the dignity of causality even to creatures."[53]

52. In *ST* I, q. 22, a. 1, co., Thomas begins his overall discussion of divine providence with these comments: "It is necessary to attribute providence to God. For all the good that is in created things has been created by God, as was shown above. In created things good is found not only as regards their substance, but also as regards their order towards an end and especially their last end, which, as was said above, is the divine goodness. This good of order existing in things created, is itself created by God. Since, however, God is the cause of things by his intellect, and thus it behooves that the type of every effect should pre-exist in the divine mind: and the type of things ordered towards an end is, properly speaking, providence." It is worth noting here that this account of providence underscores God's intentional act of creation *and* God's immediate, purposeful direction of creation for specific ends. Thomas repeats this same line of argument when introducing predestination. He writes: "Hence, properly speaking, a rational creature, capable of eternal life, is led towards it, directed as it were, by God. The reason of that direction pre-exists in God; as in Him is the type of the order of all things towards an end, which we proved above to be providence" (I, q. 23, a. 1, co.).

53. *ST* I, q. 22, a. 3, co.: "Quantum autem ad secundum, sunt aliqua media divinae providentiae. Quia inferiora gubernat per superiora; non propter defectum suae virtutis, sed propter abundantiam suae bonitatis, ut dignitatem causalitatis etiam creaturis communicet." To this line of thinking, Lonergan writes: "But according to St. Thomas, all motion is effected according to the divine plan, and this plan calls for a hierarchic universe in which the lowest things are moved by the middle-most and the middle-most by the highest. Not only did St. Thomas at all times clearly and explicitly affirm a mediated execution of divine providence, but he even argued that there would be no execution of divine providence unless God controlled the free choices of men and of angels through whom the rest of creation was administered. This position leaves no room

God governs by moving creatures directly and indirectly. Governance and *auxilium* thus seem to go hand-in-hand; in the economy of salvation, divine *auxilium* moves the recipient to be converted, to persevere, and even to love God and neighbor.[54] Such acts are the effects of the divine will, and they are executed by the application of motion.

When discussing predestination, Thomas adds that God's movement of the elect need not be seen as destroying their contingency or freedom. He writes: "Nevertheless the order of providence is infallible, as was shown above (I.22.4). So therefore the order of predestination is also certain; and nevertheless free-will is not destroyed by which the effect of predestination comes about contingently."[55] God's movement is efficient and infallible, yet it preserves creaturely freedom. Proper knowledge of God through the habit of faith and proper love of God and others through the habit of charity always depend on the contingency of choice, yet Thomas sees operative and cooperative *auxilia* as those ongoing applications of motion to the recipient which inspire or motivate free actions infallibly conducing to the end of eternal life.

---

for the theory that God gives each agent some ultimate actuation to constitute it as here and now acting" (*Grace and Freedom*, 73–74). See also Brian J. Shanley, "Divine Causation and Human Freedom in Aquinas," *American Catholic Philosophical Quarterly* 72 (1992): 100–122.

54. In the order of salvation, *auxilium* constitutes a means by which God can be said to have immediate and efficient causality over creation. In the treatise on grace, Thomas will connect the work of secondary agents with "gratuitous grace" (*gratia gratis data*). For example, in I-II, q. 111, a. 1, co., Thomas writes: "Now the order of things consists in this, that things are led to God by other things, as Dionysius says (*Coel. Hier.* iv). And hence since grace is ordained to lead me to God, this takes place in a certain order, so that some are led to God by others. And thus there is a twofold grace, one whereby man himself is united to God, and this is called *sanctifying grace*, [and] the other is that whereby one man cooperates with another in leading him to God, and this gift is called *gratuitous grace*, since it is bestowed on a man beyond the capability of nature, and beyond the merit of the person" (translation modified). So, God provides gratuitous graces for the sake of moving others to justification and sanctification, which are effects of God's predestining will.

55. *ST* I, q. 23, a. 6, co.: "Et tamen providentiae ordo est infallibilis, ut supra (q.22 a.4) ostensum est. Sic igitur et ordo praedestionis est certus; et tamen libertas arbitrii non tollitur, ex quia contigentur provenit praedestinationis effectus." Thomas maintains his position in the discussion of the will's movement in I-II, q. 10, a. 4, co., where he writes: "[Divine providence] moves all things in accordance with their conditions; so that from necessary causes through divine motion, effects follow of necessity; but from contingent causes, effects follow contingently. Since, therefore, the will is an active principle, not determinate to one thing, but having an indifferent relation to many things, God so moves it, that he does not determine it of necessity to one thing, but its movement remains contingent and not necessary, except in those things to which it is moved naturally." Thomas continues (in ad 1) that God only moves the will contingently because it would be repugnant to human nature to move it by necessity.

Thomas's position reflects important metaphysical insights gained in *SCG* and confirmed in *ST*. In these later works, Thomas does not assign the infallibility of providence and predestination to the sphere of divine foreknowledge; instead, he sees it as a direct effect of God's active willing. God, as transcendent cause, moves all things to act by the application of motion—according to the plan in the divine mind—so that God not only knows the ends of all things but moves them to those ends. Divine providence promotes rightly ordered willing—operatively and cooperatively—in the elect so that even the contingent motion of the elect must be related to that of divine *auxilium* or God as ultimate cause.[56] For the elect, these acts unfold infallibly through *auxilium*. They nevertheless can have cooperative effects, and therefore, in a real sense, allow for human freedom in the movement to glory.

Just as scholars have noted the developed emphasis of *auxilium* in *ST* over its use in *In Sent.* or *De Ver.*, so one can track a parallel emphasis on God's efficient causality in terms of providence and predestination in these same works. By the time of *SCG*, Thomas has advanced his view of God's causation to be more than an effect of formal causation; instead, it is efficient through God's transcendent and metaphysical application of motion to the entire cosmos.[57] This corresponding shift in efficient

56. Lonergan concludes that by the time of *SCG* Thomas had synthesized Aristotelian conceptions of premotion and divine providence so that God is the efficient and immediate cause of discrete movements in providence. Thomas accomplishes this by setting transcendent divine power outside the temporal order. Lonergan writes in *Grace and Freedom*: "The Thomist higher synthesis was to place God above and beyond the created orders of necessity and contingence: because God is universal cause, His providence must be certain; but because He is transcendent cause, there can be no incompatibility between terrestrial contingence and the cause of certitude of providence" (79). He subsequently adds: "Only when St. Thomas settled down to the vast task of thinking out the Christian universe in the *Contra gentiles* did he arrive at the truth that divine providence is an intrinsically certain cause of every combination or interference of terrestrial causes. By the same stroke would he arrive at the practically identical truth that God applies every agent to its activity. Accordingly, we are led to infer that the essence of the idea of application is the Aristotelian premotion as informed by the Thomist causal certitude of divine providence: '*Deus igitur per suum intellectum onmia movet ad proprios fines* [God therefore moves all things to their proper end through his intellect]'" (80).

57. Noting the general development of Thomas's thinking on causation, Lonergan notes that Thomas in *In Sent.* and *De Ver.* sees God's causation on a "creation-conservation" model where "what causes the substance also causes the active potency; what causes the active potency also causes what the latter causes—indeed, causes the causation itself" (*Grace and Freedom*, 86). As Thomas develops a stronger sense of Aristotelian premotion in the later works, including *SCG*, *De Pot.*, and ultimately *ST* I, Thomas comes to see God's motion or application as a more direct and efficient cause of all movement in the cosmos. Lonergan writes: "Once St. Thomas had

causality underscores Thomas's mature commitment to see all providential outcomes as depending on God's immediate will and thus *auxilium*.
Apart from a vigorous notion of *auxilium*, accounts of grace are left to
rely on the habitual form as the sole cause moving the wayfarer forward on the journey; in that conception, God provisions the wayfarer
with capacities that the person must initiate and use. God is the formal
(and final) cause of the wayfarer's salvation, but God recedes in terms
of efficient causality.[58] One can see depictions of this sort in Thomas's
contemporaries, including Saint Bonaventure, whose system has a wider
conceptual space for disposing oneself to meritorious human action.[59]
A lack of emphasis on efficient causality—expressed through something
like *auxilium*—often leads to accounts of sanctification where more
agency is affirmed in the human actor, something Thomas tends to restrict in the treatise on grace.[60] His mature metaphysics and parallel

---

grasped a theory of providence compatible with Aristotelian terrestrial contingence, he began at
once to argue that the creature's causation was caused not merely because of creation and of con-
servation but also because of application, instrumentality, cosmic hierarchy, and universal finality"
(87). The concept of premotion thus allows Thomas to establish God as moving things toward
their ends through "application" or movement; moreover this movement can unfold through instrumental causes but has a final end in mind which God effects as efficient cause.

58. In *God's Grace*, Wawrykow notes that Thomas favored such a position in the *Sentences* commentary; while discussing the contributions of Lonergan to the discussion of grace, he
writes: "In the *Scriptum*, Thomas followed his thirteenth-century predecessors in stressing habitual grace as a *formal* cause.... Yet, as form, habitual grace also endows the human person
with new being (*esse*), a kind of participation in the divine. And since *agere sequitur esse*, in the
Scriptum Thomas also can describe habitual grace as an *efficient* cause. Habitual grace and the
virtues infused with this grace incline the human person to acts of a distinctively supernatural
cast" (*Grace and Freedom*, 44).

59. Bonaventure will speak consistently of sanctifying grace in habitual terms which not only
make the recipient pleasing but also make their acts acceptable to God. This habitual transformation thereby raises the efficacy of the graced wayfarer so that they become the meritorious agent
of a variety of acts, including, potentially, conversion. See, for example, Bonaventure's comments
at the beginning of his treatment of grace in part V.2 of the *Breviloquium*, which addresses grace
as a gift from God. He writes: "At the same time, grace is a gift by which the soul is perfected
and becomes the bride of Christ, the daughter of the eternal Father, and the temple of the Holy
Spirit. This could in no way happen except by the ennobling condescension and condescending
nobility of the eternal Majesty through the gift of his own grace. Finally, grace is a gift that
purifies, illumines, and perfects the soul; that vivifies, reforms, and strengthens it; that elevates
it, likens it, and joins it to God, and thereby makes it acceptable to God. This is a gift of such
kind that it is rightly and properly called 'the grace that makes pleasing [*gratia gratum faciens*].'"
Bonaventure, *Breviloquium*, trans. Dominic Monti (St. Bonaventure, N.Y.: Franciscan Institute
Publications, 2005).

60. In *ST* I-II, q. 114, Thomas rejects condign merit of eternal life (as a reward earned by

account of grace acknowledge that God alone is the efficient cause of such progress by the provision of operative and cooperative auxilia.[61] Thomas's conception of God as transcendent cause in the discussion of providence and predestination thus adds a metaphysical framework for the role of *auxilium* in his mature theology of grace.

Auxilium and the Sacraments

The metaphysics that undergird *ST*'s teaching on providence and pre-destination are not divorced from the economy of salvation and the gospel narrative. Specifically, God's will to save some unfolds through created nature and the saving action of Jesus. Thus the *Tertia Pars* presents Christ as the way of return and the sacraments as instruments of grace that draw the wayfarer into full union or *reditus ad Deum*.[62] Thomas's general exposition of the sacraments (*ST* III, qq. 60–65) illustrates the way that the sacraments might be thought to (1) constitute effects of divine *auxilium* and (2) confirm Thomas's view of God as efficient cause in human salvation. In *ST* III, q. 62, Thomas treats grace as the principal effect of the sacraments. He argues that the sacraments must do more than signify grace; they must instrumentally cause its effects in the re-

---

the wayfarer himself) (a. 3), merit of the first grace (a. 5), merit for someone else (a. 6), merit of restoration after a fall (a. 7), and merit of final perseverance (a. 9). In each of these cases, Thomas recognizes that some operative *auxilium* has effected the outcome so that God must be recognized as the primary agent of the act. Notably, Thomas affirms congruent merit of eternal life (a. 3) and merit of increases in charity (a. 8); in these cases, the wayfarer has cooperated as a determining agent under the conditions of divine ordination such that he may receive a just reward for his efforts. In addition to Wawrykow's *God's Grace*, which is decisive on the restriction of merit in Thomas's theology of grace, Michael Root offers a very helpful discussion of Thomas's narrow affirmation of merit in "Aquinas, Merit, and Reformation Theology after the *Joint Declaration on the Doctrine of Justification*," *Modern Theology* 20 (2004): 5–22.

61. Lonergan summarizes: "Operation in time presupposes a premotion. But this premotion affects indifferently either the mover or the moved. Its function is simply to bring mover and moved in the right relation, mutual disposition, spatial proximity for motion naturally to ensue. When combined with the fact that God is the first mover in the cosmic hierarchy and that, as universal cause, God cannot be frustrated, this law of premotion yields the theorem that God applies all agents to their activity" (89).

62. For discussion of the place of the *Tertia Pars* in the order of the *Summa*, one that notes the limitations of an *exitus-reditus* model and argues for Christ, particularly in his humanity, as a critical axis on which the *Summa* turns, see a concise summary in Corey L. Barnes's *Christ's Two Wills in Scholastic Thought: The Christology of Aquinas and Its Historical Contexts* (Toronto: Pontifical Institute of Mediaeval Studies, 2012), 183–92.

cipient. Having first argued that God alone can confer grace, Thomas explains how the causality of the sacraments is itself an effect of God's movement. He writes: "But the instrumental cause does not act by the power of its form, but only through the motion by which it is moved [*motum quo movetur*] by the principal agent. Whence the effect is not to be compared to the instrument but to the principal agent just as a couch is not compared to the axe, but to the art which is in the mind of craftsman."[63] Toward the goal of securing the efficient instrumental causality of sacraments, Thomas deploys the critical language of motion; a sacrament confers grace "only through the motion by which it is moved by the principal agent." If one sees the sacraments as instrumentally and efficiently causal, it follows that they convey *auxilium* by virtue of their separated instrumentality.[64]

---

63. *ST* III, q. 62, a. 1, co.: "Causa vero instrumentalis non agit per virtutem suae formae, sed solum per motum quo movetur a principali agente. Unde effectus non assimilatur instrumento, sed principale agente: sicut lectus non assimilatur securi, sed arti quae est in mente artificis." Liam G. Walsh, OP, offers a helpful introduction to Thomas on the sacraments in "Sacraments," in *The Theology of Thomas Aquinas*, 326–64. See also John P. Yocum's "Sacraments in Aquinas," in *Aquinas on Doctrine*, 159–81. Thomas's contemporary, Bonaventure, resists an approach to sacraments as instrumental causes, instead relying on their divine institution for their efficacy, In *Breviloquium* VI:1.1, "The Source of the Sacraments," Bonaventure writes: "Therefore, these sacraments are called 'vessels of grace' and the 'cause' of grace. This is not because grace is substantially contained in them or causally effected by them, for grace dwells only within the soul and is infused by none but God. Rather, it is because God has decreed that we are to draw the grace of our healing from Christ, the supreme Physician in and through these sensible signs 'although God has not restricted his power to the sacraments.'" Without the working concept of *auxilium*, Bonaventure lacks a category for speaking of the sacraments as efficient instrumental causes in themselves.

64. Walsh relates Thomas's stress on sacramental causality to the overarching affirmation of divine causality found in his doctrine of God: "A particular feature of the relationship between God and humans that is important for sacramental theology is divine causality. When Aquinas analyzes the action of God in the *Prima Pars*, he proposes a remarkable integration of its final, formal, and efficient components. In crude terms, God never does anything without having an end in view and without generating a form for what is to reach that end. Where there is divine energy, there is, inseparably, divine design and divine desire…. And when God is acting in humans, made in his own image and for the purpose of coming to know and love him, the action of humans is God-formed and God-directed, as well as being God-moved" (330–31). In *ST* III, q. 62, a. 5, Thomas further defines the sacraments as separated instrumental efficient causes which extend from the conjoined efficient causality of Christ's human nature and its sacrificial action in his passion. He writes: "Now the principle efficient cause of grace is God Himself, in comparison with Whom Christ's humanity is as a united instrument, whereas the sacrament is as a separate instrument. Consequently, the saving power must needs be derived by the sacrament from Christ's Godhead through His humanity" (co.). The very purpose of the incarnation is to give life, that is, which again approximates the language of divine *auxilium*. Thomas writes: "The

Thomas's identification of *auxilium* as part of sacramental grace is vital to his overall vision of the sacramental life. Sacraments must do more than signify a particular final end; they must move the recipient to that end.[65] As such, sacraments not only infuse habits but also actualize them; Thomas writes: "If sacramental grace adds nothing above the grace of the virtues and gifts, it is in vain for the sacraments to be conferred on those already having the virtues and gifts. But in God's works nothing is in vain."[66] The argument made here resonates with earlier arguments from *ST* I-II, q. 109 which held that grace cannot merely infuse forms into the recipient *ad infinitum*. Thomas concludes: "Therefore just as the virtues and gifts, above grace commonly so called, adds a certain ordered perfection determined by power of the appropriate acts, so sacramental grace, above grace commonly so called and above the virtues and gifts, adds a certain divine *auxilium* for gaining the end of the sacrament."[67] Beyond *gratia communiter* and the habitual effects of the gifts and the virtues, Thomas again insists that God provides *auxilium*, this time to attain the special ends which the sacraments themselves prefigure. Divine *auxilium* here gives Thomas conceptual space in which to explain how sacraments cause grace and quicken the recipient to progression in the life of grace. The Eucharist exemplifies this in an edifying way.

Among the Eucharist's names such as viaticum or sacrifice, Thomas recognizes the Eucharist by the name "sacrament of charity," which illustrates its effects as both habitual and an *auxilium*.[68] Thomas argues that

---

Word, forasmuch as He was in the beginning with God, quickens souls as principal agent; but His flesh, and the mysteries accomplished therein, are as instrumental causes in the process of giving life to the soul" (ad 1).

65. Here again, an appreciation of the relationship between efficient and final causality is helpful; see Walsh's warning against separating sacramental efficient causality from formal and final causality in "Sacraments," 327–28.

66. *ST* III, q. 62, a. 2, s.c.: "Sed Contra est quod, si gratia sacramentalis non addit aliquid super gratiam donorum et virtutum, fustra sacramenta habentibus et dona et virtutes conferrentur. In operibus autem Dei nihil est frustra."

67. Ibid., co.: "Sicut igitur virtutes et dona addunt super gratiam communiter dictam quandam perfectionem determinate ordinatam ad proprios actus potentiarum, ita gratia sacramentalis addit super gratiam communiter dictam, et super virtutes et dona, quoddam divinum *auxilium* ad consequendum sacramenti finem."

68. In *ST* III, q. 73, a. 4, Thomas argues for the fittingness of various names for the sacrament, including Eucharist, viaticum, sacrifice, and communion. Thomas has already introduced *sacramentum caritatis* in q. 73, a. 3, ad 3, where he writes: "Hence, as Baptism is called

the Eucharist infuses greater formal perfection in the wayfarer through the gift of charity; this is a habitual and cooperative gift that depends on the recipient's cooperative disposition.[69] Proper reception of the sacrament progressively (and cooperatively) expands the wayfarer's capacity to love so that even some *bonum superexcendens*, such as loving one's enemy, is formally possible in the recipient. Thomas does not, however, limit the effect of the Eucharist to formal perfection. He writes: "And for that reason, through this sacrament insofar as its power is concerned, not only is the habit of grace and of virtue conferred, but it is excited into action [*excitatur in actum*] according to 2 Cor. 5:14: 'the charity of Christ presses us.'"[70] Here, then, Thomas connects the sacramental experience of the Eucharist to the conceptual distinctions of both habitual grace and *auxilium*. Without God's movement pressing the recipient to love, the formal capacity to love one's enemy remains in potency. This conclusion is particularly striking because Thomas acknowledges the Eucharist as viaticum which heals and moves the wayfarer throughout the journey, in part, by a love that cooperatively presses or moves the elect to glory.[71]

The Eucharist empowers wayfarers to reach final glory by signifying the end, infusing virtue, and reducing the recipient to action. When the recipient cooperates with such graces, Thomas affirms that the Eucharist communicates certain interim rewards. The most obvious example is that, by the cooperative motion of the sacrament of charity, the wayfarer is rewarded with increases in habitual charity.[72] Charity may manifest itself in

---

the sacrament of life, so the Eucharist is termed the sacrament of Charity, which is the *bond of perfection* (Col. iii. 14)."

69. In *ST* III, qq. 79–80, Thomas will address the disposition of the wayfarer as critical to receiving the full effects of the Eucharist. Mortal sin impedes the reception of the *res tantum* while venial sin can inhibit the full effects of charity. See esp. III, q. 70, aa. 3 and 8, and q. 80, a. 1.

70. *ST* III, q. 79, a. 1, ad 2. "Et ideo per hoc sacramentum, quantum est ex sui virtute, non solum habitus gratiae et virtutis confertur, sed etiam excitatur in actum: secundum illud Cor. 5,14: *Caritas Christi urget nos*." Thomas continues: "Et inde est quod ex virtute huius sacramenti anima spiritualiter reficitur, per hoc quod anima delectatur, et quodammodo inebriatur dulcedine bonitatis divinae: secundum Cant. 5,1: Comedite, amici, et bibite; et inebriamini, carissimi."

71. In *ST* III, q. 73. a. 4., co., Thomas writes: "With regard to the future it has a third meaning, inasmuch as the sacrament foreshadows the Divine fruition, which shall come to pass in heaven; and according to this [the Eucharist] is called 'Viaticum,' because it supplies the way of winning thither." Thomas reinforces the notion of the Eucharistic viaticum, as food for the journey, in the discussion of effects in *ST* III, q. 79, a. 2, ad 1.

72. Note that Thomas affirms this effect in the treatise on grace, especially in *ST* I-II, q. 114, a. 8, co.; for example, Thomas writes: "As stated above, whatever the motion of grace reaches to,

virtuous acts of patience, humility, obedience, or mercy, all of which allow the wayfarer to participate with and follow Christ to union with the Father. Beyond growth in virtue, Thomas also concludes that venial sins may be forgiven as a kind of interim cooperative reward. When considered in light of the language from the treatise on grace, this makes perfect sense. Those disordered or concupiscent actions that do not cause a fall into a state of sin can be healed and moved into a right order by sacramental grace. God at times provides gifts, such as the operative *auxilium* of perseverance or an infusion of habitual charity, to overcome the realities and effects of venial sins. At other times, the wayfarer may cooperate with grace in the remission of venial sins by acting with the motion of the mover, here expressed through the instrumentality of the sacrament. Inspired by the Eucharist, one can follow its motion in love for God and others rather than selfishness. Thomas writes: "Yet the reality [*res*] of this sacrament is charity, not only insofar as habit but also insofar as act, which is excited [*excitatur*] in this sacrament; and by this means venial sins are absolved."[73] Thomas's use of the word *res* is telling as it gestures at the *res tantum* of the sacrament; that is, that principal real effect of the sacrament is charity, yet the effect is not merely of the habit of charity. The sacrament also excites the love, moving one to act. The term *excitatur* was used earlier in Thomas's general discussion of the effects of the sacraments (*ST* III, q. 62) when specifically referring to divine *auxilium*. *Auxilium* is integral to the effect of the Eucharist. The gift of charity conveyed in the Eucharist not only infuses charity but excites or "inspires the good wish" by which the recipient unites herself to God and others through love. Thomas's discussion of the Eucharist reveals another point (or points) on the journey which depends on *auxilium*: the remission of venial sins.

---

falls under condign merit. Now the motion of a mover extends not merely to the last term of the movement, but to the whole progress of the movement. But the term of the movement of grace is eternal life; and progress in this movement is by the increase of charity of grace according to Proverbs (4:18): 'But the path of the just as a shining light, goeth forward and increaseth even to perfect day,' which is the day of glory. And thus increases of grace falls under condign merit." This same language of motion is maintained when speaking of the effects of the Eucharist, particularly as sacrament of charity.

73. *ST* III, q. 79. a. 4. co.: "Res autem huius sacramenti est caritas, non solum quantum ad habitum, sed etiam quantam ad actum, qui excitatur in hoc sacramento: per quod peccata venialia solvuntur." In the subsequent article (a. 5), Thomas will remind readers, however, that the Eucharist may not remit the entire debt of punishment caused by venial sin; penance remains integral to full satisfaction.

Thomas's mature appreciation of *auxilium* further expands the way in which one may appreciate the role of the Holy Spirit in the life of grace and the wayfarer's progress. At its foundation, sanctifying grace must be understood as the effect of the saving action of the incarnate Son and the ongoing mission of the Holy Spirit in the cosmos.[74] Thomas frequently associates particular effects of habitual grace with the Holy Spirit. The most patent are the gifts of the Holy Spirit which produce fruits in the recipient (see *ST* I-II, qq. 68 and 70), though the created effects of sacraments, such as charity, would also lend themselves to such a connection.[75] Moreover, Thomas associates the Spirit with gratuitous graces (*gratia gratis data*) which are given to some for the sake of leading others to God; in those cases, gifts like prophecy are effects of the Spirit conferring grace on some.[76] It would thus seem that Thomas most directly associates the work of the Holy Spirit with the created effects of habitual grace. This reading is correct, yet it does not exclude a consideration of the way in which *auxilium* "inspires the good wish" or presses the recipient to love. These effects may also be thought of as the work of the Spirit.

One way to establish this connection is to attend to Thomas's language of *instinctus* which he frequently connects to the Holy Spirit.[77] In Thomas's discussion of the gifts of the Holy Spirit, he returns to a

74. Speaking, for example, of the grace of the New Law, Thomas writes: "As stated above, the New Law consists chiefly in the grace of the Holy Spirit, which is shown forth by faith that works through love. Now men become receivers of this grace through God's Son made man, Whose humanity grace filled first, and thence flowed forth to us" (*ST* I-II, q. 108, a. 1, co., translation modified).

75. Eric Luijten makes a strong case that Thomas identifies the work of the Holy Spirit, including the infusion of habitual graces, as central to the sacrament of penance; for his findings on the sacramental causality of the Holy Spirit, see *Sacramental Forgiveness as a Gift from God: Thomas Aquinas on the Sacrament of Penance* (Leuven: Peeters, 2003), 184–91. Gilles Emery, OP, speaks of the Holy Spirit's mission thus: "Saint Thomas is speaking here of a 'sealing' (*sigillatio*) of the divine persons: the theological gift of love, which is a shared likeness in the personal property of the Spirit, offers us the possibility of entering into relationship with the Son in a mode comparable to that of the Spirit, by imitating the Spirit (Love which proceeds from the Son)." "Trinity in Creation," in *The Theology of Thomas Aquinas*, 58–76, at 68.

76. Thomas distinguishes between sanctifying grace and gratuitous grace in *ST* I-II, q. 111, aa. 1 and 5. In q. 111, a. 4, s.c., Thomas connects the gratuitous graces explicitly to the Holy Spirit as a way of promoting the fittingness of their enumeration by the Apostle.

77. This connection relies on an important study by Jan Hendrik Walgrave, "Instinctus Spiriti Sancti: een proeve tot Thomas-interpretatie," *Ephemerides Theologicae Lovanienses* 5 (1969): 417–31. Luijten also offers a helpful discussion entitled "The 'instinct' of the Holy Spirit and the conversion of the sinner" (*Sacramental Forgiveness*, 71–75).

familiar theme in this study: "But inspiration denotes a certain exterior motion. For it ought to be considered that there is a twofold principle of movement in man, an interior one which is reason; but another exterior one which is God, as was said above."[78] First acknowledging a kind of twofold movement in human beings, which again approximates to *ST* I-II, q. III, a. 2, Thomas acknowledges that human beings depend on exterior motion from God, in addition to their rationality, in order to be moved to act. In the case of the gifts, the gifts not only capacitate the recipient's form or nature so that it may act intrinsically through reason; they also dispose one to respond to God's extrinsic motion. Thomas writes:

And these perfections are called gifts, not only because they are infused by God, but also because through them man is disposed to becoming promptly movable by divine inspiration, according to Isaiah 50:5: "The Lord has opened my ear, and I do not resist God; I have not gone back." And also the Philosopher says in the chapter *On Good Fortune* that for those who are moved by Divine instinct, it does not help to take counsel according to human reason, but only to follow their inner instinct, because they are moved by a principle better than human reason.[79]

Without using the explicit language of *auxilium*, which he introduces only later in *ST* I-II, q. 109, Thomas here sketches the basic function of the gifts of the Holy Spirit as (1) imparting a habit of responding readily to divine motion or instinct and (2) affirming God's exterior motion in the order of grace, this time in actualizing the gifts of the Spirit.[80] The gifts include God's application of motion to the recipient, inclining them to action or inspiring the good wish which Thomas goes so far as

---

78. *ST* I-II, q. 68, a. 1, co.: "Inspiratio autem significat quandam motionem ab exteriori. Est enim considerandum quod in homine est duplex principium movens: unum quidem interius, quod est ratio; aliud autem exterius, quod est Deus, et supra dictum est (q.9 a.4,6); et etiam Philosophus hocdicit, in cap. *De bona fortuna.*"

79. Ibid.: "Et istae perfectiones vocantur dona: non solum quia infunduntur a Deo, sed quia secundum ea homo disponitur ut efficiatur pompte mobilis ab inspiratione divina, sicut dicitur Is. 50,5: *Dominus aperuit mihi aurem; ego autem non contradico, retrorsum non abii.* Et Philosophus etiam dicit, in cap. *De bona fortuna,* quod his qui moventur per instinctum divinum, non expedit consiliari secundum rationem humanam, sed quod sequantur interiorem instinctum: quia moventur a meliori principio quam sit ratio humana."

80. In ibid., ad 3, Thomas adds: "Likewise, the gifts, as distinct from infused virtue [an effect of habitual grace], may be defined as something given by God in relation to his motion; something, to wit, that makes man to follow well the promptings of God."

to insist is necessary for salvation.[81] Having established the notion of a divine instinct preparing one to act, Thomas connects the *instinctus* to the Holy Spirit, arguing that the gifts allow one to act when prompted by the inspiration of the Spirit. He returns to the argument that, in the order of grace, human beings need supernatural motion by which to act. Thomas writes: "But in those things directed to the supernatural end, towards which [human] reason, formed by the theological virtues, moves in an incomplete manner, that motion of reason does not suffice unless the instinct and motion [*instinctus et motio*] of the Holy Spirit attends, according to Romans 8:14–17: 'Those who act by the Spirit of God are children of God … and if children, heirs also.'"[82] The instinct or motion by which persons respond to God—which is necessary to attain glory—is the motion of the Holy Spirit.[83] The student of Thomas who progresses to the end of the *Prima Secundae* receives further language by which to describe such motion (i.e., "auxilium divinum"). This exploration of the gifts and the notion of *instinctus* allows one to argue

81. See *ST* I-II, q. 68, a. 2.

82. See ibid., co.: "Sed in ordine ad finem ultimum supernaturalem, ad quem ratio movet secundum quod est aliqualiter et imperfecte formata per virtutes theologicas; non sufficit ipsa motio rationis, nisi desuper adsit instinctus et motio Spiritus Sancti; secundum illud Rom. 8.14.17: *Qui Spiritu Dei aguntur, hi filii Dei Sunt; et si filii, et haeredes; et Ps.* 142.10 dicitur: *Spiritus tuus bonus deducet me in terram rectam*; quia scilicet in haereditatem illius terrae beatorum nullus potest pervenire, nisi moveatur et deducatur a Spirito Sancto."

83. Walgrave argues that the extrinsic motion of the Spirit's *instinctus* amplifies and orders the internal freedom of the person who responds: "The instinct (of the Holy Spirit) comes from outside but works from inside: it is *exterior* by its origin, but *interior* by its way of working within us. The more perfect its work, the more interiorized it becomes; and our will and the Holy Spirit work together as if they were forming a unique principle. The growth of motion received by our spirit does not diminish the very notion of freedom. Indeed, under the New Law, the instinct of the Holy Spirit becomes in us our own instinct. The instinct of the Holy Spirit builds up the very movement of the free will" ("Instinctus," 430), quoted in Servais Pinckaers, OP, *The Pinckaers Reader: Renewing Thomistic Moral Theology*, ed. John Berkman and Craig Steven Titus (Washington, D.C.: The Catholic University of America Press, 2005), 386. This accords very nicely with Thomas's argument that the infused gifts, which perfect nature, incline one to be increasingly (1) responsive to the Holy Spirit and (2) able to cooperate with such motion, thus meriting certain divine rewards. It also parallels Lonergan's insistence that *auxilium* be understood as a movement which includes prior operative and subsequently cooperative effects, a motion that progressively aligns the divine and human wills so that the distinction between operative and cooperative effects fades, at least, in emphasis: "Note this adaptation of the speculative materials of instrumental and voluntary theory into a doctrine of grace not only implies that conversion is but a single instance of *gratia operans*, but also involves that good performance is but one instance of *grataia cooperans*" (137).

reasonably that Thomas does not restrict the work of the Spirit's mission in the cosmos to the infusion of habitual gifts. Rather, it includes the application of motion to the elect which moves some to conversion, perseverance in the life of grace, and cooperation in meritorious acts.[84] Thomas's mature appreciation of divine motion understood as *auxilium* again provides a tool to express concretely the ways in which the church's sacramental life and the *missiones ad extra* of the divine Persons lead the elect to eternal glory.

Conclusion

The role of *auxilium* in Thomas's treatise on grace and its antecedents and effects in the other parts of *ST* illumine much about Thomas's sense of God, the created world, and the relation of the human person to God. This study has sought to demonstrate the reach of *auxilium* beyond the treatise of grace into other areas of his mature thought, thus suggesting that it functions as a consistent thematic in his systematic presentation of the Christian faith. Three brief points bear mention by way of conclusion and as material for further consideration. First, the developed stress on *auxilium* in Thomas's mature work cannot be undervalued. It is informed by his mature metaphysics of God as efficient cause through the application of motion to the cosmos. More importantly, however, it enriches Thomas's treatment of sanctifying grace so that his reader sees God's grace as more than an infusion of habits that the wayfarer must actualize.

Second, this emphasis on *auxilium* affirms God's constant presence on the wayfarer's journey. It connotes the movement of the Holy Spirit in both operative and cooperative moments on the journey, and moreover, it insists that no part of progress on the journey, especially meritorious action, can be accomplished apart from God's movement in the graced individual. If all salutary human acts can be associated with God's presence and movement, the wayfarer's journey becomes itself

---

84. In affirming the centrality of the gifts, Thomas notably suggests that the effects of habitual grace are not sufficient for glory: "By the theological and moral virtues, man is not so perfected in respect of his last end, as not to stand in continual need of being moved by the yet higher promptings of the Holy Ghost, for the reason already given" (*ST* I-II, q. 68, a. 2, ad 2).

an intimate movement into greater union with God. Thus, in order to really understand Thomas's vision of the Christian life, a rich account of *auxilium* is needed, not merely as a second category of grace but as a pattern for the ends and means of the journey itself which Thomas consistently maintains in discussions of providence and predestination, grace, the virtuous life, and the sacramental life. Finally, Thomas's stress on divine *auxilium* affirms God as the primary agent in human salvation. Even with cooperative grace, there is no motion of the free will that is detached from the divine will, and thus no act of charity can be said to be effected independently from God's motion. If that is true, there can be only limited and highly qualified claims of condign merit, and even congruent merit can be said to be possible only by the motion of the Spirit inspiring the free will to act. Thomas's presentation of *auxilium* thus affirms God as not only the formal author of salvation but also its efficient, final, and constant cause.

13

Aquinas and Scotus on God as Object of Beatific Enjoyment

AARON CANTY

In his *Compendium theologiae*, Thomas Aquinas claims that resurrected human beings experience the vision of God "according to His essence."[1] This experience possesses three components, namely seeing, enjoying, and comprehending God: "In the vision of God, therefore, who is goodness and truth itself, it is necessary for there to be love or delightful fruition, as well as comprehension. Hence, the last chapter of Isaiah says, 'You shall see and your heart shall rejoice.'"[2]

At least partly on account of the controversies regarding the beatific vision in the thirteenth and fourteenth centuries, scholarly attention has tended to focus on this topic.[3] This attention is certainly justified considering the condemnation by the chancellor and theology faculty of the University of Paris in 1241 of the view that the divine essence will not be seen by the blessed in heaven,[4] and the Council of Vienne's con-

---

1. "Non autem in quibuscumque spiritualibus actibus ultimus hominis finis consistit, sed in hoc quod Deus per essentiam uideatur, ut supra ostensum est" (*Comp. Theol.*, chap. 163).

2. "In uisione igitur Dei, qui est ipsa bonitas et ueritas, oportet sicut comprehensionem ita dilectionem seu delectabilem fruitionem adesse, secundum illud Ys. ult. 'Videbitis, et gaudebit cor uestrum'" (*Comp. Theol.*, chap. 165).

3. See Christian Trottman, *La vision béatifique: Des disputes scolastiques à sa définition par Benoît XII* (Rome: École française de Rome, 1995), 3–26.

4. See *Chartularium universitatis Parisiensis*, ed. H. Denifle and É. Châtelain (Paris: Delalain, 1889), no. 128, 1:170–72.

demnation (1311) of the assertion that the soul does not need the *lumen gloriae* to see and enjoy God.[5] Of even greater historical significance is the fourteenth-century controversy regarding the nature of the beatific vision, when Pope John XXII opined that souls would not experience the beatific vision until the last judgment.[6] Scholastic theologians, however, wrote about numerous other topics that pertained to the soul's eschatological experience of God.

One of those topics is beatific enjoyment, or fruition, the second of the three aspects mentioned by Thomas in the *Compendium*. This aspect of the heavenly experience of God pertains to the will and, for Thomas, follows beatific vision. Although enjoyment is a common category for Scholastic theologians, there was disagreement about its ordering to other aspects of the experience of God, such as vision and comprehension. The reason for this disagreement depended, at least partially, on a theologian's system of metaphysics and philosophical anthropology.

One author whose anthropology differs significantly from that of Thomas is John Duns Scotus. While the former prioritizes the intellect over will, the latter takes the opposite position, and these differences have consequences in their respective eschatologies, especially as they relate to their theories of the blessedness of the soul. This essay will examine their respective theories of beatific enjoyment and show how they are grounded in their philosophical anthropologies.[7]

Aquinas

Aquinas examines *fruitio* or enjoyment in a number of places, including the *Sentences* commentary[8] and his *Quodlibet* VII,[9] but this treatment

---

5. See Decree 28 of the Council in *Conciliorum Oecumenicorum Decreta*, 3rd ed., ed. J. Alberigo et al. (Bologna: Istituto Per Le Scienze Religiose, 1973), 383–84.

6. See Christian Trottmann and Arnaud Dumouch, *Benoît XII: La vision béatifique* (Paris: Doctor angélique, 2009), 13–117.

7. The theological development of beatific enjoyment from Thomas to Scotus is beyond the scope of this essay, but see Severin Valentinov Kitanov, *Beatific Enjoyment in Medieval Scholastic Debates: The Complex Legacy of Saint Augustine and Peter Lombard* (Lanham, Md.: Lexington Books, 2014), 48–60, 73–90, 107–14, 178–92, 253–60.

8. See *In Sent.* I, d. 1, q. 1, a. 1; q. 2, aa. 1–2; q. 4, a. 1; IV, d. 49, q. 4, aa. 2 and 5.

9. See *Quodl.* VII, q. 2, although this question pertains primarily to the *fruitio* of Christ's soul during his passion.

will focus on the *Summa Theologiae*. In the *Prima Pars* of the *ST* Thomas
links enjoyment with vision and comprehension. These three qualities
are *dotes* (gifts) of a glorified soul. Thomas explains:

"Comprehension" is one of the three prerogatives of the soul, responding to
hope, as vision responds to faith, and fruition responds to charity. For even
among ourselves not everything seen is held or possessed, forasmuch as things
either appear sometimes afar off, or they are not in our power of attainment.
Neither, again, do we always enjoy what we possess; either because we find no
pleasure in them, or because such things are not the ultimate end of our desire,
so as to satisfy and quell it. But the blessed possess these three things in God;
because they see Him, and in seeing Him, possess Him as present, having the
power to see Him always; and possessing Him, they enjoy Him as the ultimate
fulfilment of desire.[10]

As Thomas reflects on the state of the blessed in heaven, he conceives of them experiencing three things: the vision of God, the possession or attainment of God, and the enjoyment of God. Although these
three qualities exist simultaneously in the blessed, there is an ontological
priority based on the structure of the human person. The intellect sees
God, and the will attains and enjoys God.

Thomas's ordering of vision, comprehension, and enjoyment corresponds with his discussion of the ordering of the theological virtues in
the *Secunda Secundae*.[11] These virtues are "theological" in the sense that
they allow human beings to "adhere to God,"[12] but while they are all

10. "Et hoc modo *comprehensio* est una de tribus dotibus animae, quae respondet spei; sicut
visio fidei, et fruitio caritati. Non enim, apud nos, omne quod videtur, iam tenetur vel habetur:
quia videntur interdum distantia, vel quae non sunt in potestate nostra. Neque iterum omnibus
quae habemus, fruimur: vel quia non delectamur in eis; vel quia non sunt ultimus finis desiderii
nostri, ut desiderium nostrum impleant et quietent. Sed haec tria habent beati in Deo: quia et
vident ipsum; et videndo, tenent sibi praesentem, in potestate habentes semper eum videre; et
tenentes, fruuntur sicut ultimo fine desiderium implente" (*ST* I, q. 12, a. 7, ad 1). This and all
subsequent quotations from *ST* are taken from the translation of the Fathers of the English
Dominican Province, with occasional adaptations (New York: Benziger Brothers, 1947).

11. *ST* II-II, q. 17, aa. 7–8.

12. "Respondeo dicendum quod virtus aliqua dicitur theologica ex hoc quod habet Deum
pro obiecto cui inhaeret. Potest autem aliquis alicui rei inhaerere dupliciter: uno modo, propter
seipsum; alio modo, inquantum ex eo ad aliud devenitur. Caritas igitur facit hominem Deo inhaerere propter seipsum, mentem hominis uniens Deo per affectum amoris. Spes autem et fides
faciunt hominem inhaerere Deo sicut cuidam principio ex quo aliqua nobis proveniunt. De Deo
autem provenit nobis et cognitio veritatis et adeptio perfectae bonitatis. Fides ergo facit hominem Deo inhaerere inquantum est nobis principium cognoscendi veritatem: credimus enim ea

infused simultaneously and exist together, there is a certain connatural ordering to them. Thomas explains in *ST* II-II, q. 17:

Absolutely speaking, *faith* precedes hope. For the object of hope is a future *good*, arduous but possible to obtain. In order, therefore, that we may hope, it is *necessary* for the object of hope to be proposed to us as possible. Now the object of hope is, in one way, *eternal happiness*, and, in another way, the Divine assistance, as explained above: and both of these are proposed to us by *faith*, whereby we come to *know* that we are able to obtain *eternal life*, and that for this purpose the Divine assistance is ready for us, according to *Heb. xi. 6:* "He that cometh to God, must *believe* that He is, and is a rewarder to them that seek Him." Therefore it is evident that *faith* precedes hope.[13]

In order to hope for something, one must know what it is to some extent. Hence in this passage, Thomas argues that faith allows people to know that they can obtain eternal life by means of grace. Once this fact is known, hope of eternal life encourages and elicits a love for God,[14] which is a response to the communication of God's blessedness.[15] This love infused by God is a virtue which unites individuals with God and gives them peace, mercy, and joy.[16] In heaven, the vision of God's essence leads to the perfect enjoyment of God, which is the highest good that man can experience.[17]

Thomas's most extensive discussions of enjoyment in the *Summa* can be found in I-II, qq. 3–5 and 11–12. The *Prima Secundae* addresses man "as the principle of his actions"; qq. 3–5 pertain to man's destiny, while qq. 11–12 are in the section on human acts.

---

vera esse quae nobis a Deo dicuntur. Spes autem facit Deo adhaerere prout est nobis principium perfectae bonitatis: inquantum scilicet per spem divino auxilio innitimur ad beatitudinem obtinendam" (*ST* II-II, q. 17, a. 6).

13. "Respondeo dicendum quod fides absolute praecedit spem. Obiectum enim spei est bonum futurum arduum possibile haberi. Ad hoc ergo quod aliquis speret, requiritur quod obiectum spei proponatur ei ut possibile. Sed obiectum spei est uno modo beatitudo aeterna, et alio modo divinum auxilium, ut ex dictis patet. Et utrumque eorum proponitur nobis per fidem, per quam nobis innotescit quod ad vitam aeternam possumus pervenire, et quod ad hoc paratum est nobis divinum auxilium: secundum illud Heb. 11 [6]: *Accedentem ad Deum oportet credere quia est, et quia inquirentibus se remunerator est.* Unde manifestum est quod fides praecedit spem" (*ST* II-II, a. 7).

14. Although see how Thomas understands the relationship between hope and charity when considering them in the *ordo generationis* and the *ordo perfectionis* in *ST* II-II, q. 17, a. 8.

15. "Amor autem super hac communicatione fundatus est caritas. Unde manifestum est quod caritas amicitia quaedam est hominis ad Deum" (*ST* II-II, q. 23, a. 1).

16. See *ST* II-II, q. 23, a. 1, and qq. 28–30.

17. See *ST* II-II, q. 23, a. 7.

The third question addresses beatitude or ultimate happiness. Thomas explains that happiness can be considered from the point of view of the cause and object of happiness or from the point of view of happiness as experienced by the subject:

First, there is the thing itself which we desire to attain: thus for the miser, the end is money. Secondly there is the attainment or possession, the use or enjoyment of the thing desired; thus we may say that the end of the miser is the possession of money; and the end of the intemperate man is to enjoy something pleasurable. In the first sense, then, man's last end is the uncreated good, namely, God, Who alone by His infinite goodness can perfectly satisfy man's will. But in the second way, man's last end is something created, existing in him, and this is nothing else than the attainment or enjoyment of the last end. Now the last end is called happiness. If, therefore, we consider man's happiness in its cause or object, then it is something uncreated; but if we consider it as to the very essence of happiness, then it is something created.[18]

Happiness is an end, therefore, not in the sense that God is an end, but in the sense that the enjoyment of God follows the attainment of God. God is an uncreated end, but enjoyment is something created in the soul when the soul attains what it has ultimately desired.

Thomas explains further, however, in a. 4, that the essence of happiness is attaining the end, whereas the *per se* accident is enjoyment.

At first we desire to attain an intelligible end; we attain it, through its being made present to us by an act of the intellect; and then the delighted will rests in the end when attained. So, therefore, the essence of happiness consists in an act of the intellect: but the delight that results from happiness pertains to the will. In this sense Augustine says (*Conf.* x. 23) that happiness is "joy in truth," because joy itself is the consummation of happiness.[19]

---

18. "Respondeo dicendum quod, sicut supra dictum est, finis dicitur dupliciter. Uno modo, ipsa res quam cupimus adipisci: sicut avaro est finis pecunia. Alio modo, ipsa adeptio vel possessio, seu usus aut fruitio eius rei quae desideratur: sicut si dicatur quod possessio pecuniae est finis avari, et frui re voluptuosa est finis intemperati. Primo ergo modo, ultimus hominis finis est bonum increatum, scilicet Deus, qui solus sua infinita bonitate potest voluntatem hominis perfecte implere. Secundo autem modo, ultimus finis hominis est aliquid creatum in ipso existens, quod nihil est aliud quam adeptio vel fruitio finis ultimi. Ultimus autem finis vocatur beatitudo. Si ergo beatitudo hominis consideretur quantum ad causam vel obiectum, sic est aliquid increatum: si autem consideretur quantum ad ipsam essentiam beatitudinis, sic est aliquid creatum" (*ST* I-II, q. 3, a. 1).

19. "Nam a principio volumus consequi finem intelligibilem; consequimur autem ipsum per hoc quod fit praesens nobis per actum intellectus; et tunc voluntas delectata conquiescit in fine

In other words, the essence of happiness pertains to the intellect and the correlative accident of happiness pertains to the will. This position not only reinforces the priority of intellect over will, but also the priority of vision and comprehension over enjoyment.

Thomas focuses an entire article in q. 4 on the relationship between vision and delight. In q. 4, a. 2 Thomas draws on Aristotle and arguments from motion to reinforce the priority of vision:

> The Philosopher discusses this question (*Ethic.* x. 4), and leaves it unsolved. But if one consider the matter carefully, the operation of the intellect which is vision must rank before delight. For delight consists in a certain repose of the will. Now that the will finds rest in anything can only be on account of the goodness of that thing in which it reposes. If therefore the will reposes in an operation, the will's repose is caused by the goodness of the operation. Nor does the will seek good for the sake of repose; for thus the very act of the will would be the end, which has been disproved above: but it seeks to be at rest in the operation, because that operation is its good. Consequently it is evident that the operation in which the will reposes ranks before the resting of the will therein.[20]

Thomas asserts that the will rests in the goodness of the intellect's operation of vision. Therefore, even though both the will and intellect act in the effort to attain the final end, only the intellect continues to operate upon the attainment of the end. The will, which had been directing the intellect toward God, now rests in the act of vision and ceases to direct the intellect.

Because blessedness consists of seeing God, an operation of the speculative intellect and not the practical intellect, and because all the blessed see God, questions remain regarding the role of the body in ex-

---

iam adepto. Sic igitur essentia beatitudinis in actu intellectus consistit, sed ad voluntatem pertinet delectatio beatitudinem consequens; secundum quod Augustinus dicit, X Confess., quod beatitudo est *gaudium de veritate*; quia scilicet ipsum gaudium est consummatio beatitudinis" (*ST* I-II, q. 3, a. 4).

20. "Respondeo dicendum quod istam quaestionem movet Philosophus in X Ethic., et eam insolutam dimittit. Sed si quis diligenter consideret, ex necessitate oportet quod operatio intellectus, quae est visio, sit potior delectatione. Delectatio enim consistit in quadam quietatione voluntatis. Quod autem voluntas in aliquo quietetur, non est nisi propter bonitatem eius in quo quietatur. Si ergo voluntas quietatur in aliqua operatione, ex bonitate operationis procedit quietatio voluntatis. Nec voluntas quaerit bonum propter quietationem: sic enim ipse actus voluntatis esset finis, quod est contra praemissa. Sed ideo quaerit quod quietetur in operatione, quia operatio est bonum eius. Unde manifestum est quod principalius bonum est ipsa operatio in qua quietatur voluntas, quam quietatio voluntatis in ipso" (*ST* I-II, q. 4, a. 2).

periencing God and how the experience of God might vary from saint to saint. Thomas says that in this life the body is essential for human happiness because the intellect needs phantasms in order to operate. A disembodied soul, however, can experience God without the mediation of the body, and in order to have perfect happiness the soul does not need a body:

The intellect needs not the body for its operation, save on account of the phantasms, wherein it looks on the intelligible truth, as stated in the First Part. Now it is evident that the Divine Essence cannot be seen by means of phantasms, as stated in the First Part. Wherefore, since man's perfect Happiness consists in the vision of the Divine Essence, it does not depend on the body. Consequently, without the body the soul can be happy.[21]

The body is necessary, however, from a certain point of view. It is not necessary for the essential perfection of the soul, but it is necessary for its "well-being" (*bene esse*). Here is how Thomas explains it in the reply to the fifth objection: "The desire of the separated soul is entirely at rest, as regards the thing desired; since it has that which suffices for its appetite. But it is not wholly at rest, as regards the desirer, since it does not possess that good in every way that it would wish to possess it. Consequently, after the body has been resumed, happiness increases not in intensity [*intensive*], but in extent [*extensive*]."[22] The soul is happy insofar as it enjoys God, but it is not completely at rest because it "does not possess that good in every way that it would wish to possess it." A comment in the reply to the fourth objection clarifies this position further.

Separation from the body is said to hold the soul back from tending with all its might to the vision of the Divine Essence. For the soul desires to enjoy God in such a way that the enjoyment also may overflow into the body, as far as possible. And therefore, as long as it enjoys God without the fellowship of the body,

21. "Nam intellectus ad suam operationem non indiget corpore nisi propter phantasmata, in quibus veritatem intelligibilem contuetur, ut in Primo dictum est. Manifestum est autem quod divina essentia per phantasmata videri non potest, ut in Primo ostensum est. Unde, cum in visione divinae essentiae perfecta hominis beatitudo consistat, non dependet beatitudo perfecta hominis a corpore. Unde sine corpore potest anima esse beata" (*ST* I-II, q. 4, a. 5).

22. "Ad quintum dicendum quod desiderium animae separatae totaliter quiescit ex parte appetibilis: quia scilicet habet id quod suo appetitui sufficit. Sed non totaliter requiescit ex parte appetentis: quia illud bonum non possidet secundum omnem modum quo possidere vellet. Et ideo, corpore resumpto, beatitudo crescit non intensive, sed extensive" (*ST* I-II, q. 4, a. 5, ad 5).

its appetite is at rest in that which it has in such a way that it would still wish the body to attain to its share.[23]

This passage is very important for understanding beatific enjoyment because here Thomas says that the soul desires (*appetit*) to "enjoy God in such a way that the enjoyment also may overflow into the body." From previous passages, it is clear that enjoyment is experienced by the will and not the intellect, and here Thomas envisions enjoyment overflowing (*per redundantiam*) into the body. Even if a disembodied soul experiences perfect enjoyment of God, it still desires its separated body to share in that perfect enjoyment.

Another question related to the vision and enjoyment of God is how the saints experience God differently if they all see him without the mediation of phantasms or the body. Thomas addresses this question in I-II, q. 5, a. 2. In that question, Thomas claims that two things are necessary for beatific happiness, namely the final end and the enjoyment of the end. To the extent that all the blessed experience the same final end, they have the same experience, but what makes each person's experience different is the beatific enjoyment that results from attaining the final end. As Thomas puts it, "One man can be happier than another; because the more a man enjoys this Good the happier he is. Now, that one man enjoys God more than another happens through his being better disposed or ordered to the enjoyment of Him. And in this sense one man can be happier than another."[24] The disparity in enjoyment is based on the difference in each person's will. Thus, even though each person will be perfectly happy because of his vision of God, some of the saints can be more happy than others because of their experience of enjoyment in their wills and their bodies. This variation is based on different levels of participation in the divine nature.

---

23. "Et sic separatio a corpore dicitur animam retardare, ne tota intentione tendat in visionem divinae essentiae. Appetit enim anima sic frui Deo, quod etiam ipsa fruitio derivetur ad corpus per redundantiam, sicut est possibile. Et ideo quandiu ipsa fruitur Deo sine corpore, appetitus eius sic quiescit in eo quod habet, quod tamen adhuc ad participationem eius vellet suum corpus pertingere" (*ST* I-II, q. 4, a. 5, ad 4).

24. "Sed quantum ad adeptionem huiusmodi boni vel fruitionem, potest aliquis alio esse beatior: quia quanto magis hoc bono fruitur, tanto beatior est. Contingit autem aliquem perfectius frui Deo quam alium, ex eo quod est melius dispositus vel ordinatus ad eius fruitionem. Et secundum hoc potest aliquis alio beatior esse" (*ST* I-II, q. 5, a. 2).

Scotus

John Duns Scotus treats Thomas's positions on several of these matters in his *Ordinatio* IV, d. 49, qq. 4–5.[25] Scotus's principal concern initially is whether the happiness enjoyed in heaven pertains primarily to the intellect or the will. He examines Thomas's arguments regarding the priority of intellect at length. Scotus acknowledges that the argument that happiness pertains principally to the intellect has merit. To the extent that the will desires its last end before attaining it, the will precedes the last act of the intellect in its vision of God. As soon as the intellect beholds God, the desire for God is removed and it rests in God (*quietatio in fine*).[26] Using the example of the miser, Scotus says that once desired money is obtained, the will's desire for it ceases as the intellect beholds and enjoys its coveted object.[27]

According to Scotus, this way of thinking about the relationship between intellect and will in enjoying God is deficient for at least two reasons.[28] The first is that it seems to restrict acts of the will to desiring something present to the intellect. Scotus refutes this position: "If it should be denied that every operation of the will concerns a present object except that of enjoyment [*delectatio*], this would be irrational, because if the will is operative concerning an absent object, however imperfectly known because obscure, how much more perfectly will it be able to operate when an object is present perfectly, because it is seen."[29]

25. In addition to these questions from the *Ordinatio*, see also *Lectura* I, d. 1, p. 2, q. 1, in *Opera omnia* (Vatican City: Typis Polyglottis Vaticanis, 1960), 16:86–88. Scotus does not address Thomas in particular, but there is a sustained reflection on enjoyment.

26. "'Operatio – primo coniungens fini exteriori – est per quam fit primo assecutio finis exterioris'; actus voluntatis non est talis, quia voluntatis est unus actus ante assecutionem finis, scilicet desiderium, quod est ut quidam motus ad non habitum, – 'alius eius actus est quaedam quietatio in fine.'" *Ordinatio* IV, d. 49, q. 4, in *Opera omnia* (Vatican City: Typis Vaticanis, 2013), 14:336.

27. "Istud confirmatur per exemplum in appetitu sensitivo, – quia si sensibile est finis extra, sensatio est finis intra, quia per illam primo habetur sensibile, sic ut in eo possit appetitus sensitivus quietari. Patet etiam in alio exemplo, quia 'si pecunia est finis extra, possessio pecuniae est finis intra, quam sequitur quietatio voluntatis' in pecunia dilecta" (*Ord.* IV, d. 49, q. 4 [336]).

28. For more on the priority of the will, see Robert Prentice, "The Voluntarism of Duns Scotus, as Seen in His Comparison of the Intellect and the Will," *Franciscan Studies* 28 (1968): 63–103.

29. "Quod si negetur omnis operatio voluntatis circa obiectum praesens, alia a delectatione, – hoc est irrationabile, quia si voluntas est operativa circa obiectum absens, imperfecte tamen

In Scotus's view, if the object of the will is present, it does not follow that the will ceases to will. It is possible for the will to act in a new way. The second reason is that God is not just any desirable end; God is the most desirable end possible. As such, God is most naturally to be desired and therefore to be willed. Because it is the will, and not the intellect, that directs the soul to its final end, the will has a more immediate relationship to God than does the intellect.

Scotus makes another argument drawing from Anselm of Canterbury. Scotus acknowledges that with respect to the priority of intellect or will, there can be only three positions. One position is that willing follows understanding, the second position is that understanding follows willing, and the third is that both actions occur independently. Scotus dismisses the third position on the grounds that, because both willing and understanding are ordered to the same end, they must have some relationship with each other. That leaves either the will or the intellect as having priority. Scotus cites Anselm's *Cur Deus homo* as evidence for the will's priority. The following passage is a much longer excerpt than the brief reference Scotus cites, but it provides a fuller account of why Scotus might think that Anselm is a reliable authority for prioritizing the will over the intellect:

And so it is certain that rational nature was made for the purpose of loving and choosing the supreme Good above all other things, not for the sake of something else, but for his own sake. After all, if rational nature loves the supreme Good for the sake of something else, it loves something else and not the supreme Good. Now it cannot love the supreme Good for its own sake unless it is just. Therefore, it was made rational and just at the same time so that it would not be rational in vain. Now given that it was made just so that it might choose and love the supreme Good, it was made to be just either so that it would at some time attain what it loves and chooses, or not. But if it was not made just so that it would attain what it loves and chooses in this way, its being made just, so that it loves and chooses this, would be in vain, and there would be no reason why it ever ought to attain what it loves. Therefore, as long as it continues to act justly by loving and choosing the supreme Good, which is the purpose for which it was made, it will be unhappy, because it will lack something against its will, by not having what it desires—which is altogether absurd. Consequently,

---

cognitum quia obscure, multo perfectius poterit operari circa obiectum perfecte praesens, quia visum" (*Ord.* IV, d. 49, q. 4 [341–42]). English translations from the *Ordinatio* are my own.

rational nature was made just in order that it might be happy in enjoying the supreme Good, that is, God. Therefore, human beings, who are rational in nature, were made just in order that they might be happy in enjoying God.[30]

What Scotus draws from this text and from his previous arguments is that when the will desires the final end, it is not doing this for the intellect alone, but for itself, as well. Human beings do not simply want to see God, but they also want to enjoy God. Enjoyment, as a consequence, is essential to beatific happiness.

One of Scotus's primary criticisms of the Thomistic arguments pertains to the concept of motion. Thomas had argued that the will "rests" upon attaining its desired end.[31] The implication of this position is that the enjoyment which follows vision is not essential to the happiness experienced by the blessed. Scotus criticizes this understanding of rest:

If rest is taken for the delight that follows a perfect operation, I concede that that rest precedes the perfect attainment of the end. If, however, rest is taken for the restful act conjoined to the end [*pro actu quietativo in fine*], I say that the act of loving, which naturally precedes delight, rests in that way, because the operative power does not rest in the object, except through a perfect operation through which it attains its object. And then that proposition, "the first or per-

---

30. "Rationalem naturam a deo factam esse iustam, ut illo fruendo beata esset, dubitati non debet. Ideo namque rationalis est, ut discernat inter iustum et iniustum, inter bonum et malum, inter magis bonum et minus bonum. Alioquin frustra facta esset rationalis. Sed deus non fecit eam rationalem frustra. Quare ad hoc eam factam esse rationalem dubium non est. Simili ratione probatur quia ad hoc accepit potestatem discernendi, ut odisset et vitaret malum, ac amaret et eligeret bonum, atque magis bonum magis amaret et eligeret. Aliter namque frustra illi deus dedisset potestatem istam discernendi, quia in vanum discerneret, si secundum discretionem non amaret et vitaret. Sed non convenit ut deus tantam potestatem frustra dederit. Ad hoc itaque factam esse rationalem naturam certum est, ut summum bonum super omnia amaret et eligeret, non propter aliud, sed propter ipsum. Si enim propter aliud, non ipsum, sed aliud amat. At hoc nisi iusta facere nequit. Ut igitur frustra non sit rationalis, simul ad hoc rationalis et iusta facta est. Quod si ad summum bonum eligendum et amandum iusta facta est, aut talis ad hoc facta est, ut aliquando assequeretur quod amaret et eligeret, aut non. Sed si ad hoc iusta non est facta, ut quod sic amat et eligit assequatur, frustra facta est talis, ut sic illud amet et eligat, nec ulla erit ratio cur illud assequi debeat aliquando. Quamdiu ergo amando et eligendo summum bonum iusta faciet, ad quod facta est, misera erit, quia indigens erit contra voluntatem, non habendo quod desiderat; quod nimis absurdum est. Quapropter rationalis natura iusta facta est, ut summo bono, id est deo, fruendo beata esset. Homo ergo qui rationalis natura est, factus est iustus ad hoc, ut deo fruendo beatus esset." Anselm, *Cur Deus homo*, in *Opera omnia*, ed. F. S. Schmitt (Edinburgh: Thomas Nelson and Sons, 1946), l. 2, c. 1, trans. Thomas Williams in Anselm, *Basic Writings* (Indianapolis, Ind.: Hackett, 2007), 290.

31. See *ST* I-II, q. 11, a. 3.

fect knowledge of an object precedes the rest in an object" is false, even if it has the appearance of truth from a comparison to motion. In motion, something moveable follows an end and finds rest in that end, since motion to an end precedes rest in that end. But this comparison to what has been proposed is invalid because this operation is simultaneously perfectly intellective and at rest, because the rest occurs in the perfect knowledge of its object.[32]

In this passage Scotus rejects the dichotomy of motion and rest and asserts that rest can refer to a restful act. The act of loving perfectly is such a restful act. In the motion of external objects, motion and rest oppose each other. With respect to loving perfectly, however, the power of the will to love rests only through the act of knowing God perfectly. Because the act of knowing perfectly does not cease, neither does the act of loving.

What Scotus has established by the end of *Ordinatio* IV, d. 49, q. 4 is that beatific happiness is something that pertains principally to the will and that the will loves the good as good and not as known. In addition to articulating these positions, Scotus also has noted that the will directs the intellect to its end and that the intellect can only be a partial cause of the will's act of willing.

The question of enjoyment is addressed in q. 5. Based on the positions he has previously established, Scotus affirms that enjoyment is necessary for beatific happiness. In fact, beatific happiness is nothing other than a perfect act of the will, which he equates with enjoyment. The primary problem that Scotus addresses in the first part of q. 5 is what kind of act of the will corresponds with enjoyment, because there are several acts the will can perform and not all of them lead to enjoyment. The will can not will (*nolle*), but this could not lead to happiness because there could be no willing its final end. If the will wills on account of what is willed or on account of the good of what is willed, that is the

---

32. "Si enim accipitur 'quietatio' pro delectatione consequente operationem perfectam, concedo quod illam quietationem praecedit perfecta consecutio finis; si autem accipitur 'quietatio' pro actu quietativo in fine, dico quod actus amandi, qui naturaliter praecedit delectationem, quietat isto modo, quia potentia operativa non quietatur in obiecto nisi per operationem perfectam, per quam attingit obiectum. Et tunc illa propositio 'quietationem in obiecto praecedit assecutio obiecti prima, id est perfecta,' falsa est, habens tamen apparentiam veritatis ex comparatione ad motum quo mobile assequitur terminum, et ad quietem in illo termino, siquidem motus ad terminum praecedit quietem in termino. Sed haec comparatio ad propositum non valet, quia eadem operatio hic est assecutiva perfecte et quietativa, quia quietatio est in perfecta assecutione obecti" (*Ord.* IV, d. 49, q. 4 [341]).

love of friendship. If the will wills on account of the one willing or on account of the good of the one willing, that is the love of concupiscence. In other words, the will can love something for its own sake or for the sake of something else. It is only the love of something for its own sake that is true enjoyment.

While this position may seem sensible in light of the alternatives, the problem with this view is that anyone in the present life can experience this kind of enjoyment. This fact leads to a question regarding the difference between enjoyment in this life and enjoyment in heaven. Thomas had simply made the distinction between imperfect and perfect enjoyment. Imperfect enjoyment is when the soul possesses its end in intention but not in reality, whereas perfect enjoyment is when the soul possesses its end in reality. In both cases, the kind of charity that precedes and accompanies enjoyment is the same; that is, there are not different species of charity.[33]

Even if Thomas makes perfect vision of God the prerequisite for beatific enjoyment, nonetheless for Scotus it seems more probable that the enjoyment of earthly life and the enjoyment of heaven are two different species. The reason for this supposition is that if there is only one species of charity, it is theoretically possible for a wayfarer to have more charity than one of the blessed. If, through God's absolute power, a wayfarer like the Virgin Mary were to experience the vision of God, that person could experience greater enjoyment in this life than one of the least saints in heaven.[34] Also, if someone were to have the vision of God without charity, there could be no supernatural enjoyment.[35] Although these examples are highly speculative, because they are nonetheless logically possible in Scotus's view, Scotus believes that the enjoyment of God in this life is qualitatively different from the enjoyment of God in

---

33. See *ST* I-II, q. ii, a. 4.

34. "Pone ergo quod per quattuor gradus; possibile est fruitionem viatoris crescere per quattuor gradus, quia et cognitionem. Cum igitur et cognitio eiusdem speciei tot gradus habeat quot et fruitio, posita tamen intensione cognitionis, possibile est fruitionem cognoscentis proportionaliter intendi; ergo adhuc possibile est viatorem esse beatum; ergo et possibile est viatorem pertingere ad illum gradum et esse beatum. Consimiliter potest argui de aliquo gradu dato fruitionis beatificae, a quo distat supremus gradus viatoris (puta beatae Mariae) per aliquot gradus; tamen si est eiusdem speciei infra speciem fruitionis beatificae descendatur ad minus et minus, – tandem erit aliqua beatifica aequalis isti non beatificae vel minor ea" (*Ord.* IV, d. 49, q. 5 [362–63]).

35. *Ord.* IV, d. 49, q. 5 (363–64).

heaven.[36] Thus, the two principles that one learns from IV, d. 49, q. 5 are: (1) that happiness is nothing other than the enjoyment of God through the love of friendship; and (2) that the enjoyment of the saints in heaven is qualitatively different from the enjoyment of wayfarers.[37]

Conclusion

The study of Thomas and Scotus on the question of beatific enjoyment is illuminating. First, setting aside their differences, they both argue from the same sources: Augustine, Aristotle, and scripture. Thomas cites more scriptural texts and Scotus uses Anselm as a supplement to Augustine, but in their use of Aristotle and Augustine, Thomas and Scotus rely often on the same passages or very similar ones. Second, the respective theological anthropologies of Thomas and Scotus lead to very different conclusions regarding beatific happiness and enjoyment.

To summarize these differences briefly, one can say that for Thomas beatific enjoyment follows beatific vision. The vision occurs in the speculative intellect, and once the soul has possessed God in this vision and has experienced happiness, it experiences enjoyment in the will, which then overflows into the person's resurrected body. All the saints experience the same happiness, because they share the same vision, but they do not experience the same enjoyment. For Scotus, however, vision is not as important as it is for Thomas. In fact, the will is related more

36. For more on the role of the intellect and the will in Scotus's understanding of beatific vision and enjoyment, see Guido Alliney, "Libertà e contingenza della fruizione beatifica nello scotismo del primo 300," *Veritas: Revista de Filosofia* 50, no. 3 (2005): 95–108; Thomas J. Clarke, "The Background and Implications of Duns Scotus' Theory of Knowing in the Beatific Vision" (PhD diss., Brandeis University, 1971), 252–83; Manzano Guzmán, "El humanismo implicado en la comprensión escotista de la visión beatifica," in *Regnum hominis et regnum Dei*, ed. C. Bérubé (Rome: Societas Internationalis Scotistica, 1978), 1:85–94. See also Christian Trottman, "Vision béatifique et intuition d'un objet absent: des sources franciscaines du nominalisme aux défenseurs scotistes de l'opinion de Jean XXII sur la vision différée," *Studi medievali* 34 (Third Series), no. 2 (1993): 653–715.

37. Robert Prentice examines at length Scotus's understanding of the role of the will in the blessedness of the human person. See "Scotus' Voluntarism as Seen in His Concept of the Essence of Beatitude," in *Studia mediaevalia et mariologica*, ed. C. Balić (Rome: Antonianum, 1971), 161–86. See also Mary Beth Ingham, CSJ, "*De Vita Beata*: John Duns Scotus, Moral Perfection and the Rational Will," in *Proceedings of "The Quadruple Congress" on John Duns Scotus, Part 3: Johannes Duns Scotus 1308–2008*, ed. L. Honnefelder et al. (Münster/St. Bonaventure, N.Y.: Aschendorff / Franciscan Institute Publications, 2010), 379–89.

immediately to God as final end than is the intellect. One implication of this position is that the soul does not experience happiness as a result of vision, but only as a result of enjoyment. Beatific happiness is beatific enjoyment, and because the saints can experience different degrees of enjoyment, they can experience different degrees of happiness. Much has been written comparing Thomas and Scotus on the relationship between intellect and will, but examining their differences through an eschatological prism highlights some of the less well-known consequences of their respective positions on the intellect and the will and how the human person relates to God.[38]

---

38. For more on beatific enjoyment in Scotus's contemporaries and successors, see William Duba, "The Beatific Vision in the *Sentences* Commentary of Gerald Odonis," *Vivarium* 47 (2009): 348–63; Mark G. Henninger, "Henry of Harclay on the Contingency of the Will's Fruition," in *Proceedings of "The Quadruple Congress" on John Duns Scotus, Part 3: Johannes Duns Scotus 1308–2008*, ed. L. Honnefelder et al. (Münster/St. Bonaventure, N.Y.: Aschendorff/Franciscan Institute Publications, 2010), 463–77; Severin V. Kitanov, "Durandus of St.-Pourcain and Peter Auriol on the Act of Beatific Enjoyment," in *Philosophical Debates at Paris in the Early Fourteenth Century*, ed. Stephen F. Brown, Thomas Dewender, and Theo Kobusch (Leiden: Brill, 2009), 163–78; Severin V. Kitanov, "Peter of Candia on Demonstrating that God is the Sole Object of Beatific Enjoyment," *Franciscan Studies* 67 (2009): 427–89; Arthur Stephen McGrade, "Ockham on Enjoyment – Towards an Understanding of Fourteenth Century Philosophy and Psychology," *Review of Metaphysics* 34, no. 4 (1981): 706–28; Christian Trottmann, "La vision béatifique dans la seconde école franciscaine: de Matthieu d'Aquasparta à Duns Scot," *Collectanea Franciscana* 64 (1994): 121–80; and Christian Trottmann, "Guiral Ot, de l'éternité au temps et retour. Conjectures à partir du *De multiformi visione Dei*," in *The Medieval Concept of Time: Studies on the Scholastic Debate and Its Reception in Early Modern Philosophy*, ed. Pasquale Porro (Leiden: Brill, 2001), 287–317.

Primary Sources

Works of Thomas Aquinas

Thomas Aquinas. *Basic Writings of Saint Thomas Aquinas*. Edited by Anton C. Pegis. 2 vols. New York: Random House, 1945.

———. *The Division and Methods of the Sciences: Questions V and VI of his Commentary on the De trinitate of Boethius*. Translated by Armand Maurer. 4th edition. Toronto: Pontifical Institute of Mediaeval Studies, 1986.

———. *In Aristotelis librum De anima commentarium*. Edited by A. M. Pierotta. Turin: Marietti, 1959. English translation: *Commentary on Aristotle's De Anima*, translated by Kenelm Foster, OP, and Silvester Humphries, OP. Notre Dame, Ind.: Dumb Ox Books, 1994 (1951).

———. *In duodecim libros Metaphysicorum Aristotelis expositio*. Edited by M. R. Cathala and R. M. Spiazzi. Turin: Marietti, 1950. English translation: *Commentary on the Metaphysics of Aristotle*, translated by John P. Rowan. Chicago: Henry Regnery, 1961.

———. *In octo libros Physicorum Aristotelis Expositio*. Edited by P. M. Maggiolo. Turin: Marietti, 1954. English translation: *Commentary on Aristotle's Physics*, translated by Richard J. Blackwell, Richard J. Spath, and W. Edmund Thirlkel. Notre Dame, Ind.: Dumb Ox Books, 1999.

———. *Opera Omnia*. Edited by the Leonine Commission. Rome: Leonine Commission, 1882–. Vols. 4–12, *Summa theologiae*. Vols. 13–15, *Summa contra Gentiles*. Vols. 22.1, 22.2, 22.3, *Quaestiones disputatae de veritate*. Vol. 24.2, *Quaestio de spiritualibus creaturis*. Vol. 25.1, *Quaestiones de quolibet*. Vol. 50, *Super Boetium De Trinitate*.

———. *Quaestiones disputatae de potentia*. Edited by M. Pession. Turin: Marietti, 1953.

———. *Quaestiones disputatae de veritate*. Edited by R. M. Spiazzi. Turin: Marietti, 1953. English translation: *On Truth*, translated by Robert W. Mulligan, SJ, et al. 3 vols. Chicago: Henry Regnery, 1952–54.

———. *Scriptum super libros Sententiarum.* Vols. 1 and 2 edited by P. Mandonnet. Paris: Lethielleux, 1929. Vols. 3 and 4 edited by M. F. Moos. Paris: Lethielleux, 1933 and 1947.

———. *Summa Contra Gentiles.* Edited by C. Pera. Turin: Marietti, 1961. English translation: *The Summa Contra Gentiles of Saint Thomas Aquinas,* translated by the English Dominicans. 4 vols. New York / London: Benziger / Burns, Oates, and Washbourne, Ltd., 1923–29.

———. *Summa Theologiae.* Edited by Instituti Studiorum Medievalium Ottaviensis. Ottawa: Commissio Piana, 1953. English translation: *The Summa Theologica of St. Thomas Aquinas,* translated by the English Dominicans. 3 vols. New York: Benziger, 1947–48.

Other Works

Alberigo, J., et al., eds. *Conciliorum Oecumenicorum Decreta.* 3rd edition. Bologna: Istituto Per Le Scienze Religiose, 1973.

Albertus Magnus. *Commentarium in II librum sententiarum.* Edited by P. Jammy, t. 15: *Commentarii in II. et III. Lib. Sentent.* Lyon: Claudii Prost. et al., 1651.

———. *Summa theologiae.* Edited by P. Jammy, t. 17: *Prima Pars Summae Theologiae.* Lyon: Claudii Prost. et al., 1651.

Alexander of Hales. *Summa Theologica.* Edited by Pp. Collegii S. Bonaventurae. 5 vols. Quaracchi: Ex Typographia Collegii S. Bonaventurae, 1924–48.

Anselm of Canterbury. *Cur Deus homo.* In *Opera Omnia,* edited by F. S. Schmitt, 2:42–133. Edinburgh: Thomas Nelson and Sons, 1946. Translation: Anselm, *Basic Writings,* translated by Thomas Williams, 237–326. Indianapolis, Ind.: Hackett, 2007.

Aristotle. *Metaphysica.* Edited by W. Jaeger. Oxford: Oxford University Press, 1978. Translation: *Metaphysics,* translated by Hugh Tredennick. Cambridge, Mass.: Harvard University Press, 1989.

Augustine. *De civitate Dei.* Edited by Bernardus Dombart and Alphonsus Kalb. Turnhout: Brepols, 1955.

———. *De doctrina Christiana.* Edited by J. Martin. CCSL 32. Turnhout: Brepols, 1962.

Balthasar, Hans Urs von. "Denys." In *Studies in Theological Style,* translated by Andrew Louth et al., vol. 2 of *The Glory of the Lord: A Theological Aesthetics,* edited by Joseph Fessio and John Riches, 144–210. San Francisco, Calif.: Ignatius Press, 1984.

Barth, Karl. *Church Dogmatics.* 14 vols. Edited by Geoffrey William Bromiley and Thomas F. Torrance. Edinburgh: T and T Clark, 1936–77.

Bonaventure. *Breviloquium.* Translated by Dominic Monti. St. Bonaventure, N.Y.: Franciscan Institute Publications, 2005.

Cajetan. *Commentaria, Summa theologiae*, vol. 5. Rome: Leonine Commission, 1882–.

Denifle, H., and É. Châtelain, eds. *Chartularium Universitatis Parisiensis*, vol. 1. Paris: Ex typis fratrum Delalain, 1889.

Hegel, G. W. F. *Hegel's Logic*. Translated from *The Encyclopaedia of the Philosophical Sciences* by William Wallace. Oxford: Clarendon, 1975.

John Damascene. *De fide orthodoxa. Versions of Burgundio and Cerbanus*. Edited by E. M. Buytaert. St. Bonaventure, N.Y.: Franciscan Institute, 1955.

John Duns Scotus. *Opera Omnia*. Edited by Pacifico M. Perantoni, Carolus Balic, Barnaba Hechich, and Josip Percan. 21 vols. Vatican City: Typis Polyglottis Vaticanis, 1950–.

Kant, Immanuel. *Critique of Pure Reason*. Translated by Norman Kemp Smith. New York: St. Martin's, 1965.

————. *Prolegomena to Any Future Metaphysics*. Translated by Paul Carus, revised by James W. Ellington. Indianapolis, Ind.: Hackett, 1977.

Peter Lombard. *Sententiae in IV libris distinctae*. Edited by Ignatius Brady, OFM. 2 vols. Grottaferrata: Editiones Collegii S. Bonaventurae ad Claras Aquas, 1971–81.

Richard Fishacre. *In secundum librum sententiarum*. Edited by R. James Long. Munich: Verlag der Bayerischen Akademie der Wissenschaften, 2008.

Secondary Sources

Aertsen, Jan A. *Nature and Creature: Thomas Aquinas's Way of Thought*. Leiden: Brill, 1988.

————. "Method and Metaphysics: The *via resolutionis* in Thomas Aquinas." *New Scholasticism* 63, no. 4 (1989): 405–18.

————. *Medieval Philosophy and the Transcendentals: The Case of Thomas Aquinas*. Leiden: Brill, 1996.

————. "La scoperta dell'ente in quanto ente." In *Tommaso d'Aquino e l'oggetto della metafisica*, edited by Stephen Brock, 35–48. Rome: Armando Editore, 2004.

Agamben, Giorgio, and Emanuele Coccia, eds. *Angeli: Ebraismo, Cristianesimo, Islam*. Vicenza: N. Pozza, 2009.

Alliney, Guido. "Libertà e contingenza della fruizione beatifica nello scotismo del primo 300." *Veritas: Revista de Filosofia* 50, no. 3 (2005): 95–108.

Ashley, Benedict M., OP. "The River Forest School and the Philosophy of Nature Today." In *Philosophy and the God of Abraham: Essays in Memory of James A. Weisheipl, OP*, edited by R. James Long, 1–15. Toronto: Pontifical Institute of Mediaeval Studies, 1991.

————. *The Way toward Wisdom: An Interdisciplinary and Intercultural Introduction to Metaphysics*. Notre Dame, Ind.: University of Notre Dame Press, 2006.

Barnes, Corey L. *Christ's Two Wills in Scholastic Thought: The Christology of Aquinas and Its Historical Contexts*. Toronto: Pontifical Institute of Mediaeval Studies, 2012.

———. "Natural Final Causality and Providence in Aquinas." *New Blackfriars* 95, no. 1057 (2014): 349–61.

Bérubé, Camille. *La Connaissance de l'individuel au Moyen Âge*. Montréal / Paris: Presses de l'Université de Montréal / Pressees Universitaires de France, 1964.

Blanchette, Oliva. *The Perfection of the Universe According to Aquinas: A Teleological Cosmology*. University Park: Pennsylvania State University Press, 1992.

Blondel, Maurice. *Action (1893)*. Translated by Oliva Blanchette. South Bend, Ind.: University of Notre Dame Press, 1984.

Bonino, Serge-Thomas, OP. *Les anges et les démons. Quatorze leçons de théologie catholique*. Paris: Parole et silence, 2007.

Bos, E. P., and A. C. van der Helm. "The Division of Being over the Categories According to Albert the Great, Thomas Aquinas and John Duns Scotus." In *John Duns Scotus: Renewal of Philosophy*, edited by E. P. Bos, 183–96. Amsterdam: Rodopi, 1998.

Bouillard, Henri. *Conversion et grace chez S. Thomas d'Aquin. Etude historique*. Paris: Aubier, 1944.

Brown, Christopher M. *Aquinas and the Ship of Theseus: Solving Puzzles about Material Objects*. London: Bloomsbury Academic, 2005.

———. "Artifacts, Substances, and Transubstantiation: Solving a Puzzle for Aquinas's View." *The Thomist* 71, no. 1 (2007): 89–112.

———. "Souls, Ships, and Substances: A Response to Toner." *American Catholic Philosophical Quarterly* 81, no. 4 (2007): 655–68.

Burnyeat, M. F. "Aquinas on 'Spiritual Change' in Perception." In *Ancient and Medieval Theories of Intentionality*, edited by Dominik Perler, 129–53. Leiden: Brill, 2001.

Burrell, David B. "Act of Creation with its Theological Consequences." In *Aquinas on Doctrine: A Critical Introduction*, edited by Thomas Weinandy, OFM Cap., Daniel Keating, and John Yocum, 27–44. London: T and T Clark, 2004.

Bynum, Terrell Ward. "A New Look at Aristotle's Theory of Perception." In *Aristotle: De Anima in Focus*, edited by Michael Durrant, 90–109. New York: Routledge, 1993.

Cassirer, Ernst. *An Essay on Man*. New Haven, Conn.: Yale University Press, 1944.

Cessario, Romanus, OP. "Is Thomas's *Summa* Only About Grace?" In *Ordo sapientia et amoris*, edited by Carlos-Josaphat Pinto de Olivera, 197–207. Fribourg: Universitatsverlag Freiburg Schweiz, 1993.

———. "The Spirituality of St. Thomas Aquinas." *Crisis Magazine* 14 (July/August 1996): 14–16; available at insidecatholic.com.

Chenu, Marie-Dominique. *Toward Understanding Saint Thomas*. Chicago: Henry Regnery, 1964.

———. "Body and Body Politic in the Creation Spirituality of Thomas Aquinas." *Listening: A Journal of Religion and Culture* 13 (1974): 214–32.

———. "Les passions vertueuses. L'anthropologie de saint Thomas." *Revue philosophique de Louvain* 72, no. 13 (1974): 11–18.

Chesterton, G. K. *Saint Thomas Aquinas*. Garden City, N.Y.: Image Books, 1956.

Clarke, Thomas J. "The Background and Implications of Duns Scotus' Theory of Knowing in the Beatific Vision." PhD diss., Brandeis University, 1971.

Clarke, W. Norris, SJ. *Person and Being*. Milwaukee, Wis.: Marquette University Press, 1993.

———. *The One and the Many: A Contemporary Thomistic Metaphysics*. Notre Dame, Ind.: University of Notre Dame Press, 2001.

Colberg, Shawn. "Aquinas and the Grace of Auxilium." *Modern Theology* 32, no. 2 (2016): 187–210.

Colish, Marcia. "Early Scholastic Angelology." *Recherches de théologie ancienne et médiévale* 62 (1995): 80–109.

Connell, Richard J. *Substance and Modern Science*. Houston, Tex.: Center for Thomistic Studies, 1988.

Contat, Alain. "Le figure della differenza ontologica nel tomismo del Novecento." *Alpha Omega* 11, no. 2 (2008): 77–129 and 213–50.

Cullen, Christopher M. "Alexander of Hales." In *A Companion to Philosophy in the Middle Ages*, edited by Jorge J. E. Gracia and Timothy B. Noone, 104–8. Malden, Mass.: Blackwell, 2003.

Davies, Brian. "Aquinas, God, Being." *Monist* 80, no. 4 (1997): 500–521.

———. "Kenny on Aquinas on Being." *The Modern Schoolman* 82, no. 2 (2005): 111–29.

———. *Thomas Aquinas's* Summa Theologiae: *A Guide and Commentary*. Oxford: Oxford University Press, 2014.

De Finance, Joseph. *Être et agir dans la philosophie de Saint Thomas*. 3rd edition. Rome: Presses de l'Université Grégorienne, 1965.

Deely, John. *Four Ages of Understanding*. Toronto: University of Toronto Press, 2001.

———. *The Impact on Philosophy of Semiotics*. South Bend, Ind.: St. Augustine's Press, 2003.

Dewan, Lawrence, OP. "Thomas Aquinas, Creation and Two Historians." *Laval théologique et philosophique* 50, no. 2 (1994): 363–87.

———. "Thomas Aquinas and Being as a Nature." *Acta Philosophica* 12, no. 1 (2003): 123–35.

———. *Form and Being: Studies in Thomistic Metaphysics*. Washington, D.C.: The Catholic University of America Press, 2006.

Di Noia, J. Augustine. "*Imago Dei—Imago Christi*: The Theological Foundations of Christian Humanism." *Nova et Vetera* 2, no. 2 (2004): 267–78.

Diepen, Hermann. "La psychologie humaine du Christ selon saint Thomas d'Aquin." *Revue thomiste* 50 (1950): 515–62.

Doig, James. *Aquinas on Metaphysics: A Historico-Doctrinal Study of the Commentary on the Metaphysics*. The Hague: Martinus Nijhoff, 1972.

Donceel, Joseph, SJ, ed. and trans. *A Maréchal Reader*. New York: Herder and Herder, 1970.

Doolan, Gregory T. "Substance as a Metaphysical Genus." In *The Science of Being as Being: Metaphysical Investigations*, edited by Doolan, 99–128. Washington, D.C.: The Catholic University of America Press, 2012.

———. "Aquinas on the Metaphysician's vs. the Logician's Categories." *Quaestiones Disputatae* 4, no. 2 (2014): 133–55.

Duba, William. "The Beatific Vision in the *Sentences* Commentary of Gerald Odonis." *Vivarium* 47, no. 2 (2009): 348–63.

Dulles, Avery, SJ. "Criteria of Catholic Theology." *Communio* 22, no. 2 (1995): 303–15.

Elders, Leo. *Faith and Science: An Introduction to St. Thomas's* Expositio in Boethii De Trinitate. Rome: Herder, 1974.

Emery, Gilles, OP. "Trinity in Creation." In *The Theology of Thomas Aquinas*, edited by Rik Van Nieuwenhove and Joseph P. Wawrykow, 58–76. South Bend, Ind.: University of Notre Dame Press, 2005.

Fabro, Cornelio. *Metaphysica*. Unpublished manuscript. Progetto Culturale Cornelio Fabro dell'Istituto del Verbo Incarnato, 1947–49.

———. "The Transcendentality of *Ens-Esse* and the Ground of Metaphysics." *International Philosophical Quarterly* 6, no. 3 (1966): 389–427.

———. "L'*esse* tomistico e la ripresa della metafisica." *Angelicum* 44, no. 3 (1967): 281–314.

———. *L'uomo e il rischio di Dio*. Rome: Editrice Studium, 1967.

———. *Tomismo e pensiero moderno*. Rome: Pontificia Università Lateranense, 1969.

———. "Dibattito congressuale." *Sapienza* 26, nos. 3–4 (1973): 371–432.

———. "Il nuovo problema dell'essere e la fondazione della metafisica." *Rivista di filosofia neoscolastica* 66, nos. 2 and 4 (1974): 475–510.

———. *La svolta antropologica di Karl Rahner*. Milan: Rusconi, 1974.

———. "Problematica del tomismo di scuola." *Rivista di filosofia neoscolastica* 75, no. 2 (1983): 187–99.

———. *Introduzione a san Tommaso*. Milan: Ares, 1997.

———. *La prima riforma della dialettica hegeliana*. Edited by Christian Ferraro. Segni: EDIVI, 2004.

———. *La nozione metafisica di partecipazione secondo s. Tommaso d'Aquino*. Opere complete 3. Segni: EDIVI, 2005.

———. *Percezione e pensiero*. Opere complete 6. Segni: EDIVI, 2008.

———. *Partecipazione e causalità*. Opere complete 19. Segni: EDIVI, 2010.

Ferraro, Christian. "La conoscenza dell'*ens* e dell'*esse* dalla prospettiva del tomismo essenziale." *Doctor Angelicus* 5 (2005): 75–108.

Feser, Edward. *Aquinas: A Beginner's Guide*. Oxford: Oneworld Publications, 2009.

Fields, Stephen M., SJ. *Being as Symbol: On the Origins and Development of Karl Rahner's Metaphysics*. Washington, D.C.: Georgetown University Press, 2000.

———. "God's Labor, Novelty's Emergence: Cosmic Motion as Self-Transcending Love." In *Love Alone Is Credible: Hans Urs von Balthasar as Interpreter of the Catholic Tradition*, edited by David L. Schindler, 1:115–40. Grand Rapids, Mich.: Eerdmans, 2008.

Freddoso, Alfred J. "The Vindication of St. Thomas: Thomism and Contemporary Anglo-American Philosophy." *Nova et Vetera* 14, no. 2 (2016): 565–84.

Garrigou-Lagrange, Reginald, OP. *Reality: A Synthesis of Thomistic Thought.* Translated by Patrick Cummins. St. Louis, Mo.: Herder, 1950.

Garrigues, Jean Miguel. "La conscience de soi telle qu'elle était exercé par le Fils de Dieu fait homme." *Nova et Vetera* (French edition) 79, no. 1 (2004): 39–51.

———. "L'instrumentalité rédemptrice du libre arbitre du Christ chez saint Maxime le Confesseur." *Revue thomiste* 104 (2004): 531–50.

Geiger, L.-B. "Abstraction et séparation d'après s. Thomas." *Revue des sciences philosophiques et théologiques* 31 (1947): 3–40.

Gilson, Étienne. *The Spirit of Mediaeval Philosophy.* New York: Sheed and Ward, 1940.

———. *Réalisme thomiste et critique de la connaissance.* Paris: Vrin, 1947.

———. *Being and Some Philosophers.* Toronto: Pontifical Institute of Mediaeval Studies, 1952.

———. *Le Thomisme.* 5th edition. Paris: Vrin, 1957.

———. *The Arts of the Beautiful.* New York: Scribner, 1965.

Glutz, Melvin A. "Being and Metaphysics." *The Modern Schoolman* 35, no. 4 (1958): 271–85.

Gondreau, Paul. *The Passions of Christ's Soul in the Theology of St. Thomas Aquinas.* Münster: Aschendorff, 2002.

———. "The 'Inseparable Connection' between Procreation and Unitive Love (*Humanae Vitae*, §12) and Thomistic Hylemorphic Anthropology." *Nova et Vetera* 6, no. 4 (2008): 731–64.

———. "The Passions and the Moral Life: Appreciating the Originality of Aquinas." *The Thomist* 71, no. 3 (2007): 419–50.

Gorce, M. "La somme théologique d'Alexandre de Hales est-elle authentique?" *New Scholasticism* 5, no. 1 (1931): 1–72.

Goris, Harm. "Divine Foreknowledge, Providence, Predestination, and Human Freedom." In *The Theology of Thomas Aquinas*, edited by Rik Van Nieuwenhove and Joseph P. Wawrykow, 99–122. South Bend, Ind.: University of Notre Dame Press, 2005.

Goyette, John. "St. Thomas on the Unity of Substantial Form." *Nova et Vetera* 7, no. 4 (2009): 781–90.

Grillmeier, Aloys. *Christ in Christian Tradition: From the Apostolic Age to Chalcedon (451)*, vol. 1. Translated by J. Bowden. 2nd edition. Atlanta: John Knox Press, 1975.

Guzmán, Manzano. "El humanismo implicado en la comprensión escotista de la visión beatifica." In *Regnum hominis et regnum Dei*, vol. 1, edited by C. Bérubé, 85–94. Rome: Societas Internationalis Scotistica, 1978.

Haight, Roger. *Dynamics of Theology*. New York: Paulist, 1990.

Hardy, Edward Rochie, ed. *Christology of the Later Fathers*. Philadelphia: Westminster, 1954.

Harkins, Angela Kim, Kelley Coblentz Bautch, and John C. Endres, SJ, eds. *The Fallen Angels Traditions: Second Temple Developments and Reception History*. Washington, D.C.: Catholic Biblical Association of America, 2014.

Harkins, Franklin T. "The Embodiment of Angels: A Debate in Mid-Thirteenth-Century Theology." *Recherches de théologie et philosophie médiévales* 78, no. 1 (2011): 25–58.

Heidegger, Martin. *Introduction to Metaphysics*. Translated by Gregory Fried and Richard Polt. New Haven, Conn.: Yale University Press, 2000.

Henninger, Mark G. "Henry of Harclay on the Contingency of the Will's Fruition." In *Proceedings of "The Quadruple Congress" on John Duns Scotus, Part 3: Johannes Duns Scotus 1308–2008*, edited by L. Honnefelder et al., 463–77. Münster / St. Bonaventure, N.Y.: Aschendorff / Franciscan Institute Publications, 2010.

Ingham, Mary Beth, CSJ. "*De Vita Beata*: John Duns Scotus, Moral Perfection and the Rational Will." In *Proceedings of "The Quadruple Congress" on John Duns Scotus, Part 3: Johannes Duns Scotus 1308–2008*, edited by L. Honnefelder et al., 379–89. Münster / St. Bonaventure, N.Y.: Aschendorff / Franciscan Institute Publications, 2010.

Johann, Robert O. *The Meaning of Love: An Essay Towards a Metaphysics of Intersubjectivity*. Westminster, Md.: Newman, 1955.

John, Helen James. *The Thomist Spectrum*. New York: Fordham University Press, 1966.

Johnson, Elizabeth A. "The Maleness of Christ." *The Special Nature of Women? / Concilium* 6 (1991): 108–15.

Johnson, Mark. "Did St. Thomas Attribute a Doctrine of Creation to Aristotle?" *New Scholasticism* 63, no. 2 (1989): 129–55.

Johnstone, Brian V. "The Debate on the Structure of the *Summa theologiae* of St. Thomas Aquinas: From Chenu (1939) to Metz (1998)." In *Aquinas as Authority: A Collection of Studies Presented at the Second Conference of the Thomas Instituut te Utrecht, December 14–16, 2000*, ed. Paul van Geest, Harm Goris, and Carlo Leget, 187–200. Leuven: Peeters, 2002.

Jordan, Mark D. *Ordering Wisdom: The Hierarchy of Philosophical Discourses in Aquinas*. Notre Dame, Ind.: University of Notre Dame Press, 1986.

Kane, William H. "Abstraction and the Distinction of the Sciences." *The Thomist* 17, no. 1 (1954): 43–68.

Kelly, J. N. D. *Early Christian Doctrines*. San Francisco, Calif.: Harper and Row, 1978.

Kenny, Anthony. *Aquinas*. Oxford: Oxford University Press, 1980.

————. *Aquinas on Mind*. London: Routledge, 1993.

————. *Aquinas on Being*. Oxford: Oxford University Press, 2002.

Kent, Bonnie. *The Virtues of the Will: The Transformation of Ethics in the Late Thirteenth Century*. Washington, D.C.: The Catholic University of America Press, 1995.

Kerr, Fergus, OP. *After Aquinas: Version of Thomism*. Oxford: University of Oxford Press, 2002.

————. "The Varieties of Interpreting Aquinas." In *Contemplating Aquinas: On the Varieties of Interpretation*, edited by Fergus Kerr, 27–40. London: SCM Press, 2003.

Kitanov, Severin Valentinov. "Durandus of St.-Pourcain and Peter Auriol on the Act of Beatific Enjoyment." In *Philosophical Debates at Paris in the Early Fourteenth Century*, edited by Stephen F. Brown, Thomas Dewender, and Theo Kobusch, 163–78. Leiden: Brill, 2009.

————. "Peter of Candia on Demonstrating that God is the Sole Object of Beatific Enjoyment." *Franciscan Studies* 67 (2009): 427–89.

————. *Beatific Enjoyment in Medieval Scholastic Debates: The Complex Legacy of Saint Augustine and Peter Lombard*. Lanham, Md.: Lexington Books, 2014.

Klima, Gyula. "On Kenny on Aquinas on Being: A Critical Review of *Aquinas on Being* by Anthony Kenny." *International Philosophical Quarterly* 44, no. 4 (2004): 567–80.

Klubertanz, George P., SJ. "St. Thomas and the Knowledge of the Singular." *New Scholasticism* 26, no. 1 (1952): 135–66.

————. *St. Thomas Aquinas on Analogy: A Textual Analysis and Systematic Synthesis*. Chicago: Loyola University Press, 1960.

————. *Introduction to the Philosophy of Being*. 2nd edition. New York: Appleton-Century-Crofts, 1963.

Knasas, John F. X. *The Preface to Thomistic Metaphysics: A Contribution to the Neo-Thomist Debate on the Start of Metaphysics*. New York: Peter Lang, 1990.

————. "Materiality and Aquinas' Natural Philosophy: A Reply to Johnson." *The Modern Schoolman* 68, no. 3 (1991): 245–57.

————. "Thomistic Existentialism and the Proofs *Ex Motu* at C. G. I, 13." *The Thomist* 59, no. 4 (1995): 591–616.

————. *Being and Some Twentieth-Century Thomists*. New York: Fordham University Press, 2003.

Krapiec, A. M. "Analysis formationis conceptus entis existentialiter considerati." *Divus Thomas (Piac.)* 59 (1956): 320–50.

Labourdette, M.-M. "Aux origines du péché de l'homme d'après saint Thomas d'Aquin." *Revue thomiste* 85 (1985): 357–98.

Lafleur, Claude, and Joanne Carrier. "Abstraction, séparation et tripartition de la philosophie theorétique: quelques élements de l'arrière-fond farabien et artien de Thomas d'Aquin." *Recherches de Théologie et Philosophie médiévales* 67, no 2 (2000): 248–71.

Lafont, Ghislain. *Structures et méthode dans la "Somme théologique" de saint Thomas d'Aquin.* Paris: Les Éditions du Cerf, 1996.

Lea, Henry C. *Materials toward a History of Witchcraft.* Edited by Arthur C. Howland. 3 vols. New York: T. Yoseloff, 1957.

Lonergan, Bernard J. F., SJ. *Grace and Freedom: Operative Grace in the Thought of St. Thomas Aquinas.* Edited by J. Patout Burns. London: Darton, Longman and Todd, 1971.

———. *Insight: A Study of Human Understanding.* San Francisco, Calif.: Harper and Row, 1978.

Long, R. James. "The Beginning of a Tradition: The *Sentences* Commentary of Richard Fishacre, OP." In *Mediaeval Commentaries on the Sentences of Peter Lombard,* vol. 1, edited by G. R. Evans, 345–57. Leiden: Brill, 2002.

Long, R. James, and Maura O'Carroll, SND. *The Life and Works of Richard Fishacre OP: Prolegomena to the Edition of his Commentary on the Sentences.* Munich: Verlag der Bayerischen Akademie der Wissenschaften, 1999.

Long, Steven A. "The Order of the Universe." In *Dio creatore e la creazione come case commune,* edited by Serge-Thomas Bonino and Guido Mazzotta, 117–36. Vatican City: Urbanania University Press, 2018.

Lozano, Adrián. *La primera captación intelectual como fundamento del proceso de abstracción del universal según Santo Tomás de Aquino: una interpretación desde Cornelio Fabro, Étienne Gilson, Jacques Maritain y Léon Nöel.* Rome: Pontificia Università Lateranense, 2006.

Luijten, Eric. *Sacramental Forgiveness as a Gift from God: Thomas Aquinas on the Sacrament of Penance.* Leuven: Peeters, 2003.

MacIntyre, Alasdair. *After Virtue.* 2nd edition. Notre Dame, Ind.: University of Notre Dame Press, 1984.

———. *Whose Justice? Which Rationality?* Notre Dame, Ind.: University of Notre Dame Press, 1988.

Maréchal, Joseph, SJ. *Le point de départ de la métaphysique.* 5 vols. 2nd edition. Brussels / Paris: Desclée de Brouwer / Éditions universelle, 1923–26; 2nd edition, 1944–49.

Maritain, Jacques. *Ransoming the Time.* Translated by Harry Lorin Binsse. New York: Scribners, 1941.

———. *The Degrees of Knowledge.* Translated by Gerald B. Phelan. New York: Scribner, 1959.

———. *A Preface to Metaphysics: Seven Lectures on Being.* New York: New American Library, 1962. Originally published as *Sept leçons sur l'être et les premiers principes de la raison speculative.* Paris: Téqui, 1934.

———. *Existence and the Existent.* Translated by Lewis Galantiere and Gerald B.

Phelan. New York: Vantage Books, 1966. Originally published as *Court traité de l'existence et de l'existant*. Paris: Paul Hartmann, 1947.

———. "Réflexions sur la nature blessée et sur l'intuition de l'être." *Revue Thomiste* 68 (1968): 5–41.

Mattison, William. "Virtuous Anger? From Questions of *Vindicatio* to the Habituation of Emotion." *Journal of the Society of Christian Ethics* 24, no. 1 (2004): 159–79.

Maurer, Armand. "A Neglected Thomistic Text on the Foundation of Mathematics." In his *Being and Knowing: Studies in Thomas Aquinas and Later Medieval Philosophers*, 33–41. Toronto: Pontifical Institute of Mediaeval Studies, 1990.

———. "Thomists and Thomas Aquinas on the Foundation of Mathematics." *Review of Metaphysics* 47, no. 1 (1993): 43–61.

McCool, Gerald A., SJ. *From Unity to Pluralism: The Internal Evolution of Thomism*. New York: Fordham University Press, 1989.

McGrade, Arthur Stephen. "Ockham on Enjoyment—Towards an Understanding of Fourteenth Century Philosophy and Psychology." *Review of Metaphysics* 34, no. 4 (1981): 706–28.

McInerny, Ralph. "Notes on Being and Predication." *Laval théologique et philosophique* 15, no. 2 (1959): 236–74.

———. *Being and Predication*. Washington, D.C.: The Catholic University of America Press, 1986.

———. *Praeambula Fidei: Thomism and the God of the Philosophers*. Washington, D.C.: The Catholic University of America Press, 2006.

Millán-Puelles, Antonio. *La lógica de los conceptos metafísicos*, Tomo I: *La lógica de los conceptos trascendentales*. Madrid: RIALP, 2002.

———. *La lógica de los conceptos metafísicos*, Tomo II: *La articulación de los conceptos extracategoriales*. Madrid: RIALP, 2003.

Moleski, Martin X., SJ. "Retorsion: The Method and Metaphysics of Gaston Isaye." *International Philosophical Quarterly* 17, no. 1 (1977): 59–83.

Mondin, Battista. "La conoscenza dell'essere in Fabro e Gilson." *Euntes Docete* 50, nos. 1–2 (1997): 85–115.

Montagnes, Bernard. *The Doctrine of the Analogy of Being according to Thomas Aquinas*. Translated by E. M. Macierowski and edited by Andrew Tallon. Milwaukee, Wis.: Marquette University Press, 2004.

Morard, Martin. "Une source de saint Thomas d'Aquin: le Deuxième Concile de Constantinople (553)." *Revue des sciences philosophiques et théologiques* 81 (1997): 21–56.

Moreno, Antonio. "The Nature of Metaphysics." *The Thomist* 30, no. 2 (1966): 109–35.

———. "The Subject, Abstraction, and Methodology of Aquinas' Metaphysics." *Angelicum* 61, no. 4 (1984): 580–601.

Morerod, Charles. *The Church and the Human Quest for Truth*. Ave Maria, Fla.: Sapientia Press, 2008.

Muck, Otto, SJ. "The Logical Structure of Transcendental Method." *International Philosophical Quarterly* 9, no. 3 (1969): 342–62.

Newman, John Henry Cardinal. *Apologia Pro Vita Sua*. New York: Doubleday, 1989.

Nickelsburg, George W. E., and James C. VanderKam. *1 Enoch: A New Translation Based on the Hermeneia Commentary*. Minneapolis, Minn.: Fortress Press, 2004.

Nicolas, Jean-Hervé. *Synthèse dogmatique. De la Trinité à la Trinité*. Fribourg: Éditions Universitaires, 1985.

O'Brien, Thomas C. *Metaphysics and the Existence of God*. Washington, D.C.: Thomist Press, 1960.

Oliva, Adriano. *Les débuts de l'enseignement de Thomas d'Aquin et sa conception de la sacra doctrina, avec l'édition du Prologue de son commentaire des* Sentences. Paris: Vrin, 2006.

Olivera, Javier Pablo. *El punto de partida de la metafísica de Santo Tomás de Aquino, según Cornelio Fabro*. Rome: Pontificia Università Lateranense, 2007.

O'Meara, Thomas. "Grace as a Theological Structure in the Summa Theologiae of Thomas Aquinas." *Recherches de théologie ancienne et médiévale* 55 (1988): 130–53.

Owens, Joseph, CSSR. "The Range of Existence." In *Proceedings of the Seventh Inter-American Congress of Philosophy*, 44–59. Québec: Les Presses de L'Universite Laval, 1967.

———. "Aquinas on Knowing Existence." *Review of Metaphysics* 29, no. 4 (1976): 670–90.

———. *St. Thomas Aquinas on the Existence of God: The Collected Papers of Joseph Owens*. Edited by John R. Catan. Albany: State University of New York Press, 1980.

———. *An Elementary Christian Metaphysics*. Houston, Tex.: Center for Thomistic Studies, 1985.

———. *Cognition: An Epistemological Inquiry*. Houston, Tex.: Center for Thomistic Studies, 1992.

Pangallo, Mario. *L'essere come atto nel tomismo essenziale di Cornelio Fabro*. Vatican City: Libreria Editrice Vaticana, 1987.

Peréz de Laborda, Miguel. "Il ruolo della *compositio* in metafisica." In *Tommaso d'Aquino e l'oggetto della metafisica*, edited by S. Brock, 49–64. Rome: Armando Editore, 2004.

Pesch, Otto-Hermann. "Thomas Aquinas and Contemporary Theology." In *Contemplating Aquinas: On the Varieties of Interpretation*, edited by Fergus Kerr, OP, 185–216. London: SCM Press, 2003.

Pieper, Josef. *Guide to Thomas Aquinas*. San Francisco, Calif.: Ignatius Press, 1991.

———. *In Defense of Philosophy: Classical Wisdom Stands up to Modern Challenges*. Translated by Lothar Krauth. San Francisco, Calif.: Ignatius Press, 1992.

Pinckaers, Servais, OP. *The Pinckaers Reader: Renewing Thomistic Moral Theology*. Edited by John Berkman and Craig Steven Titus. Washington, D.C.: The Catholic University of America Press, 2005.

Porro, Pasquale. "Tommaso d'Aquino, Avicenna, e la struttura della metafisica." In *Tommaso d'Aquino e l'oggetto della metafisica (Studi di filosofia 29)*, edited by Stephen Brock, 65–87. Rome: Armando, 2004.

Prentice, Robert. "The Voluntarism of Duns Scotus, as Seen in His Comparison of the Intellect and the Will." *Franciscan Studies* 28 (1968): 63–103.

———. "Scotus' Voluntarism as Seen in His Concept of the Essence of Beatitude." In *Studia mediaevalia et mariologica*, edited by C. Balić, 161–86. Rome: Antonianum, 1971.

Putallaz, François-Xavier. *Le sens de la réflexion chez Thomas d'Aquin*. Paris: J. Vrin, 1991.

Rahner, Karl, SJ. *The Christian Commitment: Essays in Pastoral Theology*. Translated by Cecily Hastings. New York: Sheed and Ward, 1963.

———. "Aquinas: The Nature of Truth." Translated by Andrew Tallon. *Continuum* 2, no. 1 (1964): 60–71.

———. "The Theology of the Symbol." In his *Theological Investigations* 4, translated by Kevin Smyth, 221–52. Baltimore, Md.: Helicon, 1966.

———. *Spirit in the World*. Translated by William V. Dych, SJ. New York: Herder and Herder, 1968.

———. *Hearer of the Word: Laying the Foundation for a Philosophy of Religion*. Translated by Joseph Donceel, SJ. New York: Continuum, 1994.

Ramirez, Santiago, OP. *Edicion de las Obras Completas de Santiago Ramirez, OP, Tomo II, De analogia*. 4 vols. Edited by Victorino Rodriguez, OP. Madrid: Institute de Filosofia "Luis Vives," 1970.

Ramos, Alice. "Activity and Finality in Saint Thomas." *Angelicum* 68, no. 2 (1991): 231–54.

———. "Beauty and the Perfection of Being." *Proceedings of the American Catholic Philosophical Association* 71 (1997): 255–68.

———. *Dynamic Transcendentals: Truth, Goodness, and Beauty from a Thomistic Perspective*. Washington, D.C.: The Catholic University of America Press, 2012.

———. "A Metaphysics of the Truth of Creation: Foundation of the Desire for God." *Proceedings of the American Catholic Philosophical Association* 69 (1995): 237–48.

Rand, E. K. *Cicero in the Courtroom of St. Thomas Aquinas*. The Aquinas Lecture, 1945. Milwaukee, Wis.: Marquette University Press, 1946.

Ratzinger, Joseph. *Theology of the Liturgy: The Sacramental Foundation of Christian Existence. Collected Works*, vol. 11. Edited by Michael J. Miller, translated by John Saward, Kenneth Baker, SJ, Henry Taylor, et al. San Francisco, Calif.: Ignatius Press, 2014.

Reed, Annette Yoshiko. *Fallen Angels and the History of Judaism and Christianity: The Reception of Enochic Literature.* Cambridge: Cambridge University Press, 2005.

Renard, Henri. "What Is St. Thomas' Approach to Metaphysics?" *New Scholasticism* 30, no. 1 (1956): 63–84.

Reynolds, Philip L. *Food and the Body: Some Peculiar Questions in High Medieval Theology.* Leiden: Brill, 1999.

Robiglio, Andrea. "Gilson e Fabro. Appunti per un confronto." *Divus Thomas* 17, no. 2 (1997): 59–76.

Romera, Luis. *Pensar el ser: Análisis del conocimiento del "Actus essendi" según C. Fabro.* Bern: Peter Lang, 1994.

Root, Michael. "Aquinas, Merit, and Reformation Theology after the *Joint Declaration on the Doctrine of Justification.*" *Modern Theology* 20, no. 1 (2004): 5–22.

Rota, Michael. "Substance and Artifact in Thomas Aquinas." *History of Philosophy Quarterly* 21, no. 3 (2004): 240–59.

Rousselot, Pierre, SJ. *Intelligence: Sense of Being, Faculty of God.* Translated by Andrew Tallon. Milwaukee, Wis.: Marquette University Press, 1999 (1908).

Schenk, Richard. "*Omnis Christi actio nostra est instructio.* The Deeds and Sayings of Jesus as Revelation in the View of Thomas Aquinas." In *La doctrine de la révélation divine de saint Thomas d'Aquin,* edited by L. Elders, 103–31. Vatican City: Libreria Editrice Vaticana, 1990.

Schmidt, Robert W. "L'emploi de la séparation en métaphysique." *Revue philosophique de Louvain* 58 (1960): 373–93.

Seckler, Max. *Instinkt und Glaubenswille nach Thomas von Aquin.* Mainz: Matthias Grünewald, 1961.

Sentis, Laurent. "La lumière dont nous faisons usage. La règle de la raison et la loi divine selon Thomas d'Aquin." *Revue des sciences philosophiques et théologiques* 79 (1995): 49–69.

Shanley, Brian J. "Divine Causation and Human Freedom in Aquinas." *American Catholic Philosophical Quarterly* 72, no. 1 (1992): 100–122.

———. *The Thomist Tradition.* Dordrecht: Kluwer Academic, 2002.

Sheehan, Thomas. *Karl Rahner: The Philosophical Foundations.* Athens: Ohio State University Press, 1987.

Simon, Yves. *The Definition of Moral Virtue.* Edited by Vukan Kuic. New York: Fordham University Press, 1986.

Sisko, John E. "Material Alteration and Cognitive Activity in Aristotle's *De Anima.*" *Phronesis* 41, no. 2 (1996): 138–57.

Slakey, Thomas J. "Aristotle on Sense Perception." In *Aristotle: De Anima in Focus,* edited by Michael Durrant, 75–89. New York: Routledge, 1993.

Smith, Vincent. "The Prime Mover: Physical and Metaphysical Considerations." *Proceedings of the American Catholic Philosophical Association* 28 (1954): 78–94.

Spanneut, Michel. "Influences stoïciennes sur la pensée morale de S. Thomas d'Aquin." In *The Ethics of St. Thomas Aquinas: Proceedings of the Third Symposium* on *St. Thomas Aquinas' Philosophy*, edited by L. J. Elders and K. Hedwig, 50–79. Vatican City: Libreria Editrice Vaticana, 1984.

Steinberg, Leo. *The Sexuality of Christ in Renaissance Art and in Modern Oblivion*. Second revised and expanded edition. Chicago: University of Chicago Press, 1996.

Stump, Eleonore. *Aquinas*. London: Routledge, 2003.

Symington, Paul. "Thomas Aquinas on Establishing the Identity of Aristotle's Categories." In *Medieval Commentaries on Aristotle's Categories*, edited by Lloyd Newton, 119–44. Leiden: Brill, 2008.

———. *On Determining What There Is: The Identify of Ontological Categories in Aquinas, Scotus and Lowe*. Piscataway, N.J.: Ontos, 2010.

Te Velde, Rudi. "Understanding the *Scientia* of Faith: Reason and Faith in Aquinas's *Summa Theologiae*." In *Contemplating Aquinas: On the Varieties of Interpretation*, edited by Fergus Kerr, OP, 55–74. London: SCM Press, 2003.

———. *Aquinas on God: The 'Divine Science' of the* Summa Theologiae. Aldershot: Ashgate, 2006.

Torrell, Jean-Pierre, OP. "La causalité salvifique de la résurrection du Christ selon saint Thomas." *Revue thomiste* 96 (1996): 179–208.

———. *Le Christ en ses mystères. La vie et l'oeuvre de Jésus selon saint Thomas d'Aquin*. 2 vols. Paris: Desclée, 1999.

———. "'Imiter Dieu comme des enfants bien-aimés.' La conformité à Dieu et au Christ dans l'oeuvre de saint Thomas." In Jean-Pierre Torrell, *Recherches thomasiennes, Études revues et augmentées*, 325–35. Paris: J. Vrin, 2000.

———. *Aquinas's Summa: Background, Structure, and Reception*. Translated by Benedict M. Guevin, OSB. Washington, D.C.: The Catholic University of America Press, 2005.

———. *Saint Thomas Aquinas*, vol. 1: *The Person and His Works*, translated by Robert Royal. Revised edition. Washington, D.C.: The Catholic University of America Press, 2005. Vol. 2, *Spiritual Master*, translated by Robert Royal. Washington, D.C.: The Catholic University of America Press, 2003.

Trottman, Christian. "Vision béatifique et intuition d'un objet absent: des sources franciscaines du nominalisme aux défenseurs scotistes de l'opnion de Jean XXII sur la vision différée." *Studi medievali* 34 (Third Series), no. 2 (1993): 653–715.

———. "La vision béatifique dans la seconde école franciscaine: de Matthieu d'Aquasparta à Duns Scot." *Collectanea Franciscana* 64 (1994): 121–80.

———. *La vision béatifique. Des disputes scolastiques à sa définition par Benoît XII*. Rome: École française de Rome, 1995.

———. "Guiral Ot, de l'éternité au temps et retour. Conjectures à partir du *De multiformi visione Dei*." In *The Medieval Concept of Time: Studies on the Scholastic Debate and Its Reception in Early Modern Philosophy*, edited by Pasquale Porro, 287–317. Leiden: Brill, 2001.

Trottmann, Christian, and Arnaud Dumouch. *Benoît XII. La vision béatifique*. Paris: Doctor angélique, 2009.

VanderKam, James C. "1 Enoch, Enochic Motifs, and Enoch in Early Christian Literature." In *The Jewish Apocalyptic Heritage in Early Christianity*, edited by James C. VanderKam and William Adler, 33–101. Assen: Van Gorcum, 1996.

Verbeke, Gerard. *The Presence of Stoicism in Medieval Thought*. Washington, D.C.: The Catholic University of America Press, 1983.

Villagrasa, Jesús. "La *resolutio* come metodo della metafisica secondo Cornelio Fabro." *Alpha Omega* 4, no. 1 (2001): 35–66.

Walgrave, Jan Hendrik. "Instinctus Spiriti Sancti: een proeve tot Thomas-interpretatie." *Ephemerides Theologicae Lovanienses* 45, no. 3 (1969): 417–31.

Wallace, William. *The Elements of Philosophy*. New York: Alba House, 1977.

Walsh, Liam G., OP. "Sacraments." In *The Theology of Thomas Aquinas*, edited by Rik Van Nieuwenhove and Joseph P. Wawrykow, 326–64. South Bend, Ind.: University of Notre Dame Press, 2005.

Wawrykow, Joseph P. "Perseverance in 13th-Century Theology: the Augustinian Contribution." *Augustinian Studies* 22 (1991): 125–40.

———. *God's Grace and Human Action: 'Merit' in the Theology of Thomas Aquinas.* South Bend, Ind.: University of Notre Dame Press, 1995.

———. "Grace." In *The Theology of Thomas Aquinas*, edited by Rik Van Nieuwenhove and Joseph P. Wawrykow, 192–221. South Bend, Ind.: University of Notre Dame Press, 2005.

Weinandy, Thomas G., OFM Cap. *Does God Suffer?* Notre Dame, Ind.: University of Notre Dame Press, 2000.

Weisheipl, James A. "The Relationship of Medieval Natural Philosophy to Modern Science: The Contribution of Thomas Aquinas to its Understanding." *Manuscripta* 20, no. 3 (1976): 181–96.

White, Thomas Joseph, OP. "The Voluntary Action of the Earthly Christ and the Necessity of the Beatific Vision." *The Thomist* 69, no. 4 (2005): 497–534.

Wilhelmsen, Frederick D. *The Metaphysics of Love*. New York: Sheed and Ward, 1962.

———. *El Problema de la trascendencia en la metafísica actual.* Pamplona: EUNSA, 1963.

Wippel, John F. *Metaphysical Themes in Thomas Aquinas*. Washington, D.C.: The Catholic University of America Press, 1984.

———. "Thomas Aquinas's Derivation of the Aristotelian Categories (Predicaments)." *Journal of the History of Philosophy* 25, no. 1 (1987): 13–34.

———. *The Metaphysical Thought of Thomas Aquinas: From Finite Being to Uncreated Being*. Washington, D.C.: The Catholic University of America Press, 2000.

———. *Metaphysical Themes in Thomas Aquinas II*. Washington, D.C.: The Catholic University of America Press, 2007.

———. "Aquinas on Creation and Preambles of Faith." *The Thomist* 78, no. 1 (2014): 1–36.

Wood, Rega. "Early Oxford Theology." In *Mediaeval Commentaries on the Sentences of Peter Lombard*, edited by G. R. Evans, 1:289–343. Leiden: Brill, 2002.

Yocum, John P. "Sacraments in Aquinas." In *Aquinas on Doctrine: A Critical Introduction*, edited by Thomas Weinandy, OFM Cap., Daniel Keating, and John Yocum, 159–81. London: T and T Clark, 2004.

Zimmermann, Albert. *Ontologie oder Metaphysik? Die Diskussion über den Gegenstand der Metaphysik im 13. und 14. Jahrhundert*. 2nd edition. Leuven: Peeters, 1998.

CONTRIBUTORS

AARON CANTY is professor of religious studies at Saint Xavier University, where he teaches courses in systematic and historical theology. He is author of *Light and Glory: The Transfiguration of Christ in Early Franciscan and Dominican Theology* (The Catholic University of America Press, 2011); co-editor, with Franklin T. Harkins, of *A Companion to Job in the Middle Ages* (Brill, 2017); and has published numerous articles on medieval theology, spirituality, and exegesis.

SHAWN M. COLBERG is associate professor of theology at Saint John's University and School of Theology-Seminary. His areas of scholarship include High Scholastic theology with an emphasis on the theology of Thomas Aquinas and Bonaventure. He has published widely in journals.

CHRISTOPHER M. CULLEN, SJ, is associate professor of philosophy at Fordham University. His area of study is medieval philosophy with a focus on Bonaventure and Thomism. He is the author of a systematic study of the Seraphic Doctor's philosophy and theology, entitled *Bonaventure* (Oxford University Press, 2006). Additionally, he has written on Bonaventure's principal mentor, Alexander of Hales, and on his important disciple John Peckham. He co-edited a collection of essays on the French philosopher and Neo-Thomist Jacques Maritain, entitled *Maritain and America* (2009).

GREGORY T. DOOLAN is associate professor of philosophy at the Catholic University of America. His areas of specialty are metaphysics, Thomism, and medieval philosophy. He is editor of the volume *The Science of Being as Being: Metaphysical Investigations* (The Catholic University of America Press, 2012); and author of *Aquinas on the Divine Ideas as Exemplar Causes* (The Catholic University of America Press, 2008).

STEPHEN M. FIELDS, SJ, is professor of philosophy of religion and systematic theology at Georgetown University. He is the author of *Analogies of Transcendence: An Essay on Nature, Grace, and Modernity* (The Catholic University of America Press, 2016); and *Being as Symbol: On the Origins and Development of Karl Rahner's Metaphysics* (Georgetown University Press, 2000).

PAUL GONDREAU is professor of theology at Providence College, Rhode Island. His areas of specialty are Christology, marriage and human sexuality, Thomism, and theology of disability. He is associate editor of the theological journal *Nova et Vetera*, and author of *The Passions of Christ's Soul in the Theology of St. Thomas Aquinas* (Aschendorff, 2002).

FRANKLIN T. HARKINS is associate professor of historical theology and professor ordinarius at Boston College School of Theology and Ministry. He specializes in Scholastic theology and exegesis with a particular interest in Thomas Aquinas, Albertus Magnus, the Victorines, and Peter Lombard and the *Sentences* tradition. He is the author of *Reading and the Work of Restoration: History and Scripture in the Theology of Hugh of St. Victor* (PIMS, 2009); is co-editor, with Aaron Canty, of *A Companion to Job in the Middle Ages* (Brill, 2017); and has published numerous articles and essays on medieval theology and exegesis.

JAMES M. JACOBS is professor of philosophy and chair of pre-theology studies at Notre Dame Seminary in New Orleans, Louisiana. He specializes in Thomistic natural law ethics. His most recent articles have appeared in *Nova et Vetera* and *Heythrop Journal*.

JOHN F. X. KNASAS is professor of philosophy at the Center for Thomistic Studies at the University of St. Thomas in Houston, Texas. His areas of interest include Aquinas, metaphysics, cosmological reasoning, the Neo-Thomistic revival, philosophy of culture, philosophical psychology, and ethics. His various publications include *Being and Some Twentieth-Century Thomists* (Fordham University Press, 2003); *Thomism and Tolerance* (Scranton University Press, 2011); *Aquinas and the Cry of Rachel: Thomistic Reflections on the Problem of Evil* (The Catholic University of America Press, 2013); and *Thomistic Existentialism and Cosmological Reasoning* (The Catholic University of America Press, 2019).

STEVEN A. LONG is ordinary/full professor of theology in the Ave Maria University Graduate Theology program, and an ordinary member of the Pontifical Academy of St. Thomas Aquinas. He is the author of *The Teleological Grammar of the Moral Act* (Sapientia Press, 2007); *Natura Pura: On the Recovery of Nature in the Doctrine of Grace* (Fordham University Press, 2010); and *Analogia Entis: On the Analogy of Being, Metaphysics, and the Act of Faith* (University of Notre Dame Press, 2011). In addition, he co-edited, with Roger Nutt and Thomas Joseph White, OP, *Thomism and Predestination: Principles and Disputations* (Sapientia Press, 2016).

JASON A. MITCHELL is assistant professor of philosophy at Gannon University in Erie, Pennsylvania. He earned his PhD in philosophy at the *Regina Apostolorum* Pontifical Athenaeum in Rome (2010), with a thesis on "Being and Participation: The Method and Structure of Metaphysical Reflection according to Cornelio Fabro."

ALICE RAMOS is professor of philosophy at St. John's University in Queens, New York. Her most recent publication is *Dynamic Transcendentals: Truth, Goodness, and Beauty from a Thomistic Perspective* (The Catholic University of America Press, 2012).

RUDI A. TE VELDE teaches philosophy at the School of Catholic Theology of Tilburg University, The Netherlands, and holds an endowed chair in the Philosophy of Thomas Aquinas in Relation to Contemporary Thought. He is senior member of the Thomas Instituut te Utrecht, Tilburg University. His publications include *Participation and Substantiality in Thomas Aquinas* (Brill, 1995); and *Aquinas on God* (Ashgate, 2006).

JOHN F. WIPPEL is Theodore Basselin Professor in the School of Philosophy at the Catholic University of America. His recent books, all published by the Catholic University of America Press, include *The Metaphysical Thought of Thomas Aquinas: From Finite Being to Uncreated Being* (2000); *Metaphysical Themes in Thomas Aquinas II* (2007); and the edited volume *The Ultimate Why Question: Why Is There Anything at All Rather than Nothing Whatsoever?* (2011).

INDEX